D1345834

Turned Out Nice Again

Turned Out Nice Again

THE STORY OF BRITISH LIGHT ENTERTAINMENT

Louis Barfe

Atlantic Books

LONDON

First published in Great Britain in 2008 by Atlantic Books,
an imprint of Grove Atlantic Ltd.

1 3 5 7 9 10 8 6 4 2

A CIP catalogue record for this book is available from the British Library.

ISBN 978 1 84354 380 0

Typeset by Ellipsis Books Limited, Glasgow
Printed in Great Britain by MPG Books Ltd, Bodmin

Atlantic Books
An imprint of Grove Atlantic Ltd
Ormond House
26–27 Boswell Street
London WC1N 3JZ

For Sir Bill, who was there, and for Susannah,
Primrose and Lyttelton, who were here

Contents

List of Illustrations

Canterbury Hall. © Illustrated London News Ltd/Mary Evans Picture Library.

Dan Leno. Author's collection.

The Co-Optomists. © BBC/Corbis.

Horace Percival and Tommy Handley. © BBC/Corbis.

The Windmill Girls. Mary Evans Picture Library.

Nude revue bill. Author's collection.

The Goons. © BBC/Corbis.

Take It From Here rehearsal. Popperfoto/Getty Images.

Danny Kaye programme cover. Author's collection.

Danny Kaye programme. Author's collection.

Poster for The Crazy Gang's *Young in Heart*. Author's collection.

Poster for Billy Cotton's band. Author's collection.

Poster for Mike and Bernie Weinstein's *Showtime!* Author's collection.

Poster for Dickie Henderson's *Light Up the Town*. Author's collection.

The Albanian Eurovision delegation. Courtesy of Terry Henebery.

Ernest Maxin, Kathy Kirby, Bill Cotton Junior and Tom Sloan. BBC Photo Library/Referns.

That Was the Week That Was. Author's collection.

The George Mitchell Minstrels. Author's collection.

Dusty Springfield. Dezzo Hoffman/Rex Features.

Duke Ellington. David Redfern/Redferns.

Shirley Bassey and Tommy Trinder. Getty Images.

Bruce Forsyth and Sammy Davis Junior. Getty Images.

Rolf Harris. ITV/Rex Features.

Michael Parkinson and Harry Stoneham. Author's collection.

Peter Cook and Dudley Moore. Author's collection.

Eric Morecambe and Ernie Wise. Courtesy of Barry Fantoni.

The Comedians. Courtesy of Granada.

Les Dawson. Getty Images.

Lord Grade, Fozzie Bear and Frank Oz. Getty Images.

Jimmy Savile. Getty Images.

The Price is Right board game. Author's collection.

Noel Edmonds and Mr Blobby. New Group/Rex Features.

Strictly Come Dancing. © Topfoto/PA.

Introduction

What is light entertainment? Over the years, the term has baffled even its most distinguished practitioners. Scriptwriter Denis Norden once noted the glee with which its detractors asked 'whether "Light Entertainment" fell into the same insubstantial category as "Light Refreshments" and "Light Housework"'. Norden also recalled Eric Maschwitz – novelist, songwriter and a distinguished head of BBC Television's LE department – 'loath[ing] the term and ... prowl[ing] his office in shirtsleeves and thin red braces enquiring "What is it meant to be the opposite of? Heavy Entertainment? Or Dark Entertainment?"'[1]

Although inextricably linked with television, the expression predates broadcasting. It first occurs in *The Times* in September 1796, in a review of a Haymarket Theatre production called *A Peep Behind the Curtain*. By the early twentieth century, it had come to describe the genteel, frothy productions that dominated the West End stage. In 1945, James Agate published an anthology of his theatre reviews called *Immoment Toys: a survey of light entertainment on the London stage, 1920–1943*.

In broadcasting terms, however, light entertainment is a development from the earthier productions of the variety theatre and music hall, and as radio and television have expanded and diversified, the concept of 'variety' has expanded and diversified too. In the forties and fifties, when television was growing up in public, it meant acts or 'turns': magicians; whistlers; light-opera singers; crooners; women who couldn't sing very well, but had big knockers (one female singer's bill matter was a coarse, leering 'All this and four octaves!'); performing animals; animals whose unique selling point was their refusal to perform (dog owners will know that deadpan is not their natural tendency); and comedians who claimed to have a giraffe in a shoebox.

Since then, the broadcast definition of variety has expanded to include quiz shows, 'people' shows, chat shows and talent shows. In the sixties and seventies, television became the dominant force in entertaining the nation, and, before the fragmentation of audiences caused by home video and the advent of satellite television, an exceptional programme could capture and captivate half the UK population.

As a child growing up in the late seventies and early eighties, I absorbed it all. One of my earliest memories is of Tom O'Connor presenting Thames Television's *London Night Out*, complete with the *Name That Tune* quiz segment. *The Muppet Show*, *The Good Old Days* and *The Morecambe and Wise Show* and anything featuring Les Dawson were required family viewing. The *Royal Variety Performance* and the *Eurovision Song Contest* were (and are) non-negotiable annual appointments to view. When Tommy Cooper took his final, fatal bow on *Live From Her Majesty's*, I was watching the show with my great-grandmother, unsure of what had happened until the newsflash immediately after. Family holidays were spent in British seaside resorts where real live variety lived on in pier theatres – on one jaunt, when I was nine, I was taken to see Tommy Trinder doing his stand-up act, as well as Jimmy Edwards and Eric Sykes in the comic play *Big Bad Mouse*. Trinder addressed his audiences as 'You lucky people'. It wasn't until adulthood that I realized how lucky I'd been to see him and Edwards in action while I could.

As I moved from impressionable youngster to objectionable teenager, I turned my back on old-school entertainment in favour of rawer, more alternative fare. It was that period just after *The Young Ones* when Brucie and Tarby were being painted as, at best, cosy old farts gagging their way round the golf course, and, at worst, close friends of the common enemy, Mrs Thatcher. Bob Monkhouse was just a smarmy game show host, a fake-tanned snake oil salesman. One

Christmas, a violent row blew up because I wanted to watch something dangerous and alternative, while the rest of my family wanted to watch Russ Abbot. Majority rule and family gerontocracy had their way, so I sat with them all, declaring Abbot to be about as funny as piles and determined not to laugh. I lasted about three minutes before cracking a smile. Now, on Christmas Day, I rue my posturing, there being vast stretches of tedium in the modern festive schedules during which I'd happily crawl across broken glass for a glimpse of Bella Emberg dressed as Wonder Woman.

By the early nineties, television had turned its back on the old-school entertainers, but in doing so revealed the alternatives to be the new establishment. Ben Elton was on the way to writing musicals with another common enemy, Andrew Lloyd-Webber. Stephen Fry was rapidly becoming the human equivalent of a much-loved listed building. Meanwhile, Bob Monkhouse showed his true colours as a clever, thoughtful man of comedy with an incendiary performance on *Have I Got News For You*, and a funny, and unexpectedly candid autobiography. At this point, I realized I'd been a fool. It's perfectly possible to love both Adrian Edmondson and Bruce Forsyth. After all, what was *Saturday Live* if not *Sunday Night at the London Palladium* with knob and fart jokes?

Variety has been pronounced dead many times, but the truth is that the genre will never truly die. It just keeps evolving. What follows is the story of that evolution, from Victorian singalongs to the Saturday night spectaculars.

CHAPTER ONE

Empires, moguls and a man called Reith

The acme of light entertainment was reached between 8.55pm and 10pm on Christmas Day 1977, when 28 million viewers tuned into BBC1 to watch the *Morecambe and Wise Christmas Show*. From the opening spoof of US cop show *Starsky and Hutch*, to the closing sequence in which Elton John played the piano in an empty studio – TC8 at BBC Television Centre, to be precise – for Eric and Ernie dressed as the studio cleaners, over half the nation was present. Variety had come a long way in the century and a quarter since its birth.

The birth took place at the Canterbury Arms in Lambeth and, in time, Charles Morton, the Canterbury's licensee, became known as 'the father of the halls'. Morton, born in Hackney in 1819, had been in the pub business since his early twenties; he had been landlord of the Canterbury, situated just south of the River Thames between St Thomas's Hospital and the railway line into the newly built Waterloo station, since December 1849. At his previous establishment in Pimlico, he'd gained a reputation for providing good entertainment, mostly in the form of 'free and easies', 'harmonic meetings' or 'sing-songs' – evenings where the drinkers, almost all of them male, would get up and give a song, accompanied on the pub's piano. He continued these attractions at the Canterbury, adding ladies' evenings by popular demand, and their success was such that the tavern's parlour soon proved inadequate.

Four skittle alleys at the rear of the public house were swept away to allow a suitable venue to be built, and on 17 May 1852, the Canterbury Hall opened its doors for the first time, allowing larger audiences to be accommodated. The bill was very much as it had been in the pub, with singers called forward by the chairman, accompanied on the grand piano and a harmonium on the stage. As important as the singing was the opportunity to enjoy a pipe, a glass of porter and convivial company. Such was the demand that by 1856, a bigger, better Canterbury Hall had to be built. Ingenious planning and construction allowed entertainment to continue uninterrupted through the building works. The new Canterbury was opened in its entirety on 21 December 1856. This was an age when pub design was ornate to the point of suffocation, and the second Canterbury took its cue from this tradition. It was noted for 'its architectural merits, and the general propriety and beauty of its decorations ... the careful blending of colour; and the large amount of glass judiciously distributed about over the building imparts lightness and character to a room of more than ordinary dimensions ... The customary evening attendance at this popular resort, we understand, extends to 1000 persons.'[1]

In these early days, the bill consisted largely of 'songs, glees, madrigals, etc.'[2] with comedy very low on the bill. Influential as Morton was, he was not the first to use the name 'music hall'. In November 1848, publican Richard Preece had renamed the Grand Harmonic Hall of the Grapes in Southwark Bridge Road the Surrey Music Hall. Then, in 1851, Edward Winder changed the name of the Mogul Saloon in Drury Lane to the Middlesex Music Hall. He was also preceded slightly by restaurants that laid on entertainment and invited musical contributions from diners; these were known as 'song and supper rooms' and had sprung up from the 1830s onwards.

The first, and best known, of the song and supper rooms was at 43 King Street, which had once been a private house belonging to Sir Thomas Killigrew, founder of the Theatre Royal, Drury Lane. Since 1774, it had operated as a hotel, known as Joy's, until it was taken over by W.C. Evans, comedian at the Covent Garden theatre. Known, rather pedantically, as 'Evans's (late Joy's)', it offered bed and breakfast at a guinea a week, and a table d'hôte at 6pm every day for just two shillings. 'A fine HAUNCH and NECK of VENISON ready this day' said the advertisement in *The Times* – the nosh being top of the bill. Almost as an afterthought, the ad explained that there was 'The Harmonic Meeting every evening as usual; Mr. Evans in the chair.'[3]

The song and supper rooms were resolutely male, and a flavour of the resentment this must have caused at home can be found in 'Mr Caudle joins a club – The Skylarks', written in 1845 for the then new humorous periodical *Punch* by Douglas Jerrold, who frequented Evans's:

How any decent man can go and spend his nights in a tavern . . . There was a time when you were as regular at your fireside as the kettle. That was when you were a decent man, and didn't go amongst Heaven knows who, drinking and smoking, and making what you think your jokes. I never heard any good come to a man who cared about jokes . . . The Skylarks, indeed! I suppose you'll be buying a 'Little Warbler' and at your time of life, be trying to sing . . . Nice habits men learn at clubs! There's Joskins: he was a decent creature once, and now I'm told he has more than once boxed his wife's ears . . . Going and sitting for four hours at a tavern! What men, unless they had their wives with them, can find to talk about, I can't think. No good, of course.[4]

The early manifestations of the Canterbury Hall bore no resemblance to a theatre. Their design was somewhere between a banqueting hall and a concert hall with a platform for performers at the end. There was no sign of a proscenium arch, boxes or a raked floor – and for good reason. Music halls were not permitted to put on theatrical entertainment, and the Lord Chamberlain's men were always on hand to make sure that the drama in the halls and taverns remained strictly off-stage.

A degree of liberalization finally occurred with the passing of the Theatres Regulation Act in 1843, which allowed places of entertainment to apply for theatrical licences, under the jurisdiction of the Lord Chamberlain's office. Before 1843, only the theatre at Covent Garden, on the site of the present Royal Opera House, and the original Theatre Royal at Drury Lane were allowed to stage plays. Drury Lane had opened in 1663, just three years after the restoration of the monarchy, and even this limited provision was improvement on the times of Cromwell, when the 'playhouses were pulled down and actors branded as vagabonds'.[5] Unlicensed premises were allowed to present monologues, songs or ballets – anything musical or involving a single dramatic performer seemed to be permissible – but even a brief extract from a play was out of the question. Scripts (such as they were) of these performances evaded the Lord Chamberlain's prim pencil, entertainment venues without a theatrical licence being instead controlled by the Disorderly Houses Act of 1751, a law originally intended to regulate brothels. With provision of public entertainment regarded as on a par with whoring, the idea of performers as disreputable individuals was sown early.

Some have suggested that the 1843 Act prohibited the serving of food and drink at places with theatrical licences, but it actually says nothing specific about this. It is more likely that the respectable types who ran the theatres thought that it was rude in the extreme to be guzzling shellfish, gnawing on a pig's trotter and hollering for ale while some poor chap was strutting and fretting.

The transpontine success of Morton's new hall inspired entrepreneurs north of the river. The Seven Tankards and Punch Bowl in Holborn became Weston's Music Hall in November 1857. John Wilton, publican of the Prince of Denmark near Tower Bridge, found his existing premises too cramped and opened his own hall in 1858 – happily still extant, with its horseshoe-shaped balcony and barley sugar columns. The Royal Standard at Victoria spawned the first of the halls that would eventually become the Victoria Palace. The Panopticon of Science and Art on Leicester Square became the Alhambra Palace in 1858. In 1863, Samuel Vagg, known professionally as Sam Collins, took over the Lansdowne Arms and Music Hall in Islington, renaming it Collins'.

Soon, Morton was heading north himself. He spied the ideal opportunity when the Boar and Castle on Oxford Street, an old coaching inn with a sizeable yard, came onto the market in 1860. Aided by the expertise of architects Finch, Hall and Paraire, he built the first Oxford Music Hall, which opened on 26 March 1861. Still very much a concert hall, rather than a theatre, it burned down twice, first in February 1868 and again in November 1872, but each time it was rebuilt bigger and better, with the design gradually becoming more theatre-like. The turning point in the evolution of hall design came in 1885, with the opening of the London Pavilion, the first music hall to offer tip-up seats as opposed to benches and tables.

As the building form developed during the late nineteenth and early twentieth century, specialist architects came to prominence. Bertie Crewe made a significant contribution, including the Kingston Empire and the Golders Green Hippodrome, as did the partnership of Oswald Wylson and Charles Long, who designed the Chelsea Palace and last incarnation of the Oxford. However, by far the most prolific and celebrated of all the architects was Frank Matcham, who, by the time of his death in 1920, had initiated over eighty music halls and altered as many. Born in Devon in 1854, the son of a brewer's clerk, he began his career as an apprentice in the architectural practice of Jethro Robinson. Ever sensible and practical, he married Robinson's daughter and took over the firm on his father-in-law's death in 1878. Matcham had a great flair for planning – the sight lines in a Matcham building are uniformly excellent from the very cheapest seats upwards – but he remained budget-conscious, designing the best auditorium he could within the constraints, often at the expense of the exterior treatment. For all his economy and sound structural knowledge, though, he was an interior stylist par excellence. His critics condemned him as architecturally illiterate, pointing to his lack of academic training, but while it's fair to say that his interiors were often a mishmash of styles, from Oriental to Renaissance and back again, they somehow made sense as a whole.

While entrepreneurs like Morton had tended to concentrate on a handful of halls at a time, later proprietors like Sir Oswald Stoll and Moss Empires built nationwide chains, and Matcham's modus operandi found great favour with these operators. Manchester-born Edward Moss had begun his career as a variety theatre proprietor in Edinburgh in 1877, aged 25. His theatres came to be regarded as the 'number one' halls, the circuit – thirty halls strong by 1925 – being known to performers as 'the tour'. His peak as a promoter of new hall building came in 1900 with the opening of the Hippodrome on Charing Cross Road, a circus theatre where audiences could thrill to the sight of twenty-one forest-bred lions, or a man riding a turtle in the giant water tank. Moss was knighted in 1905 for his services to entertainment and charity, but died just seven years later. His *Times* obituary reported that his 'ambition was to be a country gentleman and sportsman', the rather sniffy implication being that a variety theatre proprietor could never be a gentleman.[6]

Oswald Stoll, Australian by birth, had begun his career as an impresario in Cardiff in 1889 with the takeover of Leveno's music hall, which he renamed the Empire. This was a popular choice in an age when the world map was predominantly red. Before long, he had a chain of eight halls, all run with a high moral tone. On his death in 1942, *The Times* noted that his Cardiff experience 'of rowdy audiences made him determine to do all he could to raise the status of music halls and make them places of family entertainment', the paper having evidently got used to the idea of show business types as worthwhile human beings in the thirty years since Moss's death.[7]

Stoll's career peaked with the opening of the Coliseum on St Martin's Lane in 1904, an Italian Renaissance-style 2,358-seater on which Matcham was encouraged to pull out all the stops. The building was revolutionary in the most literal sense, from the mechanized glass globe at the top of the facade to the concentric rings of the revolving stage, which could run in any combination of directions. This technological marvel even allowed horse races to be staged in the theatre. Slightly less impressive was the truncated railway that carried royal visitors from their carriage to the foyer; it failed to work satisfactorily and was soon removed.

From the grandest halls, like the Coliseum, down to the plainest provincial venues, each variety theatre had a dedicated support staff – prop men, wardrobe mistresses, set builders and stagehands, who put the shows together and took them apart again. Peter Prichard, who later became an artists' agent, was brought up in a family of such craftsmen and women:

At the turn of the century, the theatres had their own carpenters, because they made all their own scenery and things like that. My grandfather had been a stage carpenter when it was a profession, but he went from theatre to theatre. My grandmother's bid to fame was that she had been wardrobe mistress on Buffalo Bill's last tour of England. Her sister, my great aunt, had a boarding house [in west London] and some of the cast lodged with her. She said that it included the American Indians who were in the show, because they weren't allowed in the hotels. We had a lot of the props still in the cellar, but we were bombed. We had a load of spears, bows, arrows and shields of the Red Indian period that were left there.[8]

As the buildings, the management and the skills of the support staff developed through the second half of the nineteenth century, so did the entertainment on offer. One of the earliest professional entertainers was W.G. Ross, who forged his reputation in the song and supper rooms with the song 'Sam Hall, the Condemned Sweep'. He contrived to get the audience on his side with this tale of woe, only to chide them at the end of each verse.

Into the 1860s and 1870s, the performers remained mostly singers and almost exclusively male. William Randall was a hit at the Canterbury and the Oxford with seaside ditties like 'On the Sands!'. Meanwhile, just as the US was abolishing slavery, E.W. Mackney[9] was making a name in London as 'the Negro Delineator', the first 'blackface' singer in a line that would continue through Eugene Stratton, G.H. Chirgwin and G.H. Elliott[10] and well into the television age as part of the *Black and White Minstrel Show*.

The first female performers were making their breakthrough at this time, among them 'serio-comic' vocalists like Annie 'The Merriest Girl That's Out' Adams. She helped pave the way for Vesta Victoria, whose signature song was 'Waiting at the Church', and Ada Reeve – as well as for the one female music hall performer who remains almost a household name nearly a century after her death. Born Matilda Alice Victoria Wood in Hoxton in 1870, Marie Lloyd became the archetypal music hall female. Her torrid private life (she married three times, never wisely nor too well) was a fitting background for her repertoire of flirtatious, risqué songs, such as 'I'm a Bit of a Ruin That Cromwell Knocked About a Bit', 'Don't Dilly Dally on the Way' and the almost-certainly penis-related 'Wink the Other Eye'. In particular, 'Don't Dilly Dally on the Way', written for Lloyd by Charles Collins and Fred W. Leigh, would have spoken to working class urban audiences, depicting as it did a moonlight flit to avoid paying the rent:

> We had to move away
> 'Cos the rent we couldn't pay.
> The moving van came round just after dark.
> There was me and my old man,
> Shoving things inside the van,
> Which we'd often done before, let me remark.
> We packed all that could be packed
> In the van, and that's a fact,
> And we got inside all that we could get inside.
> Then we packed all we could pack
> On the tailboard at the back,
> Till there wasn't any room for me to ride.
>
> My old man said: 'Foller the van,
> And don't dilly-dally on the way.'
> Off went the van wiv me 'ome packed in it,
> I walked be'ind wiv me old cock linnet.
> But I dillied and dallied,

8

Dallied and dillied,
Lost me way and don't know where to roam.
And you can't trust a 'Special',
Like the old-time copper,
When you can't find your way home.

Another option for female music hall performers was to pretend to be men. Vesta Tilley and Ella Shields were just two of them, but the field was led by Hetty King – billed, with justification, as 'the world's greatest male impersonator'. Dressed in a top hat and evening suit, King popularized the song 'Give Me the Moonlight', and in her later years became a mentor to crooner Frankie Vaughan, who was always ready to acknowledge her influence.

The modern concept of the comedian was also beginning to emerge. The greatest of all early practitioners was Dan Leno (real name: George Galvin), who had begun his career as a clog dancer before moving into more verbal forms of entertainment. His meandering, frequently surreal act included comic songs with long, spoken digressions such as this cynical rumination on an all too recognizable tourist trade from his 1901 recording of 'The Beefeater':

There's no place on the face of the earth like the Tower of London. If you've never been there, go again. It's a glorious place. Everything old. Now in the first place when you visit the Tower of London, it's free, but you have to pay a shilling to go in. The first ancient item you see is the man that takes the money at the door. Then you pass through the refreshment room, which is the oldest refreshment room in the Tower, and the only one, and there are some very ancient items in the refreshment room, such as the buns, ginger beer, the barmaids and whatnot.[11]

Not far behind Leno was the droll George Robey, billed as 'the Prime Minister of Mirth' and the first music hall performer to receive a knighthood. Then there was Little Tich, as Harry Relph was professionally known, whose diminutive stature was at odds with the length of his boots. In the north of England, comedians tended to play naïve, going for the sympathy laugh. The king of the 'gowks', as these near-simpleton characters were known, was George Formby senior, with his catchphrase 'Coughing better tonight', a reference to the chest condition that would eventually kill him, and songs like 'John Willie, Come On', in which the protagonist failed to notice that he was being propositioned by a prostitute. After his death in 1921, his whole act was taken on by his son. By the thirties, however, Formby junior had found his own voice, in risqué songs performed to his own banjolele accompaniment, and was on his way to a level of stardom his father had never achieved, thanks to the medium of film. He also established his own memorable catchphrase, declaring that things had 'turned out nice again', even when they obviously hadn't.

Unsurprisingly, given the supper club clientele, one of the main characters of the early music hall had been the high-flyer, either down on his luck, or, as in George Leybourne's 'Champagne Charlie' characterization, 'good at any time of day or night, boys, for a spree'. Slowly, however, as audiences expanded, a more earthy, working class element began to be depicted on stage. The authentic cockney dialect (a curious, nasal whine only distantly related to the modern 'cockney' dialect of Estuary English) was heard loud and clear from the likes of the 'coster comedians', who were so called because they acted and sounded like market traders or costermongers. The pioneer was Albert Chevalier, the 'Coster Laureate'. However, his contemporary Gus Elen is better remembered and documented. Having survived into the age of the talkies, he left a permanent record of his act – including his passionately-sung tribute to the goodness of beer, 'Half a Pint of Ale' – in a series of short films for British Pathé.

Throughout the history of music hall and variety, from the early days at the Canterbury to the circuits over fifty years later, the comedians and singers tended to be the big draws, but it was the speciality acts that helped ensure that variety remained varied. The rule of thumb was that the stranger the performance, the more memorable it was.

Take the magician Kardoma, whose act was summed up admirably in his bill matter: 'He fills the stage with flags.' He sometimes filled it with flowers, according to his mood and availability of stock. Or perhaps 'Checker' Wheel – 'The man with the educated feet' – whose star turn was to tap dance in roller skates.

Among the best known of all the 'spesh' acts were the acrobatic troupes like the Five Delevines, who made a speciality out of contorting their bodies into letters of the alphabet, and the Seven Volants. Where these acts were all about feats of agility, others dealt in futility, such as Banner Forbutt, an Australian trick cyclist who, in 1937, managed to stay upright on a stationary bicycle for two hours and thirty-nine minutes. His countrywoman, the contortionist Valentyne Napier, became a massive draw; billed as 'the Human Spider', she performed on a web bathed in ultraviolet light. Many spesh acts came from overseas, but others were not all that they seemed. Rex Roper, the lasso-spinning cowboy act, was authentically Western – from Bristol, that is.

Some forms of dance came under the speciality heading, such as the adagio work performed by the Polish act, the Ganjou Brothers and Juanita, in which Juanita entered on a pendulum hung from the flies, before being thrown all around the stage with great skill by the three brothers.[12] Far less strenuous, but no less skilful, was the sand-dancing of Wilson, Keppel and Betty, who, in their cod-Egyptian garb, shuffled in unison to the strains of 'The Old Bazaar in Cairo'. When booked for appearances in Germany their utterly innocent act was disapproved of by the Nazis because of the bare legs on show.

Then there were the magicians, from the suave David Devant to the unfortunate Chung Ling Soo (in real life, the resolutely Caucasian, American-born illusionist William Robinson), who was killed on stage at the Wood Green Empire on 23 March 1918, when his bullet-catching trick went horribly wrong. Animal acts always went down well, from Captain Woodward's Performing Seals to Hamilton Conrad and his Pigeons, via a plethora of dog acts, such as Maurice Chester's Performing Poodles, Darcy's Dogs and Cawalini and his Canine Pets. The best documented of all the dog acts was Duncan's Collies, inherited by Vic Duncan from his father in 1927 and active well into the fifties. Duncan's dogs had amazing balance, instilled by teaching them to stand on their hind legs on the back of a chair. Highlights of the act included a dog rescuing a baby (in reality, a doll) from what appeared to be a burning building, and a car accident scenario that must have taken years of training. This involved one dog driving a car and another playing dead under the front wheels, while a third, the canine passenger of the car, stood on hind legs at a public telephone calling for an ambulance.

There were even more curious acts on the scene, such as quick-change artists who could reappear in fresh garb in the time it took them to walk behind a screen. One of these was Wilf Burnand, who took to the stage dressed as Scottish singer Harry Lauder, complete with kilt, stick and tam-o'-shanter. Behind the screen he went, emerging barely seconds later as G.H. Elliott in blackface, repeating the trick once again to emerge as Marie Lloyd. Not a word was spoken in Burnand's act. It was all down to his costume changes and the orchestra playing musical cues associated with each of the artists he evoked.[13]

The relative freedom afforded to the music hall meant that material could tackle subjects that might have been deemed unsuitable in a more tightly regulated medium. It was possible to be topical. For example, one song highlighted the expediency and hypocrisy of mainland dwellers' attitudes to the Irish, as the nineteenth century gave way to the twentieth. At this time, there was a great deal of anti-Irish feeling in England, largely inspired by Charles Stewart Parnell's campaign for Home Rule and his subsequent divorce scandal. One performer, ventriloquist Fred Russell, may even have changed his name to avoid being tainted by association, as his grandson, Jack Parnell, explains: 'Charles Stewart Parnell was a pretty bad name in this country, so I believe my grandfather changed his name because of that. My father's stage name was Russ Carr, but I don't think there was any particular reason for that, it was just a stage name.'[14] However, in the Boer War, the Dublin Fusiliers played a vital role, which prompted

Albert Hall and Harry Castling to write a song for the performer Pat Rafferty, called 'What Do You Think of the Irish Now?':

> You used to call us traitors,
> Because of agitators,
> But you can't call us traitors now![15]

Around this time, during the early 1900s, Marie Lloyd was at the head of a phalanx of performers who used their freedom to highlight earthier concerns. Lloyd's risqué repertoire included innuendo-laden songs like 'She'd Never Had Her Ticket Punched Before', a tale of an innocent abroad on the railways, but with seemingly lewd undercurrents:

> The man said, 'I must punch your ticket', spoke sharp, I suppose,
> Said she, 'Thou punch my ticket, and I'll punch thee on thy nose'.[16]

Off-stage, her life was a mess of feckless husbands and freeloaders abusing her considerable generosity, but professionally, Lloyd was a very canny operator. Summoned to defend her material by the London County Council licensing committee, she sang one of her supposedly offensive songs very demurely, then an apparently innocent and acceptable song in a lascivious manner, with plenty of winking. Filth, as Tom Lehrer later put it, was in the mind of the beholder.

Lloyd also used her clout to improve conditions for acts less well-off than herself. A life on the halls was hardest for those lower down the bill – known as 'down among the wines and spirits' due to their placement in the printed programme – but it wasn't a picnic for the stars. In London, a big name would rush, by carriage, between several halls in one night. A typical night for Marie Lloyd began with an 8.30 appearance at the Middlesex, saw her heading south to the Canterbury for 9.10, to the Royal Cambridge at Shoreditch for 10.10, and ended with a bill-topping performance at the Oxford at 10.45. When Dan Leno died in 1904, aged just 43, his *Times* obituary observed that his 'mind and body, it seems, were worn out by overwork'.[17] The effort had not been entirely wasted, though. Leno was the biggest star of his day and, on the day of his funeral, a crowd three deep and three miles long came to pay its last respects, as his body processed to the Lambeth Cemetery in Tooting.

The lesson of Leno's demise was not learned, and proprietors tried to get even more out of the artists they booked. In October 1906, Walter Gibbons, proprietor of the Empires at Islington and Holborn, the Clapham Grand and the Brixton Empress among others, bought the Brixton Theatre. He tried to capitalize on its proximity to the Empress by making acts double up at the two halls. Not surprisingly, the performers cried foul and went on strike. The location of this disagreement was significant. Many London-based music hall performers had made their homes in Brixton and Streatham, because of the all-night tram service, so Gibbons's action was a high explosive device landing in their back yard.

Most of the other proprietors weren't far behind Gibbons in their desire to squeeze even more value out of the talent. Many added matinees without extra pay and placed punitive barring clauses in contracts, preventing artists from appearing at halls within a certain radius, during a set time period. For a performer such as the tragedian John 'Humanity' Lawson, it meant that 'if I enter into contract for say, two years' time, the law decides that in that particular district of anything from three to ten miles, I must not ply my calling'.[18]

Gibbons made emollient noises about extra pay for matinees, and closing the extra theatre, but these turned out to be time-buying manoeuvres while he consulted other proprietors about how best to screw more work out of the turns. Before long, aided by the newly formed Variety Artists' Federation, the whole profession was on strike. Marie Lloyd handed out leaflets to highlight the reasons for the industrial action, while Gus Elen could be found picketing outside the Canterbury, singing an adapted version of his song 'Wait Until the Work Comes Around':

> If yer don't get stars,
> The public stop out!
> That's a' argyment what's sensible and sound
> Get yer stars back – pay your bandsmen
> Treat your staff a bit more handsome
> Or your dividends will never come around. [19]

The stars' decision to come out on strike was a magnanimous gesture. The likes of Lloyd were earning £80 a week, at a time when a skilled labourer wouldn't expect to earn much more than that in a year. When managers attempted to squeeze more out of their performers, it was the lowest-paid – such as the pit musicians, some of whom were on as little as £1 a week – who had it worst. With the involvement of the big names, the strike proved very effective. An arbitrator was appointed, work was resumed, and in June 1907 an improved contract was offered, including payment for matinees and more reasonable barring clauses. The episode gained the VAF members the nickname 'Very Awkward Fellows', but it forced managers to ease off in their exploitation of talent.

For all the improving efforts made by Stoll and others during the latter years of the nineteenth century, the music hall was still not regarded as respectable. In particular, by the mid-1890s, the Empire and the Alhambra theatres on Leicester Square had developed reputations as dens of vice. The Empire's promenade, it was said, was full of gentlemen with little or no interest in the show and ladies who were happy to offer other distractions at a price. The reputation was largely unjustified. As early as 1866, the Alhambra's manager had told a Parliamentary Select Committee that approximately 1 per cent of his 3,500-strong audience were prostitutes, and that it was impossible to stop them buying tickets for shows.[20]

It fell to Mrs Laura Ormiston Chant, the Mary Whitehouse of her day and a fully paid-up member of the great and good with connections in the Liberal Party, to order a clean-up. When, in October 1894, Empire proprietor George Edwardes applied to the London County Council for a new licence as a matter of routine, Mrs Ormiston Chant blocked it 'on the ground that the place at night is the habitual resort of prostitutes in pursuit of their traffic, and that portions of the entertainment are most objectionable, obnoxious, and against the best interests and moral well-being of the community at large'.[21]

In particular, she objected to the suggestive, flesh-coloured tights worn by the ballet dancers on stage. A Miss Shepherd, one of the Empire dancers, spoke up for her colleagues, stating that 'their lives were as pure and honourable, and their calling as respectable, as those of Mrs Ormiston Chant and her friends', adding that her work at the Empire had allowed her to 'make the last days of her widowed mother happy', which moved some of those present to cheer. Mr T. Elvidge, secretary of the Theatrical and Music-Hall Operatives Union, also spoke up, estimating that the closure of the Empire would affect, 'directly and indirectly . . . not fewer than 10,000 working people'.[22] Mrs Ormiston Chant, who had visited the Empire five times, and claimed she had been accosted frequently by men who mistook her intentions and availability, remained unconvinced.

Edwardes declared the Empire closed on 26 October 1894, citing the regulatory mess. However, it was eventually decided to award the licence on condition that the serving of drinks in the auditorium should cease, and that the promenade should be 'abolished'. In practice, this meant that it was to be hidden from the auditorium by a temporary canvas screen. Very temporary, as it transpired. On the night of the grand reopening, it was torn down by promenaders, including the young Winston Churchill. Fragments were then carried out into the London night. The public had given Mrs Ormiston Chant a very robust answer.

The music hall finally achieved a measure of legitimacy on 1 July 1912 at the Palace Theatre, on London's Cambridge Circus. It was, as Sir Oswald Stoll said, the night when 'the Cinderella of the Arts' finally went to the ball: the first *Royal Variety Performance*. There had long been music hall fans in the ranks of the royal family, in particular King Edward VII, who took his love of stage folk further than most – actress

Lillie Langtry being one of his mistresses. However, the normal procedure had been to summon favoured performers for a private 'command' performance at a royal residence. Dan Leno had been a particular favourite. In the fields of opera and ballet, royal galas were well established, and it was finally decided to extend the same patronage to variety.

Almost all of the big names of the day were present, if not in a performing capacity then as a walk-on in the 'Variety's Garden Party' finale; among them were coster comedian Gus Elen, 'blackface' performer G.H. Chirgwin, illusionist David Devant, the Australian comedienne Florrie Forde, musical theatre star Lupino Lane, Scottish singer Harry Lauder, comedian George Robey and the acrobatic Delevines. There were two notable absentees. Elen's counterpart Albert Chevalier was omitted for unknown reasons, while Marie Lloyd was not invited for the sin of being too vulgar. It has been suggested that it was at least partially a payback for her vocal support of the 1907 strike. Lloyd responded in a typically robust manner, by declaring that all of her performances were by command of the British public.

1912 was also the year when the music halls came under the jurisdiction of the Lord Chamberlain for the first time, clearing up a decades-old anomaly and allowing one-act plays to be presented in variety bills. Unfortunately, 1912 was also to be the peak of music hall, its rise checked by the enforced hiatus of the First World War. The last of London's great variety theatres had already been built, with the opening of the Matcham-designed Palladium in 1910. The form of the shows was also changing, with the old order of a chairman introducing a disparate selection of turns being replaced by packaged, star-led shows.

The first generation of entrepreneurs and proprietors had given way to a new breed. Walter Gibbons's interests had formed the basis of the General Theatres Corporation, which was taken over by the fledgling Gaumont-British movie outfit in 1929. In charge of GTC was George Black, the Birmingham-born son of an early cinema entrepreneur, who had come to London in 1928 to take the job. When GTC took over the Moss circuit in 1932, Black's empire (or rather Empires) expanded massively, making him just about the most powerful man in entertainment at the time. Only slightly less exalted was his general manager Val Parnell, the son of ventriloquist Fred Russell. Sir Oswald Stoll held onto his circuit until his death in 1942, when he was succeeded by the superbly named Prince Littler.

The Moss/GTC and Stoll circuits were known as the 'number one' halls, and below them was a clear hierarchy for performers to scale or descend according to fashion and favour. Leading the 'number twos' was the Syndicate Halls circuit. 'Syndicates were second-rate, really, although they had very, very influential theatres like the Metropolitan, Edgware Road and the Empress, Brixton, etc.,' explains Peter Prichard. Each circuit had bookers, who carved fearsome reputations among the talent. 'The booker at Moss Empires was Cissie Williams, [it was] Miss [Florence] Leddington at Syndicates, and at Stoll's, it was Harry Harbour's father [Sam Harbour], then Harry Harbour.'[23]

Among the stars that the new variety bosses brought forward was Harry Tate, who would be one of the hits of the second *Royal Variety Performance* in 1919, and a major draw until his death in 1940. He was the doyen of sketch comedians with routines such as 'Motoring', 'Golfing', 'Fishing' and 'Selling a Car', in which, accompanied by a cheeky young boy who was too clever for his own good (portrayed, at one point, by a young Hughie Green), he played a clueless, yet devious buffoon with an all too mobile moustache. In reality, Tate was clean-shaven, and the moustache was a prop, clipped to his nose, allowing him to wiggle it, milking every last drop of laughter from a situation.

Later came the Crazy Gang – consisting of Bud Flanagan and Chesney Allen, Jimmy Nervo and Teddy Knox, Charlie Naughton and Jimmy Gold – who were to take up residency at the London Palladium for much of the thirties, transferring to the Victoria Palace after the Second World War. None of this success was expected, however, when the group was formed in a fit of pique by George Black. Black was all-powerful, and thought nothing of tying up most of his major talent with a blocking clause stating that, following an appearance at one of General Theatre Corporation's West End houses, an act could not appear at any other central venue. He kept the acts he really wanted in work and thus prevented them appearing for Stoll or any rivals. Everyone involved was happy, including the Glaswegian double act Naughton and Gold. However, when Charlie Naughton and Jimmy Gold returned from an Australian tour in 1931, they found themselves outside the barring period and in a position to accept an approach from Stoll to play his Alhambra in Leicester Square. Their agent pointed this out to Black suggesting that if he could guarantee them a week at the Palladium, they wouldn't take the Stoll offer. Black responded by giving them their week in Argyll Street, as long as they didn't mind sharing the bill with Nervo and Knox, not to mention Billy Caryll and Hilda Mundy, who appeared on that first bill, but didn't become part of the famous gang. Furthermore, the show would not consist of their usual, separate acts. All three turns would work together. The week commencing 7 December was to be 'Crazy Week'.[24]

Naughton and Gold went crazy. They were generally wary of the whole set-up and particularly suspicious of Jimmy Nervo and Teddy Knox, whom they had suspected of stealing their material in the past. Moss Empires' general manager Val Parnell mollified Naughton and Gold, and the booking went ahead. Naughton and Gold were very much the senior partners, having been together as an act since 1908. Jimmy Gold was the writer of the pair, coming up with a lot of the material. Charlie Naughton was, in Roy Hudd's recollection, the 'little, pot-bellied butt of all the sketches ... He never had much to say but just walking on as Spartacus or Friar Tuck or Thisbe was enough.'[25] Unfortunately, recordings of their work haven't aged well, and they come across as a typical, fair-to-middling, cross-talking double act of the era:

GOLD: Here we are, Charlie, here we are. Loch Ness.
NAUGHTON: Loch Ness, we'll soon catch this monster.
GOLD: I think it's a myth.
NAUGHTON: A myth?
GOLD: You know what a myth is?

NAUGHTON: Oh yes, a moth's sweetheart.

GOLD: Not at all, it's a beast, a monster. Now you know what a monster is?

NAUGHTON: Yes, I married one.

GOLD: It isn't a woman I tell you, it's a beast.

NAUGHTON: That's the wife all right.

GOLD: It's a big fish, and I know all about big fish. My father had a fish shop in Aberdeen.

NAUGHTON: Haddie? [A pun on finnan haddie, a smoked haddock dish popular in Aberdeen.]

GOLD: Yes he had.

NAUGHTON: Yes, and I know all about fish, and I know about fish roe, such as cod roe, hard roe, soft roe and Rotten Row.

GOLD: Rotten Row's not a fish.

NAUGHTON: It's a pla[i]ce.[26]

Nervo and Knox were a decade younger than Naughton and Gold and had been together since only 1919.[27] Both were acrobats by training, and at this point in their career were best known for their slow-motion wrestling act. As if this weren't enough talent on one bill, Nervo and Knox insisted on bringing in 'Monsewer' Eddie Gray, juggler, prankster, wearer of the most expressive false moustache this side of Harry Tate, and the true inventor of Franglais.

Black's main motivation was to make life difficult for Stoll, but 'the results genuinely surprised him ... the theatre was packed'.[28] Repeat bookings followed, and in June 1932, another act was added to the formula. Bud Flanagan and Chesney Allen were singers of sentimental songs and purveyors of corny jokes rather than knockabout comedians. Apart from concerns that their presence would slow the show down, Bud Flanagan's pushiness, born of an absolute knowledge of his own worth, irritated Nervo, Knox, Naughton and Gold. Parnell again smoothed things over and the incumbents began to accept Bud and Ches. So did the audiences, and the new line-up was even more successful than the original. The sketches were important, but the main thing was the interplay between the comedians, frequently violent and disruptive as it was. 'Buckets of water and paste fell on performers' heads in the middle of their act,' remembered Maureen Owen in her history of the Crazy Gang. 'Audiences were asked to laugh at the spectacle of one person causing bodily injury to another or breaking up a skilled act.'[29] The audiences didn't care for health and safety and so, over the next decade, the Crazy Gang became the biggest stars in variety, as well as great favourites of the royal family, continuing the long line of patronage.

Meanwhile, the 'Cheeky Chappie' Max Miller, in a suit made from what appeared to be a pair of curtains, stood slightly stooped by the footlights, and conspired with the audience to continue the legacy of bawdiness left by some earlier music hall performers. Even Miller's racier jokes seem tame by today's standards, such as the one about the girl of 18 who swallowed a pin, but didn't feel the prick until she was 21. Just to be safe, though, he made sure the audience knew what they were getting with the equivalent of the modern broadcaster's 'strong language' disclaimer. He offered them the choice between the white book (clean jokes) and the blue book (his more risqué material). They always chose the blue book.

Aside from pure comedy acts like Miller and the Crazy Gang, show bands were also carving out a niche for themselves by incorporating a comedic element in their act. Jack Payne and Henry Hall both went from being hotel bandleaders to national figures in the early years of broadcasting. They capitalized on this fame with touring shows, while shrewd Lancastrian Jack Hylton and bluff, matey Londoner Billy Cotton took their dance bands onto the variety stage. Hylton's main calling card had been his recording associations with HMV and Decca, while Cotton had begun his bandleading career at the Palais, Southport in 1925, where he had popularized a dance craze called the Black Bottom. By 1928, his band was resident at the newly opened Astoria in London's Charing Cross Road, and was also recording for the Regal label, and Cotton himself was on his way to becoming a household name.

Not all of the talent was home-grown, though. In 1933, Duke

Ellington's orchestra headlined at the London Palladium, followed in 1935 by Louis Armstrong, known as Satchmo (short for 'Satchelmouth'). Although the sanitized jazz of the British dance bands was popular, the authentic item was still too advanced for mass consumption at this point. 'The great British public stayed away in their thousands,' recalled musician and scriptwriter Sid Colin in 1977. 'For the jazzers, the tour became a pilgrimage, and they followed Satchmo from theatre to theatre, often watching and listening marooned in a desert of empty seats.'[30]

Until the early twentieth century, live entertainment was the only type available, but the all-powerful bookers eventually had to contend with competition, which came initially from cinemas. The earliest movie shows had been items in variety bills, but films soon justified their own dedicated buildings and a new approach to showmanship. In the larger, plusher picture palaces, such as the four Astorias built in the inner London suburbs at Brixton, Streatham, Finsbury Park and on the Old Kent Road in the late twenties and early thirties, variety acts played second fiddle to the latest sensations from Hollywood. By 1939, there were an estimated 5,500 cinemas in Britain, although the peak of cinema attendances was not reached until 1946, with 1.6 billion, or 31 million patrons weekly. When, in the twenties, broadcasting entered the fray, the variety world viewed it more as a threat than an opportunity.

Since its foundation in 1922, the BBC's stated *raison d'être* has been to educate, inform and entertain.[31] For much of its early history, however, entertainment was emphatically the junior partner. Until 1927, 'BBC' stood for British Broadcasting Company; it was a private business, set up by a consortium of radio manufacturers so that their customers would have something to listen to on their crystal sets. It might have been in the best interests of these parties to make programming as populist as possible, but the new venture was both tightly regulated by the General Post Office (the government agency responsible for telecommunications) and subject to the iron will of its general manager, John Charles Walsham Reith. A son of the manse to whom religion remained vitally important throughout his life, Reith was a Scot by birth, an engineer by training and didactic by inclination.

Acrobats, jugglers and other visual performers could hardly be expected to make much of an impact on the new medium of sound broadcasting, but Reith's distaste for levity meant that, at first, comedians hardly figured either, with the schedules consisting largely of talks and music. At the lighter end of programming, the dance bands employed at the major London hotels were early to the microphone, most notably Carroll Gibbons and his Savoy Orpheans – which was an easy job for the outside broadcast team, the Savoy hotel being next to the BBC's studios in the Institute of Electrical Engineers building at Savoy Hill. Not much further away was the Hotel Cecil, where Jack Payne's band had the residency. In February 1928, Payne joined the Corporation as its director of dance music and his band became the BBC Dance Orchestra.

Reith's wariness towards performers was echoed by the uncertainty many variety managers, agents and performers felt about broadcasting. It was possible to tour with the same act for years, but radio was seen as a voracious consumer of new material, with the added disincentive of poor remuneration. Many bookers put clauses in artists' contracts forbidding them from broadcasting. Walter Payne, head of Moss Empires, refused to have anything to do with the BBC until 1925, when a limited amount of co-operation began. As a result, the wireless had mostly to make do with second-rate or untried performers. One of these was a Liverpudlian comedian, Tommy Handley, who began his broadcasting career in a revue called *Radio Radiance* in 1924. With the wealth of experience he was able to gain in these pioneering days, he didn't remain second-rate for long, and within fifteen years of his radio debut, he was the top broadcasting comedian.

For a long time, the BBC avoided frivolity altogether on Sundays. Taking 1 November 1924 as a typical Sabbath, broadcasts on 2LO – the BBC's London station – began at 3pm with Big Ben, followed by a march from the Band of Princess Patricia's Canadian Light Infantry, and continued through the classical repertoire, culminating in two broadcasts by De Groot and his Piccadilly Orchestra including highlights from Verdi and Wagner. As the twenties gave way to the thirties, the BBC was forced to take the lighter end of its output more seriously because of the growth of commercial stations like Radio Paris, Radio Normandie and Radio Luxembourg, which were beaming their signals over from the Continent. Free of regulation and the wrath of Reith, they had no need to be solemn. Unsupported by licence fee funding, they took in advertising, and manufacturers were keen to get their names on variety shows. Davy Burnaby, one of the stars of the long-running *Co-Optimists* revue of the twenties, could be found on Radio Luxembourg in the mid-thirties, leading the 'Rinsoptimists' in a show sponsored by Rinso detergent. His merry band included the young Welsh banjoleist Tessie O'Shea. Meanwhile, George Formby – son of the bronchial northern turn and purveyor of cheeky, but never smutty comic songs – was a regular in *Feen-A-Mint Fanfare*, sponsored by one of the leading laxatives of the day. Without much competition from Reith's organization, the continental stations had the lion's share of the Sunday listenership.

The development of variety at the BBC had also been hampered by the absence of a dedicated executive. Although a revue and vaudeville department was created in March 1930, it remained the province of the director of drama, initially R.E. Jeffrey, 'an ex-actor of the boldly extrovert school'.[32] Eventually the mantle passed to bearded, swordstick-toting Val Gielgud, brother of actor John. The most important early innovator in radio drama, he regarded his variety responsibilities as a nuisance, and was greatly relieved, in 1933, when Reith took them away and gave them to Gielgud's friend, Eric Maschwitz, editor of the *Radio Times*.

Maschwitz was ideally suited to being the BBC's first director of variety, being as much a lyricist, playwright and novelist as he was a journalist. Born in Birmingham, he was educated at Repton and Cambridge, devoting more time to his Footlights membership and his extra-curricular writing than to his studies, so that he considered himself lucky to have scraped through his finals.[33] He moved to London after graduation, published his first novel and married the revue artist Hermione Gingold, which gave him a thorough grounding in handling performers. In need of more regular work, he had, at the suggestion of his friend Lance Sieveking, another pioneering BBC producer, applied to join the Company, becoming an assistant in the outside broadcast department in 1926. This proved to be a very temporary appointment, as his writing skills made him the ideal internal candidate for the job of managing editor at the *Radio Times*, keeping the brilliant but disorganized editor Walter Fuller in line. Unfortunately, Fuller died of a heart attack within weeks of Maschwitz's appointment, and he suddenly found himself in the editor's chair.

Maschwitz's dual song- and playwriting careers began while he was still at the *Radio Times*, as a favour to Val Gielgud – his main selling point being that as a BBC staff member he wouldn't need extra payment for such work. He wrote a technically complex radio play based on Compton Mackenzie's novel *Carnival*, which 'used so many studios that we practically tied Savoy Hill in knots'.[34] Nonetheless, it was judged a success and soon Gielgud was in need of a musical. Maschwitz had been introduced to an impecunious young composer called George Posford, and they collaborated on a show called *Good Night, Vienna*. Maschwitz admitted that 'the story included almost every sugary cliché imaginable' but praised Posford's 'fresh and tuneful' score.

To their surprise, the morning after the broadcast, film producer Herbert Wilcox called offering £200 for the film rights. It became one of the first musical talkies to be made in Britain, starring Jack Buchanan and Anna Neagle, the future Mrs Herbert Wilcox. It was a success in West End cinemas, but a possibly apocryphal story suggests it was less well received elsewhere. Passing a south London cinema where it was showing, Maschwitz is reported to have asked the commissionaire how it was faring. 'About as well as *Good Night, Lewisham* would do in Vienna' came the reply.

Maschwitz liked to present himself as a dilettante, to whom things happened largely by happy accident. This belies his considerable natural talent, charm and ability to negotiate a path through the already problematic politics of the BBC. Broadcasting House had opened in 1932, and Colonel G. Val Myer's design was perfect for broadcasting in all but one regard: its size. Even from the outset, it was too small for the Corporation's ever-expanding activities, which included the start of the Empire Service (later External Services, now World Service) that year. When Maschwitz took over in 1933, variety had two dedicated studios in the basement of the new building – BA for general 'vaudeville' programmes, BB for the use of the BBC Dance Orchestra, under the direction of Henry Hall since February 1932. Nonetheless, Maschwitz 'began to gaze longingly across Langham Place at St George's Hall'.[35]

Once the home of David Devant and John Nevil Maskelyne's magic shows, it had been dark for some time, and Maschwitz suggested that the variety department should take it over. Initially sceptical, the engineers conducted acoustic tests and declared that it was not merely adequate for broadcasting but perfect. Maschwitz moved his gargantuan desk (actually a boardroom table that had been rejected by the BBC governors) and his staff into the building. This phalanx included new, dedicated producers like John Watt, brought over from the BBC's Belfast outpost by Gielgud; former schoolmaster Bryan Michie, who went on to discover Morecambe and Wise for his *Youth Takes A Bow* show; and Harry S. Pepper and John Sharman, a pair of hoofers who had both learned their trade in concert parties.

The decision to get out was a mark of Maschwitz's shrewdness. He noted that, at Broadcasting House, the BBC was 'undoubtedly on the way to becoming a trifle "grand"', with the weekly Programme Board meeting assuming 'the hushed solemnity of a Cabinet conference'. St George's Hall provided 'a pleasant sense of escape' for the variety department, described variously by Maschwitz as 'surely the most assorted and co-operative collection of characters ever assembled', and 'my band of incorrigible bohemians'.[36] Unsurprisingly, they thrived in the old theatre atmosphere, away from the sleek, austere modernity of BH – as the new building was and remains known to BBC staff.

Apart from the dance bands, early radio variety had consisted of revues, concert parties and monologues, and these continued well into the thirties with *Music Hall*, produced by John Sharman, and Harry S. Pepper's *Kentucky Minstrels*. This programme was very much a continuation of the family business for Pepper, son of Will C. Pepper, who had been running blackface minstrel concert parties since the 1890s. Although no make-up was needed for the radio version, the songs remained the same, drawing on the Stephen Foster catalogue. Not that Pepper was always looking to the past for inspiration. He was the main instigator of *Monday Night at Seven* and its successor *Monday Night at Eight*, a portmanteau show combining variety, the 'Inspector Hornleigh Investigates' detective stories and 'Puzzle Corner', hosted by fellow producer Ronnie Waldman.

There was innovation in the air too. Producer Max Kester introduced Marx Brothers-style humour to the British airwaves in *Danger – Men at Work*, which he also wrote, while John Watt pioneered a semi-documentary approach in *Songs from the Shows*, where the stories behind famous compositions were explained. Despite these great strides, variety moguls like GTC boss George Black were at best dubious of broadcasting. From October 1928, Black had allowed live relays from the Palladium and the venture was successful enough for Oswald Stoll to join in shortly after. However, in 1931, when the economic downturn had kicked in fully, Black pulled out. It took all of Maschwitz's charm and persuasion to restore relations and show the variety moguls that broadcasting was an additional shop window for their artists, not a rival outlet, allowing relays to resume.

The most lasting success of the Maschwitz era was a show he created himself, the Saturday evening magazine programme *In Town Tonight*, 'devised to provide a shop window for any topical feature that might bob up'. The first edition was something of a shambles, apart from the final item, where the bandleaders of the day returned to the ranks and played (as they had at the silver wedding party of Christopher Stone, the first presenter to make a feature of playing gramophone records on the radio). It improved quickly and remained a fixture in the

Saturday evening radio schedules until September 1960. Most memorable of all was its opening sound montage, featuring a Piccadilly flower-seller yelling the programme's title, and sound effects of the London traffic, all of which came to a halt when announcer Freddie Grisewood issued the command 'STOP!', making way for Eric Coates's evocative 'Knightsbridge March'.

In the summer of 1937, Maschwitz accepted an offer from Metro-Goldwyn-Mayer to become a Hollywood screenwriter. His four years as director of variety had turned the BBC from a grudging provider of jollity into an entertainment powerhouse, and it was John Watt's job to carry on the work.

The radio had represented a major change in the way the British people were entertained. Previously, making your own entertainment had been a popular option. In pre-music hall days, better-off families often had a piano or a harmonium in the front parlour, around which everyone would congregate to sing. Poorer families usually had no such luxury, but banjos, ukuleles and harmonicas could be found reasonably cheaply, while rhythmic accompaniment could be improvised on a pair of spoons or bones. The music halls, variety theatres and later the cinemas provided entertainment for all, with seats at prices that ranged from reasonable to exorbitant. Most importantly, it was mass entertainment, entertaining thousands at a time. However, broadcasting could entertain millions at a time without them having to leave their homes. Of course, those in miserable, drab abodes will have wanted to leave them as often as possible and enter the escapist world of the local Empire or Gaumont, but as living standards improved, this became less of an issue. Broadcasting also represented good value. A radio licence cost ten shillings a year at a time when the cheapest seat in the Odeon Leicester Square was two shillings and sixpence. This counted for a lot in the depression that stretched from 1929 to the start of the Second World War.

★

During Maschwitz's reign at St George's Hall, the development of a new mass medium had been gathering momentum. Between 1924 and 1930, John Logie Baird's experiments in television had progressed from transmitting a crude image of a Maltese cross a few yards to sending real drama and variety, of an admittedly limited nature, over long distances. The picture had only 30 lines of resolution, compared with the 625 in a modern standard-definition television image, but it proved a source of fascination to the early adopters of the day, who built their own sets or bought a Baird 'Televisor' for 25 guineas. The only thing Baird was missing was a decent-sized transmitter, and the obvious answer was to approach the BBC. Unfortunately, the appeal of television wasn't so obvious to Reith, who took against Baird in no uncertain terms, while the Corporation's chief engineer Peter Eckersley admitted to grave misgivings over the technical quality of Baird's efforts. So the initial approach was rebuffed.

Eventually, after much negotiation, the BBC agreed to facilitate test transmissions from 30 September 1929, using the 2LO radio transmitter on the roof of Selfridges department store, for half an hour each morning with additional trials after closedown. At first, sound and vision could not be transmitted simultaneously, 2LO having only one frequency. Consequently they were broadcast in alternating two-minute chunks. The twain met when the twin-wavelength Brookmans Park transmitting station replaced 2LO in early 1930, and soon the first play with synchronized sound and vision was broadcast – a production of *The Man with the Flower in His Mouth* by Luigi Pirandello. By 1932, the experiments had moved from Baird's premises on Long Acre into the new Broadcasting House.

Entertainment found a home within the new medium from the off, and the gents from St George's Hall were roped in to organize the pioneering shows, originated in the basement of Broadcasting House. One example of an early TV variety show was *Looking In*, broadcast on 21 April 1933 at 11.12pm. Written by John Watt, with music by Harry S. Pepper, it featured Anona Winn – later to become famous as one of the panellists on *Twenty Questions* – and a dance act by the Paramount

Astoria Girls.[37] The 30-line transmissions continued until September 1935, but the need for higher definition was obvious. A wing of the Alexandra Palace building in Wood Green was acquired for studios and a transmitter mast. The Palace, known to the public as Ally Pally, but in the abbreviation-heavy BBC as AP, had been built in 1873 as an exhibition centre and show place. It was intended to be north London's answer to the Crystal Palace in Sydenham, but was a white elephant from the start. Its lowest ebb came during the First World War when it was used as an internment camp for prisoners of war and other enemy aliens.

When television arrived at AP, the technology was far from finalized. Baird had developed a system capable of 240 lines, initially using a messy and cumbersome process involving a film camera from which the film was developed instantaneously, but by the time he achieved this, he no longer had the field to himself. In 1931, the HMV and Columbia record companies had merged to form Electric and Musical Industries, or EMI. HMV had been an early leader, but by the time of the merger, the Columbia side of the company was making the running in research and development, thanks to a restless inventor called Alan Dower Blumlein. By the early thirties, Blumlein had invented a system of electric recording that beat the existing American-made Westrex system hands down without infringing a single patent, and had developed the method of stereo disc recording that would finally be adopted by the industry in 1958. To focus on television, EMI joined forces with the Marconi company, with work proceeding at EMI's Central Research Laboratories in Hayes, under Isaac Shoenberg. By 1936, Shoenberg's team, in which Blumlein played a vital role, had succeeded in producing a purely electronic system, and one that was capable of a 405-line picture using cameras known as Emitrons. A date of 2 November 1936 was set for the launch of the BBC's new high-definition television service, using the Baird and Marconi-EMI systems on alternate weeks. Baird won the toss to go first.

However, the planners had reckoned without the first director of television, Gerald Cock, who as head of outside broadcasts for BBC

Radio, had been used to turning thoughts into action quickly. He decided that the Radiolympia exhibition in August 1936 would be an ideal showcase for the new service. The technicians insisted the equipment wouldn't be ready and the producers said there wouldn't be enough programme material, but, somehow, programme chief Cecil Madden conjured up the required elements and the service was on air over two months early, broadcasting both to the exhibition from Alexandra Palace and from the exhibition itself. After a hiatus, while the lessons of the experiment were absorbed and limited test transmissions took place, the launch proper went ahead as planned. At 3pm on 2 November, the Baird system went on air with speeches from BBC chairman R.C. Norman, Postmaster General the Rt Hon. G.C. Tryon, Television Advisory Committee chairman Lord Selsdon, and Baird chairman Harry Greer. Then, accompanied by the BBC Television Orchestra under the baton of Hyam 'Bumps' Greenbaum, Adele Dixon sang a song composed for the occasion, called 'Television is Here':

> A mighty maze of mystic, magic rays
> Is all about us in the blue,
> And in sight and sound they trace
> Living pictures out of space
> To bring a new wonder to you.

Following Miss Dixon were the black American dancers Buck and Bubbles. Television had launched with a variety show. A bill of only two acts, but the intent was clear. Greenbaum conducted a sound-only orchestral interlude between 3.30pm and 4pm, when it was back to the top for the benefit of viewers on the Marconi-EMI system. So, the second programme on British television was a repeat.

Baird's system was capable of high-quality pictures, but it was held back by the intermediate film technique, which limited camera movement and angles, while also requiring a large investment in film stock and processing. Moreover, the 'Spotlight' announcement studio required the announcers to wear heavy make-up. Intermediate film was only a stopgap while Baird developed suitable electronic cameras, but the Marconi-EMI system had already achieved this with its Emitrons, so from February 1937, the Baird system transmissions were discontinued.

In terms of programming, one of television's earliest successes was the magazine programme *Picture Page*, created and produced by Madden, and first broadcast as a test in the hiatus between Radiolympia and the full launch. *Picture Page* was effectively *In Town Tonight* in vision, with topical items and guests introduced by the Canadian actress Joan Miller. Miller 'connected' the viewers with the various guests, on a prop switchboard with a television screen in the front panel. No actual recordings of the pre-war run survive,[38] but the odd *Picture Page* item does exist on the demonstration film that was shown each morning before live programmes started. One of these includes a gorgeous moment where announcer Leslie Mitchell is shown how to eat healthily from the nation's hedgerows by an aged military gentleman. Sprinkling his chickweed liberally with pepper, Mitchell almost chokes on his first mouthful.

That *Picture Page* was a small-scale variety show masquerading as an interview programme is underlined by the other programme Miller and Madden worked on: *International Cabaret*. In it, as the title suggests, continental speciality acts working in London's clubs trekked up to AP to perform for the tiny number of viewers lucky or rich enough to afford a television set. Miller linked the acts from her switchboard, which now featured a placard saying 'Grand Hotel' instead of a television screen. The edition of 12 March 1937 showcased The Bryants (billed as 'silent comics'), an acrobatic outfit called the Seven Menorcas, singer and dancer Lu Anne Meredith and the Knife-Throwing Denvers.

Unencumbered by the mutual suspicion of the early days of wireless, even the big stars came up from the West End to feed the new medium. Stanley Lupino and Laddie Cliff, with pianist Billy Mayerl – billed by the *Radio Times* as 'the Three Musketeers of musical comedy'[39] – were televised from Alexandra Palace in late January 1937, just as their show *Over She Goes* was packing them in at the Saville Theatre. Mayerl made a return visit to Ally Pally in March for a self-explanatory series called *Composer at the Piano*.

Older performers also got a look-in, with *Old Time Music Hall*, produced by Harry Pringle. One edition in March 1937 starred Fred 'I'm the Black Sheep of the Family' Barnes[40] and Harry Champion, both of whose stars had shone brightest in the days before variety. Meanwhile, Harry S. Pepper transferred his radio minstrelsy to television with *The White Coons Concert Party*, first transmitted on 23 January 1937. Along with Pepper and Doris Arnold on their two pianos, and banjo dervish 'Lightning' Joe Morley, comedian Tommy Handley – already a wireless veteran – made his first television appearance.

The size and scope of the shows was limited by the size of the studios: Alexandra Palace A (the Marconi-EMI studio) and B were both 70 feet by 30 feet. Really big shows could be staged by linking them, but performers had to rush down the corridor separating the studios between scenes. Another limitation was the technology of the time, the Emitron cameras having a limited depth of field. However, taking an outside broadcast unit to a theatre enabled larger-scale spectacles to reach the small screen. One such outing was organized for 12 September 1939, for the premiere of the new musical comedy *I Can Take It* at the Coliseum, starring husband and wife performers Jessie Matthews and Sonnie Hale. Viewers were promised 'a medley of boiled shirts, fashionable dresses, wisecracks, and opulence'[41] as distinguished guests were accosted in the foyer by announcer Leslie Mitchell; this was to be followed by fellow announcer Lionel Gamlin interviewing Matthews and Hale in their dressing room and then, finally, the opening of the show itself.

Sadly, the viewers would have seen nothing but blank screens. On 1 September 1939, in anticipation of the declaration of war, the Television Service closed down. The primary reason was the fear that the Alexandra Palace transmitter would be an invaluable navigational aid for the Luftwaffe. The instruction was to close at noon, but a Mickey Mouse cartoon, *Mickey's Gala Premiere*, went out as planned at 12.05pm, followed by the test card for fifteen minutes, then closedown.[42]

★

War brought television to a temporary halt but it didn't kill off radio completely, though rationalization was required. The National and Regional Programmes were merged immediately into a single programme – the Home Service – transmitted nationally on just two wavelengths. Again, the idea was to fox the Luftwaffe. If all transmitters were using the same frequency, it would be harder to use them for directions. The variety department was evacuated, at first to Bristol, its work now of vital importance in maintaining morale. Through the disarray of the move, organist Sandy MacPherson almost single-handedly kept the schedules going from the Compton theatre organ in St George's Hall, playing tuneful light music wherever a gap had opened up. Once the new shop was set up, the pre-war hits continued their runs.

The biggest hit was the comedy show *Bandwaggon,* starring 'big-hearted' Arthur Askey and Richard 'Stinker' Murdoch. The series had started badly in January 1938, facing cancellation after only three shows. It was rescued when its stars took over the writing themselves and moved the bulk of the action to a fictitious flat on the roof of Broadcasting House, where they lived with a menagerie that included a goat called Lewis and a cockerel called Gerald (almost certainly an homage to the BBC's director of television, Gerald Cock). Characters such as the charlady Mrs Bagwash and her daughter Nausea were introduced, along with catchphrases like 'Ay theng yew' and 'proper humdrum', and soon the show became a firm favourite. The two stars were contrasting, but complementary characters: Askey was an earthy Liverpudlian concert-party performer with a love of corny jokes, while the Cambridge-educated Murdoch was urbane and well-spoken. However, they accounted for only twenty minutes of each show (which sometimes lasted an hour, sometimes forty minutes), the rest consisting of fairly straight items like 'Mr Walker Wants To Know', in which an actor called Syd Walker presented moral dilemmas and asked 'What would you do, chums?'

This slot was ideal in wartime, as it could be used to underline matters of national importance, such as security. In the show of 30 September 1939, barely a month after the outbreak of war, Walker demonstrated the dangers of listening to gossip. The rumour was out that the Germans had sunk HMS *Rodney*. Eventually, it emerges that a small freighter has been sunk, but that the captain and all the crew have been saved. The captain's name? Rodney.

War changed the flavour of the comedy slightly too. In peacetime, head of variety John Watt had commented that 'it is said that there are only six jokes in the world, and I can assure you that we cannot broadcast three of them'. (Proscribed topics included marital infidelity, stuttering and deafness, although Watt was unsure how deaf people were able to complain about programmes they couldn't hear.) By October 1939, he'd decided that there had been 'an addition to the list of permissible jokes in the person of Hitler'.[43] In the same show as Mr Walker's careless talk dilemma, Murdoch and Askey made full use of the concession:

MURDOCH: Let's tell them the joke about old Nasty's father and mother.

ASKEY: No, the censor had that out this morning, if I remember rightly.

MURDOCH: Yes, in any case, Big, remember what we agreed. We were going to give old Nasty a rest this week and talk about something else for a change.

ASKEY: Yes, but I feel you'd like to say something about him, you know. He's pinched a lot of our publicity, hasn't he? I mean, he's had his name in the paper every day this week.

MURDOCH: Anyway, Mrs Bagwash isn't worried about him.

ASKEY: Oh, she doesn't care a hoot. She said to me this morning 'It's no good those Germans sitting up in those balloons over London trying to frighten us, because they can't.'[44]

This influential series came to an end in November 1939, and the job of entertaining the nation fell to other comedy shows, such as *Happidrome* and *Garrison Theatre*. Three service-based comedy shows played an important part too: from the fictitious HMS *Waterlogged* came *Navy Mixture* with Eric Barker and Jon Pertwee; the Army contributed *Stand Easy* with Charlie Chester; while the Royal Air Force pitched in with the most enduring of the three, the sublime, whimsical *Much Binding in the Marsh*, written by its stars, Kenneth Horne, and, on vital war work, Richard Murdoch.

However, the true successor to *Bandwaggon* in the listeners' affections had begun in July 1939, under a title borrowed from a newspaper headline about 'Old Nasty': *It's That Man Again*. That man was Askey's fellow Liverpudlian Tommy Handley, by now a consummate radio performer. With almost everyone apart from the *Daily Express* acknowledging that war was just around the corner, Ted Kavanagh's pun-laden, quick-fire scripts included a German spy character, Funf, from the second show; he was played by Jack Train, speaking sideways into a glass tumbler for a telephone effect. Just how quick-fire *ITMA* was is remembered by John Ammonds, who joined the BBC as a 29-shillings-a-week sound effects operator in 1941, aged 17. After a month's training in London, he received the call to go west:

> They said 'How do you fancy going to Bristol for a month?' I didn't realize that would be the start of about thirty years in light entertainment. We did *ITMA* live. It makes me shudder to think of that now. Most of the effects were done at the microphone because we couldn't time it on disc. That was an incredible experience with all the teamwork. I've got a picture of me somewhere, blowing bubbles into a bowl for the 'Don't forget the diver' sound effect. Horace Percival [who played the Diver] on one side, Tommy on the other and me with a BBC soup bowl. It was very fast-moving for its time, although all the puns are a bit tiresome now.[45]

It soon became apparent that Bristol was not the safe haven that the BBC variety department had hoped for. Ammonds remembers the air raids being worse than those he'd experienced in London. One night, the sound effects library took a direct hit. Thankfully, no one was hurt, but a safer berth was soon found at Bangor on the north Wales coast, and the variety department moved there in April 1941. Ammonds's memories of the place are very fond: 'I spent an incredible two and a half years in Bangor, learning show business. No university could give me the instruction I had in that time. I was working with Jack Buchanan, Evelyn Laye, Robb Wilton and all these big stars of the time.'

Bangor proved to be ideal until London was deemed safe enough again in the summer of 1943, though Ammonds does recall one incident there:

> One night, a German bomber must have got lost coming back from bombing Belfast, and jettisoned a couple of bombs on Bangor. We were in the middle of transmission, from a church hall. On the archive recording, suddenly you hear this crunch. They took us off the air, because they didn't want the Germans to know where we were. Charlie Shadwell was conducting, Kay Cavendish and Paula Green were singing 'It Ain't What You Do, It's the Way That You Do It', and the German pilot must have taken heed.[46]

By May 1944, *ITMA* had the ears of 40 per cent of the listening public, and it was credited with a major role in keeping morale high on the home front. Once the euphoria of victory had passed, however, it became clear that the world of variety had changed forever.

CHAPTER TWO

A wizard time for all

Victory in Europe came on 8 May 1945, and the response was a massive national sigh of relief, followed by the sort of party that can only come after nearly six years of having very little to celebrate. Hubert Gregg, who had written 'Maybe It's Because I'm a Londoner', wrote a song about getting lit up when the lights went on in London, and many followed the lyrics to the letter. Trafalgar Square was awash with drunken revellers, some up lamp-posts, others in the fountains. For the first few hours of peace, at least, the nation was happy to entertain itself.

The post-war era of radio variety began at 8.30pm on Thursday 10 May 1945, with *V-ITMA*, purporting to be a live relay from the seaside town of Foaming at the Mouth. It opened with an exhortation to wave flags and greet Mayor Handley as he gave a speech from the balcony of the town hall. Some of the local urchins chose to greet the Mayor with their catapults while other more civic-minded children suggested that he was 'a jolly decent chap' who was 'going to give us a wizard time'.[1] For the next four years until his untimely death, Tommy Handley did give the nation a wizard time, and when he passed on, his was a hard act to follow.

ITMA and radio variety adjusted to peacetime conditions very swiftly, despite losing many humorous targets with the demise of the Nazis. Radio was still the dominant entertainment medium, television being off-air until the summer of 1946 and, even then, some years away from being a mass medium. Live variety was important, but it took a couple of years of peace to get back to full strength in its metropolitan heartland, while in the provinces it never regained its former glory.

Many stage performers had been working in theatres of war, entertaining the troops at the behest of the Entertainments National Service Association (ENSA). Slowly, the West End began to regain an element of its pre-war vitality with the return of some of the biggest names. The Palladium passed on the reunion of the Crazy Gang, which proved to be the gain of the Victoria Palace. On 17 April 1947, Bud Flanagan, Jimmy Nervo, Teddy Knox, Charlie Naughton and Jimmy Gold opened in *Together Again*, as big a success as any of their earlier shows. *The Times* welcomed their return fulsomely, declaring that 'together, these comedians are irresistible. Gravity, which may hold its own against Flanagan or against Nervo and Knox or against Naughton and Gold, cannot co-exist with the mere idea of them as a gang.' This was no hyperbole. By 1949, all of the Crazy Gang were getting on a bit, with Naughton and Gold in their early sixties, but their miscreant child tendencies remained fully intact and, on their night, they were quite able to defy the forces of nature, being one themselves.

When *Together Again* came to an end on 29 October 1949, bandleader Billy Cotton and ample Welsh singer 'Two Ton' Tessie O'Shea brought in their touring show, *Tess and Bill*, to fill the gap. Agent Leslie Grade offered both stars the option of a salary or a percentage, as Billy Cotton's son Sir Bill Cotton remembers:

> My father said 'I'll take the salary if you don't mind,' because he had to pay twenty men at the end of the week. He'd lost quite a bit of money by then. She took a percentage. They went round and round the country, and it was a hell of a good combination. Tessie O'Shea was wonderful. She was a pain in the arse, but she was a great performer. Eventually, she put the show in at the Victoria Palace. She'd got 65 per cent of it or something, and the old man said to her 'You're very silly.' They booked Jimmy Wheeler and Reg Dixon to come in with them, to boost it, but by this time, they'd been to the Metropolitan Edgware Road twice, the

Golders Green Hippodrome twice and all the London theatres. The old man said 'They won't pay a pound or whatever it was to see a show that they've already seen for 4s 6d.' It didn't do very well.[2]

Cotton's agent Leslie Grade was part of a new breed of variety agents. For much of the history of show business, artist representation had been the province of a plethora of one-man (or woman) operations in miniscule offices on or just off London's Charing Cross Road. Turns would call at a grille in the door, ask if there was any work for them and be informed either one way or the other without necessarily entering the office. There were a few large agencies, with correspondingly magnified clout. Harry Foster's agency in particular stood out from the herd, partly because it had expanded by taking over another significant rival, Hymie Zahl's Vaudeville Agency. It was also the London affiliate of the gargantuan William Morris agency in the US. So, when Val Parnell brought Danny Kaye over to headline at the Palladium, the deal was done through Foster's.

However, in the years immediately after the Second World War, Lew Grade and his brother Leslie had built up an agency that was, in time, to dominate show business. The Grade ascendancy is the classic immigrant success story – Lew proving that a clever Russian Jewish boy could come from nothing to be one of the most powerful men in his chosen field. With rumours of pogroms circulating and the certainties of old Russia disintegrating, Isaac and Olga Winogradsky had left the Ukrainian town of Tokmak in 1912, with their two sons, five-year-old Louis and two-year-old Boris, and ended up in Whitechapel, east London. Back home, Isaac had been the proprietor of a couple of very early cinemas, but in Whitechapel he had to find work in clothing factories, where the hours were long and the pay was low. In 1916, a third son, Lazarus, was born, and by 1921 Isaac had his own workshop, elevating the family from grinding poverty to merely extreme poverty.

Louis had distinguished himself at school, particularly with figures, but had reluctantly been drawn into the family business. His head for arithmetic soon got him out of the machine room into book-keeping for a larger textile company, but his heart was never in it. His escape came in the mid-twenties with the Charleston craze. He and Bernard (as Boris had become, after a period as Barnet) were naturals at the new dance, and showed their skills extensively in the local ballrooms. They won almost every competition they entered and eventually turned professional. For professional purposes, Louis anglicized his name to Louis Grad, but when a poster for a Paris engagement misspelled his surname as 'Grade', he kept the misspelt version.

By 1935, after nearly a decade on the stage, the physical nature of the work was getting to him. He also realized that the Charleston had a finite shelf life and that he wasn't a good enough dancer for anything else. So he decided to become an agent, joining the office of Joe Collins, then a show business colossus, now better known as the father of Joan and Jackie. He proved so good at the job that the firm became Collins & Grade. The secret of his success was being at his desk by 7am. By the time Collins arrived, his partner had done a morning's worth of deals already. Bernard, who had adopted the stage name Delfont, joined briefly before striking out on his own. Then kid brother Leslie, as Lazarus had become, came in as office boy before he too went into business on his own. When Leslie was called up for service in the RAF, it looked like his agency would have to close, but big brother stepped in. Lew's own military service had been cut short by water on the knee – an industrial injury for a dancer – so he was available. Moreover, his relationship with Collins had become fractious, so he was looking for a way out. With £10,000 invested by cinema owners Sid and Phil Hyams, Lew and Leslie Grade Ltd was founded and Leslie went to war knowing his business was in safe hands.[3] When they were reunited, the agency went from strength to strength.

They were a contrasting pair. Leslie was quiet, Lew was a larger-than-life character, who enjoyed playing the part of the mogul, complete with a gigantic cigar. While no one of his stature could ever be completely free of enemies, Lew Grade inspired a great deal of loyalty and affection from across the board. If the Grade organization was a dictatorship, as rivals sometimes alleged, it was a largely benign one. The business side of things was important, but it was just the means. Entertainment was the end.

Everyone had a Lew Grade story, many of which were apocryphal. One that wasn't, by his own admission, involved a juggler at the Finsbury Park Empire. Grade asked the performer how much he was getting. 'Twenty-five pounds' a week came the answer. Grade replied that this was preposterous, and that he could easily get forty. 'Who's your agent?' Grade asked. Came the reply: 'You are, Mr Grade.' Lew got the headlines, but Peter Prichard, who began as an office boy with Hymie Zahl in 1947 and worked for the Grades from 1954, is in no doubt about the quiet one's status. 'Leslie was the best of all of them,' he asserts.

As well as representing the biggest names, the Grades had another ace in the hole. Traditionally, circuit bookers and promoters built the bills, leaving the agencies to take their 10 per cent. With business in decline, though, the bookers wanted to reduce their risks, as Peter Prichard explains:

The whole of light entertainment changed during the war. The theatres weren't taking the gambles. They were frightened of opening because of the bombing. People like the Grades convinced the theatres to let them package the shows. The risks were high, but the rewards were good – 65/35 was about right. You had the power then of putting your own shows in, but you were still governed by the actual theatre companies. They wouldn't take anything, they'd only take what they wanted. 'We don't want that act, we've had a bad report.' But the agents, really, became producers. The only one who didn't was Harry Foster, because he didn't believe in it. He'd send his acts to Leslie Grade for him to package. That was a problem for Foster's, but all the others took the gamble.[4]

By the end of *Tess and Bill*'s run, Billy Cotton's bankability had increased massively, due to radio exposure. He and the band had been broadcasting regularly since the early thirties, but on 5 February 1949, the first *Billy Cotton Band Show* had gone out. This programme was to cement Cotton's reputation as something of a national treasure, and was to be one of the first all-new shows of post-war radio variety. For the next twenty years, his theme tune 'Somebody Stole My Gal' and his raucous shout of 'Wakey Wakey!' – inspired by the musicians' lethargy on that first Sunday morning after a week of late nights on the road – became synonymous with the smell of roast beef, as Cotton Junior acknowledges:

> If they'd put that show on at about four o'clock in the afternoon, it would have come and gone without anybody noticing. But it just happened that he hit on that catchphrase, which was an accident. It gave the wife the thing of saying to the husband or to the children 'be home before Billy Cotton shouts "wakey wakey"'. And then what followed was half an hour where nobody had to listen, really. It just created an atmosphere of jollity in the room.[5]

Other shows came along to refresh the radio variety roster, keep the millions listening and continue fostering a national sense of unity, as the wartime warhorses came to their natural ends. The direct replacement for *ITMA*, starting in April 1949, just three months after Handley's death, was *Ray's a Laugh*. It was a sketch show with situation comedy elements, starring Ted Ray with a supporting cast that occasionally included the young Peter Sellers. Ted Ray, like George Formby, hailed from Wigan, but they were very different performers. Formby relied on songs rather than patter, whereas Ray (real name, Charles Olden) was a gag merchant, although he did have musical leanings, having begun his performing career by inverting his surname and going out as 'Nedlo the Gypsy Violinist'. *Ray's a Laugh* was one of the major hits of post-war radio comedy and ran from April 1949 to January 1961, but while Ray was undoubtedly a skilled comedian, the material was safe, domestic and gentle, as one listener, John Fisher, recalls:

> One joke particularly stays in my mind. One weekend, Ted Ray and Kitty

Bluett, to whom he was married on the show, went to Paris. Kitty said to Ted, 'I'm just going downstairs to look at the magazines.' He said, 'Darling, you can look at magazines at home.' She replied, 'In French, magazine means shop.' That was the standard.[6]

It fell to *Take It From Here* to push back the boundaries, with scripts by Frank Muir and Denis Norden that combined cleverness and erudition with a dogged refusal to let a good pun pass by. (In a sketch about the return from university of a Punch and Judy man's son: 'You were very lucky to get him in at the Royal College of Puppets and Marionettes.' 'Well, naturally I had to pull a few strings.'[7]) Before his wartime service in the Royal Air Force, Norden had been one of the youngest cinema managers in London, working for a period at the cavernous, luxurious Trocadero, Elephant and Castle. Muir had no previous show business form, but both emerged into civilian life intent on becoming comedy writers. Fate brought them together in the Cinephone arthouse cinema on Oxford Street, when they were the only people to laugh at an apparently straight line of dialogue. Both were tall, urbane, witty, clever men, and these qualities came through in the comedy they wrote together.

The series had grown out of a Forces-based radio show called *Navy Mixture*, which had featured the Australian comedienne Joy Nichols and, oddly for a Navy show, an RAF veteran, 'Professor' Jimmy Edwards. Edwards possessed a very distinguished war record, a handlebar moustache and a masterfully comic way with a trombone and a music stand. In particular, he could get belly laughs simply by spinning the top of the music stand as if it were a radar dish,[8] and treating the trombone as though it were a rifle at a clay pigeon shoot. He played up to his real-life reputation as an enthusiastic drinker with props such as a xylophone with a note that turned into a beer pump, despatching the resulting liquid with glee, with the line 'You go join your friends. All rendezvous in Jim's tum.' Then there were the signature gags, many of them patently Muir and Norden creations, from their combination of erudition and groanworthiness. Peering at sheet music, he wondered aloud about the piece's provenance: 'Paganini? Paganini? Oh, page nine.' His on-stage character was bombastic, but strangely lovable.

To go with Muir, Norden, Edwards and Nichols, Australian comedian and occasional *Navy Mixture* performer Dick Bentley was enlisted. Later Nichols left to be replaced by June Whitfield, then at the start of her career as one of the most versatile comic actresses Britain has ever seen; singer Alma Cogan, 'the girl with the laugh in her voice', was also signed up. With this versatile cast, *Take It From Here* (or *TIFH*, pronounced TIFE) majored in parodies of movies of the day. For many, though, the highlight of the programme was 'The Glums', a weekly slice of life from the home of a work-shy, bibulous patriarch (Edwards), his five-watt bulb of a son, Ron (Bentley), and Ron's screechy but well-meaning fiancée, Eth (Whitfield).

Another post-war radio variety smash was *Educating Archie*, which is best described as an early sitcom despite the presence of variety show elements like musical interludes. As the title suggests, the situation for the comedy was the education of a naughty schoolboy called Archie, but Archie Andrews was no ordinary schoolboy. If his performance had ever been described as 'wooden', it would have been no more or less than the truth, as he was a ventriloquist's dummy. The man with his hand up Archie's back was Peter Brough, like Kenneth Horne of *Much Binding in the Marsh* fame, a businessman who went into entertainment.[9]

During the show's ten-year run, from June 1950 to February 1960, the job of educating Archie was taken on by a series of 'tutors', beginning with the Australian comedian Robert Moreton. Later, the tutorial role was taken on by Tony Hancock, at the start of his radio career, and Max 'I've arrived, and to prove it, I'm here' Bygraves. A female foil was also on hand, in the form of Beryl Reid or Hattie Jacques, both skilled comic actresses rather than variety performers. It was Reid who, rather cruelly, highlighted Brough's worst professional shortcoming. Asked if you ever saw his lips move, she replied 'Only when Archie's speaking.' Although the idea of a ventriloquist making his name on radio seems odd to modern, multimedia-savvy eyes and ears, there had been a precedent in the US, with Edgar Bergen and his dummy Charlie McCarthy. Indeed, the lack of visibility was a positive boon to the technically limited Brough.

He stood in stark contrast to Arthur Worsley, arguably the best 'vent' act Britain ever produced. Active on the halls from the fifties and later on television, Worsley never spoke as himself, leaving his dummy Charlie Brown to do all the talking. Lesser ventriloquists make a joke out of their inability to say 'bottle of beer', but Worsley mastered the difficult plosive 'B' without ever moving his lips. Such was Worsley's skill that it was almost possible to suspend disbelief and think that the dummy really was speaking independently. One sound engineer is reputed to have asked Worsley to move the microphone closer to Brown's mouth. And yet Worsley never became a major star, while Brough did, as well as being a shrewd exploiter of early merchandizing opportunities.

Not all of the big post-war radio variety shows followed the sketch and situation template. Others were purer variety shows, interspersing stand-up comedy and other acts. Broadcast weekly from factory canteens, *Workers' Playtime* had begun in May 1941 as a morale booster, at the instigation of minister of labour Ernest Bevin, and continued until October 1964. A spot on the show was an important first broadcasting step for many acts, although many remembered that a mention of the foreman's name always got a bigger laugh than any gag, however well timed.

If *Workers' Playtime* was the Ford Model T of pure radio variety, the Rolls Royce was *Variety Bandbox*, which began in February 1944 and ran continuously until April 1951, returning for a final hurrah between October 1951 and September 1952. The show was built around a resident comedian, the longest lasting of whom was Frankie Howerd, although Derek Roy, Reg Dixon and Beryl Reid also served. One 1950 edition of the show began with the organastics of Jerry Allen before Howerd's first appearance, giving bandleader Billy Ternent an English lesson:

HOWERD: Now let's turn to grammar. Example 1. 'I were glad to come in here tonight.' That's wrong, isn't it? 'I were glad to come in here tonight.'

TERNENT: Of course it is. It should be 'I were glad to come in here this evening.'

HOWERD: 'I were glad.' Is that right?

TERNENT: Yes.

HOWERD: Think! Oh, thrice think!

TERNENT: Well, you was glad, wasn't you? . . . I'll bet you can't conjugate.

HOWERD: At my peril, what is conjugate?

TERNENT: The next station to Notting Hill Gate.[10]

This exchange was followed by a six-minute spot from Australian soprano Barbara Lee, then it was the turn of 'one of the up-and-coming personalities that the last year or so's broadcasting has produced' – Peter Sellers. He began his act with a pantomime called 'Sellerinda', in which he played all the parts, including impressions of most of his *Ray's a Laugh* colleagues and the cast of *Much Binding in the Marsh*. From the recording, it is clear that the studio audience is in fits, but heard more than five decades after its original transmission, this seems to be more to do with the repetition of the various characters' catchphrases and the cracking pace at which Sellers rattles through them. That said, the voices are uncanny. In time, his material would improve.

Closing the show was 'that unfailing prophet of doom and destruction, the fugitive from Wagga Wagga', Bill Kerr, with his musings on the potentially unpleasant contents of postage stamp adhesive:

I don't suppose you know what was in the stuff you were licking, and I don't suppose the people that make it know what they're mixing. As long as it's sticky, it's all right. I don't want to worry you, but flypaper's sticky. You know what that does to flies, and they only walk on it. [11]

The BBC's North region, with its base in Manchester, was also an important contributor to the radio variety schedules, under the direction of entertainment head Ronnie Taylor. Taylor had the respect of performers and producers because he had been a writer himself and, like Eric Maschwitz, he combined executive life with an impressive output of highly broadcastable scripts. One of Taylor's young producers was John Ammonds, who had moved north to get away from the hierarchy of Aeolian Hall, the new, post-war premises of the variety department in London. 'A job came on the [notice]board for "Variety producer, Manchester, North region",' Ammonds relates. 'I thought it would be a good thing, because I didn't want to do dance bands and *Music While You Work*, and the chance of a scripted show coming up was a bit remote. I talked it over with my wife and applied.'

On the interview board were Taylor, and the regional head of programmes, B.W. Cave-Browne Cave. 'A marvellous name. I'd met Ronnie once, at Aeolian Hall. They asked all sorts of questions, then the chairman turned to Ronnie and said "Are there any questions you'd like to ask Mr Ammonds?" and Ronnie said "No, I know John's work terribly well." That was fairly typical, as I found out later, and I got the job. Ronnie was marvellous. I have no hesitation in saying that he was the nicest and cleverest boss I ever worked for at the BBC.' Ammonds's first production starred Ken Platt, a magnificently lugubrious comedian, whose catchphrase was 'I'll not take my coat off – I'm not stopping'. 'Ronnie said "I've had to go ahead and cast it, I think you'll be quite pleased." His mother was Thora Hird, and his girlfriend was played by Billie Whitelaw, so it wasn't a bad cast.'[12]

★

All of the big post-war hit shows were broadcast on the Light Programme, which had been complementing the Home Service since 29 July 1945. Early in the war, it had been conceded that more entertainment for the Forces was needed, and so, on 7 February 1940, the Forces Programme was born, becoming the General Forces Programme in 1944. Unsurprisingly, this relatively breezy, cheerful network proved popular with non-military audiences, so in peacetime, the GFP gave way to the Light.

The idea of a 'light' network would have been unthinkable in the Reith era. The Reithian-model BBC had been built deliberately on mixed programming. A red-nosed variety show could be followed by an improving talk, with the hope that some listeners might forget to switch off, and thus be educated almost by osmosis. While the idea of hiving off all of the ghastly lowbrow shows was superficially appealing, it reduced the chances of such serendipity. Or, as one radio producer summed it up, rather sniffily:

> If one wanted to keep one's listening light, one had merely to retune one's set when something serious came along [. . .] The creation of the Light Programme ... quickly put an end to all that. As the natural successor to the Forces Programme, the Light catered for those who wanted levity all the time, purely for background listening . . . No longer was it necessary to take evasive action if one wanted to avoid the first rate.[13]

Comments like these were unfair, as, in reality, the old-model BBC, admirable though it was at the start of broadcasting, would have carried on haemorrhaging listeners to the revitalized continental stations. The Light Programme was a ratings success from the start, and while there was a lot of light musical filler like *Music While You Work*, some of the comedy output, like *Much Binding in the Marsh*, truly deserved to be described as first rate. The BBC soon realized that having one very popular network would buy the goodwill to attempt other, less popular, but artistically worthwhile, works elsewhere, and set up a third network alongside the Home Service and Light Programme for this very purpose. The inauguration of the Third Programme on 29 September 1946 did create a clear hierarchy: Light – lowbrow, Home – middlebrow, Third – highbrow. Although the bulk of the Third Programme's output was music and drama, it opened with a comedy programme: an arch, self-referential satire on the whole business of radio called *How to Listen*, written by and starring the humorist Stephen Potter, with help from the comedienne Joyce Grenfell.

While experimentation was allowed on the Third Programme, the mainstream variety output was expected to conform to stringent regulations. These were enshrined in the famous 'green book', as the *BBC Variety Programmes Policy Guide for Writers and Producers* was known. Issued in 1949, it is best known for declaring:

There is an absolute ban upon the following:

Jokes about:
  Lavatories
  Effeminacy in men
  Immorality of any kind

Suggestive references to:
  Honeymoon couples
  Chambermaids
  Fig leaves
  Prostitution
  Ladies' underwear, e.g. winter draws on
  Animal habits, e.g. rabbits
  Lodgers
  Commercial travellers

Extreme care should be taken in dealing with references to or jokes about:
  Pre-natal influences
  Marital infidelity

Good taste and decency are the obvious governing considerations. The vulgar use of such words as 'basket' must also be avoided.[14]

The 'green book' has been held up over the years as an example of the stuffiness and lack of humour exhibited by the BBC. In fact, its author, head of variety Michael Standing, was all too conscious of its absurdity. In 1976 he admitted to comedy writer Barry Took that he 'had a chuckle when he was writing it', but Standing observed that while 'many of the things in it must today seem absolutely ludicrous ... public standards at that time were very different from now'.[15]

Standing's fiefdom was Aeolian Hall in Bond Street, to which the variety department had decamped on its return from wartime evacuation in Bristol and Bangor. A return to St George's Hall was out of the question, as it had succumbed to Luftwaffe bombs on 11 May 1941. Aeolian Hall was to remain the home of BBC radio entertainment until 1975. Under Standing was the assistant head of variety, a bluff Australian called Jim Davidson. A former musician, he took special interest in the dance band programmes, but showed his knowledge to be patchy. He interrupted one BBC Show Band session with a request for 'arco brass' – 'arco' being the musical term for bowed strings. Cyril Stapleton, the conductor, was well used to Davidson's ill-informed interference and told the brass to switch to cup mutes.

One radio producer of this time stood out as a beacon of forward thinking. Patrick Kenneth Macneile Dixon, known universally as Pat, was the Oxford-educated son of a Glasgow University professor. A journalist and an advertising copywriter before joining the BBC in 1940, his professional institutionalization completely failed to eradicate his rebellious streak. Reputed to have a Confederate flag hung on his office wall at Aeolian Hall, he was the first call for the less conventional thinkers in entertainment. Among other achievements, he produced *Third Division* for the Third Programme, a Muir and Norden-scripted sketch show that included Peter Sellers's first performance of 'Balham: Gateway to the South', a spoof travelogue of the unlovely south London suburb that found a wider and very appreciative audience when it was resurrected for the 1958 Parlophone LP *Best of Sellers*.

It was Dixon who first recognized the talent of the newly demobbed Spike Milligan, who was, with Sellers, Harry Secombe and Michael

Bentine, part of a group that congregated at a Victoria pub called the Grafton Arms, run by scriptwriter and ex-Army major Jimmy Grafton. Dixon urged his seniors to give Milligan, Sellers, Secombe and Bentine a chance. However, the job of producing the resulting radio show – called *Crazy People*, after the original title of *The Goon Show* was rejected by the upper echelons – was given to a junior colleague, Dennis Main Wilson. Roger Wilmut, chronicler of the Goons' history, suggests that 'the combination of an avant-garde producer [like Dixon] and crazy comedy' was too rich for the variety bosses' blood,[16] but if so, they had seriously misjudged Wilson, himself one of the great eccentrics of broadcasting. One of his later colleagues, Roger Ordish, remembers him as 'a wonderful man' and 'mad' to boot, a trait that seemed to show through most obviously in his speech patterns:

Dennis had this wonderful way of talking that was semi-comprehensible. Digressions within digressions within digressions. He had some sort of nervous breakdown. Afterwards, he was working on a series with Barry Humphries, who asked 'This nervous disorder, how, precisely, did it manifest itself?' Dennis replied 'Barry, I won't bore you. Needle nardle noo, voom voom, the Goons, Neddie Seagoon, voom voom voom, I started to talk nonsense.' I remember once, at the BBC Club, in a dramatic gesture, he seized me by the shoulder while explaining something, and tore my shirt accidentally. 'Roger! I'll buy you a new one ... As I was saying ...' carrying on, with the shirt flapping in the breeze.[17]

Born in Dulwich, Wilson had joined the BBC's European Service in 1941, before being called up into the Royal Armoured Corps. Despite his anti-establishment tendencies, Wilson gained a commission in the Armoured Cavalry. After the war, while working for the Control Commission in the British Zone of occupied Germany, he found himself back in radio as head of light entertainment at the newly established Nordwestdeutscher Rundfunk, under the controller Hugh Carleton Greene. Returning to London and the BBC, Wilson found a berth in the variety department, overseeing auditions of the numerous comedians who were emerging from the Forces.

One was the comedian and scriptwriter Bob Monkhouse, who recalled Wilson giving off 'a definite whiff of March Hare' when they first met, during an audition at Aeolian Hall.[18] The regular auditioner was, according to Monkhouse, given to tough marking. Five per cent was a pass, and 20 per cent was the highest he ever awarded. Minding the shop on the day of Monkhouse's audition and unfamiliar with the procedure, Wilson gave the comedian 101 per cent and promptly collapsed, missing a Gershwin medley by Monkhouse's RAF colleague, the jazz pianist Stan Tracey. This, then, was the man that the BBC, in its infinite wisdom, regarded as a safe pair of hands to keep the wild and wonderful Milligan in check.

The first series was well received and a second series followed, but with one major difference – *Crazy People* was dropped in favour of *The Goon Show,* the title Milligan had wanted all along. The path was clear for a revolution in radio comedy. Never before had logic been dispensed with so comprehensively. Never before had regular characters been killed off week after week only to reappear almost immediately ('You dirty rotten swine . . .'). Never before had a Wurlitzer theatre organ been driven across the Sahara desert, changing key as it changed gear. However, while much has been made of the revolutionary effect of *The Goon Show*, and quite rightly too, it retained some elements of the traditional BBC comedy show. It had a live announcer to top and tail – first Andrew Timothy, then the put-upon and much-loved Wallace Greenslade, who claimed to be above it all, but would always end up being dragged into the action, to the detriment of his dignity. The early shows contained several sketches separated by musical items, but even when the series moved over to one continuous narrative per show, the musical items remained: a spot from Dutch jazz harmonica virtuoso Max 'Conks' Geldray and a vocal number from the Ray Ellington Quartet.

Where *The Goon Show* differed was by having, in Milligan, a writer who regarded nothing as sacred. Numerous others, including the cast, co-writers and rebellious BBC producers, were only too happy to help him in his quest, but Milligan was the show's life force and conscience. It was aided too by being phenomenally popular, which meant that the BBC couldn't simply bury it. The influence this popularity brought was not merely internal. Just as, later, the Beatles inspired more young boys to pick up guitars than just about any band before or since, *The Goon Show* was responsible for a whole generation of comedians and comic writers.

What made such an uncompromising, surreal show such a massive hit? The timing counted for a lot. After years of grinning and bearing it for the sake of morale, the nation was ready for something iconoclastic. At the start of its run in 1951, austerity was still the order of the day, and some vital supplies were still on the ration. So, it was a release to hear the Goons blowing things (and, to be fair, each other) up and generally painting authority as something to be mocked. *The Goon Show* often followed a simple pattern: Neddie Seagoon, played by Harry Secombe, would be tempted by an improbable or heroic scheme, only to end up broke, broken or both. However, because every show got from the start point to its illogical conclusion in vastly differing ways, they were never criticized for being formulaic. The authority figures were cowards, most notably the corrupt, yellow-bellied Major Dennis Bloodnok. Some of the characters – such as the George Sanders-esque con man Hercules Grytpype-Thynne and his lackey Count Jim Moriarty – were out for whatever they could get. Their pickings diminished greatly as the series went on, rendering them ever more destitute, to great comic effect. Meanwhile, others like Eccles and Bluebottle displayed a touching faith in authority and humanity. Arguably, the masterstroke was to have Seagoon oscillating wildly between the two: constantly outclassed by Grytpype-Thynne's evil intelligence, but only too happy to take advantage of Eccles and Bluebottle when it suited his needs. In its own gloriously warped way, all human life was there in *The Goon Show*.

The Goon Show was a trailblazer in another sense, as it put the spotlight on the writers in a way that no show had done before. For most of variety's history, writers had been at best unsung heroes, at worst downtrodden skivvies. Not for nothing did Denis Norden once describe writers as 'comedians' labourers', while *Hancock's Half Hour* co-creator Alan Simpson remembered that when he and Ray Galton got their first BBC break, 'writers were hardly heard of in those days'.[19] Even with the huge hit status of *ITMA*, it is unlikely that the name Ted Kavanagh meant much to most of the listening public. George Formby insisted on a co-writing credit on all of his hit songs, despite contributing nothing to the compositional process. The punters were allowed to think that their favourite stars came up with all of their own funnies, and it was a potent belief, as Eric Sykes discovered when he began writing for Frankie Howerd and asked producer Bryan Sears for a credit in the *Radio Times*. 'He patted me on the shoulder and he smiled the smile of a hungry crocodile, and then he said "All Frank's fans believe he makes it up as he goes along. Ergo, if they had an inkling that it was all written for him he'd lose an awful lot of his fans."'[20] Sykes knew Sears wasn't bluffing, as his own father, a massive Howerd fan, truly believed that Howerd was ad-libbing all the time and had trouble comprehending that anyone, least of all his own son, could be responsible for the words Howerd spoke.

In the fifties, however, the situation changed. Frank Muir and Denis Norden – described by Alan Simpson as 'the governors' – were regular panel game personalities. Eric Sykes became a household name when he began performing as well as writing – having been jointly responsible, with dance-band singer turned scriptwriter Sid Colin, for most of the hit run of *Educating Archie*. Meanwhile, Ray Galton and Alan Simpson made occasional appearances in the radio episodes of *Hancock's Half Hour* and had their pictures in the credits of the television version. The growing power of the writers was encapsulated in Associated London Scripts, the agency-cum-talent nursery-cum-dosshouse that Milligan, Sykes, Galton, Simpson and Howerd established in premises over a greengrocer's in Shepherd's Bush.

Also in the front rank of comedy writers at this time was the partnership of Bob Monkhouse and Denis Goodwin. The pair had been contemporaries at Dulwich College, but they did not meet until adulthood. Monkhouse had sold his first jokes at the age of 14, by waiting outside the stage door of his local theatre, the Lewisham Hippodrome. After being demobbed from the RAF, he had established himself as a comedian, using his uniform, at the suggestion of Peter Brough, to win the audience's sympathy. However, that wasn't enough to win over one tough audience on a radio broadcast from the East End, after which Monkhouse was sure his career was in ruins. Fortunately, it transpired that the listening millions had missed hearing him dying on his feet as the network had faded the programme early in favour of a cricket commentary. The following week, he did a new act based on interruptions, and was a smash hit. Moreover, as he was making his name as a performer, he and Goodwin were building a reputation as reliable suppliers of comic material to the profession, producing gags and scripts to order for radio personalities Tommy Trinder, Bernard Braden and Cyril Fletcher, among many others. The likes of Muir, Norden, Galton, Simpson, Monkhouse, Goodwin and Sykes would, in time, establish comedy writers as celebrities in their own right.

★

As engineers, producers and performers returned from the war, it became possible to think about the resumption of the BBC Television Service. The pre-war equipment needed a fair bit of work to get it back into shape. A similar effort of refurbishment was required in televisually equipped homes, as sets were tested to see if they had survived seven years in mothballs. They were few in number: by 1947, only 14,560 television licences had been issued, at £2 a time, compared to 10.8 million radio licences, which were still only 10 shillings a year. On 7 June 1946, Jasmine Bligh, one of the original television announcing team, stepped from a car outside Alexandra Palace and asked viewers if they remembered her. A repeat of *Mickey's Gala Premiere* followed, but the big spectacle was on the following day, when outside broadcast units relayed the Victory Parade.

Although some expertise had been built up before the war, everyone involved in television in the immediate post-war era was a pioneer, pushing and stretching the aged equipment until it broke. At first, however, the programme content of the revived service remained roughly the same as it had been before hostilities. *Picture Page* returned, the simple single-act shows of the pre-war era also came back and the pre-war *International Cabaret* concept was refined by producer Henry Caldwell into a package under the title *Café Continental*. 'Anything to do with France was Henry,' recalls Yvonne Littlewood, then a secretary at Alexandra Palace. *Café Continental* was presented in the round, with the audience situated on tables around the wall of the set. The opening shot each week took the viewer into the 'club', as if emerging from a carriage, greeted by Père Auguste – a real-life Kensington restaurateur – who hosted the show with Hélène Cordet. At the end, the opening was reversed, and the guest would be ushered back to their carriage, with the closing caption being written on the blind. The gloved hand that came into shot to pull the blind shut was invariably that of a burly scene shifter, rather than a continental lady of leisure.

One of the problems that held television light entertainment back in the immediate post-war era had also hampered the early history of radio entertainment, namely, the absence of specialist producers. Heavyweight drama producers like George More O'Ferrall, Michael Barry and Robert Barr sometimes had to turn their hands to producing variety shows. Even the head of the Television Service, Maurice Gorham, took a hands-on interest, at one point questioning whether it was right to pay a male dancer £25 a week, considerably more than many staff members. The Light Entertainment department didn't exist until 1948, when a radio executive, Pat Hillyard, was seconded to become the first head of LE. There was also a lot of snobbery within the Corporation, a hangover from the high-minded pre-war days. Variety was a necessary evil, and television was the BBC equivalent of the salt mines. To work in television variety at this time was virtually to be a pariah.

Fortunately, as with radio, pioneering specialists with a great belief in entertainment and the possibilities of the medium began to emerge. The first was Michael Mills, who had joined the BBC before the war as a sound effects operator, but gone to serve in the Royal Navy, with an attachment to the Free French Navy. Yvonne Littlewood, who had been a secretary at Broadcasting House before moving to Alexandra Palace as secretary to the personnel assistant, remembers Mills's arrival well:

> He was supposed to be back on 1 January [1947], and he was three days late. When Michael joined, because he'd been doing kind of revue-type shows for the Navy, they gave him a title of 'producer, light entertainment'. Drama producers such as George More O'Ferrall, Michael Barry and Robert Barr – who was a good writer – used to come to Michael and say 'I've got this variety show and I don't know what to do about it,' and Michael used to say 'Well, I'd start with a running order if I were you, and this is the sort of running order I'd do.' He was fumbling around himself, but they'd all say 'Thank you, you've helped me so much.' He said it was really the blind leading the short-sighted.[21]

Mills gained a reputation as a ferociously hard worker and also something of a firebrand. Unhappy with his allotted personal assistant, whom he felt couldn't keep up, he found himself begging the personnel office for extra support, where his pleas were fielded by Miss Littlewood:

> Michael was a real whirlwind and I think this lady, who was married and lived in Muswell Hill, found him heavy weather, and she certainly didn't want to do late hours. He used to ring me up endlessly saying 'I've got this running order for tomorrow and I've got nobody to type it.' I said 'Michael, we don't have anybody to send you.' Eventually I got so fed up with it, I said 'If you will stop ringing me up and wait until 5.30, I'll come and do it myself, but please don't ring me up any more.' And so I went and did it, the best I could. Anyway, then, this lady finally decided she'd had enough, she resigned and quick as a flash I applied for her job. I remember Mr Budd [Miss Littlewood's boss in the personnel office] asking 'What do you want to go and work in production for?' I replied that was really why I had joined the BBC. He said 'Well, you know you'll have to be downgraded if you go to production from the job you're

doing now.' I said 'So be it.' My salary went down from £4 16s 10d a week to £4 12s 10d. The first show I did for Michael was on 14 June 1947, called *Variety Express*, and we lasted eight years together.[22]

Another early specialist was Bill Ward, who had been a pre-war television sound mixer, before moving into production. With no precedents and no one initially to tell them whether they were going wrong, Mills and Ward set the standard for television entertainment, and set it as high as their limited resources would allow.

One of Mills's most memorable early programmes was a full production of the Vivian Ellis musical *Jill Darling* in February 1949, which stretched the facilities at Ally Pally to their full extent and possibly a little more. 'We did act one in studio A, then we had a mini-interval, during which we all went to studio B, where we did the second act. While we were in there doing the second act, they changed the scenery in A and we went back to do act three in A. Can you imagine doing something like that live?' asks Littlewood. To complicate matters further, Mills decided that the studio was of an inadequate size for some of the long shots, so he 'used to open the sliding door and put the camera in the passage, so he could get the shots. He was always pushing forward the boundaries, and they realized we'd have to move.'[23]

Meanwhile, Bill Ward was responsible for *How Do You View?*, a Terry-Thomas vehicle that was the first successful and truly original comedy show on British television. Thomas, whose real name was Thomas Terry Hoar-Stevens, had begun as a film and cabaret performer before the Second World War, developing the upper-crust cad character that would sustain him through the rest of his career. Running for five series between 1949 and 1952, it was an early satire on the medium itself, with Thomas supported by his butler Moulting, played by Herbert C. Walton, and his chauffeur Lockit, played by the young Peter Butterworth. Some of the comedy came from the fact that Thomas could not really afford either; indeed, he did not have a car. Leslie Mitchell, already a TV veteran, interviewed Thomas about various fictitious experiences, the first time that a straight announcer had crossed over to the comedy side, but certainly not the last. In one edition, Thomas claimed to be an expert on old London street cries. The first series was written by the star, but later Talbot Rothwell – yet to find 'infamy'[24] as the most prolific writer of *Carry On* screenplays – and Sid Colin took over.

Other producers were less successful in their attempts to make a splash. In particular, designer Richard Greenough, who had helped create the sets for *How Do You View?*, recalls producer Walton Anderson's disastrous production of *Carissima*, transmitted on 25 November 1950:

> We had two days in both studios at Alexandra Palace. We did an act in each, and there must have been a short interval while they all rushed down the corridor. It all went very well for the first day and part of the second day when he realized he was never going to get through it. The decision was taken in the end to just do it, and the first two-thirds were very good, but the last bit, which hadn't been rehearsed, wasn't. One of the sets hadn't been put up, and people were a bit hysterical at the end of it.[25]

A far worse crime, in official circles, than making cast and crew hysterical and putting a botched show on the air was the fact that the whole affair had gone £579 10s 3d over budget. This was a considerable overspend, considering that the average house price at the time was around £1,900. As late as 1953 the total budget for three months of light entertainment was £42,166, a large proportion of which went on orchestrations. Producers were encouraged to use stock arrangements wherever possible to cut costs, but the desire to do things properly made LE an expensive business. In 1952, programme controller Cecil McGivern suggested replacing some multi-artist variety bills with single-artist shows using the biggest international stars, indicating that they would probably cost roughly the same.

Along with Anderson, Richard Afton was another producer of the pioneer era apparently incapable of reaching the heights of Ward and Mills, but his relative inadequacy didn't stop him from being an ogre. His main contributions to the schedules tended to be straightforward variety bills, usually relayed from a theatre as an outside broadcast (OB). When he tried anything more advanced, he came a cropper, as Richard Greenough suggests:

> He was a monster. I worked a lot with him. Well, I got landed a lot with him, really. He was all right, provided he could aim three cameras at an act. At Alexandra Palace, he did a rather complicated sitcom with Norman Wisdom, about a school [*Cuckoo College*, a one-off sixty-minute show transmitted on 13 May 1949]. There were four rooms with a corridor in between. He succeeded in missing every single shot, so all the gags never got seen, because he was always late with it. But sticking cameras in front of something, that was kind of fine. He was good at getting a bill together and he created the Television Toppers [a dance troupe]. He married the one at the end, as I remember.[26]

It was one of Afton's shows that resulted in animals being banned from the studios, after the Ministry of Agriculture had to approve the dressing room for a dog act. Producer T. Leslie Jackson later had to get special permission to use a one-man band with a monkey as a contestant on *What's My Line*.

Pat Hillyard was not the ideal leader for this bold, experimental outfit. Cecil McGivern, the autocratic, awkward controller of the television service, realized this all too well and, at one point, upbraided Hillyard for being too much of an administrator – one of the BBC's infamous 'grey men' – and not enough of an impresario. A breakthrough came when Hillyard brought his radio colleague Ronnie Waldman over to television, primarily as a producer, but also, nominally, as his deputy. It was a blessing in disguise for all concerned when, in October 1950, Hillyard took three months' medical leave and left Waldman in charge as acting head of LE. Hillyard never returned to the job – once he had recovered, he rejoined the radio variety department, becoming its head in December 1952.

The Oxford-educated, theatre-trained Waldman was the impresario the department needed so desperately, and an able administrator too.

He had to be. For all Hillyard's efforts, Waldman's first impression was that he had inherited a department close to collapse. Waldman had an ear for comedy, an eye for a lavish spectacle and, always important, a sure hand when it came to BBC politics. He knew that budgets were not elastic, but he was willing to fight for enough money to enable his producers to do their jobs properly. He knew that inexpensive programmes had their place, but that to do everything on the cheap was a false economy. In 1951, he rebuffed vigorously an attempt by the grey men to impose a cost of £725 an hour on all light entertainment programming. Waldman knew the value of proven hits, but was quick to press the case for innovation. In short, he was an inspirational figure for a directionless department, the right man in the right job at the right time.

He had the good fortune to arrive in television just as the obvious need for alternative facilities was being met, allowing the scope and scale of productions to be expanded. In 1949, the BBC bought thirteen acres upon which to create a purpose-built television studio complex. The land was part of the former Franco-British Exhibition site at Shepherd's Bush, the famous White City from which the greyhound stadium and the tube station took their name. Unfortunately, post-war building restrictions meant that work could not begin immediately. So, as a temporary solution (albeit one that was to last for nearly forty-two years), the redundant Gaumont-British film studios in nearby Lime Grove were purchased for £230,000 from the Rank Organization, which was concentrating its production at the Pinewood Studios in Buckinghamshire.

The first Lime Grove studio was opened for children's programmes on 21 May 1950 by Mrs Attlee, wife of the Prime Minister. It was named studio D, continuing the sequence from Alexandra Palace. In all, there would be four studios at Lime Grove: D, E, G and H. One studio was designated F, but it was never used for production, instead becoming the main scenery store. The absence of studio C is explained by the BBC's love of initials and acronyms. The central control room, through which all output was routed to the transmitters, was referred to as the

CCR, and senior engineers felt that a studio C would result in confusion. (There had in fact been a pre-war plan to use the derelict theatre at Ally Pally as a studio, for which the designation C was to have been used.)

Studio G was chosen as the home of light entertainment, and it came into use on 23 December 1950, with a programme called *Gala Variety*, produced by Michael Mills, hosted by comedian Bill Fraser and featuring singer Dolores Gray, ventriloquist Peter Brough and his dummy Archie Andrews, comic Jimmy James and a young magician called Tommy Cooper. At 112 feet by 54 feet, studio G was a vast improvement on the cramped studios at AP, if a little narrow, something that would prove less than ideal for audience shows. For now, though, Mills and designer Richard Greenough revelled in their new-found freedom. The set resembled a squared-off circus ring, with all action taking place in the centre. Mills had Fraser make his big entrance in a sports car 'just to show we had the room'.[27]

The following year was Festival of Britain year, and the nation began the curious business of harking back to the Great Exhibition of 1851, while looking forward to the bright future. Mills caught the spirit of nostalgia with a series called *The Passing Shows*, which made full use of the new studios. Each of the five programmes covered a decade in the history of entertainment from the turn of the century onwards. Whereas most entertainment shows before had been, by necessity, modest, these were big, ambitious productions, as was Mills's subsequent series of dramatized biographies of entertainment legends such as C.B. Cochran and music hall star Marie Lloyd. Frank Holland, then the assistant property master, remembered the prop store being 'filled from floor to ceiling with props for a *Passing Show*. Just one show . . .'[28] All of these sets needed to be changed while the show was live on-air. No wonder the designer described them as 'terrifying . . . the scene boys had their shirts sticking to them'. Happily, they came off without a hitch. 'Yes, they were memorable,' Yvonne Littlewood recalls. 'They were enormous for that time, but they were very successful. They drove everybody crazy, but they were good.'[29]

At this point, in 1951, there were ten light entertainment producers employed by BBC Television: Richard Afton, Walton Anderson, Henry Caldwell, T. Leslie Jackson, Bill Lyon-Shaw, Michael Mills, Douglas Moodie, Graeme Muir and Bryan Sears. Based at Lime Grove, their output was supplemented by contributions from the regions. Bristol had a young man called Duncan Wood, on his way to becoming one of the best situation comedy producer/directors there has ever been. In Glasgow, there was Eddie Fraser, while Broadcasting House in Leeds had local boy and ex-Army major Barney Colehan. Colehan had come over from radio, where he had been producer of *Have a Go!* with Wilfred Pickles. His first network contribution was an outside broadcast of Victorian-style music hall from the City Varieties Theatre in Leeds. *The Good Old Days* remained a big hit show until his retirement in 1983.

These men grew in stature and expertise as the medium they worked in became more prominent. In the earliest days of television, the paucity of receivers in use meant that mistakes could be made without ending a performer's career. By 1953, however, 2,142,452 households had television licences, a 15,000 per cent increase on six years earlier. There had been two motivators behind the growth. One was gradual, as the transmitter network was rolled out nationwide. The Sutton Coldfield mast brought TV to the Midlands and a little further afield (with reception reported in Longridge, Lancashire, 115 miles away) from 17 December 1949. The northern transmitter at Holme Moss followed on 12 October 1951, then the Scottish station at Kirk O'Shotts on 14 March 1952, before Wenvoe brought television to Wales and the west of England from 15 August 1952. The other cause was more sudden: many people acquired sets in time to watch the Coronation of Queen Elizabeth II.

The broadcasting effort for the Coronation was mostly concentrated on the outside broadcast of the ceremony and procession, but the light entertainment department also did its bit with a show called *All Our Yesterdays*. Co-written by producer Michael Mills and veteran Ealing screenwriter Angus MacPhail, it presented excerpts of entertainment from the previous four Coronation years, beginning with Queen

Victoria's accession in 1837, before coming to the present day. Pat Kirkwood revived her triumphant Marie Lloyd depiction from *The Passing Shows* for the 1911 segment. Yvonne Littlewood gives a flavour of the show: 'We restaged things from the early part of the century like [excerpts from the musical comedies] *Flora Dora* and *Tell Me Pretty Maidens*, and, when we got up to date, which was 1953, there were excerpts from London shows that were running, like the original *Guys and Dolls* and *South Pacific* with Wilbur Evans. [We had] Max Adrian and Moira Fraser doing a thing, and a musical in the West End, *Love from Judy* with Jeannie Carson. We did all this live. It's an absolute mystery to me how we did it.'[30]

It was into this increasingly professional creative hothouse that younger producers like Brian Tesler came. Tesler had the distinction of being the department's first graduate trainee. 'Graduates in those days went into news and current affairs, to work with [deputy head of talks] Grace Wyndham Goldie,' he explains. His own entrée had been through Forces Radio in Trieste during his National Service, working in student revue at Oxford, and composing some successful songs with his friend and contemporary Stanley Myers, later to become an acclaimed film composer. 'We sold half a dozen songs in about ten minutes to two music publishers,' Tesler recalls. 'They were recorded and used on television.' This experience proved crucial when Tesler applied to the Corporation, while in his final year of study. The appointments officer at Broadcasting House didn't even make eye contact with the young would-be producer until the end of the interview:

He was just asking me questions, filling in a form, and at the end of it said 'Is there anything else you want to tell me that might be of interest?' and I said 'Well, I have written some songs and they have been recorded and broadcast.' And he stopped, and for the first time, looked up at me and said 'Broadcast? On the BBC?' He suddenly started paying attention, and arranged for me to meet Ronnie Waldman.[31]

In his final term at Oxford, Tesler tipped Waldman off about an open-air revue he was staging, featuring a young Maggie Smith, whose father was a local schoolteacher. Waldman sent Graeme Muir, an actor turned producer, who took his wife, the actress Marjorie Mars, with him for the evening. Tesler, showing early signs of the shrewdness that would take him to the top of the executive tree in television, 'got Graeme and Marjorie plastered on champagne, and he gave Ronnie a rave review'. But Tesler was to find other senior producers more cynical about his credentials: 'They were old pros, and the only reason they thought I, as a graduate with no show business experience at all, could have got into the BBC light entertainment department was because I had to be the illegitimate son of Ronnie Waldman himself. "Why else? They're both Jewish, they're both dark, he's got to be, there's no question about it."'[32]

New producers cut their teeth on fifteen-minute, single-act shows, mostly under the *Starlight* banner, and Tesler was no exception, beginning with a show at Alexandra Palace with Pat Kirkwood. 'After that, I did a couple of small shows there, including one with Pet Clark. We all did Pet Clark,' he observes. He began on a six-month attachment, after which the normal procedure was to enter the pool of available producers, unless he somehow proved to be indispensable.

Fortunately, his salvation came from one of the sub-genres emerging within light entertainment, the panel game. In 1950, Mark Goodson and Bill Todman – US producers who would come to dominate the game show format market – had set the benchmark with *What's My Line*, where a panel of celebrities tried to guess the jobs done by various members of the public, aided only by a short mime and their own hunches. At the BBC, the task of making the show less brash for genteel British viewers fell to T. Leslie Jackson, remembered by his colleague Tesler as 'a strange, interesting and very lovely man'. The chosen host was Irish sports commentator Eamonn Andrews, and while the show made his name in Britain, the real star was on the panel. Panellist Gilbert Harding, already a familiar voice on radio from his appearances on *Twenty Questions* and *The Brains Trust*, became known and loved by the television audience, despite or possibly because of his extreme grumpiness.

One of the main virtues of the panel game was its relative cheapness. No lavish set was necessary. At the outset, *What's My Line*'s total weekly budget was a mere £200, compared to £2,500 for a *Passing Show*. The fees were £20 for the regular panellists and 18 guineas for other panellists. The chairman received between 20 and 25 guineas, and the guest celebrity – whom the blindfolded panellists had to identify – could count on 10 guineas for their exertions. Other shows were needed when *What's My Line* took a breather, and Tesler took the lead:

In 1953, during my six months, *What's My Line* was having its first ever summer break. Once it started, it had been on continuously. Ronnie Waldman introduced me to another old friend of his, Gordon Crier, a great radio name who worked then for an advertising agency. He said 'Get together with Gordon Crier and come up with a game. He has some good ideas.' He had an idea called *Why?* It was very simple. You had the host, a team playing the adults, and a team who were going to be the children. A parent would make a statement such as 'You're to do this or that', the child would say 'Why?' and they had to justify it. Somehow, the host decided who had won within a certain time. Madness. We had Richard Attenborough, Brenda Bruce, Bob Monkhouse, Bill Brown the politician. Terrific cast, lousy idea. We thought it went all right, but only just. Of course the public wanted *What's My Line*, and if it was going to be something else, it had to be something as good. Patently it wasn't. The switchboard was swamped with complaints. Of course, the title was an absolute gift to the critics, and in those days television was very important. It was front-page news. 'This show went on last night. Why?'

The next day, I was called in by Cecil McGivern, the first time I'd met him. I said 'I'm sorry about last night.' He said 'Don't be sorry. You've got to try new things. Keep persevering with it. It's got the germ of an idea. It'll never be as good as *What's My Line*, but it's a different show. How old are you?' I said I was 24. He said 'Right, be 24. Don't try and copy other people. We want young ideas in the business.' I went out of his office on an absolute high. I thought 'What a marvellous guy,' because he had a terrible reputation for being tough and brutal.

Instead of sending me into the pool, Ronnie said 'We need some new panel games, I'll keep you on for six months, however long it takes to find some new games.' So we advertised to the public, asking them to send any ideas in. One of them was the germ of *Guess My Story*, and there were several others, such as *Tall Story Club*. We did a run of six weeks and we got at least three games out of that run and I went on to produce two of them.[33]

Tesler was also involved in comedy, notably *And So To Bentley*, a Frank Muir and Denis Norden-written sketch vehicle starring Australian comedian and *Take It From Here* regular Dick Bentley. Like *How Do You View?*, television itself was a frequent target for the series. Announcers were drafted into the action alongside Bentley and his supporting cast, which included Peter Sellers. One edition charted the progress of Cyril Purseglove, a television weatherman who rather let fame get to him. Not that it was Muir and Norden's first satire of the medium. In January 1951, they had scripted *Here's Television,* with the groansome subtitle *Comparisons are In-Video*. At the time, a short animated film showing the Alexandra Palace and Sutton Coldfield transmitter masts against a map of the British Isles made frequent appearances on BBC television. Muir, Norden and Michael Mills opened their show with a new version, in which washing wafted in the breeze on a line lashed between the two.

On *And So To Bentley*, Tesler collaborated with another young producer. Ernest Maxin learned his craft not in university revue, but on the variety stage. Maxin's violinist father had passed on his musical skills to his son, while his maternal grandparents had run a boarding house for theatricals in Leeds, as a result of which Harry S. Pepper was a friend of the family:

He came round to visit us one evening at teatime. I was practising, he heard me playing a little Bach and Mozart on the piano and he said to my mother and father 'You know, we'll take the kid on tour with us. We'll black him up and we'll make him a minstrel.' My father said 'No, *mein* boy is going to be a classical pianist,' but my mother said 'How much, love?'[34]

Maxin spent the next three years touring with Pepper's company, getting a thorough grounding from the other acts in everything from tap dancing to timing a gag, before he fell foul of the child performer's main occupational hazard:

We were at the Sheffield Empire and Harry rang my parents, to say 'I'm sorry, Dora and Max, but the kid's washed up in the business, he's not getting the laughs any more.' I was too big. It was funny when my feet didn't touch the floor. I was nine, but I looked about thirteen. So you're looking at the only guy who was washed up at nine without a pension.[35]

Nonetheless, Maxin continued performing through his school years, and devoured every Hollywood musical that he could. When he left school, he became a professional actor and dancer. One engagement was an Australian tour of the Tennessee Williams play *A Streetcar Named Desire* with Vivien Leigh. A BBC booker came out to try and entice Leigh to work for television. She said no, but the booker suggested that Maxin should go and see them on his return. He saw this as his golden opportunity:

From when I was with the minstrels, I wanted to be a producer and a director. Harry S. Pepper sometimes used to throw his coat over his shoulders, and I saw myself being like that. I didn't feel I was ready for films, but I'd seen some television and I was excited by it. I thought it was the right progression.[36]

As suggested, he presented himself at Lime Grove upon his return to Blighty, but found the response muted at first:

I must have created a great impression, because they didn't even know who I was. Then, they remembered. Bill Lyon-Shaw was there, in Ronnie Waldman's office, and I'd worked with him on a show in the theatre. Bill saw me and said 'I know him. He's an actor, a dancer and if you want any music scores done . . .' He always had a cigarette on the end of his mouth. He asked 'Why are you here, old boy?' and the cigarette would go up and down. I said I wanted to be a producer. He said 'Good, we'll encourage you.' Ronnie Waldman, whom I loved dearly, a wonderful guy, said 'Wait a minute, we've got to pay him.' Bill said 'Seriously, I think he'd be very useful. He's got a good pedigree from the theatre. Tell me, what's your favourite form of entertainment?' I said 'Going to the movies.' He said 'That's what we want.'[37]

Education apart, Tesler and Maxin had other things in common, not least geography, as Tesler grew up in Walthamstow, near Maxin in Leyton. They became firm friends from the moment they met on the directors' training course at Luxborough House off Marylebone Road, as recalled by Tesler:

It had been sort of a sixth-form college. The lecture rooms had desks where two people sat side by side. On the very first morning, I'm looking around all these people, who I later discover included David Attenborough, Michael Peacock, Paddy Foy and lots of other names.[38] This tough-looking thickset guy, who looked as if he was a boxer, came over to me, looked down at me and said 'Are you a Jewish boy?' I said 'Yes.' He said 'Can I sit with you?' So Ernest and I sat together. I think that's so typically Ernest and shows you what a sweet, sweet man he is.[39]

The young men of LE soon made their mark by leaping on every technical innovation that arrived in the studios. Tesler and Maxin, in particular, were praised for their inventive use of new camera tricks like overlay and inlay, where images from two sources could be combined.

To be shamelessly immodest, I went further than most people [Tesler explains]. I used inlay and overlay more than anybody else did, and before anybody else did. That's how the Silhouettes, the successors to the Television Toppers, got their name. We wanted a new name and they'd just done a Ted Heath show with me in which they did dance numbers, as shadows, leaping about on instruments all over the place, in silhouette.[40]

Maxin sometimes favoured more traditional enhancements to the visual experience, something that got him into trouble when he had a studio's linoleum floor varnished to make it look glossy. 'Ronnie told me off like crazy for that,' he admits. 'It ruined the floor, but it looked terrific on the screen.'[41] Once the bollocking had been administered, the firm but fair Waldman had the floor replaced with a finish that could be painted in any way required, and Maxin was given as many spectaculars as he could handle.

The expansion in the number of producers mirrored a significant expansion in the Television Service's light entertainment output, to around 450 productions a year, or an average of nine per week. The organization moved on 23 September 1953 from Lime Grove to the scenery block at Wood Lane, the first part of the new Television Centre to be completed.

Thankfully, the available studio space had increased as well, with the acquisition of the Empire variety theatre on Shepherd's Bush Green. It had been built for Oswald Stoll in 1903, to the design of Frank Matcham, but declining audiences were forcing circuits to rationalize. Previously, theatres and music halls had been hired by the BBC on an ad hoc basis for shows, including the Bedford in Camden Town, but the decision had been made to acquire a theatre. The BBC had the option either of buying the Empire or buying the lease of the 1902-vintage, W.G.R. Sprague-designed King's Theatre on Hammersmith Road. The latter was in better condition, and, at £85,000, nearly half the Empire's £150,000 asking price, but the former was freehold. That swung the decision, as did its proximity to Lime Grove and the future

Television Centre site; not to mention Prince Littler's willingness to accept an offer of £120,000. This figure seems massive, but, in May 1953, the theatre had been hired by the BBC for a week, at a cost of £1,000, for a Richard Afton-produced gala and an edition of *What's My Line*. So it paid for itself in just over two years. It closed as a music hall on 26 September 1953, and the BBC took vacant possession on 29 September. The budget did not yet extend to equipping it fully, so at first it was run on a drive-in basis, using outside broadcast cameras and control vans.

In the early days of television entertainment, studio size made it impossible and undesirable to have live studio audiences. As soon as space allowed, however, audiences were tested, and it was found that they could have a beneficial effect on programmes, as Brian Tesler's experience on *Ask Pickles* – an early wish-fulfilment programme, preceding *Jim'll Fix It* and *Surprise Surprise* by a couple of decades – shows:

One week when studio D at Lime Grove was not available, they said 'You'll have to go into the Shepherd's Bush Empire. You don't have to do it in front of an audience, but it's the only place we've got.' We thought 'Why not do it in front of an audience?' The warmth that an audience brought to *Ask Pickles* in the Shepherd's Bush Empire was extraordinary. I said 'I don't want to do it without an audience any more.'

And So To Bentley was done without an audience, and it got lousy ratings. Charlotte Mitchell was the girl of the show, and her nanny came to see the show [at Lime Grove] in the little viewing room by reception downstairs. We'd done a send-up of a Ruritanian romance, with Dick Bentley as the ageing student prince, who couldn't get the girl, because she was a commoner. We went downstairs afterwards, and the nanny came towards Charlotte in tears. And Charlotte said 'What's the matter?' The nanny said 'Oh it was so sad. He wanted to marry you, but he couldn't,' and I suddenly realized that people were taking these satires seriously, because they didn't know it was meant to be funny.[42]

★

While light entertainment on radio and television went from strength to strength in the forties and fifties, the story of live variety in the immediate post-war era was one of more mixed fortunes. Having let the Crazy Gang go to the Victoria Palace, mistakenly believing that their glory days were past, the London Palladium management under Val Parnell tried to keep attendances up by importing the biggest names from the US. The first to come over was Hollywood song-and-dance star Mickey Rooney in January 1948, causing *The Times*'s critic to observe that he 'plays the trumpet lustily, the drums with abandon, and the piano occasionally. He works too hard for his effects, but there is something engaging about him when he relaxes.'[43] Perhaps because of this, his season was a flop, and ended midway through its last week.

The next act in, however, was a runaway success. Danny Kaye, who had just starred in the film *The Secret Life of Walter Mitty*, took the Palladium stage on 2 February, and at the same time took London by storm. In the first half of the show, audiences were treated to the comedy of Ted Ray – on the verge of radio stardom, and, according to *The Times*, the only one of the supporting cast who 'rises above a dreary and sometimes distasteful mediocrity'.[44]

After the interval, it was Kaye's turn. His forty-five-minute spot took up the whole second half of the show, something that eventually became the norm for visiting megastars. Initially very nervous, he admitted as much to the audience, and the rapturous applause that ensued broke any ice that there might have been. One of the high spots of his act was mimicking a tone-deaf crooner, but *The Times*'s critic observed that for the most part 'he just fools about, with a microphone before him and a band behind, dancing a little occasionally, chatting with the conductor, interrupting his own singing, and generally making fun of himself and everyone else'. All of this, however, was to good effect. *The Times* concluded that 'Mr. Kaye is a most successful and agreeable clown.'[45]

In June 1948, jazz giant Duke Ellington returned to the Palladium for the first time since 1933. Unfortunately, a long-standing dis-agreement between the Musicians' Union and the American Federation of Musicians meant that he could not bring his orchestra with him, so he and cornet player Ray Nance had to undertake the engagement to the accompaniment of a British trio. The musicians were led by (Canadian-born) bassist Jack Fallon, with Tony Crombie on drums and Malcolm Mitchell on guitar. As good as they undoubtedly were, Ellington was always at his best with his full band behind him. Those who saw the show got variety in the truest sense of the word, with Ellington's sophisticated music being complemented by the Stockton-on-Tees-born comedian Jimmy James. A teetotaller who was universally recognized by his peers as the best drunk act on earth, his act on the Ellington bill involved introducing his stooge, the long-faced, deadpan, stammering Eli 'Bretton' Woods (played by James's nephew, Jack Casey), as his new discovery. The nature of Woods's unique talent varied, according to the late Roy Castle, who remembered one occasion:

Our Eli was a whistling contortionist. 'He whistles "Bird Songs at Eventide" and does the splits at one and the same time.' Jimmy paused to take a quick drag, but just before the fag got to his mouth he added, 'And if the sirens go, he'll probably do *three*!'[46]

On another night, Woods, 'dressed in an ill-fitting suit and a Davy Crockett hat', was introduced as 'The Singing Skunk Trapper'. Castle eventually joined the act himself, as James's second stooge, always billed as Hutton Conyers, a role played by several comedians through the years. Perhaps James's best-remembered routine revolves around Conyers' fiercely guarded shoebox and its unlikely contents:

CONYERS: Is it you that's putting it about that I'm barmy?
JAMES: Me? Good heavens, no. Why should I do that?
CONYERS: Well is it him?
JAMES [to Woods]: Is it you?
WOODS: I don't want any.

75

JAMES: He doesn't want any. We got a load in last Friday. [To Woods] You must have some left.

WOODS: How much are they? . . .

CONYERS: I've been to South Africa . . . Just before I came home, they gave me a lovely present.

JAMES: Did they? What did they give you?

CONYERS: Two man-eating lions.

JAMES: Oh yes? Did you fetch them home? Where do you keep them?

CONYERS: In this box.

JAMES: Two lions in there? I thought I heard a little rustling . . . [To Woods] Go and get two coffees . . . He's got two lions in that box.

WOODS: How much are they?

JAMES: He doesn't want to sell them . . . He's got a giraffe in there with the lions.

WOODS: Is it black or white?

JAMES: What colour's the giraffe?

WOODS: The coffee, I mean.[47]

Written down, this may well seem baffling and unfunny. Seen and heard, as is possible thanks to its presence in Tyne Tees Television's opening show in 1959, it's a tour de force of misunderstanding and mangled logic, with the accompaniment of James's beautifully timed grimaces, asides and puffs on his cigarette. It's a world away from the laboured puns of most of James's contemporaries. James is a reasonable man caught between two idiots, who manage to leave him wondering if he's not an idiot as well ('there'll be enough room in the van for the three of us'). When Conyers claims to have an elephant in the box too, a gift from the Indians, James asks if it's male or female. Woods interjects with the reasonable enough suggestion that the information would matter only to another elephant. James's reply is majestic. He fixes the stammering adult in the Davy Crockett hat with a glare and says 'I'll stop you going to those youth clubs.' Duke Ellington's reaction to his colleague's act was, sadly, not recorded, but it would be nice to think that he loved James as madly as he professed to love his audiences.

Provincial halls didn't have the Palladium's luxury of being able to import exotic stars from the US. In some cases, it was tried, but ended in failure, such as Frank Sinatra's poorly patronized engagement at the Bristol Hippodrome. Even central London competitors struggled. When dancer turned agent and promoter Bernard Delfont tried to put on American stars at the London Casino on Old Compton Street (now the Prince Edward Theatre), Parnell's greater resources and willingness to pay top dollar at the Palladium nearly put Delfont out of business at the start of his career.

For some outside the capital, nudes provided the answer, inspired by Vivian Van Damm's success at the Windmill Theatre. This venue, just off London's Shaftesbury Avenue – then, as now, the main thoroughfare of theatreland – had opened in 1909 as the Palais De Luxe cinema, but in 1931 it was taken over by a rich widow called Mrs Laura Henderson and turned into a theatre. A brief period of legitimacy, in the form of plays, didn't pay, so Henderson found a new manager in Van Damm, who reopened the Windmill on 4 February 1932 with a new concept – Revuedeville.

It was a novelty from the start, by virtue of providing non-stop entertainment, as cinemas had been doing for some time. With seats at 1s 6d and 2s 6d, the five performances a day meant that whenever you turned up, you were guaranteed a show, with musical numbers and comedians such as Van Damm's first discovery, John Tilley. However, the novelty soon wore off, as rival theatres in better locations presented their own non-stop variety shows. Van Damm fought back with what he called 'living tableaux':

My idea was that perfectly proportioned young women should be presented in artistic poses, representing a frieze entablature or a famous classical painting. Standing perfectly still, they would of course form part of the glamorous stage decor. This was a revolutionary idea in British show business.[48]

Even more revolutionary was the fact that they should be largely naked. The standing still was less an attempt to turn flesh and blood into *trompe l'oeil* and more a necessity imposed by the Lord Chamberlain's office, which took a very close interest in events at the Windmill. They decided if costumes were decent or indecent, or whether the fan dancers were letting their fans slip 'accidentally' more than was acceptable. The Windmill, aptly, sailed close to the wind and got away with as much as it could. Van Damm's daughter Sheila, who took over the running of the theatre on her father's death in 1960, remembered with gratitude that the Lord Chamberlain's men gave her advance notice of their inspections and always walked from their base at St James's Palace, giving her time to check that all was seemly.

Vivian Van Damm is remembered as a benign dictator figure, whose word was law. He looked upon his girls with a fatherly eye, and insisted that the comedians should not fraternize with them – although when a relationship came to his attention, he would let it pass if he thought it a good pairing. Similarly, when he said no in an audition, that was it. Unless, of course, you were Bruce Forsyth. Before Forsyth finished his dance routine, VD (as Van Damm was inevitably known to the irreverent) said he'd seen enough. Forsyth insisted on seeing it through to the end. Despite, or perhaps because of his impertinence, Forsyth got the job.

By the early fifties, the Windmill was famous for its girls, the fact that it had remained proudly and defiantly open throughout the war, and for the vast number of young comedians who began their careers there. They included Forsyth, Michael Bentine, Jimmy Edwards, Arthur English, Tony Hancock, Bill Kerr, Alfred Marks, Bill Maynard, Harry Secombe and Peter Sellers. (Spike Milligan, infamously and perhaps unsurprisingly, failed the audition.) The 'living tableaux' brought out the worst in some of the customers, some choosing to masturbate under cover of a newspaper. A member of staff kept close watch on the aroused hordes with a pair of binoculars (a luxury that was strictly verboten in the opposite direction) ejecting any offenders. Kenneth More, before he became an actor of note, worked at the Windmill, binocular duty being among his responsibilities.

The Windmill formula was replicated nationwide, with touring and resident troupes. In Birmingham, the Aston Hippodrome billed itself as 'The Windmill Theatre of the Midlands', and presented the likes of Pauline Penny and her 'Pennies from Heaven' troupe. Once, when appearing at Collins's Music Hall on Islington Green, Penny had made the mistake of performing in front of a wind machine. Word of the effect it had on her luxuriant pubic bush soon got around, resulting in a full house, some punters rushing up from the Angel to catch the phenomenon. Paul Raymond was a magician on these strip bills, but he soon saw that his talents would be better used packaging and promoting the shows. Thus was a multi-million-pound Soho porn and property empire born.

The rest of the live variety profession was, however, suffering. The growing popularity of television and the cinema undoubtedly had some effect on the decline of the halls, but they cannot accept the total blame. Housing standards were improving, making nights in more attractive for many of the population. Another culprit was entertainment tax, which had been introduced in 1916 as a cash cow for a nation at war, but which had gradually become more punitive over the years. For example, at the start, the tax took a shilling for each ticket over 7s 6d in price. By 1950, it was 1s 1d for each ticket over 2s 9d. The cinema, which accounted for 93 per cent of all entertainment tax receipts by the end of the Second World War, was hit hardest, but the live side took a considerable knock as well. A theatre in South Kensington closed in November 1949 with losses of £7,000, which was almost exactly the amount of entertainment tax its operators had paid since opening.

By the mid-fifties, variety theatres were closing for conversion or, more often, demolition. Declining receipts, combined with the sudden increase in speculative development, following the relaxation of wartime building restrictions, made the decision easy, and proprietors were made lucrative offers for sites that were no longer earning their keep. Kingston Empire, which had opened at the tail end of the variety theatre building boom in 1910 (and was where Gracie Fields was working when she married her first husband in 1923), closed in March 1955, to be gutted and converted into a supermarket.

However, as one set of outlets dwindled, another grew to take variety to a greater number of people than ever before.

CHAPTER THREE

Strictly commercial

After the long years of austerity, the fifties saw the British people heading into a period of relative affluence. There was money to spend, and with the end of rationing, there were things to spend it on. The drive to rebuild exports had relaxed a little, meaning that luxury goods were available to buy at home once again. 'Make do and mend' was giving way to rampant consumerism. It wasn't quite time for prime minister Harold Macmillan to declare that 'most of our people have never had it so good',[1] but the movement towards that memorable utterance was distinct. In fact, it wasn't quite time for Harold Macmillan, for in October 1951, the electorate had ejected Clement Attlee's radical Labour government in favour of the Conservatives under the 76-year-old Sir Winston Churchill.

This, then, was the political and social background for the birth of British commercial television, funded by advertising. There had been rumblings about commercial broadcasting since before the foundation of the BBC, but these began to grow louder and louder after the Second World War. When the BBC's Royal Charter came up for renewal in 1946, the decision was taken to maintain the existing system until 31 December 1951; after that, other possibilities were open to discussion. The three most prominent voices in favour of breaking the BBC's monopoly came from the Conservative backbenches. John Rodgers, Ian Orr-Ewing[2] and John Profumo were all part of the new intake of

MPs from the 1950 General Election, the first to be honoured with any television coverage of the results. Two of them also had vested interests: Rodgers had come into Parliament from the advertising agency J. Walter Thompson, while Orr-Ewing was a consultant to a television equipment manufacturer. To be completely fair, Orr-Ewing spent most of his life lobbying against monopolies and restrictions of one sort or another. On top of this, he was a television man through and through. Armed with an Oxford physics degree and a radio ham's licence, he had joined EMI as a trainee in 1934, just as the final development of the 405-line television system was going on. He then moved, in 1937, to the BBC to work in the outside broadcast department.

Away from this triumvirate of radical thinkers, the parliamentary reaction was mixed. The Labour Party were all against the idea, as were elements within the Conservative Party. In particular, Prime Minister Churchill was less than enthusiastic, referring to the mooted enterprise as a 'tu'penny Punch and Judy show'.[3] Others had decidedly odd motives for wanting to see an element of competition in broadcasting. Lord Woolton, the chairman of the Conservative Party and the man who as wartime Minister of Food gave his name to a notoriously unappetizing pie, argued in favour of commercial television because he feared that the BBC might fall under communist influence at some point. Most vocal of the Labour naysayers was Christopher Mayhew MP, whose face was so regularly seen on BBC television that he was known to his detractors as the honourable member for Lime Grove. He wrote a pamphlet called 'Dear Viewer' arguing that programme quality would suffer, and was the prime mover in the National Television Council, a coalition of the great and the good who were willing to weigh in against the vulgarizing evil of commercial television. Their number included Lady Violet Bonham-Carter, Festival of Britain director Sir Gerald Barry, Lord Halifax and Eric Fletcher. The latter, a parliamentary colleague of Mayhew's, was also vice president of the Associated British Pictures Corporation, one of the two major British film-making and cinema-owning combines, and pledged the part-time assistance of an ABPC publicity man for the Council's work.

Above: Charles Morton's
Canterbury Hall,
Lambeth, 1856

Right: Dan Leno, 1903

The Co-Optimists concert party makes a broadcast at the BBC's Savoy Hill studios in August 1930. On the far left, standing, is Davy Burnaby; immediately below him is the young Stanley Holloway. The focus of their attention is the Round-Sykes 'meat safe' microphone

It's those men again: Horace Percival tries to get through to wartime favourite Tommy Handley during a broadcast of *ITMA* in January 1944

Above: The Windmill Girls performing in clothed mode for the BBC cameras at Alexandra Palace

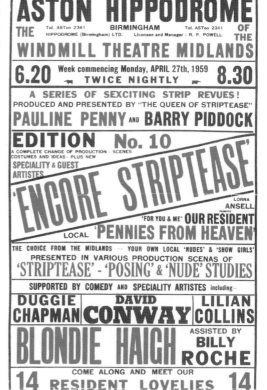

Right: Penny drops 'em: a provincial nude revue bill, 1959

Early Goons: Harry Secombe, Michael Bentine, Spike Milligan and Peter Sellers in riotous assembly around an AXBT ribbon microphone, May 1951

Jimmy Edwards, Wallas Eaton and June Whitfield rehearsing for *Take It From Here* at the Paris Cinema, London, 1954

The pro-commercial interests soon organized themselves into a countervailing lobby, under the banner of the Popular Television Association. The leading lights on this side of the debate were Charles Orr Stanley, overlord of the electronic equipment manufacturers Pye; Sir Robert Renwick, an industrialist with a background in electricity generation; and Norman Collins, journalist, popular novelist, a former controller of the Light Programme and the controller of BBC Television from December 1947 to October 1950. The Association was a lobbying front for a serious, well-organized company called the Associated Broadcasting Development Company Ltd, or ABDC, which had been incorporated on 6 August 1952 and was run by Stanley, Renwick and Collins.

Collins's exit from the BBC in 1950 was part principle, part pique. The principle was an unshakeable belief in the possibilities of the medium of television, which he felt could only be realized by maintaining a certain distance from radio and its practices. TV was not merely to be illustrated wireless. Throughout his three years in the job, Collins had been the ideal administrator for a fledgling creative enterprise and also a great evangelist for television. The pique resulted from Collins being passed over for the director of television post in favour of George Barnes, because director general Sir William Haley didn't think him suitable. Apart from the obvious personal slight, Barnes, as head of the spoken word and the Third Programme, had never dirtied his hands with the junior medium before. Broadcasting House had looked down on television from the start, but appeared to be taking an interest now that the service was gaining in credibility and professionalism. When Barnes's appointment was confirmed, Collins was asked to stay on as controller. He requested a couple of hours to consider his position, time that he instead used to call his many Fleet Street contacts with the news of his principled resignation and the fact that he would be throwing a party at the Savoy that night to celebrate his liberation. The BBC issued counter-publicity to the effect that Collins hadn't shown any interest in leaving until being passed over for the directorship, but Collins had outflanked the Corporation.

As a natural Conservative with television experience and a fair amount of charisma, Collins was the perfect frontman for the commercial television campaign. He set about the task with zeal, touring the country to preach to the unconverted and allay their worst fears. As both sides lobbied like mad through 1952 and 1953, the proposals for commercial television went through two White Papers, resulting in the Television Bill. As the Television Act, this passed onto the statute books on 30 July 1954, but it had been heavily revised during its progress through Parliament. The main change was the abandonment of the proposed £750,000 grant to prevent commercial TV from having to be too commercial. Instead, the Independent Television Authority (ITA) was trusted to maintain decency by regulation, under the stewardship of chairman Sir Kenneth Clark and director general Sir Robert Fraser, a former civil servant.

A federal, regional structure was adopted for the new Independent Television (ITV) service, with regional franchises to be awarded to programme contractors for fixed periods. On 25 August 1954, a tiny classified advertisement appeared on the front of *The Times*, inviting 'those interested in becoming PROGRAMME CONTRACTORS in accordance with the Television Act' to 'give a broad picture of the types of programme they would provide, their proposals for network or local broadcasting of their programmes, some indication of their financial resources, and the length of contract they would desire'.[4] On 26 October 1954, the first successful contractors, for London, the Midlands and the North – giving 60 per cent coverage of the UK – were announced. Each region was split, to prevent one dominant player emerging and taking all of the advertising revenue, with one company taking Monday–Friday, and another taking Saturday and Sunday.

The London weekday franchise, set to begin less than a year later, on 22 September 1955, was awarded to a consortium of Broadcast Relay Services and Associated Newspapers, a combination to be known as Associated-Rediffusion. London weekends and the weekday Midlands contract, beginning in February 1956, went to the Collins/Stanley/Renwick ABDC grouping, while weekends in the Midlands and North were awarded to Kemsley-Winnick, an alliance between *Sunday Times* owner Lord Kemsley,[5] former dance-band leader Maurice Winnick and Isaac Wolfson of Great Universal Stores. Their weekday counterpart in Lancashire and Yorkshire, which came on air in May and November 1956 respectively, was the Granada theatres group, led by the Bernstein brothers, Sidney and Cecil. After these pioneers had reached the airwaves successfully, further regions were added, achieving near-national coverage by 1962. Scottish Television had launched in 1957, then Southern came along in 1958, followed by Anglia in the east of England in 1959, then came Ulster, Westward, Border and Grampian. The roll-out finished in the Channel Islands in 1962, with the launch of the tiny Channel Television.

Among the disappointed applicants was the Incorporated Television Programme Company Ltd, headed by Prince Littler of Stoll Theatres, commercial radio producer Harry Alan Towers, Palladium boss Val Parnell and the powerful agent Lew Grade. Littler professed himself 'amazed to learn that no facilities have been offered to us, and we can think of no valid reason for this in view of our experience in the entertainment world and the talent at our disposal'.[6] In fact, it was the talent at the group's disposal that counted against them, as the ITA felt it would put them in far too strong a position. As powerful as the Stoll Theatre and Moss Empire interests were, it was the amazing reach of Grade's agency business that most alarmed the regulators.

The Grades dominated live variety, while the other disappointed applicant for a commercial television franchise had a commanding position in the field of film-making and exhibition. Perhaps surprisingly, given that its vice president Eric Fletcher was a leading lobbyist against commercial TV, the Associated British Picture Corporation had applied – chairman Sir Philip Warter and Pathé division chief Howard Thomas having become convinced of television's potential. Nevertheless, the ITA described the ABPC submission as 'half-hearted'.[7] In his speech at ABPC's 1954 AGM, Warter declared that the board had 'considered it advisable to safeguard the Corporation's interest by applying for a licence'[8] while regarding the Cinemascope widescreen process as the future of the business.

Both the ABPC and Grade's Incorporated Television Programme Company were to have a second chance, much to the new Authority's embarrassment. The ABDC bid had Norman Collins's television expertise, Charles Orr Stanley's technical know-how and Robert Renwick's business gravitas, but it proved to be short on capital. On 11 March 1955, just over six months before the first programmes were due to go out on the London transmitter, it was announced that ABDC would be merging its interests with the vanquished applicant ITPC. Prince Littler of ITPC became chairman of the combined group, known as the Associated Broadcasting Company (ABC), with Collins demoted to deputy chairman. If Collins was ever bitter about the situation, he did his best not to show it, no doubt mollified by the considerable riches the venture eventually brought him.

Meanwhile, the Kemsley-Winnick consortium suffered from Lord Kemsley's almost complete lack of interest in the venture, the main impetus having come from the Kemsley group's editorial director Denis Hamilton and Kemsley's stepdaughter, Ghislaine Alexander. She had appeared as a panellist on *What's My Line* and furnished the initial introduction to Winnick, who administered the show's format rights in the UK. Unfortunately, Kemsley's sons did not share their stepsister's enthusiasm, and also developed a personal antipathy towards partner Isaac Wolfson. Worst of all, Kemsley had never got on with Winnick. Getting cold feet, Wolfson withdrew, then Kemsley followed in February 1955 – a bare twelve months before the first Midlands programmes were set to take to the air – leaving Winnick without financial backing. Hamilton tried to talk Kemsley (described by one of his journalists, Godfrey Smith, as 'a frightful old twit really'[9]) round, but his mind was made up. Winnick begged the ITA to give him time to find new backers, but it was decided to re-advertise the contracts. On 13 September 1955, barely more than a week before the launch of the London station, the ITA gave Kemsley-Winnick's franchises to ABPC, who arranged to take on the equipment ordered for the abortive company. ABDC had decided to launch as ABC, but had to change its name to Associated TeleVision, or ATV, after only three weeks. The reason was that the late entrant, ABPC, had already used the ABC name for its national chain of cinemas, and wanted to use the same branding for its television subsidiary.

Another early snag was the abortive plan to share transmission sites with the BBC. It soon became apparent that the existing masts could not carry both sets of transmitting aerials. Astonishingly, given the time available, suitable alternative sites were found, at Croydon, Lichfield and on Rivington Moor in Lancashire (later better known as Winter Hill), and the already tight schedule was maintained. Studio space being urgently required, all except Granada chose to adapt existing buildings. Associated-Rediffusion took over the former Fox film studios at Wembley, as well as Frank Matcham's Granville Theatre at Walham Green, while ATV converted the Wood Green Empire into a studio and set up a transmission control centre in Foley Street. Both shared office accommodation in the former Air Ministry building on Kingsway, where Associated-Rediffusion also had studios, and they also briefly shared the tiny Viking film studio in Kensington. ABC had expendable cinemas in the shape of the Astoria in Aston for its Midlands studio, which it would share with ATV, and the Capitol at Didsbury for its northern outpost. Elsewhere in Manchester, architect Ralph Tubbs – best known for the Dome of Discovery and the Skylon at the Festival of Britain – was erecting the UK's first purpose-built television studios for the Bernsteins.

As important as the premises and technology, if not more so, were the staff. The obvious source of production talent was the BBC and so the defections began, lured by the promises of better money and instant promotion. One relatively junior BBC LE producer, Dickie Leeman, had left in 1954 in preparation for the new venture. Senior producer Bill Ward moved over to ATV, as did designer Richard Greenough, who became the new company's head of design:

I would never have got that promotion at the BBC. Peter Bax had died in 1952, Richard Levin became head of design in 1953 and I was not his favourite [whereas] I was with Peter Bax. I had worked with Bill [Ward] quite a lot, and I think I went to ATV because of Bill. It was better paid, better altogether for me, one way and another. Wood Green Empire was a much better studio than Shepherd's Bush. The proscenium was 40 feet wide instead of 30, and we built the stage way out to under the circle, with an orchestra pit.[10]

On a wing and a prayer, Associated-Rediffusion and ATV were ready for their opening night, 22 September 1955. Although it was a Thursday, the weekday and weekend contractors treated the debut as a joint venture, sharing the programming burden. This made sense, as Associated-Rediffusion's strengths were to be in drama and documentaries rather than light entertainment, with ATV making an almost perfect complement. The first night began with a short film about the establishment of the service and the city it would be serving, narrated by Cecil Lewis – a reassuring voice from the past, having been one of the founding fathers of the BBC. Similarly soothing was the presence of Leslie Mitchell, announcing for Associated-Rediffusion as he had at the start of BBC TV nearly nineteen years before. Then, at 7.15pm, it was live to the Guildhall for the opening ceremony, relayed by Associated-Rediffusion, complete with speeches from the Lord Mayor of London, Sir Kenneth Clark and Postmaster General Sir Charles Hill. Finally, at 8pm, the new service began to show its true colours with a Bill Ward-produced variety show, transmitted live by ATV from Wood Green.[11] The host was bandleader turned disc jockey Jack Jackson, with radio favourite Billy Cotton and his band, Australian zither-playing cutie Shirley Abicair, and Leslie 'The Memory Man' Welch as guests.

The variety show was interrupted at 8.12pm by a novelty act: the first commercial break in British television history. Introduced by Jack Jackson with the words 'This is what you've been waiting for', a tube of toothpaste in a block of ice was pronounced to be 'tingling fresh', giving Gibbs SR the honour of being the first product in that inaugural £1,000-a-minute break. Next came *Café Continental*'s Hélène

Cordet, with a spoof panel game in which both sides declared that Cadbury's was their favourite drinking chocolate. An advertisement for margarine rounded off the first spot and then it was back to Wood Green. The big show was followed by drama from Associated-Rediffusion, boxing from ATV and then back to Associated-Rediffusion for a visit to the opening-night gala cabaret, with George Formby at the Mayfair Hotel.

The critical response to the first night was almost wholly favourable, even from parts of the media that had grave reservations about the whole enterprise. *Daily Express* proprietor Lord Beaverbrook had taken against ITV from the outset, largely, it is believed, because he was informed that he wouldn't get a sniff at a franchise. As a result, the *Daily Express* declared on 22 September that 'the whole set-up is futile in its present form'. It was pointed out that the new service 'can count on 400,000 sets at the most', compared to 4,767,000 receiving the BBC, although it was not pointed out that the BBC had nearly achieved national coverage, whereas ITV was available in London only. The *Express* also argued that advertisers got poor value for their money compared with newspaper advertising. Once advertisers realized this, would the new venture 'be able to pay the heavy price of good programmes? The standards are bound to deteriorate rapidly by comparison with the BBC.'[12] The following day, however, even the *Express* reviewer praised the 'general slickness', found the variety show 'brilliant, but brassy', declared the Mayfair Hotel relay to be 'on a level with good class BBC' and thought the boxing 'excellent'. In the minus column, the news was 'scrappy', the drama 'poor quality' and the ads 'irksome when the novelty had gone'.

In contrast, the *Daily Mirror* had used its leader column on 22 September to wish ITV the best of luck, while stressing that it had no connections with any TV companies. Indeed, it had passed on the chance to invest in ABDC when Collins had been at his most desperate for backers. The *Mirror*'s success had been based on giving the public what it wanted, and it supported ITV as a kindred spirit:

The **politicians** have pummelled it.

The **bishops** have belted it.

The **killjoys** have caned it.

But from today only the verdict of Mr and Mrs Televiewer matters.[13]

And the next day, TV correspondent Clifford Davis pronounced it a 'slick, fast-moving evening of entertainment', with even the Edith Evans/John Gielgud extract from *The Importance of Being Earnest* proving 'a rare treat in TV drama'. Davis saved his scorn for the ceremonial part of the evening:

THE BIG LET DOWN was that boring opening. Why did ITV have to go all high-hat and pompous instead of setting the screen sizzling from the start?

It was BAD SHOWMANSHIP to waste so much time instead of getting on with the job in hand – the job that ITV has been brought in to do – to ENTERTAIN.

Why inflict on viewers all those sombre sayings and meaningless platitudes [. . .]?[14]

The answer to Davis's question was simple. ITV wanted to make a good impression with everyone, from the lowest brow to the highest hat. Commercial television had been viewed by its detractors as a vulgar, Americanized influence on the British people. The presence of imported shows on ITV like *I Love Lucy* and *Dragnet*, and the move away from sedate panel games towards quiz shows with cash prizes suggested that this view was not entirely unfounded. The sombre, none-more-British opening ceremony was a response to these sniffy critics before the real business could get under way, secure in the knowledge that all viewers would sit through just about anything having spent a fortune on sets capable of receiving the new channel.

Deciding what to watch was made easier by that night's lacklustre opposition from the BBC. On television, the Guildhall ceremony went head to head with *Disneyland: the Donald Duck Story* (imported from

America, ironically enough), while there was a concert of Schubert and Beethoven on the Home Service, the record programme *Family Favourites* on the Light, and the poems of Laurence Binyon on the Third. The BBC managed to steal some of the new venture's coverage by killing off Grace Archer in *The Archers*, but as this had happened a full fifteen minutes before ITV went on the air, it had no effect on ratings.

ITV's first game show came on the second night, in the form of *Take Your Pick* with Michael Miles. Hughie Green's *Double Your Money* began on the following Monday. Both shows and their presenters had come to Associated-Rediffusion from Radio Luxembourg. In *Take Your Pick*, contestants who answered three questions successfully were allowed to choose the key to one of thirteen numbered boxes. In some were things worth winning. In others were booby prizes. At various junctures, Miles offered to buy the key, leaving the contestants to ponder the chances of the box contents being better than the offer. It was *Deal or No Deal* with added general knowledge and the bonus of the fiendish Yes/No interlude, where Miles fired personal questions at contestants who were not allowed to respond with 'yes' or 'no'. The merest hint of either and they were gonged off. *Double Your Money*, in contrast, was a relatively pure quiz. Contestants chose a specialist subject from a board on which the options were displayed. The first question was worth £1, the second worth £2, and so on up to £32. Those who got to £32 entered a difficult final 'Treasure Trail' round, the theoretical top prize for which was £1,000.

The first edition of *Double Your Money*, a rare survival from those early days, makes very interesting viewing. 'Mugging' is a show business term for any form of attention-seeking gurning in performance, and here Hughie Green – Canada-raised and that rarest of creatures, a child performer who had continued to be successful in adulthood – gives a mugger's masterclass. Every comment to a contestant is accompanied by a sideways look at the camera, with either a wink, a grin or a grimace, as appropriate.

The contestants seem chosen to cover all the bases. The first is an

Arsenal football club clerk who knows a lot about geography and makes it into the Treasure Trail round. Green asks if there are any Arsenal fans in, and gets a massive cheer, unsurprisingly, as the show was made at the Highbury studios run by Norman Collins's High Definition Films company. The second is a young female physiotherapist, all A-line skirt and horn-rimmed glasses, who goes away with nothing after faltering on the third question – the name of Winston Churchill's poodle (which was Rufus).

Then it's the turn of the married couples. A young couple, married only five weeks, answer questions on the RAF, the husband having recently emerged from his two years' National Service. He looks barely out of short trousers, his telephonist wife seems the archetypal young fifties wife, happy to defer to her husband in all matters. Green observes that it'll be a different matter in five years. The stars of the show, however, are a couple from the East End of London. Married since 1900, he is 78, she is 73 and the sort of woman that Irene Handl made a career of playing in films like *I'm All Right, Jack* and *Two Way Stretch*. They express no strong preference for any subject, so Green steers them into answering questions on old-time music halls. The husband gets the first question – where is the Metropolitan music hall? – wrong. Having been firm but fair with the youngsters, he can't bear to see these salt-of-the-earth septuagenarian cockneys go away empty handed. He all but gives them the right answer (Edgware Road) and the £2 and £4 answers prove easy enough. On the £8 question, concerning the identity of music hall's 'handcuff king', the old cockney can remember that the name begins with an H, but even with heavy prompting from Green, the name 'Houdini' eludes him. As a quiz show, the format would still work today, but that first edition is a snapshot of a lost age, in which dolly-bird hostesses, pimply, recently demobbed National Servicemen, and people who would have remembered the Jack the Ripper murders as local news all co-existed. It was bright, brash fun for all the family and the viewing figures reflected as much.

The instant hits of its game shows apart, A-R didn't really have much light entertainment of its own. Head of drama Peter Willes was nominally in charge, but his main interest was in new, serious writers like Harold Pinter. The company also made an impressive showing in current affairs and documentaries, through series like *This Week* and Dan Farson's various quirky but subtly investigative outings like *People in Trouble*, *Out of Step*, *Living for Kicks* and *Dan Farson Meets*. Slightly mannered presentation apart, the Farson shows that survive stand up amazingly well.

David Croft – later to become the co-creator of *Dad's Army*, *Hi-De-Hi!* and *'Allo 'Allo* – began his television career at Associated-Rediffusion as a script editor, and he soon realized that Willes 'was completely at sea in popular light entertainment', his idea of a hit show being 'anything starring Hermione Baddeley and Hermione Gingold',[15] both names from the golden age of West End revue, which had long since passed. With the recruitment of Ken Carter from the BBC as senior producer, there were some attempts to build up a light entertainment presence for A-R, most notably American director Richard Lester's efforts to bring the success of *The Goon Show* to the small screen with Spike Milligan and Peter Sellers in *The Idiot Weekly, Price 2d*. The experiment was successful enough to result in two further Milligan/Sellers series: *A Show Called Fred* and *Son of Fred*. Making many of the wilder flights of fancy from *The Goon Show* work on television would have been impossible with the technology of the time. The surviving material from the series shows that Lester and co. went to the other extreme, showing quite clearly that these were grotty sets in a small studio, to considerable comic effect. For one item, the respected actor Valentine Dyall wandered out of the studio, down the corridor and into the canteen. There was no studio audience, only the laughter of the cast and crew.

However, the efforts of Croft, Carter and Willes were overshadowed by a decision to subcontract the majority of A-R's light entertainment commitments to Jack Hylton Television Productions Ltd, a company formed by the bandleader turned impresario. On paper, it was the dream ticket. Hylton had brought the Crazy Gang back to the West End after the war, when they were as successful as they had been before, if not more. His stage revues at the Adelphi, such as *The Talk of the Town*, which ran from November 1954 to December 1955, made good use of relatively new performers like Tony Hancock and Jimmy Edwards. His, then, was the golden touch. With Val Parnell and Lew Grade tied up in ATV, Hylton was the next best thing.

Unfortunately, for the most part, Hylton's television productions failed to realize the potential of the new medium. They looked stagey, indeed many were just outside broadcasts from existing Hylton stage shows. His first situation comedy, *Love and Kisses*, was a stage play filmed in a theatre and chopped into five parts. Material used in Hylton shows was often top drawer, but not especially original. The better scripts for the early Hylton shows were 'adapted' from Sid Caesar's *Your Show of Shows*, which had run on the NBC television network in America from 1950 to 1954, and with writers like Mel Brooks, Neil Simon, Carl Reiner and Larry Gelbart, the quality was high. Unfortunately, Hylton chose to 'borrow' the material without Caesar or NBC's knowledge. Eventually, they got wind and a licensing deal was set up.

Hylton also had a regrettable tendency to let his sexual urges influence his professional interests. He married only twice, but for most of his first, thirty-five-year marriage, he was estranged from his wife and in a relationship with another woman, while enjoying numerous affairs and dalliances. His period in television was marked by his relationship with the Italian singer Rosalina Neri. To describe her professionally as such is perhaps too kind. She was meagrely talented, but undeniably easy on the eye, although the *Daily Herald* observed that she was 'a combination of Sabrina, the young Marlene Dietrich and Marilyn Monroe – but grown to nightmare proportions'. The *Liverpool Echo* commented that she was 'without a voice to match her vital statistics', while the *Manchester Evening News* plumped for describing her simply as 'a shockingly bad singer'. Despite her deficiencies, she made many guest appearances in Hylton shows before gaining her own vehicle, *The Rosalina Neri Show*, in 1959. Her biggest problem was with the English language, to the point that 'it proved to be almost impossible to understand what she was saying' when singing in English.[16]

In fairness, Hylton had only two months between closing the A-R programme deal and the transmission of the first show on 29 September 1955. Even worse, the production of the debut offering – a filmed compilation of items from the Adelphi's *The Talk of the Town* with additional appearances by Robb Wilton, Stanley Holloway and Flanagan and Allen, under the *Jack Hylton Presents* banner – was hit by strike action. What the viewers saw prompted the *Daily Mirror*'s Clifford Davis to suggest that Hylton 'should confine his activities to the live theatre – and, for pity's sake, leave television alone'.[17]

While Hylton's shows did improve eventually, the critical reception didn't – with the bad first impressions counting for a lot. There were sketch show hits: *Alfred Marks Time*, starring comedian Alfred Marks; Arthur Askey's *Before Your Very Eyes*, which had transferred from the BBC; and, prior to his BBC TV debut, *The Tony Hancock Show*, which remains funny fifty years on, in the handful of surviving recordings. This is largely due to the all-original scripts from Eric Sykes, Larry Stephens (both fresh from collaborating with Spike Milligan on *The Goon Show*), Ray Galton and Alan Simpson. Galton and Simpson's contribution was uncredited, as they were already developing the BBC TV sitcom that would cement Hancock's star status. Particularly memorable is a spoof of *A Streetcar Named Desire*, with Hancock playing opposite June Whitfield, a comic actress whose performances have been, at worst, merely very good throughout her career. Her cries of 'Show 'em the tattoo, Brad' lead Hancock to lift his T-shirt, revealing the word 'Aldershot' clumsily daubed on his chest. Stupid maybe, obvious maybe, but funny certainly.

Other Hylton shows that found a measure of favour included the Crazy Gang's sporadic televisual outings and the occasional visits of the sophisticated French humorist Robert Dhéry. Unfortunately, these were not enough to rescue Hylton's reputation. In the *Daily Mail*, Peter Black – whose rigorous, critical, insightful, well-written reviews do much to give a flavour of television from an era when recordings are scarce – felt he understood where Hylton had gone wrong:

> Jack Hylton has very strong and personal ideas about what the television audience wants. He sees us – I'm deducing from what I have seen of his TV shows – as a typical Monday night audience at the Theatre Royal, Shuddersford . . . It is, of course, a profound misjudgement. The provincial music hall audience is so used to making the best of its bargain that it will applaud the dimmest spark of talent or even of effort.[18]

In contrast, Black argued, the television audience was 'spoiled and capricious'. It's more likely that Black was, charitably, ascribing his own high viewing and critical standards to the majority of the audience, when, in truth, they were mostly rather less discerning than a paying variety audience, reasonably happy to flump down in front of something, anything, after a hard day at work, school or wherever. His perception that Hylton had utterly misjudged the new medium was, however, more than fair.

Fortunately, Associated-Rediffusion's shortfall on the network was more than made up for by ATV. The first weekend included the debut of *Sunday Night at the London Palladium*, hosted by Tommy Trinder. The Palladium show succeeded where Hylton's early efforts failed, thanks to the prestige of the venue itself (every performer regarded the Palladium as the acme of the profession) the quality of the bill on offer and the fact that the programme was visibly live. In one of the few surviving recordings of the show, dating from 13 April 1958, the bill consists of Pinky and Perky, oddball US comedian Dick Shawn, country singer Marvin Rainwater and jazz legend Sarah Vaughan, not to mention the Tiller Girls, high-kicking their way around the stage. Something for all the family. There was also the added attraction of a game show interlude in the form of 'Beat the Clock', in which married couples competed for household goods and a shot at a cash jackpot that rose week by week if not won. At the end of the segment, the victorious couple would be asked 'Can you come back next week?' giving independent television its first original catchphrase.

The Palladium shows were supplemented by *Val Parnell's Saturday Spectacular*, which usually focused on a single star. Eric Sykes was persuaded to take on twenty-six of these shows fortnightly, primarily as a scriptwriter, despite the gruelling workload. There were 'easier ways to commit suicide', he observed in his memoirs.[19] The enticement was the galaxy of international superstars that Parnell guaranteed Sykes. 'Mentioning Bing Crosby was like saying to an alcoholic "They're open,"' Sykes confesses, visualizing the chance to hob-nob with his heroes. The series got off to a good start with jazz singer Mel Tormé, but in subsequent weeks, the parade of legends failed to materialize. Domestic stars like Tommy Steele, Dickie Valentine and Lonnie Donegan all did their bit, while Peter Sellers and Spike Milligan helped Sykes out on a couple of occasions, as did Sykes's long-standing collaborators Hattie Jacques and Deryck Guyler, but soon Sykes was contemplating 'walking up and down Oxford Street with a sandwich board asking for volunteers'.[20]

Unfortunately, the presence of the ATV powerhouse meant that the other regions tended not to get a look-in when it came to entertainment. The second biggest contributor in the early years was Granada, the northern weekday company. In a deft bit of showmanship, Sidney Bernstein had decided to give the studios at the new Manchester complex even numbers only, making it seem as though there were twice as many as there really were. Manchester would eventually have studios 2, 4, 6, 8 and 12. The former Chelsea Palace theatre was studio 10, and it was home to hit situation comedy *The Army Game* and the resolutely high-class variety show *Chelsea at Nine*, which was very much a pet project of Sidney and Cecil Bernstein's. 'They remembered the great days of the Stoll variety shows of the twenties,' recalled founding Granada executive Denis Forman, 'in which clowns, classical musicians, famous actresses and great ballerinas could all be found on the same bill.'[21]

The brothers thought that their good relations with MCA, one of the largest talent agencies in the US, would see them through, but the first show suffered from the last-minute withdrawal of an American producer, so the Bernsteins decided to become hands-on and book the best talent they could, wherever it could be found. 'The brothers attended rehearsals together . . . [and] vetted numbers for the regular song and dance troupe (the Granadiers),' Forman observed.[22] Unfortunately, this caused resentment among their fellow executives who thought that the chairman and deputy chairman should be concentrating on business, not show business. They relinquished their grip, rather tellingly nominating not head of light entertainment Eddie Pola, but Denis Forman, the urbane former head of the British Film Institute, to take over from January 1959. It was on Forman's watch that the most memorable moment of the show's run occurred, the appearance in June of Maria Callas, performing the second act of *Tosca*. Videotape recording was in its infancy at this time, and Forman had contrived to get a week ahead, enabling him to watch his great coup on holiday in south Wales. He reported back to Bernstein 'the impact Callas made [in] that farm kitchen . . . I do not believe there is any film star or actress alive who could have matched her power last night.'[23]

The company also made a big impression in the field of game shows, in which Pola, an American-born ex-hoofer, majored. To the network, Granada contributed *Criss-Cross Quiz* with Jeremy Hawk, *Spot the Tune* with Marion Ryan and *Twenty One*. NBC's original US version of *Twenty One* was the subject of a rigging scandal, after it emerged that contestant Charles van Doren had been fed answers by the production team. The press levelled similar allegations at the Granada version, and these were met with a promise of a robust legal defence, but the show and the legal action were both quietly dropped.

★

With the regions all playing to their respective strengths in programming, the new service was an instant hit. In February 1956, ITV had between a 60 and 63 per cent audience share in houses that were able to receive the programmes. Qualitative research suggested that only 16 per cent of viewers actively preferred the BBC's output. The pattern was repeated as each new ITV region launched, with an average ratio of 67 per cent of viewers opting for ITV over 33 per cent in favour of the BBC. Only the Anglia region, which took to the air on 27 October 1959, was a relative failure at first, snaring 55 per cent of the viewers to the BBC's 45 per cent.

Although each company made regional programmes for its own viewers, the top-rating shows were the networked productions from the major contractors, programmes bought by all of the regions and transmitted simultaneously across the whole of ITV. Before television, tastes in entertainment had been regionalized. The earthy comedian Frank Randle always went down best in his north-western heartland – most obviously in Blackpool, where his summer season shows dominated the Golden Mile year after year. Nowhere was the difference in tastes more noticeable than in Scotland, which had its own comedy subculture, and a famously violent dislike for comics from south of the border. Most notorious was the Glasgow Empire, the Moss circuit's Scottish showplace, where, in the words of the Scottish actor and comedian Stanley Baxter, 'English comedians came to die quietly.'[24] One of them was Des O'Connor, who faked a faint in order to win a measure of sympathy from the crowd and put a premature end to his ordeal. Mike and Bernie Winters suffered for their art as well. The act began with Mike wandering on stage with a clarinet, on which he played *Exactly Like You*. When Bernie made his entrance by sticking his head through the curtains and proffering his trademark toothy grin, a voice from the gods shouted 'Shite, there's two of them!'[25]

One of the best-loved of all Scottish comedians was Chic Murray, whose surreal, whimsical material was rendered all the more effective by being delivered in a measured, cultivated accent. (Later in life, he played the headmaster in the film *Gregory's Girl*, a perfect piece of casting if ever there was one.) Active from the forties until his death in 1985, he was the very essence of droll – indeed, when he began his performing career in an act with his wife Maidie, they were billed as 'the tall droll and the small doll'. With his ever-present cap or 'bunnet' perched on his head, he delivered lines like 'There's a new slimming course just out where they remove all your bones. Not only do you weigh less, but you also look so much more relaxed,' apparently more bemused than amused. One of his most famous routines involved a trip to a wedding in Blackpool and an encounter with a large-nosed female guest. Not sure how to greet her, he bows. She bows back, and with her nose, accidentally cuts the cake. ('The bride was in tears. So was the cake.') Unperturbed, the woman raises her massive conk in the air and begins sniffing – it transpires that she can sense that someone is boiling cabbage in Manchester.

Jack Milroy and Rikki Fulton were among Chic Murray's contemporaries, and it was as the gaudily dressed Glaswegian wide boys Francie and Josie that they made their reputations, first on stage in the *Five Past Eight* revues at the Glasgow Alhambra and then in their own series for Scottish Television.[26] Best known for their 'Are ye dancin'?' routine, their fans also never tired of what became known as 'the Arbroath gag', in which Josie – played by the lugubrious, equine Fulton – attempts to tell a simple two-line joke, but ends up taking a quarter of an hour, thanks to digressions and Milroy's interruptions. The kernel of the joke involves a visitor knocking at a door and asking if a member of the household is in. On being told 'She's at Arbroath,' the visitor replies 'Don't worry, I'll wait for her to finish,' having misheard 'Arbroath' as 'her broth' and thought that she was merely enjoying a bowl of soup. On his own, Fulton would go on to become a Hogmanay institution on BBC television in Scotland, with his annual *Scotch and Wry* sketch show.

Murray and Fulton had a modicum of success outside Scotland, but neither achieved the profile of Stanley Baxter. He had begun his career as a child actor on BBC radio, in the Scottish *Children's Hour*, before honing his craft further during his National Service while serving in an entertainment unit in Singapore that also included Kenneth Williams, future dramatist Peter Nicholls and film director-to-be John Schlesinger. After demob, he joined the company at the Citizens' Theatre in Glasgow, where he worked on dramas and comedies and became, by common consent, the best pantomime dame in the business. From the Citizens' he joined Howard and Wyndham, the dominant Scottish theatre group, performing in the *Five Past Eight* shows at the Alhambra.

He became a popular radio comedian in Scotland with shows like *Stanley Baxter Takes the Mike*, and also began to make appearances on television. By the end of the fifties, however, he was restless, and sensed that the old order of variety was on the way out. 'I decided I didn't like the way Howard and Wyndham was going, so I needed to go south,' he explains. 'I came south with no prospect of work at all. Stewart Cruickshank, who was the boss, said "Are you sure you're going? I can't promise you there'll be any work if you have to come crawling back." Full of old-world charm. So I came south in 1959. In 1960, I won the BAFTA and they all shut up.'[27]

The BAFTA in question (actually an SFTA at the time, as the name 'British Academy of Film and Television Arts' didn't come into existence until 1976) was for the best light entertainment performance; it was given to Baxter for the BBC TV revue series *On the Bright Side*, in which he starred alongside Betty Marsden, already known to millions for her sterling character performances in radio's *Beyond Our Ken*. Film roles began to come Baxter's way, including a pair of virtuoso performances in 1961's *Very Important Person*, in which he played both an inmate in a German prisoner-of-war camp and the camp's commandant. Nonetheless, he never neglected television, his own national BBC series, *The Stanley Baxter Show*, beginning in 1963, then resuming from 1967 to 1971 with a run of shows networked from BBC Scotland. The signature of the show – which was, in essence, a variety production, with musical guests between the sketches – was its clever pastiches and parodies of television and films. These were usually written by Ken Hoare and often featured Baxter playing more than one part, something that was now possible thanks to videotape recording. However, in among the universally recognized subjects for satire, Baxter also had the courage to introduce a national audience to the Scottish accent in its most undiluted form, in the long-running series of 'Parliamo Glasgow' sketches.

Baxter had been mining the comic possibilities of gutteral Glaswegian in his radio shows, with scripts by his Citizens' Theatre colleague Alec Mitchell in the style of lectures given by an 'elderly English don [who] had come up to look at Glasgow habits and language as if it were the Congo'.[28] The pair revisited the idea for television, but were asked for something more visual. Mitchell and Baxter decided that the answer lay in foreign language education programmes like *Parliamo Italiano* and *Sprechen Sie Deutsch?* They were right. With the help of a female co-presenter, Baxter explained how Glaswegians spoke in situations such as buying fruit and veg from a market stall or meeting a new boyfriend's parents for the first time. For example, a request for a drink came out as 'Whirrabooranurraglessagin?' The contrast between the prim, earnest way in which the presenters explained the phrases and the gutteral nature of the phrases themselves was comedy gold.

Back at Lime Grove, Ronnie Waldman had done much, by the late fifties, to make BBC Television's light entertainment output a polished, professional product. While the audience figures looked grim, the critics all compared the newcomer to the BBC, often unfavourably. This wasn't to say that the BBC couldn't learn some tricks from the new network, as Brian Tesler explains:

> ITV went straight to the American pattern of the same show in the same slot on the same day every week. You can make a date to watch your favourite programme. Fortnightly, you've forgotten what happened, and you had to like the programme all over again. I think the theory was that a cast couldn't be expected to learn a new script every week. The construction department couldn't possibly be expected to construct new sets weekly. It's got to be a fortnightly turnaround. And that was absolute nonsense. So you had big BBC successes, shows that Bill Ward did – such as *How Do You View?* and *Before Your Very Eyes* – they were fortnightly. My *Ask Pickles* was fortnightly. The first run of the *Billy Cotton*

Band Show was fortnightly. Things like the *Dave King Show* and so on, on Saturday night, were monthly.[29]

Before long, the BBC began to adopt weekly scheduling.

The BBC was helped by the fact that the new network didn't have a monopoly on big American names. Throughout the fifties, the BBC had been transmitting imported editions of *The Jack Benny Show*, one of the top-rated comedy attractions on US television. Eventually, Benny came over to do a special for the BBC, live from the King's Theatre, Hammersmith. Ronnie Waldman had been trying to get Benny to make a show in London for some time, but he had to battle with the star's perception of the Corporation's stuffiness. 'He wouldn't come to the BBC because he felt that all the producers wore black jackets, striped trousers and a bowler hat, and that they carried a rolled umbrella and a briefcase,' explains one who certainly didn't, Ernest Maxin. 'Jack called Ronnie and said "I've heard about this Maxin guy. They tell me he's OK. Tell me what he looks like." Ronnie said "He looks like an American." I used to have a crew cut in those days, and I went to a tailor who cut the suits in an American way. You know, [I was] Hollywood mad. Then Ronnie said "He's a Jewish boy." Jack Benny said "I'll take him."'[30]

Maxin was detailed to meet Benny at the Dorchester, where he was staying on his way to an engagement in Rome. 'I was very nervous because I admired this guy and I had an hour-long show to do live,' Maxin admits. Benny immediately put the young producer at his ease. The fact that Maxin was himself an experienced performer helped break the ice. Then the discussion turned to the show. 'He said "Tell me Ernest, you've all seen my shows here in England. How do you see me?" I said "As the public see you. They know that you're mean, and you're never older than 39." He said "Oh great, that's fine. Have you got any ideas?"'

The idea that Maxin proffered involved Benny trying to make his way through Immigration at the airport without removing his thumb from the date of birth on his passport. At desk after desk, the routine built. 'I went through it just briefly, and he was laughing his head off.

I said "Eventually, you get so disgusted, you ask for the next plane back to Los Angeles. You never come in.'" Benny liked it, and called in his writers from the next room:

> Five writers came in, walked in, like the Tiller Girls doing Jack Benny. Jack looked at me, he didn't really know what I was smiling at. I explained the idea. They said 'Yes, Jack, we think it's a great foundation for us.' I said 'But Jack, that's only the last sketch. I'd like to use your own material for the stand-up sequences.' He said 'Oh don't worry about that, that's OK. Boys, go in and write this sequence.' So they said 'Sure, Jack,' and all walked back like that. I said 'I'd better go now, Jack.' He said 'You can't go yet, the boys are writing the script. Give them forty-five minutes.' I heard them typing away. After about half an hour, they came in and said 'Jack, take a look at this.' I was in hysterics. They handed it to him, he looked at it, he started to smile and laugh, so obviously it was OK.[31]

Although the centrepiece was in place, Maxin was still worried about the rest of the show. When the script was finished, it looked set to under-run by a considerable margin. 'I said to Jack "You've got eighteen pages here. Usually we allow about a minute, a minute and a half a page. At most two minutes, allowing for laughs,"' Maxin recalls. 'He said "Really? Then I'm very sorry for your comedians." I said "Jack, the most you're going to get out of this is thirty minutes," but he wouldn't change. I thought "Well, he's the master. He knows." I said "Jack, you've got to remember you haven't got an American audience." He said "Ernest, I've been in the business longer than you. I promise you I won't let you down, and I know you won't let me down."'[32]

Still worried, Maxin shared his concerns with Waldman, who replied 'He knows more about his work than all of us put together, but remember it could be your job on the line, Ernest. You'd better have something up your sleeve. We can't put on the potter's wheel for twenty-five minutes.' Maxin knew he couldn't have a standby act to finish a Jack Benny show, so he tried to 'spread' it at rehearsals, to little avail. 'All I could make it spread without it looking slow was about three minutes,' he remembers. As the show went on the air, live, the young producer was understandably nervous:

> The captions for the previous show were going up on the screen, then 'Ladies and gentlemen, the Jack Benny Show.' He walked on the stage to tumultuous applause and just stood there, with a look that said 'So, this is the BBC? Lousy.' Eventually, the laugh started to subside, but as it got to a certain point, he turned as if to say 'What the hell are you laughing at?' off-stage, and he stood there like that. It started to subside again, and as that went, he moved his hand. Every time a big laugh came and it subsided, he'd turn. The way he did it was wonderful. We finished, as I wanted to finish it, with exactly twenty seconds to go. The last caption came up 'Produced by Ernest Maxin'. Bang. Right on time. I've got my job, I can go in on Monday. I went downstairs onto the stage. I found myself walking like him. He gave me a big kiss. He said 'I've really enjoyed this. I enjoyed rehearsals.' All the things you want to hear. We're still standing on the stage. I said 'Jack, how did you do it so that you could time it, not even five seconds out, to the second?' He said 'Ernest, I'll tell you. You know when I do that [turn around]? I've got a wristwatch on each hand.' He just kept looking at it. The thing was, if the laugh went slightly before he wanted it to go, he knew, without saying a word, how to build another laugh.[33]

As it transpired, the competition from commercial television was the final spur the department needed in its bid to be treated with respect by the Corporation's elders. Current affairs was favoured by the high-ups because it had gravitas. With Leonard Miall and Grace Wyndham Goldie running the quaintly titled 'talks' department, current affairs programming was going from strength to strength in the form of *Panorama* and the light, entertaining magazine programme *Tonight*. However, it was the mass audience brought in by the variety that allowed the BBC to continue to justify its licence fee.

The new shows that emerged in response to ITV included both the innovative and the comfortingly familiar. In the latter camp came the

Billy Cotton Band Show, a television version of the hit radio show. Cotton, as an artist represented by the Grade agency, had made six Saturday night programmes for ATV at the start, and while they proved popular enough, Cotton realized that he needed a more formatted show if he wasn't to use up all of his valuable variety schtick. His son, Bill Cotton Junior, a successful music publisher who was about to join the BBC as a trainee producer, persuaded him to give the BBC a hearing. Ronnie Waldman enticed Cotton Senior with a highly lucrative joint contract for radio and television, and gave him Brian Tesler as producer. As Tesler explains: 'It was quite a gamble. I was a revue and cabaret man from Oxford, and he was music hall. I think that was one of the reasons why Ronnie was so great. He was great at casting, unlikely casting. Bill wasn't certain we'd even speak the same language, but of course we did. It was light entertainment.'[34]

The first show went out on 29 March 1956 from the Television Theatre, opening with announcer Peter Haigh yawning, only to be roused by Billy Cotton shouting his catchphrase. The Television Toppers were present, as were Cotton's lead trumpeter Grisha Farfel, whose solos became a feature of the show over the next twelve years, and bumbling comic attraction Richard Hearne, aka Mr Pastry. Perhaps most interesting is the inclusion of an act called Morris, Marty and Mitch, the Marty in question being a young Feldman, yet to join forces with Barry Took as a scriptwriter. The mixture proved to be just the sort of thing to claw ratings back from ITV, with 54 per cent of adult viewers tuning in. The quantity was important, but the BBC also valued its own qualitative research, in the form of the Appreciation Index (AI), as decided by what would today be called a focus group. The debut *Band Show* notched up an AI of 70, 15 higher than any previous Cotton shows.[35]

★

Just under a year later, on 16 February 1957, another new show hit the air, shying away from traditional entertainment in favour of addressing emerging trends in music and fashion. Rock and roll was in the ascendant, as were teenagers – themselves an innovation, providing an interim stage between childhood and the premature middle age that had previously been expected of most respectable young citizens. *Six Five Special* was a show for them. The BBC also had the sudden need to fill the hour between 6pm and 7pm, which had previously been left fallow by both the BBC and ITV to allow parents to get their infants off to bed. During the week, this 'Toddlers' Truce' was now replaced by the news magazine *Tonight*, while on Saturdays it was the new youth show, which had been the brainchild of young producers Jack Good and Josephine Douglas, both almost fresh from Oxford. It's fair to say that Good's motivations for following the path he did differed slightly from those of most young BBC graduate trainees:

> I was summoned to the office of the head of light entertainment, Mr Ronald Waldman. 'What made you want to be a television producer?' 'Well sir, I thought that really this is a new medium and we must use it to the best advantage, to inform, to educate and to entertain.' Went down a treat. Little did they know that I'd already seen [the film] *Rock Around the Clock* . . . For me, it [rock and roll] means energy, excitement, novelty and rebellion. Being against toffee-nosed, conventional, culturally dead society. 'Kick you in the face, you Tory buggers' stuff. It seemed to me that was what a bourgeois should do. You know if you want to escape the bourgeoisie, you've got to turn your back on your own or turn your front on your own and start whacking them. It's just a natural reaction for an avant-garde bourgeois.[36]

Once again, then, it was a case of cometh the hour, cometh the man. Good caught the mood of the time perfectly. Co-hosted by co-producer Josephine Douglas and Radio Luxembourg DJ heart-throb Pete Murray, with guest appearances from former boxer Freddie Mills, scriptwriter Trevor Peacock and numerous others, not to mention an in-vision audience of jiving youngsters, it featured the latest 'hooligan music', as its detractors dubbed it at the time. Nowadays, most of the surviving hooligans have national treasure status, bus passes and a lifetime's guarantee of work on the nostalgia circuit. Some even have knighthoods. In 1957, however, they were a threat to the status quo, and so *Six Five Special* was quite unlike anything that had ever appeared on British television before. Associated-Rediffusion had a record show called *Cool for Cats*, in which professional dancers accompanied the hits of the day, but it was rather refined, as might be expected from a producer like Joan Kemp-Welch, who later brought the early works of Harold Pinter to the television screen. *Six Five Special* was anything but refined. Television was still resolutely monochrome, but simply the knowledge that singer Wee Willie Harris had dyed his hair lime green was enough to cause outrage in Tunbridge Wells and other leafy outposts where the easily disgusted set up camp.[37] Very few recordings survive, and those that do exist come across as a relay from a rather star-studded village hall hop. One existing show presages *Blue Peter* by including an incongruous feature on mountaineering between the jumping and jiving. At the time, though, it must have been revolutionary and liberating.

Good's next step was typical of many young BBC producers at the time. He went to ITV, ABC to be precise. The money was much better, but the main motivation was that he would be able to ditch the worthier aspects of *Six Five Special* in favour of rock and roll music pure and simple. On Sunday 15 June 1958, on the stage of the Wood Green Empire, *Oh Boy!* was born.[38] Good promised 'one of the fastest shows on television. Cackle is cut to the minimum. No jokes, no long "plugs" for the latest recordings . . . *Oh Boy!* will show exciting singers and bands playing exciting music to an excited audience.'[39] It made stars of singers like Cliff Richard, Marty Wilde and Vince Eager, as well as providing South African organist Cherry Wainer and the house band, Lord Rockingham's XI, with their hour in the spotlight.

★

Good had been preceded out of the door by Brian Tesler, who went to ATV in January 1957, after the Corporation rather arrogantly assumed that its own prestige was enough:

When ITV was about to start the BBC started putting people under contract. I had a two-year contract, which actually took me past the opening year of ITV. I knew nothing about the commercial world, and it frightened the life out of me. Anyway, we were all terribly complacent about ITV. How could it possibly catch on? All those awful little jingles interfering with programmes, you wouldn't want to watch interrupted programmes like that, so I was happy to stay. But at the end of that two-year period, my contract was coming up for renewal, so I went to see Leslie Page, who was in charge of personnel. He said 'Ah, Tesler, your contract's up for renewal. You've done quite well, we'd like to keep you on, we'd like to offer you another contract for two years, is that satisfactory for you?' I said 'Yes, fine, the only thing is that I'm earning £1,700 a year at the moment, could I go up to £1,800 for those two years?' He said 'Oh no. Working for the BBC is reward enough.'[40]

The conversation took place in the midst of rehearsals for a musical show with presenter Eamonn Andrews and the orchestra of Frank Chacksfield, inspired by Andrews' surprise number eighteen chart hit *Shifting Whispering Sands*. ('It was a pretty lousy song, but it made good visual material,' Tesler remembers.) Tesler returned to the studio, where his sombre mood was noticed by Chacksfield and Andrews' manager Teddy Sommerfield, as Tesler recalls:

He said 'What's the matter with you? You were very bright before you went for whatever it was you went for.' I told him and he said 'Ah, would you be interested in working for ITV?' I said 'Damn it, yes.' He went and made a phone call. He came back and said 'Well, I've talked to Lew Grade, and he'd like you to join ATV for a salary of £3,500 a year. Now I didn't think that was enough, so I got him to throw in two weeks in New York each year to study American television. What shall I say to him?' I said 'Bite his hand off.'[41]

So, the BBC lost one of its best producers for the sake of £200. The incident prompted Ronnie Waldman to take up cudgels with the personnel department over their inflexibility, pointing out the damage it could do as other valuable staff were tempted to leave. The situation improved, but BBC salaries always remained lower than those of the opposition.

Despite being the new boy, Tesler was experienced enough to work out that he was being given base metal rather than gold for his first show at ATV, a *Val Parnell Saturday Spectacular*. Bill Ward sent him to see Grade and Parnell in the office they shared at Television House in Kingsway. ('They were joint managing directors, so they shared opposite corners of an office.') In typical salesman mode, Grade enthused about the bill for Tesler's debut: Harry Worth and one of the dizzy blonde panellists from the ATV panel game *Yakety Yak*. 'Nobody else is available because it's pantomime season, but you can do a great show with those two,' Grade enthused, not entirely convincingly. Tesler was crestfallen:

I went away so miserable. I didn't want to do a variety bill. Two of the last things I'd done at the BBC had been with [comedian/song and dance man] Dickie Henderson Junior. One was a Billy Cotton show in which I had Bill and young Bill with young Dick and old Dick. The two old men and the two young men, with a very good script written by Jimmy Grafton. It had gone very well, and I had great admiration for Dickie. He was in the American idiom. He sang, he danced, he had a great sense of humour. The microphone routine was terrific, just a terrific routine. [This involved Henderson wrestling with an off-stage scene hand for ownership of a microphone lead, while trying to sing. Each time he regained some slack, it would be pulled taut again, causing him to fall over.] And he'd also been the guest on the last Pet Clark show at Riverside studios. They'd done a duet, and I thought if I can get the chance, I want to do a show with Dickie. I phoned him, I phoned Jimmy, and I said 'Look, I've got a date and I don't like what they've given me, I'd like the three of us to do a show.' They said 'Terrific idea,' so we met for lunch, and it was obvious it was going to be great.

I went back to the office and I phoned Lew. I said 'Lew, I know it was very nice of you to offer me Harry Worth, but I really want my first show to be my show. I'd like to do *The Dickie Henderson Show*.' He said 'Val won't like it.' Dickie had been the star of a series that Dickie Leeman had produced for ATV, called *Young at Heart*, that hadn't been at all successful. So I went to Bill Ward, who was head of department, told him what had happened. He said 'I'll have a word with Val.' He came back and said 'Val says all right, but it's not going to be called *The Dickie Henderson Show*, it's just going to be a *Saturday Spectacular* with Dickie Henderson.'

Showing the chutzpah that would help take him to the top of the executive tree in British television, Tesler disobeyed Parnell's strictures:

So I was very naughty, we were all very naughty. The side of Wood Green had the stage, and down where the orchestra pit had been there was just a hole. Down the other side, the side of the wall, there was an area, it was very narrow, but you could use it. I put black material with stars on it with beautiful showgirls in glossy dresses in front of it, and had the camera crabbing along the line. Terrific music, the first caption, star-studded, said 'Val Parnell presents *Val Parnell's Saturday Spectacular*'. And there was Dickie standing by a hat rack, with a clapped-out piece of cardboard that said 'The Dickie Henderson Show?' So we didn't really call it *The Dickie Henderson Show*, and it wasn't spectacular, because it had a question mark, but we got away with it. It was a very good show, it had some very good things in it, and bless his heart, Val sent me a telegram, and said 'It was a terrific show, you can do more Dickie Henderson shows in future, and they can be called *The Dickie Henderson Show*.'

That established me at ATV better than I could have expected, because I hadn't done what was expected and taken what I was given. So from then on I was able to do what I wanted to do. If they gave me stars, and they very often did, I never turned another show down, and I never had any problem with budgets.[42]

Tesler was soon given responsibility for Parnell's flagship show, *Sunday Night at the London Palladium*, known internally as *SNAP*. He wanted to tackle the show his way, and, this time, he was given his head from the off. Quite simply, he didn't want to keep Tommy Trinder as the host. 'He was getting stale, and also he was just a bit too downmarket,' Tesler argues. 'By that time, ITV was growing up very quickly. Val was happy, very happy with the change. I was very surprised that there was no resistance. I didn't know at the time, but he, for some business reason or other, wanted to get rid of Tommy anyway. He'd upset Val, somehow.'[43]

At this point in 1958, Tesler had no successor in mind, so a series of guest hosts took over *SNAP* for a month at a time, starting with Dickie Henderson. He was followed by Hughie Green, Bob Monkhouse, Alfred Marks and, most memorably, Robert Morley. 'Robert played Robert beautifully,' says Tesler. 'He hadn't heard of any of these people or what they did. It was just hilarious.' At the same time, Tesler was working on a series called *New Look*, showcasing new discoveries, 'which I loved doing. We had Roy Castle, Bruce Forsyth, Lionel and Joyce Blair, Joe Baker, Jack Douglas and Ronnie Stevens, a very capable revue actor. With Bruce, Dickie Henderson said "There's this guy, you ought to see him, he's very good." I thought he was terrific, so I put him onto *Sunday Night at the London Palladium*, just as an act, and then into *New Look*. I thought "Wow, I've got Bruce, Roy, Lionel, Joyce . . . I've got a show here."' Val Parnell had other ideas, earmarking Forsyth as the ideal replacement for Trinder on *SNAP*. 'Val saw Bruce Forsyth in the first *New Look* and said "Right, he's the one we want."'[44]

As with most 'overnight successes', Forsyth had been in the business for years. His apparently meteoric rise to the top hosting job in LE belied a long hard slog of working at the Windmill and in summer seasons. Forsyth took over with aplomb, his catchphrase – the first of many over the years – being 'I'm in charge'. Tesler has less happy memories of the opening of Forsyth's first show, though:

> I was fed up with that same bit of film at the start, the stars bursting, and I had this terrific idea. I wanted to introduce Bruce to the public and for it to be different. The idea was that we'd start with the orchestra

tuning up, so I'd start on the MD's music with 'Sunday Night at the London Palladium' written on the top. The musical director that night was Reg Cole. We'd pull out, the orchestra would be tuning up and we'd cut to the wings. There was Bruce, standing talking nervously to Jack [Matthews], the stage manager, a marvellous guy. Jack would be saying 'Don't worry Bruce, everything's going to be fine.' Bruce is saying 'Well, it's very important to me. I've never done anything like this before. I hope it's going to work.' Then I cut to all the glamorous girls coming down a metal spiral staircase, past Bruce, saying good luck. Of course, there wasn't really a spiral staircase there. Then back to the orchestra. Cue Reg. And 'Startime' [Eric Rogers' famous theme tune] would start, we'd pull back and the show would begin. Terrific. All live.

So I cue Reg for the tuning up, Reg went straight into the opening music, and I'm screaming 'Stop it! Stop it! Jack, stop him.' There was absolute bedlam for about thirty seconds. No one knew what the hell was going on. Then we didn't go back to the tuning up, alas, and so as far as the audience at home was concerned, they heard the beginning of the music and it suddenly cut dead, and suddenly we were back in the wings with Bruce and Jack, and all the rest of it happened. But that beautiful opening, which I thought was really rather good, went for a burton. Well, half a burton, anyway.[45]

The mid-fifties brain drain at the BBC was compensated for by another new intake of producers. One was Francis Essex, formerly of Amersham Repertory Theatre, who had also been behind a West End revue called *The Bells of St Martins* in 1952. The director of the show had been Bill Lyon-Shaw, and the designer had been Richard Greenough, both taking time out from their BBC work. When Michael Mills left the Television Service to return to the theatre, Essex came in the opposite direction, as Yvonne Littlewood recalls:

Michael went to work for [the theatre group] Howard and Wyndham, mainly in Scotland. He walked out of the door and left the desk the way it always was. I had been with him for eight years, quite a long time, and I was quite confused. Ronnie sent for me, and he said 'I've just taken on a new young producer, I'd like you to look after him, he's got no experience of television.' It was Francis Essex. I said give me a week, ten days to get the desk straight, deal with all Michael's files and send them off to archive. Within twenty minutes of leaving Ronnie's office, the door opened and a face peered around and said 'I think I'm going to come and work in this office with you, could I come in now and sit down, because I haven't anywhere to sit?' I said 'All right, you'd better come in then.' Francis was quite a whiz-kid, he moved ahead very swiftly.[46]

One of the programmes with which Essex made his mark was the record review show *Off the Record*, presented by veteran bandleader Jack Payne. Song pluggers – whose job was to get broadcasting bands to use their company's songs, or, where appropriate, to get recorded versions played on air – made a beeline for the programme, one of them being Bill Cotton Junior. Michael Reine, the music publishing company that he ran with composer Johnny Johnston, was doing very nicely, but Cotton could see how important television was becoming and wanted to be in the thick of it:

We were very successful, making a lot of money and doing well. Then, in 1955, when ITV was starting, Johnny decided to start to write jingles. After two or three months of this, the office was packed full of bowler-hatted advertising agents, all coming to arrange their commercials. I had a wish to be involved in television. I went to Bill Ward at ATV first. I knew the Grades very well because they were my father's agents. I said to him I'd quite like to get my feet under the table in television. He said no good coming to us, you've got to go to the BBC and get yourself trained. Ronnie Waldman was desperately trying to sign my father to a joint contract for radio and television, and I encouraged him to take the BBC offer. When I presented myself for the possibility of having a six-month training attachment, with no further obligations, Ronnie obviously thought it wouldn't do any harm in the negotiations.[47]

As important as his connections were, Cotton's progress was almost certainly aided by a guardian angel already in the department, in the form of Littlewood:

I've known Bill for a very long time. He used to come down when we were doing *Off the Record*. I remember Bill telling me over a pint in the pub, the British Prince, that he'd applied for a job on the training course and he hadn't heard anything. He was going to tell them what they could do with the training course if he didn't hear quite soon. I remember going in the next day to speak to Ronnie's secretary, a lady called Hilary Mitton. She was a bit forbidding, very businesslike and protected Ronnie all the time, but I got in to see him. I said 'I don't know if I should be saying this, but I was having a glass with young Bill' (we always called him young Bill in those days) 'and he hasn't had a reply.' I didn't say exactly what Bill said. Not long afterwards he was on the training course, and I've often wondered if I was responsible.[48]

Like all BBC light entertainment trainees in the mid-fifties, Cotton cut his teeth on fifteen-minute single-act shows, the best known of which went out under the *Starlight* banner. When he took the job, he set out one condition, namely that he was never to be asked to produce his father's show. However, when Brian Tesler left, the old man asked if the *Billy Cotton Band Show* could become a family concern. Waldman was all for it, but mindful of the younger man's concerns. Cotton Senior took the matter into his own hands, as Sir Bill recalls:

I came home one night and my father was sitting there. He'd come for supper, he brought smoked salmon, we sat down and he enchanted my late wife with his stories. He was a great storyteller. And it came to when it was time to go, and he said 'It's time that decent men were in their beds,' and he put his hat on, and his coat, and he stood in the door and said 'Oh, by the way, why won't you do my show?' So I knew I'd been hijacked. I said 'I wouldn't want to win an argument with you, but the producer has to have the final decision.' He said 'I'll never argue with you in public, we'll only ever argue in private.' Once he'd said that and a few other things, I thought I suppose I'll agree to it. I really wanted to do it, I suppose. I was a great admirer of my father.[49]

In the years that Cotton Junior produced the *Band Show* there were only two disagreements. One came 'when he booked a girl called Pamela Dennis, who'd been appearing at the Stork Club. She could sing a bit, and she looked great. When we sat there and I heard her sing, I just stopped looking at her and looked at him, and he said "I think I had too much to drink last night."'[50]

Another big production bearing the name of Bill Cotton Junior was *Perry Como Comes To London*, a one-off special in 1960. As with Jack Benny, the BBC had been showing the American crooner Como's cosy musical shows from the US network NBC – which required editing before they were suitable for British television. 'We had to take the commercials out. They were all sponsored by Kraft–Philadelphia cream cheese,' remembers Yvonne Littlewood.[51] The shows were such a success that Como decided to follow Benny to London. In preparation, Cotton went to the US and found it 'quite extraordinary how much better they were at doing these things than we were'. Nonetheless, Como's American producer Clark Jones trusted Cotton to get on with the job of setting the show up, while he directed the performances.

The show featured cameos from British personalities, beginning with character actor Richard Wattis as the immigration officer Como encountered on his way into Britain. 'We did all of it on location, with quite a lot of shooting in Covent Garden,' recalls Yvonne Littlewood, who was Cotton's production assistant on the show. 'We had Harry Secombe, Fenella Fielding, Ralph Richardson, Margot Fonteyn. We had a sequence at Woburn Abbey, it was just when the touristic thing was starting up for the houses. The only bit we did in the studio was the last segment – [with his signature tune] "Sing to me, Mr C" – in the Television Theatre.'[52]

Artistic success was one thing, but there were technical issues relating to the differing screen resolution of the UK and US TV systems, as Yvonne Littlewood explains:

> We had to make it in 525 lines because it was American. They had started doing tape editing long before we did. They brought their tape editor with them and set them up a little mini-place in Television Centre on the fourth floor. This guy came and people stood and watched him – of course it was the old knife through the tape in those days. And we had to convert it back to 405 [lines – the British standard] for us.[53]

Cotton and Littlewood's colleagues behind the camera included three young men at the start of their television careers. The floor manager was Douglas Argent, the assistant floor manager was Michael Hurll (son of Fred Hurll, the chief executive of the Scouts), and the call boy was William G. Stewart, who has a permanent reminder of the team: 'We had a group photograph taken of all of us in cricket gear with a shield in front of us saying "BBC" on it. Bill had worked it out. It read "Bring Back Como". The whole lot of us ended up as producers.'[54]

In their early days at the BBC, Bill Cotton and Francis Essex had shared an office, as well as the experienced support of Miss Littlewood. Essex's whiz-kiddery took him away very quickly, first to ATV as a producer, then to Scottish Television as controller of programmes. Thus another vacancy was created, filled in November 1958 by Stewart Morris, the son of Southan Morris, owner of a successful chain of cinemas. The plan was for Stewart to join the family business, but he rebelled and applied to the BBC:

> First of all, I wrote all these letters. Dozens of them. Ronnie Waldman interviewed me, he wrote me a wonderful letter, saying 'In order to stop wasting your time and mine, I will see you for a few minutes.' I walked up and down Frithville Gardens getting my courage up. I was asked at the selection board, if I didn't get the job, would I apply for a job as an AFM [assistant floor manager] or a PA? I said no. They said 'Why?' I said 'I don't think the two jobs necessarily need the same type of approach.'

I was very arrogant in those days. And at the end of that interview, he said 'I'll give you a job for six months' and it was £12 a week. I went straight onto the directors' course, at the end of which you had to do a thirty-minute production, for which the budget was £30. Trevor Peacock, whom you see now as an actor in the *Vicar of Dibley*, wrote it for me and appeared in it.[55]

So it was that the fully fledged Morris produced the youth-oriented music show *Drumbeat*, set up as the successor to *Dig This*, which had been the replacement for *Six Five Special*. As the end of his six months approached, Morris worried that he hadn't heard anything about a contract renewal. On the last day of his contract, he called in to see Tom Sloan, the assistant head of light entertainment. 'I walked into Tom and said "Well I've enjoyed it, thank you very much,"' Morris recalls. 'He said "What are you talking about?" I replied that my contract expired the next day. He said "Get out of here." I went back to my office in one of the caravans, the phone was going, and I had a new contract. Tom became my mentor really.'[56]

At this point in the late fifties, each programme had a producer, who also directed the cameras and often wrote the script himself. Each producer had a PA, and that was it in terms of support staff, but that was about to change. 'We were just secretaries,' Yvonne Littlewood explains, 'but along the way they discovered that producers really needed a bit more help.' This came in the form of production assistants, a job that carried far greater responsibility than its modern-day equivalent as a junior member of a large production team. Eventually, the production assistant layer in the BBC became known as production managers. Littlewood applied for one of the newly created positions:

You didn't type all the stuff, you had a secretary to do that, but you worked the floor. You did what the floor managers were doing, but you stayed with the producer throughout the production. Quite a few of us girls applied, the ones that had a lot of experience. I went for an interview – it was the head of production management, the personnel person and

Ronnie. They said 'Of course the trouble is that you've never really worked on the floor.' They were giving all these jobs to ex-floor managers. I said 'Well, I've had a lot of experience, and if I have to go on the floor and tell them where to put the scenery, well, I'll do it. If I don't do it well enough, you can make me a secretary again.' Very politely, of course. And anyway I got the job, and I had the feeling that it was only because of Ronnie who had faith in the fact he thought that I could do it and he knew how long I'd been working with Michael. I was a very dedicated person, I know that.[57]

★

In 1958, Littlewood's sponsor Ronnie Waldman decided to move on, after nearly a decade in charge of television light entertainment. He didn't move to one of the rival, commercial companies, although his experience, skills and contacts would undoubtedly have been prized greatly. Instead, he accepted the challenge of establishing the BBC's programme sales and syndication arm, a business that would eventually become known as BBC Enterprises. The internal assumption was that Waldman's deputy Tom Sloan, who had joined the department as an administrator in 1954, would get the job, but it soon became clear that Sloan had been overlooked. In 1956, the by-now Sir George Barnes had moved to become principal of the University College of North Staffordshire (now Keele University), and the job of director of television had been filled by Gerald Beadle, the former head of the West region. Beadle stayed at his club, the Saville, when in London, where he found himself sharing his concerns for the future of television with a fellow member – songwriter, radio pioneer and former director of variety at the BBC Eric Maschwitz. Since leaving the BBC for Hollywood in 1937, Maschwitz had been a wartime intelligence officer, written his memoirs and returned to the life of a jobbing songwriter. In such circumstances, the appointment of Maschwitz over Sloan's head went down very badly, as Sir Bill Cotton remembers:

Eric Maschwitz, not to put too fine a point on it, was a well-known drunk in the West End at the time. His wife owned a club, and he had decent money because of what he earned from his royalties. When his appointment was announced, we were horrified. At various times, he'd accused the BBC of being run by 'Jews and queers', despite being Jewish himself. Tom Sloan complained to the director general. He felt he had a right to complain.[58]

In fact, it soon became obvious that Maschwitz, described by Frank Muir as 'perhaps the last of the great romantics', was an inspired appointment. His administrative input was minimal, but his ability to boost morale and smooth egos was second to none. The overlooked Sloan became, in effect, the head of light entertainment in all but title, while Maschwitz, the great impresario, gave the department a dash of show business glamour and rallied the troops, as Cotton recalls:

> The two of them, actually, were ideal together. We had Tom Sloan looking after the nuts and bolts of the department, making sure that everything was happening, and Eric Maschwitz throwing the parties. He increased the morale of the department no end and he also fought our corner all through the BBC. If you did a good show, you went in to see Tom and got his plaudits, then you went in to see Eric – 'My boy, what a wonderful show.' If you did a rotten show, you went in to see Eric and you didn't go in to see Tom at all. And he'd go 'I know how you feel, have a drink.' His way of doing the job, any job, was enthusiasm, and his enthusiasm extended to confronting criticism with the truth. Sydney Newman [the Canadian producer who had joined the BBC as head of drama from ABC] had exactly the same effect on drama.[59]

In the early years, the BBC light entertainment producers had been expected to work across the department's output, but as the fifties continued, a divide between narrative comedy, such as sitcoms, and variety, meaning everything else, began to emerge. Duncan Wood was among the comedy specialists, Bill Cotton Junior and Stewart Morris were among the variety experts. In December 1957, at the end of the fourth series of *Hancock's Half Hour*, comedy spoofed variety with

Hancock's Forty-Three Minutes: the East Cheam Repertory Company, beautifully written by Ray Galton and Alan Simpson, and produced by Wood, as a ramshackle, cut-price vaudeville show. Hancock's opening monologue in particular is a fine, cynical take on the whole business of variety on television:

> The highest compliment the BBC can pay to an artist. White tuxedo, big orchestra, dancing girls . . . Of course it had to come. They couldn't keep on disappointing a man of my calibre. I told them, I said, 'I want the girls, mate, the dancers and the singers. I'm fed up of doing this half hour on my own . . . I want the music and the girls, sitting in the wings reading while they do all the work.' That's me. Then come on afterwards saying 'Thank you very much, it was great,' without the faintest idea of what they've been doing. I said to them '[. . .] I want the hour's show otherwise I shall go over to the other lot.' And they agreed. And I went over to the other lot. And here I am back with this lot. Makes you sick . . .[60]

Galton and Simpson's set-up was that there were no acts booked, Hancock's sidekick Sidney Balmoral James having spent all but ninepence of the budget on drinks for his friends. All too aware of the competition, Hancock asked 'How can I do a "Val Hancock's Monday Spectacular" on ninepence?' The answer presented itself in the shape of the theatre caretaker's stage-struck monkey, a troupe of oversized middle-aged dancers called 'The Glamazons', the Keynotes vocal group – who think they're rehearsing for Vera Lynn – and a 'trio of continental jugglers'. These turn out to be Hancock himself, with Mario Fabrizi – his handlebar moustache instantly recognizable to all lovers of British comedy films – and stone-faced stooge Johnny Vyvyan. Together they attempt a series of pathetically easy or hopelessly bungled stunts, the completion of each resulting in an outbreak of mugging from Hancock.

The highlight of the show, however, is the multi-talentless 'Arnold', played by *Hancock's Half Hour* regular John Vere. He demonstrates paper-tearing, without producing any shapes. ('I don't know, I just tear it.') He plays the spoons by clanking them together vaguely in rhythm, while singing a set of hitherto unknown lyrics to Glenn Miller's 'In the Mood':

> Mister, what d'you call it what you're doing tonight?
> Hope you're in the mood because I'm feeling all right
> Awfully glad to meet you and I hope we'll be friends
> Who wants a bucket of cement?[61]

Finally, as his big finish, he dances on glass. That is to say he stands on panes of toughened safety glass while still wearing his shoes. When Hancock points out that he was expecting bare feet and broken glass, 'Arnold' replies 'Charming. I'm not cutting my feet to ribbons for you. The man's a sadist.' The comic appeal of this forgotten gem is enhanced by the sure knowledge that, early in his career, Hancock worked on real bills as bad as this one. It is both a satire of and an homage to a lost world.

The late fifties also saw the start of one of the longest-running and, ultimately, most controversial light entertainment shows to hit the airwaves. Beginning with a special on 14 June 1958 and a follow-up on 16 August, the *Black and White Minstrel Show* had progressed to a monthly series by the following January. Designed to showcase the talents of the George Mitchell Singers, the idea had been floating around for some time. Such a show had been mounted in the Alexandra Palace days, and in April 1957, Ronnie Waldman fielded a proposal from the head of Midlands regional programmes for a 'Kentucky Minstrels' type show with the news that he was in discussions with his old radio producer colleague Harry S. Pepper. The production job fell eventually to George Inns, who had been involved in television earlier than almost anyone else – as a 16-year-old sound effects boy in radio, he had worked on Lance Sieveking's pioneering production of Luigi Pirandello's *The Man with the Flower in His Mouth* for the Baird 30-line system. He rose to become a radio variety producer, working on *In Town Tonight* and *Ray's A Laugh*, before transferring to the Television Service in 1955.

Minstrelsy had long been part of the tradition of entertainment. Inns, Waldman, Maschwitz and company saw no problem in bringing it to television, and making it one of the biggest, most lavish productions attempted so far. The emphasis was on the music, at first drawn from the traditional minstrel repertoire, by American composers like Stephen Foster. In later years, the show tackled modern West End and Hollywood musical items, leading in the seventies to the somewhat bizarre spectacle of a troupe of blacked-up men in spangly waistcoats dancing robotically and singing 'We Don't Matter At All' from the musical *It's a Bird, It's a Plane, It's a Superman*. The show also featured a resident stand-up comedian, with Leslie Crowther, Don MacLean and ventriloquist Keith Harris all serving in the role over the years. Although the make-up made it harder to identify performers and it was an ensemble production rather than a star vehicle, stars did emerge from the show, most notably the singers John Boulter, Dai Francis and Tony Mercer.

The vast majority of viewers shared the BBC's lack of reservations, making it an instant hit, and inspiring a long-running stage version at the Victoria Palace, in need of a star attraction following the Crazy Gang's retirement in 1960. Elsewhere, however, there were rumblings of discontent and, for much of its twenty-year run, the BBC came under pressure from racial lobbies to axe the show. Inns always defended the show robustly. He responded to one broadside in 1967 by saying 'How anyone can read racialism into this show is beyond me.'[62] Inns's sincerity was indubitable, but the idea that the show was born in a more innocent age is undermined slightly by an illuminating coincidence: a few days after the second show had been transmitted, the Notting Hill race riots began.

★

While this frenetic activity was going on in broadcasting, variety theatre in the West End was in its death throes, having disappeared from almost everywhere else during the previous decade. In the major showplaces of the capital, during the fifties and sixties musicals took over from music hall. Alone, the Palladium continued presenting variety bills into the eighties, before becoming a venue for musical shows. The Hippodrome on Charing Cross Road underwent a more radical transformation than most other comparable venues, though. It closed as a variety house on 17 August 1957, following the season of hit American singer Charlie Gracie. When it reopened in August 1958, it was as the Talk of the Town cabaret restaurant, with most of the 1901 Frank Matcham interior removed or hidden from view. It was a joint venture between hotelier and caterer Charles Forté, Lew Grade's brother Bernard Delfont and theatrical producer Robert Nesbitt, who came up with the concept.

After attending Repton and then Oxford University, Nesbitt had begun his career in advertising, before diversifying into writing for revues and cabaret shows. When, in 1932, the director of a show he had co-written called *Ballyhoo* became indisposed, Nesbitt asked if he could step in, and so his career as a director and producer began. By 1935, he was working with the celebrated French variety producer André Charlot on his revues, which had been running in London since 1912. He was also producing his own shows, and his first West End pantomime impressed George Black so much that he gave him several Palladium shows to produce, including one with the Crazy Gang. While the unflappable, urbane Nesbitt could produce such rough and tumble without turning a hair, his real signature was in great spectacle. The longest-legged, most glamorous dancers could always be found in Nesbitt's shows. He was a stickler for professionalism on stage and off, which extended to the modes of address used by his colleagues. 'Calling him Bob Nesbitt was like calling the Queen "Miss",' Rosalyn Wilder, his assistant for twenty years, explains. 'It was Mr Nesbitt. None of us who worked with him ever called him anything other than Mr Nesbitt. Even since he died, we still refer to him as Mr Nesbitt.'[63]

Nesbitt had gone to America to produce a show on Broadway called *Catch a Star*, which was a fearful flop, leaving him with nothing to do.

Rosalyn Wilder recounts the story of how the inspiration for the Talk of the Town came:

> He was sitting twiddling his thumbs wondering what to do and one of the mob from Las Vegas who was friendly with [impresario] Billy Rose said 'Why don't you come out to Las Vegas, it's just starting up and you might like to do a show there.' He thought why not, he went out there and produced the first floorshow. He suddenly realized that if you could sit people down and they could watch a show and eat and drink, that it might be a new way of entertaining people. He came back, saw Bernard Delfont and said 'I've done this, I think this is the way forward.' Bernard said 'Well, let's think about it and find a venue.' They came up eventually with the Hippodrome. The Hippodrome was dying. It was always a dark, dull and dingy theatre and it didn't have a very large capacity. It had acres of marble, but it was dark and brown, whereas the Palladium was always gold and crimson.[64]

Even with the combined expertise of Nesbitt and Delfont, the Talk of the Town took a while to find its feet. Rosalyn Wilder, who joined Nesbitt the year after the opening, explains: 'It started off with just the floorshow, and it wasn't a huge success. In 1961, Bernard Delfont said "Look, this isn't working, I'm going to put a star artist in. We'll do floorshow early, star artist late," and that's how we did it.' Eartha Kitt was the first big name to make an appearance, with each star appearing at the venue for a season of two weeks to a month. In isolation, Nesbitt and Delfont couldn't pay enough, but combined with television appearances and other engagements, the figures worked out very well. Most of the stars who appeared tended to be singers. 'If you put on a comedian, frankly, it was less likely to work. Jackie Mason was very much an unknown quantity at the time, but very funny. He had some wonderful routines.'[65]

There were other, smaller venues that offered dining and entertainment, such as the Pigalle restaurant on Piccadilly, and clubs like Winston's and the one owned by Latin bandleader Edmundo Ros, but the Talk of the Town was cabaret on a grand scale. Nevertheless, by the end of the fifties, the variety theatre was all but dead. Variety, however, would carry on into the next tumultuous decade, all the time adapting, improving and, yes, even swinging.

CHAPTER FOUR

'Albanie – douze points'

The sixties were a time of great liberalization. The decade began with the passing of the Betting and Gaming Act, which legalized off-racecourse bookmaking and ushered in bingo, the saviour of many loss-making theatres and cinemas. It ended with the lowering of the voting age from 21 to 18, taking in the legalization of homosexuality along the way. The Wilson government's galumphing attempts to harness the 'white heat of technology' at least acknowledged the fact that great strides were being made in the field. In particular, telecommunications forged ahead, with the inauguration of the Telstar satellite in 1962 easing the transmission of live television pictures from the US to Europe and vice versa.

On a more basic, domestic level, prosperity was on the increase. Full employment, or something quite like it, was being maintained. In February 1960, the total number of jobless was a mere 450,000. Car ownership more than doubled between 1959 and 1969, rising from 4.4 million private vehicles to 9.7 million. House building was booming, reaching a peak of 400,000 new homes a year towards the end of the decade – with the average house price rising from £2,784 in 1956–1965 to £6,757 in 1966–1975. Most importantly for the purposes of light entertainment, between 1957 and 1967, the number of television licences grew from 7 million to 14.3 million.

This was bad news for radio, which slid into second place in the

punters' affections. However, the ageing staff in radio light entertainment were not helping ensure that the medium remained up to
date. When Terry Henebery had joined BBC Radio as a 25-year-old
producer in 1958 it was still 'the days of the dance-bands and all that
jazz. Ted Heath, Lou Preager, all that was still happening,' although the
menace of rock and roll was emerging. The Light Programme's response
was to retitle its Saturday morning *Skiffle Club* as *Saturday Club* –
reflecting a more general pop music policy – under the production of
Jimmy Grant, with Brian Matthew presenting. Henebery took over
Grant's old job of producing *Jazz Club*.

In terms of comedy, there were successes like *The Navy Lark* – a
situation comedy set on HMS *Troutbridge*, a dumping ground
for the senior service's most inept sailors – and the sketch series
Beyond Our Ken, starring the unflappable Kenneth Horne. In 1965,
following the exit of writer Eric Merriman, *Beyond Our Ken* became
Round the Horne, scripted by Merriman's former collaborator Barry
Took and his new colleague, Marty Feldman. In the process of the
changeover, the show became much more risqué. However, Took
and Feldman were clever enough to ensure that those most likely
to be outraged would not understand a word of the show's coded
filth and innuendo. The characters Julian and Sandy, played by Hugh
Paddick and Kenneth Williams, were a pair of actors who popped
up each week doing different jobs to pay the bills during their 'resting'
periods. Obviously homosexual, much of their dialogue was written
in the gay patois of Polari,[1] in which good was 'bona', a face was an
'eek', a look was a 'vada', feet were 'lallies', men were 'omis', women
were 'palones' and men like Jules and Sand were 'omi-palones'.
Naturally, when they ran a legal firm, it was called 'Bona Law', while
Julian admitted 'we've got a criminal practice that takes up most of
our time'. This was, for its time, what Jules and Sand would themselves
have called 'bold'. Yet, even with hit shows like this, radio was in a
decline.

In the mid-sixties, the recruiters made a concerted effort to entice
bright young men into radio light entertainment, going direct to the

universities. One of them was Trinity College, Dublin, where, in 1963, Roger Ordish was coming to the end of his studies:

> They sent a wonderful man called Peter Titheradge, who was what was called a Light Entertainment Organizer. He came to universities just looking at people who did comedy – writing, directing or performing. He was able to say 'You can come for an interview.' That was phase one. Phase two was the interview, and it was with him, Roy Rich [Pat Hillyard's replacement as head of radio LE] and [his assistant] Con Mahoney I think. I passed that interview and was given a six-month training attachment. My first pay cheque said 'producer', which was pretty amazing. My mother said 'Where do you want to go from here? You're a BBC producer and you're 24.' I said 'Well, I don't want to be anything else.' And I never was.[2]

Junior producers were expected to learn the ropes on 'a terribly simple thing, which was little more than a disc jockey show – a daily live programme called *Roundabout*. It had a different presenter every day and it was records, live music – or pre-recorded, original music – and short interviews, funny news clippings, all that sort of stuff.'[3]

The Musicians' Union's rules of the day, which governed the amount of 'needle time' allowed on radio, resulted in a need for specially recorded music. If radio stations were allowed to play too many records, the union was concerned that its members would be done out of a job. As it transpired, the union was largely correct, and in the seventies, the BBC was eventually forced to disband many of its staff orchestras, including the famous Northern Dance Orchestra. But in the sixties, beat groups were on the rise, and younger listeners wanted to hear the original artists, not an orchestral cover version. The revitalized Radio Luxembourg was bound by no such strictures, so music fans would brave the atmospheric fading of its high-power signal on 208 metres medium wave, broadcast from the Duchy of Luxembourg, to hear the latest records as they were intended, linked in English by disc jockeys like Alan 'Fluff' Freeman, Jimmy Savile and Pete Murray. The station, known affectionately as 'Fab 208' and 'the station of the stars' was aided in its endeavours by the major record companies, such as Decca and EMI, who sponsored shows on the station to promote their latest releases. The BBC appeared even more out of touch with the latest musical trends when offshore pirate radio stations began to operate from ships and forts just outside British territorial waters. First on the air was Radio Caroline, opened on 28 March 1964 by Irish entrepreneur Ronan O'Rahilly from a converted passenger ferry anchored three miles off Frinton. In December, Wonderful Radio London – known to listeners as Big L – followed suit, and while many stations came and went, Caroline and Big L were the dominant forces, with well-organized advertising sales forces based on land in London. With audiences of several million, the pirate ships and Luxembourg were repeating the pattern of the thirties, but this time there was no world war to force the competitors off the air.

The resolution came in the form of the Marine, &c., Broadcasting (Offences) Act, which became law on 14 August 1967. It became illegal for any of the offshore stations to have a business presence in the British Isles, which made the gathering of advertising revenue very difficult. Caroline tried running its airtime sales through an office in New York, but the business soon foundered. Radio London had decided that it would be impossible to make a profit under the new legislation and closed down at 3pm on the day the Act came into effect. There was a welcoming party of over a thousand teenagers for the Radio London presenters as they arrived at Liverpool Street station after the last broadcast. In the pirates' stead, the BBC, under director of sound broadcasting Frank Gillard, was allowed to provide a new pop music service as part of a reorganization of its radio networks. From 30 September 1967, the Light Programme was to become Radio 2, with the Third Programme becoming Radio 3, the Home Service changing its name to Radio 4 and the new pop station coming in as Radio 1. Most of the presenting talent for the new venture, including Tony Blackburn, Keith Skues, Kenny Everett, Dave Cash and John Peel, came from the pirate ships, as did the style of presentation. Robin Scott, the controller of Radios 1 and 2 told *The Times* that he had 'a professional admiration for what they have done. It would be foolish to pretend that we are not using some of the techniques of the commercial stations.'[4]

The BBC radio networks would eventually reposition the medium and maintain its relevance in the television age, not least as a breeding ground for future television stars, producers and formats, but never again would it be the dominant force in broadcasting. By 1966, radio was plundering television's script archive in search of ratings, beginning with a series of sound-only remakes of the hit Galton and Simpson-written sitcom *Steptoe and Son*. The pattern of radio remaking TV hits continued with adaptations of *Dad's Army*.

It wasn't entirely doom and gloom. The sketch show *I'm Sorry I'll Read That Again* began a successful nine-year run in 1964, introducing John Cleese, Bill Oddie, Graeme Garden and Tim Brooke-Taylor to the listening public, along with their Cambridge contemporaries Jo Kendall and David Hatch. While the others went off to found Monty Python or become Goodies, Hatch became a radio producer, then head of radio light entertainment, controller of Radio 2 then Radio 4 and, eventually, the managing director of BBC Radio. Kendall, meanwhile, would go on, in the late seventies, to be a cast member of *The Burkiss Way*, an early outing for Andrew Marshall and David Renwick, on their way to becoming one of the dominant writing teams in British comedy.

Over in television light entertainment, the fifties had been a time of experimentation, while the medium tested new formats and approaches. At the start of the decade, most television entertainment had been simple, act-based shows, but the genre expanded to take in panel games, quiz shows, sketch comedy, shows built around a particular artist to reflect their career and personality in a way that would not be possible on stage, and programmes that followed the comings and goings of the popular music scene. The only major programme genre yet to make its debut was the chat show. With so many of the main elements in place, the sixties became the decade of consolidation and increased professionalism. Such gems as LE could offer would be buffed to an incredibly high sheen, particularly when colour television became a reality in 1967.

A lot of the credit for this can go to Tom Sloan, who finally took over light entertainment at BBC Television in 1961, when Eric Maschwitz manoeuvred himself into a specially created job as assistant and advisor to the controller of programmes. (This turned out to be a non-job, and Maschwitz left the BBC for Associated-Rediffusion in 1963.) Maschwitz was the nominal head until his exit, but in reality, Sloan was in charge. The romantic Maschwitz had referred to his producers as 'my ragged army' and invented affectionate nicknames for them. Frank Muir related in his memoirs how he and Denis Norden were 'Los Layabouts', while Dennis Main Wilson was 'Dr Sinister' and Graeme Muir was 'our resident gynaecologist'.[5] On taking over, the businesslike Sloan declared that 'this department has a lot of work to do and we are all professionals so you can forget any "ragged army" nonsense'.[6] Waldman and Maschwitz had both been producers and performers, whereas Sloan was an administrator. Frank Muir observed that he was 'keen on things which he felt were due to him like "discipline" and "loyalty"' and that his 'real interest lay not in the product but in the management of it'. Nonetheless, he knew the BBC system backwards, was good at getting just enough money for his staff to do their jobs properly and protecting them from interference from above.

One of Sloan's first administrative moves was to replace himself as assistant head of light entertainment, choosing Bill Cotton Junior. The appointment acknowledged informally the division of LE's labours. 'I looked after variety and Tom looked after comedy,' Sir Bill Cotton explains. 'We worked very closely together, there were never any divisions, and I used to defer to him. The division really was situation comedy and musical shows. Between the two, there were sketch shows and broken comedy shows, which could be done by either side.'[7] In 1964, the division became formalized by the appointment of Frank Muir as assistant head of light entertainment group (comedy), Cotton becoming assistant head (variety). Producers henceforth tended to be either variety producers or comedy producers.

The increased professionalism was further embodied in BBC Television Centre, which finally opened as a production facility on 29 June 1960, with a variety show from studio TC3 called *First Night*, produced by Graeme Muir. William G. Stewart was a call boy on that first production, and he remembers the excitement it caused among the normally blasé staff:

> It was a variety special, starring David Nixon and Arthur Askey. What was so funny about it was that there were two dance groups at the time – the Television Toppers and the Silhouettes. The Silhouettes were on Billy Cotton's show, and the Toppers were on every other show. I remember the buzz went round: 'They've got the Toppers and the Silhouettes.' Now you'd think of it as like Toytown, but it was exciting, like Rod Stewart *and* Elton John.[8]

Similar moves to create bespoke studio facilities were afoot at Granada in Manchester and at Associated-Rediffusion's Wembley site. At Teddington, ABC was adapting the existing film stages, which were being augmented with new blocks containing the latest technology. Meanwhile, ATV was creating a state-of-the-art four-studio television centre in the former Neptune film studios at Elstree, which had been bought from the Hollywood actor Douglas Fairbanks Junior. (These studios are really in Borehamwood, but the Elstree name had been adopted by the British International Pictures studios over the road when they were built in the twenties, and it came to signify the several studios in the area, regardless of their real location.)

Compared to the previous makeshift dwellings, these complexes were set up as factories for television. Design and building of sets happened in-house on giant paint frames – the design block at BBC Television Centre, rather cleverly, had a trench in the floor allowing scenery to be lowered for access while the painters remained at ground level. ATV at Elstree had its own rehearsal rooms in the main office block, Neptune House. Associated-Rediffusion's new studio 5 at Wembley was – and still is – the largest television studio in Britain, perfect for the giant variety spectaculars that A-R didn't really make.

In time, though, ATV's studio D at Elstree became perhaps the best of all the LE studios. The advantages it had over the competition were its permanent audience seating and its lighting trench – a simple device that allowed the white cyclorama cloth around the back wall of the studio to be lit in such a way as to give the impression of infinity. 'That took years to do,' ATV's head of design Richard Greenough recalls. 'For a long time we built the stage up on rather rickety rostrums. I say rickety . . . I don't know how they didn't collapse.'[9]

Among the most essential of the workers in these television factories were the orchestras who made the music for the shows. British session musicians had, and still have, an unparalleled reputation for accurate sight-reading, a valuable quality in the frantic world of television. The musicians themselves rarely featured in starring roles, but the conductors became well-known faces. Eric Robinson was pre-eminent at the BBC in the fifties and sixties as a conductor and arranger, providing the accompaniment for the *Black and White Minstrel Show* as well as his own series, *Music For You*. ATV used a number of musical directors in its earliest days, including 'Carry On' score maestro Eric Rogers and Cyril Ornadel. By 1958, however, with the big bands in decline, Jack Parnell – a star in his own right from his days drumming with Ted Heath and his Music and then leading his own hard-swinging band – came into Uncle Val's empire:

> If you know promoters like I know promoters, if they can get four guys making as much noise as sixteen, they're going to use them. This was before the Beatles and everything, but I could see it coming. I thought 'We've got to do something else,' and Leslie Grade said 'You've got to come off the road and bring the band into TV,' so that's what we did. The first shows I did were with the band that was off the road. The first show we did was a Max Bygraves special and we went on from that really. A lot of the guys peeled off, really, because they didn't like that

kind of work. I brought in the top session men and wound up with nearly all the Ted Heath band including Kenny [Baker], and Tom McQuater from the Squad[ronaire]s.[10] A wonderful band, that was. We made a huge reputation in America. Stars would come and only come if it was our band. I know for a fact that it was demanded by some of them that our band was on it.

At one time, in the early part of that, we were doing five live television shows a week, and the pressure was unbelievable. We had a huge team; we had four rehearsal pianists doing a show each, a whole bunch of arrangers. The main pianist was Norman Stenfalt, from the Heath band. *The Arthur Haynes Show*, oh there were loads of them. We used to do *Thursday Startime*, I think it was called, then there was *Sunday Night at the London Palladium*. We used to do a thing called *Music Shop*, on Sunday afternoons. I used to play drums on that. I was writing a lot of music for plays and background music and stuff like that. It became much easier when we could record. Easier, but not quite as exciting.[11]

While Parnell was getting established at Wood Green, on his way to becoming ATV's main musical director, another broadcasting band members were becoming personalities in their own right. Based at the BBC's Manchester outpost, the Northern Dance Orchestra – conducted variously over its life by Ray Martin, Alyn Ainsworth, George Clouston and Bernard Herrmann – had replaced the Northern Variety Orchestra in 1954 and worked extensively on radio. When the BBC bought the former Mancunian Films studio (a converted Wesleyan chapel at Dickenson Road, Rusholme) in 1954, the band was called upon to provide music for television as well, not least of which was its own series, *Make Way for Music*.

At a time when television was tightly scripted, planned and formal, these NDO shows must have seemed wild, anarchic and loose. *Make Way for Music* was born of a sudden, desperate need, which dictated the form the first show would take, as announcer Roger Moffat recalled shortly before his death in 1986:

It was a Friday and we were doing the radio show at lunchtime. [BBC North entertainment producer] Barney Colehan had arranged for the orchestra to accompany Shirley Bassey in the evening on a live television programme. Shirley had a sore throat so he came dashing down to the studio and said 'What are we going to do? Shirley can't do it.' I said 'Don't ask me, I wasn't on the television show in the first place.' He said 'Well, can you think of something?' I said 'Why don't you televise what happens in a sound show.' He said 'Thank goodness, that's a good idea. Can you come along with Les Howard and do the show, and [singer] Sheila [Buxton] and the orchestra?' I said 'Yes, all right.'

So, we all assembled to play the same programme on television that we had at lunchtime. Barney had said to the orchestral manager 'I'd like all their band jackets and smart clothes.' So, I said to Barney 'This is meant to be a televised radio show, they're all in their braces and things. You can't do that.' He said 'Well, you can't just have them looking scruffy and unshaven' . . . We all went out to the pub and I . . . said 'Forget about your jackets, fellas' . . . Barney went white when they all came on the stage about five minutes before the show. I could hear him screaming through the earphones . . . so we did it like that and it was a great success.[12]

The show was seen by head of light entertainment Eric Maschwitz on a visit to the North region, and he backed a network transfer. He insisted on the continuation of shirtsleeve order – and the braces sported by lead alto saxophonist Johnny Roadhouse became a national talking point. Colehan got into the spirit of the thing too, making frequent comments over the studio talkback, and giving the impression that the viewer was eavesdropping on a high-spirited rehearsal.

Even before *Make Way for Music*, Moffat had a fairly well justified reputation as an 'enfant terrible'. Once, during a printing strike, he declared on air that the current edition of the *Radio Times* was absolutely no use to anyone outside London. On *Make Way for Music*, his mischievous humour was free to run riot. No song announcement was complete without an affectionate insult aimed at the soloist. He opened one show by assembling several members of the band around him in a circle because 'I just thought the viewers might like to see exactly what a dope ring really looks like.'[13] Such organized chaos met with a surprising degree of approval from the powers that were. When, in 1959, the Corporation made *This Is the BBC*, a documentary film about its activities, the NDO was featured prominently, playing a superb Alan Roper arrangement of 'On Ilkley Moor Baht' 'At', while the whole BBC is shown enjoying its lunch. In his announcement, Moffat describes Roper as 'a man who's made so much money out of the coffee business, he now has a house in its own grounds'.

Make Way for Music was far from being the North region's only contribution to television light entertainment. Since July 1953, Colehan had been producing *The Good Old Days*, an outside broadcast from the stage of the City Varieties Theatre in Leeds, a proper horseshoe-shaped music hall dating from 1865. The idea behind the show was to recreate the atmosphere of those far-off nights with modern performers. The audiences, often drawn from the ranks of local amateur dramatic societies, were all decked out in period dress, and there was even a chairman, in the form of South African-born actor Leonard Sachs, to introduce the turns in the florid, loquacious way that Victorian music hall chairmen did. Colehan's other shows included *Club Night*, transmitted from northern working men's clubs, featuring the sort of music and comedy that could be expected on a club bill. Although he worked often at the Manchester studios, Colehan was never based in the north-west, working instead from Broadcasting House at Woodhouse Lane in Leeds, his home city.

In 1958, John Ammonds moved over from producing radio LE at the BBC in Manchester to become the region's main television light entertainment producer. After the directors' training course came a three-month attachment to Douglas Moodie in the LE department in London, during which he produced a series of fifteen-minute shows with Michael Holliday, one of the top pop singers of the day. His debut left room for improvement, as he admits: 'It was the first show I did, and it was live network, at 10.45 admittedly. Mike had forgotten the words. He got completely lost on the last verse. Fortunately, the band, with Johnny Pearson on piano, caught up with him and they all finished together, but I went back to my digs in Wimbledon thinking "Oh, the first real go in London and it was a disaster.'"[14] Moodie smoothed the matter over at the programme review meeting, aided by the fact that no one else present had seen the show, and Ammonds returned north to assume his new duties.

One of them was to find something suitable for bumbling comedian Harry Worth, who had so nearly failed to get Brian Tesler off to a flying start at ATV. A North region-only pilot in 1959 was successful enough to lead to a series in early 1960, written by Ammonds's benefactor Ronnie Taylor and called *The Trouble With Harry*. This was followed in the autumn by *Here's Harry*, best known for its opening title sequence, in which Worth positioned himself by a shop window and raised an arm and a leg, using the reflection to appear as though he was jumping in the air.

The growing importance of television led to a breakthrough in 1960, when the *Royal Variety Performance* was transmitted in vision for the first time. It was recorded on 16 May at the Victoria Palace by ATV and transmitted on Sunday 22 May in place of *Sunday Night at the London Palladium* and ABC's *Armchair Theatre*. The suggestion had come up before, but various ceremonial and organizational objections had been raised. It seems most likely that the final approval came as a result of the new technology of videotape recording and editing. The *Royal Variety* show was (and remains) renowned for over-running, but recording made it possible to package, schedule and transmit the show to its best advantage at last.

The bill that night had been assembled by Jack Hylton, newly freed from his association with Associated-Rediffusion. Naturally, the Crazy Gang loomed large, as the show was taking place in their theatrical home. In what *The Times* described as their 'topical novelty', the ageing miscreants appeared as 'bridesmaids gleefully recalling their part in a recent wedding', the topicality coming from the marriage of Princess

Margaret and Antony Armstrong-Jones ten days before the show. The other acts included Adam Faith (a 'beatnik' in *The Times*'s parlance), Cliff Richard 'radiating chubby good humour throughout his most sultry songs'[15] and skiffle maestro Lonnie Donegan singing 'My Old Man's a Dustman', which had only just vacated the number one spot in the chart, with his band around him dressed in coats and mufflers, as street musicians.[16]

It was a pair of American performers, however, who stole the show. One was Nat 'King' Cole, who 'sang of love and life with alternate energy and nostalgia, almost winning his battle with a band which seemed to regard beat numbers as an automatic cue for blotting out completely the singer they were supposed to be accompanying and glossy romantic pieces as an excuse for abandoning rhythm altogether'. The other was the man who personified the phrase 'all-round entertainer', Sammy Davis Junior, making his first appearance on British soil. *The Times* described him as 'a small, wiry, almost Aztec-looking man with a galvanic personality' and praised his 'electrifying' singing and his 'needle-sharp impersonations of Messrs. Cole, Laine, Martin, Lewis and ... Louis Armstrong, as they might handle "Birth of the Blues".'[17]

Davis was such a smash that he was asked to return for the 1961 *Royal* show, again televised by ATV. (From 1962 onwards, after intervention from Bernard Delfont on the BBC's behalf, the two networks alternated in presenting the *Royal Variety Performance*. To this day, the BBC produce it in even-numbered years, ITV in odd-numbered years.) Even though his impact was considerable the second time around, this time Davis had to compete with two bona fide troupers – the American comedians George Burns and Jack Benny. Burns's wife and long-time comedy partner Gracie Allen had retired from the business, so a Burns and Allen routine was tackled, with Benny in drag, playing Allen. Given that Benny could slay an audience with nothing more than a pause, the effect was predictably seismic.

The international guest stars at the *Royal Variety Performance* were not always best remembered for their performance, however, one example being Mario Lanza's involvement in the 1957 show. Grade Organization agent and personal friend Peter Prichard had been deputed to keep an eye on the singer and notorious drunk. Unfortunately, a rehearsal call caught Lanza asleep, and when Prichard tried to wake him, Lanza lashed out at his friend. Prichard described what had happened to Leslie Grade, whose first reaction was that treating one of his agents like this was unacceptable, and that Lanza should be removed from the show. Pragmatism prevailed and Grade said 'Peter, let him do his song. Then, when he comes off, hit him back.' Word of the altercation soon got out, and resulted in a *Daily Mirror* reporter doorstepping Prichard's grandmother. Having explained what had happened in the hope of eliciting more information, the reporter was told 'Oh, most probably. Peter fights all the kids in the street.' Momentarily, in his aged relative's mind, the successful theatrical agent had regressed to being a Shepherd's Bush street bruiser.

In the early sixties, ATV's dominance of light entertainment within the ITV network was beginning to be challenged by the weekend contractor for Midlands and the North, ABC Television. ABC had excelled in drama from the start, but its entertainment output had been rather directionless, with the exception of pioneering pop shows *Oh Boy!*, *Boy Meets Girls* and *Wham!!*, all produced by Jack Good. ATV had resorted to other tactics to keep ABC in its place, such as refusing some of ABC's early entries into entertainment, and thus denying them a network showing. These included a Michael Bentine revue series called *After Hours*, which ABC managing director Howard Thomas would later describe as 'one of the funniest shows that London has never seen'.[18]

The turnaround began with two coincidental events: ABC's acquisition of the former Warner Brothers film studios at Teddington, which gave the company a well-equipped base to help it snare the best talent the capital could offer, and the arrival of Brian Tesler from ATV at the end of 1959. While his three years working for Grade and Parnell had been 'very happy', he felt his hard work deserved financial recognition. Freelance work was the answer, ideally dividing his time between ATV and the BBC. Then came the big surprise:

Teddy Sommerfield got me interviews with [BBC head of light entertainment] Eric Maschwitz and [ATV programme controller] Bill Ward, who both said 'Yes, six months, marvellous, absolutely.' Teddy then said 'Oh, Howard Thomas wants to see you as well,' and I thought, 'Well, he wants some freelance work as well, so maybe I can do it next year.' I went in to see him and he said 'I want you to run features and light entertainment for me. I want you to be an executive.' I said 'Ultimately I want to be an executive, but not yet.' He said 'Well I want you to do it, think about it.' That was the end of the year, I went up with Audrey [Tesler's wife] to her family in Yorkshire, and he kept phoning up in Yorkshire. Howard kept phoning: 'Come and meet the board.' So I had a board lunch at Golden Square, then went down to the studios at Teddington. I thought 'What the hell,' went back, talked to Audrey and said yes, which upset Bill Ward and Eric Maschwitz. In fact, Bill Ward didn't speak to me for at least six months or even more, which was hilarious. We had joint meetings, me and my people, Bill and his people, and Bill would say to Muir Sutherland [ABC's programme co-ordinator] on my left 'Ask him about so and so and so and so.' I'd say to Muir 'Tell him it's OK, I'm going to do that.' Muir would say 'It's OK he's going to do that.' It was absurd. It sounds like a sketch.[19]

Tesler found the new job hard-going. 'It was hopeless. It was very difficult,' he admits. 'Howard Thomas was not a light entertainment man. He was a news, current affairs and drama man. He knew enough light entertainment to know what was good, but not enough to do it.' This became obvious when Thomas decided to write a script for a situation comedy himself. Tesler knew it was a poor effort, but realized that actually making it might have the desired effect. 'It was terrible,' Tesler says. 'I said to [producer] Philip [Jones] "Can you do this?" He said "I can't get anybody to play in this." I said "Please, it's going to make a point. It won't get on the air. Make as good a fist of it as we can just to show Howard that it really is difficult." Bless his heart, he did. We showed it to Howard. Howard agreed it was terrible and he never ever said anything again about light entertainment, ever.'

Philip Jones had come to Tesler's attention through an anomaly of television reception at the home of his wife's parents: 'They lived in Yorkshire, which was ABC territory, except I couldn't see ABC programmes, because where they lived in Sleights, there wasn't a gap in the hills all the way round. The only ITV I could see was Tyne Tees, which was how I saw the work of Philip Jones, and how I got him down to ABC.'[20] It was a lucky spot. Jones, who had begun his career at Radio Luxembourg, would go on to run light entertainment for ABC and its successor, Thames, well into the eighties. Apart from Jones, Ben Churchill and Ernest Maxin – who came over from the BBC to join his old colleague – Tesler had trouble getting the right staff for his department, many of the best producers being tied up elsewhere. So, while Tesler was busy with executive life, the producer shortages meant that he had to carry on directing shows himself.

One of his productions was a 1960 spectacular that showed ATV and the rest of the network that ABC meant business: *Sammy Davis Junior Meets the British*. The American star had been booked for his first British performances, including his *Royal Variety* show triumph and a season at the Pigalle on Piccadilly.[21] Tesler had booked Davis, through Harry Foster's agency, for the Sunday of his first week in town, and arranged a series of set pieces that included a comedy/dance routine in a hat shop, with Lionel Blair playing the upper-crust milliner, and a 'Pied Piper' sequence at Battersea funfair with a group of children from Dr Barnardo's homes. 'The idea was that part one would be Sammy doing an act with lots of impressions,' Tesler outlines. 'Part two would be the Battersea funfair thing, and part three would be his nightclub act, with the studio at Teddington set with tables filled with celebrities.'[22] The recording of the Battersea sequence went well, but the playback revealed an unforeseen hazard:

We're looking at it for the first time, and as he crosses from one exhibit to another, we pan past an entire camera crew. I said 'Oh Christ, but we've just passed an entire camera crew.' He said 'They're not going to be watching the cameras, they're going to be watching me. Fuck the camera crew.' He was right, and I don't think anybody noticed.[23]

Unfortunately, Davis's pragmatism deserted him at the start of studio rehearsals, already limited in time by Davis's tight schedule, as Tesler explains:

I had a huge white staircase constructed, with curtains at the top. The idea was that he [Davis] would do his first number, coming down the staircase. He comes into the studio on Saturday morning, sees the staircase and says 'No, I don't want that. I'll fall down the staircase and ruin the show. Get rid of it, scrap it.' So the big set piece had to go. Then, when we were rehearsing on the Sunday, we were using, for the very first time, a lavalier radio neck-mike. Because the studio was empty, there was a howlback on that precious lavalier mike, the first radio mike used in British television. He got so furious at the howlback that he tore the mike from his neck, threw it across the studio and destroyed it.

He hated everything about the day. I'm sitting in the control room at the end of rehearsals, going through notes, and the make-up lady comes in and says 'He's not going to do the show. He said he's very unhappy, he doesn't want to do the show.' So I went to his dressing room and said 'What's all this about?' 'I don't want to do the show.' I asked why, and he replied 'Because you're a bunch of inefficient cocksuckers.'[24]

Not daunted, Tesler told Davis that the British public were dying to see him in action. The star replied that they could come to the Pigalle – a physical impossibility given the likely size of the viewing audience. The producer assured the star that all would be all right on the night.

As I'm talking, I can hear the B-movie accompanying music. 'Sammy, you've got to do it. You don't like me, I'm not crazy about you. It doesn't matter. It's the audience that matters. The British audience.' Schmaltz like you've never heard in your life. At the end of which, I'm thoroughly ashamed of myself, but he says 'Yeah, well, all right, I'll do it.' He did it, and of course it was a smash. It was the last thing I did, though, because it was a bastard to do. He was a bugger. I thought at the end of that, that's it, I'm happy being an executive, I can't do both, I refuse to do both.[25]

Another important LE contribution made by ABC was the hidden camera prank show *Candid Camera*, which began a hit run on British TV in 1960. In America, it had been developed from the radio series *Candid Microphone* by its presenter Allen Funt. In the UK, the first host was Bob Monkhouse, aided by pranksters Jonathan Routh and Arthur Atkins, and producer Ronnie Taylor. It was revived periodically over the following sixteen years, finally in 1976 with Routh as the host, but the premise remained the same. Present ordinary people with extraordinary situations and film them secretly. A memorable early stunt was the car that turned up at a garage with its driver claiming it was in need of some work. On closer inspection, the car was revealed to have no engine. Silent movie legend Buster Keaton had been involved with the original US show, which thrilled Monkhouse when he went to the States to see the show being made and met his hero.

ABC's heightened profile in light entertainment brought problems with ATV. Although ITV had been set up as a free market, with the constituent companies competing for network slots and selling each other programmes, ATV regarded light entertainment as its fiefdom. 'ATV was willing enough for ABC to provide church services, race meetings and children's programmes for London networking, but they were determined to dominate all the major entertainment spots in the London week-end schedule,' ABC managing director Howard Thomas recalled in his autobiography.[26] At one point, Val Parnell tried to convince Thomas that he had no need to employ any programme-makers, but Thomas went the other way, realizing that he 'could fight with Parnell and Grade only from a position of armed strength . . .

Whenever I threatened not to network one of their programmes I had to be ready with an equally effective programme of our own to replace theirs.'[27] At one point, ATV thought that ABC wasn't paying enough for *Sunday Night at the London Palladium*. As Grade and Parnell regarded the show as a non-negotiable element of every ITV company's schedule, they believed that the odds were stacked in their favour. However, Thomas, bolstered by the growing power of his light entertainment department under Tesler, threatened to pull the Palladium show altogether and produce an alternative from ABC's newly rebuilt flagship theatre in Blackpool. In the event, the matter was resolved, but ABC made *Blackpool Night Out* anyway, and it became the summer replacement for *Sunday Night at the London Palladium* from July 1964.

Blackpool Night Out had developed from ABC's *Big Night Out*, a vehicle for Mike and Bernie Winters. Unlike many acts with a common name, Mike and Bernie were real brothers, having anglicized their proper surname, Weinstein, for professional purposes. Brought up in the north London suburb of Tottenham, both had musical inclinations from an early age. Mike played clarinet and studied at the Royal Academy of Music at the same time as jazz musician John Dankworth, while Bernie played drums, which he studied at the Tottenham campus of the University of Life. Becoming eligible for his call-up at the tail end of the war, Mike Winters had tried to join the Merchant Navy, but been dismissed by the medical officer as unfit for service. Recommended by a pianist friend, the brothers joined the Canadian Legion, which was looking for musicians for troop shows. While others spent their time square-bashing, the brothers Weinstein, by their own admission, had it cushy. 'Service as a legionnaire was the best time in my life,' Bernie Winters recalled in the pair's autobiography. 'We were only playing soldiers, but that didn't stop us getting all the perks other servicemen got in wartime ... My only rank was entertainer.'[28]

Upon being demobbed, the pair took their chances as a double act, without much success. Mike went into the schmutter trade, beginning by selling scarce nylon stockings paired up from manufacturers' seconds. Meanwhile, Bernie carried on as a solo act. An ill-advised venture into mail order scuppered Mike's clothing business and, on a whim, he decided to rejoin his brother on stage. Their first major breakthrough was a year working on a touring bill with newly minted rock and roll star Tommy Steele, as a result of which they notched up their first television appearances, on *Six Five Special*. Their next big breakthrough, in 1962, was seen only by those present at a cinema in Cleveleys [probably the Odeon], near Blackpool, when technical troubles held up the recording of ABC's *Holiday Town Parade*. Mike and Bernie filled the hiatus with twenty-five minutes of ad-libs, impressing producer Philip Jones enough to offer them their own show. It took a while for him to persuade his bosses of their appeal, but they took over *Big Night Out*. When they began their stint on the show, they were working in a summer show at Southsea with Arthur Askey. They would fly up to the ABC studios at Didsbury each week with a generous helping of material given to them by the veteran comic.

Just as the Weinstein boys were establishing themselves at ABC, another double act was making its name at ATV. Eric Morecambe and Ernie Wise were not blood relatives, but had an almost-fraternal relationship. They had met as child performers just before the Second World War, and worked together in Bryan Michie's *Youth Takes A Bow* revue in 1940. Ernest Wiseman was from Leeds, and was a junior song and dance man in the mould of Jack Buchanan. Eric Bartholomew came from the seaside resort of Morecambe in Lancashire, on the other side of the Pennines.[29] Whereas Wiseman's act aspired to and, by all accounts, achieved a sophistication beyond his years, Bartholomew's schtick was firmly in the north-western tradition of the 'gowk' or simpleton. Wearing tails, a bootlace tie, short trousers and a beret, while holding a gigantic lollipop, he sang a number called 'I'm Not All There'. Although disparate as performers, the pair became good friends. Bartholomew was usually accompanied on tour by his mother Sadie, and she effectively became Wiseman's guardian. It was Sadie's inspired suggestion that the pair channel their off-stage banter into an act.

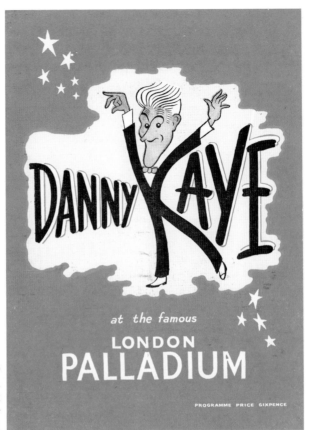

Danny Kaye returns to the London Palladium for a further triumphant season in 1955, aided by a full supporting bill

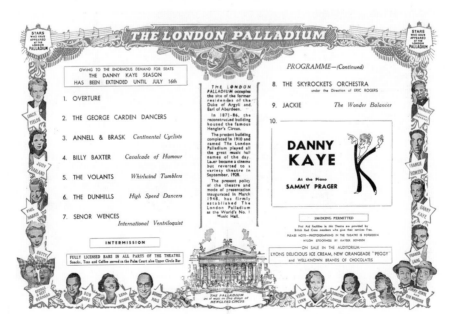

THE LONDON PALLADIUM

OWING TO THE ENORMOUS DEMAND FOR SEATS
THE DANNY KAYE SEASON
HAS BEEN EXTENDED UNTIL JULY 16th

1. OVERTURE

2. THE GEORGE CARDEN DANCERS

3. ANNELL & BRASK   Continental Cyclists

4. BILLY BAXTER   Cavalcade of Humour

5. THE VOLANTS   Whirlwind Tumblers

6. THE DUNHILLS   High Speed Dancers

7. SENOR WENCES
International Ventriloquist

INTERMISSION

FULLY LICENSED BARS IN ALL PARTS OF THE THEATRE
Snacks, Teas and Coffee served in the Palm Court also Upper Circle Bar

THE LONDON PALLADIUM occupies the site of the former residences of the Duke of Argyll and Earl of Aberdeen.

In 1871-86, the reconstructed building housed the famous Hengler's Circus.

The present building completed in 1910 and named The London Palladium played all the great music hall names of the day. Later became a cinema but reverted to a variety theatre in September, 1928.

The present policy of the theatre and mode of presentation inaugurated in March 1948, has firmly established The London Palladium as the World's No. 1 Music Hall.

THE PALLADIUM
as it was in the days of
HENGLER'S CIRCUS

PROGRAMME—(Continued)

8. THE SKYROCKETS ORCHESTRA
under the Direction of ERIC ROGERS

9. JACKIE   The Wonder Balancer

10.

DANNY
KAYE

At the Piano
SAMMY PRAGER

SMOKING PERMITTED

First Aid Facilities in this Theatre are provided by British Red Cross members who give their services Free.
PLEASE NOTE—PHOTOGRAPHING IN THE THEATRE IS FORBIDDEN
NYLON STOCKINGS BY KAYSER BONDOR

ON SALE IN THE AUDITORIUM
LYONS DELICIOUS ICE CREAM, NEW ORANGEADE "PEGGY"
and WELL-KNOWN BRANDS OF CHOCOLATES

The Crazy Gang's swansong: a poster for *Young in Heart*, 1960

Top left: Suburban London's own Cotton Club: Billy Cotton's band show reaches Finsbury Park in 1954

Top right: Meanwhile, in Blackpool in 1968, the brothers Weinstein top the bill

Right: All-round entertainer Dickie Henderson visits Great Yarmouth for the summer season in 1966

The Albanian Eurovision delegation, 1968: BBC LE producers Brian Whitehouse, Terry Henebery and Roger Ordish in heavy disguise on the roof of Television Centre. The folder reads 'Tom Sloan – Congratulations' in Russian

Ernest Maxin, Kathy Kirby, Bill Cotton Junior and Tom Sloan prepare for the 1965 Eurovision Song Contest

By the early fifties, Eric Bartholomew and Ernest Wiseman had become Eric Morecambe and Ernie Wise, with an uncommon wealth of show business experience for two men still in their mid-twenties. They had become popular radio performers, with their own series, *You're Only Young Once*, beginning on the BBC's Northern Home Service in November 1953. The script was the nominal responsibility of a writer called Frank Roscoe, but he was in heavy demand at the time, working for other Northern radio comics like Ken Platt, and some of the material was less than ideal. Fortunately, the performers could draw on their own reserves, as the show's producer John Ammonds recalls. 'Eric and Ernie used to bring their gag books to Piccadilly [the location of the BBC's Manchester headquarters until 1975] on a Sunday. In fact, Ronnie Taylor, shortly after I got the radio job, said to me "Can you work a Roneo machine? That's one of the main qualifications for the job," because on Sunday nobody was in.'[30]

Their radio success made Ronnie Waldman keen to sign them for their own BBC television series, and he travelled to the Winter Gardens in Blackpool, where they were working, to make the offer. It seemed like the final push that would propel them into the big time, but in fact it was a considerable career setback. In the absence of any recordings, *Running Wild*, which aired fortnightly for six shows from 12 April 1954, is now remembered primarily for the verdict delivered by Kenneth Bailey of the *People*: 'Definition of the week: TV set: the box in which they buried Morecambe and Wise.'[31] It seems likely that the series was nowhere near as bad as had been made out, merely mediocre: in the words of their biographer Graham McCann, 'neither unmissable nor unwatchable'. Some of the blame must be placed with producer Bryan Sears, who was not in tune with the northern comics, but the production's main shortcoming seems to have been in the writing. Sears had hoped to enlist Bob Monkhouse and Denis Goodwin, but they were unavailable – almost certainly because they were preparing their own BBC show, *Fast and Loose*, with Brian Tesler producing. This left Sears with very little time to search for alternatives, but writers were found, including Lawrie Wyman, who would go on to create *The Navy Lark* for radio. Cobbling material together might have worked on radio, but the unforgiving eye of the new medium showed the cracks all too clearly.

Rather cruelly, *Fast and Loose*, the first show of which went out just three weeks after the first *Running Wild*, in the same slot, turned out to be a hit from the off. 'The show was a high-speed smash, every gag worked,' Monkhouse later recalled,[32] but he and Goodwin were battling with similar time constraints to Morecambe and Wise, and both knew that the second show would not reach the same standard. It helped that they wrote their own material, but it also helped that they were far wilier than Morecambe and Wise. The first *Fast and Loose* was advertised as the start of a series, but at Goodwin's suggestion, Monkhouse faked a dead faint at the end of the show, and the claims of exhaustion convinced Waldman to delay the rest of the series until September 1954.

In contrast, Eric and Ernie found themselves having to rebuild their reputations almost from scratch. The experience made them determined never again to go along with advice they didn't agree with, no matter how exalted or experienced the adviser. They went back to doing spots on other people's shows, including well-received appearances on the *The Good Old Days*, BBC Television's long-running tribute to Victorian and Edwardian music hall. In 1956, they became the resident comedians on ATV's *Winifred Atwell Show*, working with the popular pianist, and aided by scripts from Johnny Speight, who seemed to understand the pair better than their previous writers.

The next breakthrough came when they enlisted Billy Marsh as their agent. Bruce Forsyth, a friend and client of Marsh's for over thirty years, described him as 'a very tough negotiator ... a showbiz legend, an agent who cared about his stars and was thrilled when things were going right for them'.[33] Marsh, a Dover-born farmer's son, had moved from working in his local theatres to working with agent Bernard Delfont in 1941. Throughout his career, he was well known for working on trust, as his colleague and successor Jan Kennedy explains. 'Billy Marsh never had a contract with any of his talent, and neither do we.

I want the talent to be happy. The first thing, after talent, is belief. If you believe in that talent, with a bit of luck and a few careful decisions, you should be able to get them up there.'[34] This was the kind of backing that Eric and Ernie needed. Marsh showed his mettle during their preliminary meeting with him by calling ATV's head booker Alec Fyne and landing them a spot on *Sunday Night at the London Palladium*.

By 1961, Marsh was convinced that Morecambe and Wise were ready for their own television series, and offered them to Lew Grade at ATV. Grade turned them down flat. He agreed that they'd come a long way from *Running Wild*, but did not think they were worth the risk. He changed his mind once Marsh began to offer them elsewhere – at one point, Eric Maschwitz was very interested in bringing them back to the BBC to make amends – and their first ATV show went out from the Wood Green Empire on 12 October 1961. On the recommendation of Ben Warriss (of the double act Jewel and Warriss), the performers had insisted on having Sid Green and Dick Hills, a pair of former schoolteachers, as their scriptwriters and Colin Clews as their producer. The recommendation was a good one, as this was to be the team that supported Eric and Ernie throughout their seven years at ATV.

Grade may also have had motives for taking on Morecambe and Wise other than the fear of competition. The actors' union Equity was threatening ITV with strike action over fees for its members, but Morecambe and Wise were members of the rival Variety Artists' Federation. Equity followed through with its threat on 1 November 1961, just three weeks after the series started. Oddly, the strike was just what the performers and their writers needed. The reception for the first couple of shows had been mixed. Morecambe and Wise themselves were unhappy with Hills and Green's large-scale sketches with sizeable casts of supporting actors. One led Morecambe to complain that he had trouble finding his partner. Suddenly, a pared-down vision was required, with the writers being pressed into service as the stooges where appropriate. The result was ideal – Eric and Ernie had the space to develop their comic personas, while the writers' initial hesitance and reluctance as performers gave them something to spark off.

Morecambe was never better than when dishing out gentle insults. By the time the series found its feet, the ghost of *Running Wild* had been well and truly laid.

In their 1960s work for ABC, Mike and Bernie Winters followed the classic double act pattern of straight man and idiot, and so to a certain degree did Eric and Ernie at this time, although the dynamic of their on-stage characters would later change and become more complex and rewarding. Hills and Green's contribution has been overshadowed somewhat by Eric and Ernie's later association with the great scriptwriter Eddie Braben, but they produced some sterling work for the ATV shows. One particularly memorable sketch cast Eric as a flamenco dancer, with Ernie as a singer:

ERIC: What are we dressed like this for?

ERNIE [in strangulated Spanish accent]: Senōr, you are the great Spanish dancer El Rico Cavallero Gonzales.

ERIC: Am I? Who's working you? [Aside] Someone's working him.

ERNIE: No joke, sir.

ERIC [also in strangulated Spanish accent]: But eet's a leeving?

ERNIE: I, sir, am Don Ernesto Philippo Manuel de Castile.

ERIC: That's a cigar. A little fat cigar.

ERNIE [gesturing to guitarist]: This here is my comrade . . .

ERIC: That's good, isn't it? A Russian Spaniard.[35]

The sketch captures perfectly Eric's role in the partnership as a disruptive element. It also underlines one of their great skills as an act: making a script sound spontaneous. Like all of their work, it will have been rehearsed to the point of destruction, but on the show, it still comes up fresh. Having been introduced to the guitarist, Eric then notices his female dancing partner:

ERIC: Who's the dolly?

ERNIE: Lil.

ERIC [incredulous]: Whaddyamean, Lil?

ERNIE: It's Lil. Come here, it's a very sad story. You see her mother went to Spain on one of those cheap trips. Need I go on?

ERIC: If you don't want the show to finish early, yes.[36]

ERNIE: She went to Spain, her mother . . .

ERIC: On one of those cheap tours.

ERNIE: She met a bull-fighting fellow.

ERIC: They're all the same. They carry their own sheets around with them. You've got to watch them.

ERNIE: The moon was out. Romance, a lot of this [mimes drinking].

ERIC: Ah, tequila, tequila. No, that's Mexico.

ERNIE: Before . . .

ERIC: . . . her mother knew where she was, it was a package deal.[37]

In an earlier ATV show, recorded at the Borehamwood studios on 2 December 1963, they had showcased a new band from Liverpool. After performing 'This Boy' and 'I Want to Hold Your Hand', the Beatles were joined on stage by Ernie, who suggested that they perform a number together. Then Eric, 'the tall handsome one with the glasses', comes to join 'the one with the short fat hairy legs', and the four with what George Harrison refers to as 'big fat hairy heads':

ERIC: Ahhhhhhhh, it's the Kaye Sisters! Fabulous. Have you dyed your hair?

ERNIE: It's not the Kaye Sisters. This is the Beatles.

ERIC [as if talking to a small and very cute furry animal]: Hello Beatles. [Normal voice] Where is he? There he is. Hello Bongo.

ERNIE: That's Ringo.

ERIC: Oh, is he there as well?[38]

The Beatles were among the first British pop stars to display their natural sense of humour. Indeed, it was their repartee that impressed record chief George Martin more than their music when they auditioned for EMI's Parlophone label. Previously, stars had been under pressure from their managers to be humble and reverent whenever they opened their mouths to do anything other than sing. John Lennon felt no such compulsion, and appears to deflate Eric momentarily with a withering putdown, before Morecambe recovers his form:

ERIC: What's it like being famous?

JOHN LENNON: Ah, it's not like in your day, you know.

ERIC: What? That's an insult that is. What do you mean not like in my day?

LENNON: My dad used to tell me about you, you know [does 'when I was knee-high to a grasshopper' gesture].

ERIC: Only got a little dad, have you?[39]

For the number that followed, a rendition of 'Moonlight Bay', the Fab Four and Ernie donned striped jackets and straw boaters, while Eric emerged from the wings in a deluxe Merseybeat wig and that quintessential piece of early Beatle fashion, a collarless Pierre Cardin jacket, shouting Beatleisms, and the odd Gerry and the Pacemakers quote, over the others. There is a story that the show's producer, Colin Clews, insisted on it going out early in the run, in case the Beatles' star faded suddenly. The fact that, by the time the show was recorded, the band had already scored three number one hits and a number two, as well as appearing at a *Royal Variety Performance*, suggests the story is apocryphal. Although the scope and extent of their career and influence was not yet apparent, it was already evident that they weren't any old transient pop fad.

The encounter with the Beatles underlines Morecambe and Wise's generosity as performers. Eric, Ernie and their writers Sid and Dick – sometimes referred to as 'Sick and Did' – knew that the quality of the show mattered more than who got the laughs, sometimes giving away the best lines to guests if they thought it would get a better response. Mike Winters had no such sense of perspective, according to Eric Geen, who wrote for Mike and Bernie in their ABC heyday:

The trouble was that Mike wanted to have as many lines as Bernie. Mike had to be on screen as much as Bernie. It was foolish. Bernie didn't worry, he was laid-back, but Mike did all the business, and whatever Mike said went. Mike blew it. He was jealous and it made it very difficult to write sketches. He didn't like other people on the show getting laughs. Also, they didn't want to do slapstick, they wanted to be more serious. If you're a comic, you can't be serious. Bernie was a funny fellow – a natural clown.[40]

★

Although Mike and Bernie Winters were entertaining enough, it's obvious that ATV had the better double act. However, the double act that headed the firm through its early years came to an end in September 1962, when Val Parnell retired as joint executive chairman. From that moment on, ATV was Lew Grade was ATV; although he was a powerful man before he even entered television, his involvement with the medium made Grade a household name. He had grasped television's potential from the start, and had withdrawn from the family agency in March 1956 to concentrate on ATV. He would remain devoted to the company until his retirement in 1977.

In an industry based on vision, Grade was one of the biggest visionaries of all. Early on, he saw the value of exporting and syndicating programmes on the American model, and ATV's success in this field was marked by three Queen's Awards to Industry for Export Achievement. ATV's main export products were the filmed adventure series made by its sister company ITC, such as *The Saint*, *The Baron*, *Danger Man* and *Man in a Suitcase*. However, ATV also managed to package entertainment shows for the American market, often using big US stars – a real case of flogging sand to the Arabs and a testament to Grade's skills as a salesman. In particular, ATV enjoyed a warm association with singer Jo Stafford, not least because her manager Mike Nidorf was an old friend of Grade's – indeed it was Nidorf who had alerted the agent to *The Times*'s announcement inviting applicants for commercial television franchises in 1954.

ATV was also early into full-scale colour production, making colour shows for export more than two years before they could be transmitted domestically.[41] In the US, NBC had been transmitting successfully and regularly in colour since 1954, so ATV made its most exportable shows in monochrome for domestic transmission and in 525-line NTSC colour, the US standard. One of the most prominent, if not actually the earliest, was *The Heart of Show Business*, recorded in 1966 and transmitted in the UK on 26 March 1967, although British viewers could see it in monochrome only. It was a charity spectacular, in aid of the victims of the collapsed slag heap at Aberfan, starring singers Shirley Bassey, Tommy Steele, Frankie Vaughan and Sammy Davis Junior, as well as the newly wed actors Elizabeth Taylor and Richard Burton. Among Taylor's duties was to introduce an acrobatic act known as Les Trois Charlies, who on closer inspection turned out to be Spike Milligan, Harry Secombe and Peter Sellers, performing in the mode of Tony Hancock's useless troupe on *Hancock's Forty-Three Minutes*, a decade earlier.

Even though the US had over a decade's head start on the UK when it came to colour television, ATV worked out very quickly that the US television companies were creating a lot of needless hassle for themselves. 'The colour cameras did need a lot of light and we were terribly misled by the Americans, because they said that the colour temperature of the lamps had to be a certain level,' explains Richard Greenough, ATV's head of visual services, as the head of design was known by 1967. 'A new lamp would only sustain that level for a few hours then it became more red. So what happened in the early days was that we'd use lamps for rehearsal, then they'd all have to be changed for recording. This was an enormous problem and expense. Then our lighting directors and the vision control people suddenly twigged the idea that if you altered the red level you were back to where you started. The moment we realized that, the lamps had their normal life and we adjusted the colour electronically. The Americans didn't seem to get that idea.'[42]

Some of the other ITV companies weren't too sure about Grade's pursuit of export dollars either. Howard Thomas of ABC 'sometimes . . .

jokingly reminded him that he should be concentrating on Birmingham, England, rather than Birmingham, Alabama'.[43] However, even those who thought that some of ATV's products were vulgar, trashy or too transatlantic for comfort had to admit that Grade himself was a man of honour. Grade was always as good as his word – a verbal contract from him was a firmer guarantee than some rivals' written contracts.

Grade's record of honour came in very useful when he found himself having to reconcile the apparently irreconcilable. In 1965, ATV bought from Prince Littler and Emile Littler the Stoll Moss group, but the acquisition had a 20 per cent voting stake in its new owner. Grade needed to find a buyer for the shares quickly, and approached Sir Max Aitken, chairman of the Express newspaper group and son of Lord Beaverbrook (one of ITV's harshest critics, who had died the previous year). Aitken was enthusiastic, but almost everyone told Grade that he'd never get the deal past the *Daily Mirror*, a major ATV shareholder since April 1956, or the Independent Television Authority. Grade's good relationship with Mirror Newspapers chairman Hugh Cudlipp, and Cecil King, chairman of the Mirror's parent company, IPC, ensured the first hurdle was overcome with ease. Grade managed to put the ITA's objections about newspaper influence in television ownership into context by pointing out that one of ITV's strongest critics was now keen to invest in it. The deal went through.

The Stoll Moss deal meant that ATV suddenly owned the London Palladium, home of its flagship entertainment show, which maintained its popularity throughout the sixties. During the twelve-year run of *Sunday Night at the London Palladium*, there were several changes of host. Bruce Forsyth became ill in September 1960, and, for nearly a year, his place as compère was taken by the virtually unknown comic Don Arrol, who described the experience as 'like working with a ghost behind me . . . it's Bruce's show'.[44] Forsyth took an unenforced sabbatical from the show in 1962, with affable Liverpool-born comic Norman Vaughan and his catchphrases, 'swinging' and 'dodgy', taking over.

★

As important as ATV's flagship variety show was, Grade viewed the export of programmes, particularly to the US networks, as a vital part of the company's future. BBC Television's light entertainment group had its own international commitments too, but Europe figured far more heavily. A BBC show – the *Black and White Minstrel Show* – was, in 1961, the first winner of the coveted Golden Rose prize for best entertainment programme at the Montreux Television Festival. Over a decade earlier, the Corporation had played a central role in setting up the European Broadcasting Union, which was instituted at a specially convened conference in Torquay on 12 February 1950, as a response to the increasing Communist domination of the existing industry forum, the International Broadcasting Organization. The final straw had come when the IBO moved its headquarters from Brussels to Prague. At the outset, the EBU's main responsibilities were technical and political, not least of which was ensuring that broadcasting stations kept to their internationally agreed frequencies. It was one of the Union's technical achievements that led to one of the most enduring elements of light entertainment programming, namely the *Eurovision Song Contest*.

Broadcasting television pictures from the continent to the UK had become a reality on 27 August 1950, when an hour-long outside broadcast had been beamed from Calais across the English Channel. By 1954, the EBU had set up a network of relays between its member broadcasters, allowing live transmission across Europe. The name 'Eurovision' was coined by George Campey, the television correspondent of the London *Evening Standard*. Such technical marvels were of limited use without programmes, though, and the idea of a song contest was mooted, with the first competition taking place in Lugano, Switzerland, in 1956. Due to a missed deadline, the UK sat out that first contest, which was won by 'Refrain', sung by Switzerland's Lys Assia, but entered in 1957.

After the 1957 contest in Frankfurt, it became a rule that the winning country would host the following year's contest, but the UK staged the Eurovision twice before winning. In 1959, Teddy Scholten took first place for the Netherlands with 'Een Beetje' ('A Little Bit'), but the Dutch declined to stage the contest in 1960, having already done so in 1958 and found it an expensive do. The UK entry, Pearl Carr and Teddy Johnson's 'Sing Little Birdie' had come second, so the BBC took over, holding the contest at the Royal Festival Hall on 29 March 1960, under producer Harry Carlisle, a panel game veteran, and director Innes Lloyd, a curious choice in retrospect as he would become best known for his distinguished work in drama. Katie Boyle made her first appearance as the host, aided by a commentary from David Jacobs. The French won, represented by Jacqueline Boyer with 'Tom Pillibi' – and won again just two years later. They passed on the honour of holding the contest a second time, and the BBC was once again asked to step in. Tom Sloan, who had finally become head of light entertainment in 1961, decided that it would be an ideal opportunity to show off the capabilities of the new BBC Television Centre, as Yvonne Littlewood explains:

> There were fifteen countries, even in 1963. We used [studios] three and four, and five for the jury.[45] We had the performance in one of the studios, three or four, with the orchestra, and the other one with the audience, the scoring and everything. Harry Carlisle looked after the general administrative side and I did all the direction. We had excellent sound [by] Len Shorey. That contest was significant for me, because singing for Luxembourg was Nana Mouskouri [with whom Littlewood worked many times subsequently]. Singing for Switzerland was Esther Ofarim, and there were other singers like Heidi Brühl and Alain Barrière, Françoise Hardy, all sorts of interesting people.[46]

Of the competitors, the voting juries were most impressed by the Danish entry – 'Dansevise' by Grethe and Jørgen Ingmann – although their victory was not without controversy. Katie Boyle had been unable to hear the votes cast by the Norwegian jury, so she decided to move on and return to them later. The audience, both in the studio and at home, had no such problems. When she returned to them, their votes had changed and were instrumental in giving neighbouring Denmark a narrow victory over Switzerland.

Finally, with Sandie Shaw's victory in the 1967 contest in Austria, the UK got to hold the contest as a winner. For most viewers, the most memorable aspect of the 1968 show at the Royal Albert Hall was 'Congratulations' by Cliff Richard being beaten by the Spanish entry, 'La La La' by Massiel, with only one point in it. It later emerged that Richard might have won, if it hadn't been for gerrymandering by operatives of Spain's General Franco. For those behind the scenes, it sticks in the memory for a quite different reason. At the Royal Albert Hall, Stewart Morris was producer/director, with Tom Sloan on hand as executive producer. Through the rehearsals, all was going like clockwork, but back at Television Centre, Sloan's deputy Bill Cotton was getting a little restless at having to keep an overworked department running while Sloan was glad-handing the continental visitors; he was also wondering if things weren't going so well that complacency was setting in. Over lunch with some of his young producers, a plan began to formulate. Roger Ordish, along with Terry Henebery and Brian Whitehouse, was one of the canteen conspirators:

> Bill said 'Tom's sitting there saying "All these bloody foreigners coming saying they want to change their rehearsal time and their accom-modation's not good enough . . ." I think he needs something to leaven it. What can you do?' We said we could be another nation.[47]

After lunch, Ordish, Henebery and Whitehouse went to costume and make-up, emerging in dark glasses, wide-brimmed hats, false moustaches and beards as the Albanian delegation. Ordish had become the group's spokesman due to his ability to speak Russian, and had called in his university friend Sue Arnold, then working on the *Daily Sketch*, to act as the group's 'interpreter'. 'We even hired a Rolls-Royce,' Ordish recalls. 'It was arranged that Tom would see it arrive and he said "Well, at least they've got some money."' Terry Henebery remembers the precise amount: £10 to hire the Roller for an evening.

The plan was to proceed to the Royal Albert Hall, where Cotton would go in first and check the lay of the land. Terry Henebery explains: 'The deal was that when we got out of that car, if Bill was at the window blowing his nose, get back in the car, because Tom's in a bad mood and it's going to go down like a cup of cold sick.'[48] AHLEG (Tel) – Assistant Head of Light Entertainment Group (Television) – was not seen to blow his nose, and so the game was afoot. As the party entered, they bowed to Sloan, who returned the gesture, which almost blew the gaff. 'Jim Moir [who was running the floor on the show] knew about it, but he wasn't part of it,' says Ordish. 'He almost gave the game away when he got the most terrible fits of giggles seeing Tom Sloan bowing to us.'[49] As the stunt escalated, so did Moir's amusement, although thankfully unseen by Sloan. Ordish continues:

I was talking gobbledegook, and our interpreter was saying 'Mr Antolini asks why can't the Albanians be called for a rehearsal?' And Tom Sloan was saying 'Tell them that Albania is not a member of the European Broadcasting Union.' Of course, when you're doing all that, you never look at people. You look at the interpreter. The next thing was to say 'Mr Antolini says that if you hear their song you will find it so beautiful that you will put it in the contest.' And then we began to sing 'Congratulations' in cod-Albanian.

It was Sloan's secretary, Queenie Lipyeat, who cottoned on quickest. 'They thought it was student rag,' Henebery recalls, 'but when it all erupted, Tom's secretary rushed across the room, whipped my moustache off and said "It's Terry Henebery."' There was then a brief pause, while they awaited Sloan's reaction. 'There's that pregnant moment, that millisecond when you think "He's going to go apeshit."' Thankfully, Sloan took it in the intended spirit. 'He said "I've been had, that's fucking marvellous."' He loved it. He adored it that we cared enough to want to do it. Because that's the way things work, isn't it? You've got to care enough about the person to do it. He paid for the Roller, made us go back to Television Centre, got us into the small bar at the Centre, and made us keep doing it for his friends in the evening. We still had all the gear on, the funny hats, the smoked glasses and the moustaches.'[50]

There is another punchline to the story. With the aid of Eurovision's excellent communications network, news of the prank spread quickly. 'They had a link-up with all of the Eurovision countries to test the lines and they'd all heard this story,' Ordish relates. 'In the practice, Albania won the Eurovision Song Contest. *Albanie – douze points*.'[51]

In the fifties and sixties, the music provision for BBC TV's light entertainment output – including the *Eurovision Song Contest* – had been dominated by the conductor and arranger Eric Robinson. As well as supplying the backing for programmes like the *Black and White Minstrel Show*, he also became a star in front of the camera with his own series *Music For You*. In contrast, his successor was rarely seen on screen, but his name is instantly recognizable to anyone who saw a set of programme credits in the seventies or eighties. Ronnie Hazlehurst had begun his professional musical career as a trumpeter in dance bands around Manchester. He joined the BBC as a staff arranger in the early sixties, and contributed musical scores to all of the big light entertainment shows, including a superb arrangement of 'Swing Low, Sweet Chariot' for a 1964 *Billy Cotton Band Show*, as well as writing the original theme tune for the Dick Clement/Ian La Frenais sitcom *The Likely Lads*. He also wrote a big band theme based around the notes 'B-B-C' for use every morning before schools programmes.

In 1968, he became the music adviser to BBC TV's light entertainment group, and from then was the dominant force in music for BBC entertainment shows. His memorable themes included *The Two Ronnies*, *Last of the Summer Wine*, *I Didn't Know You Cared* and *Some Mothers Do 'Ave 'Em*. Although he was a skilled user of harmonies – deriding one-time colleague Buddy Bregman for his over-simple arrangements – his signature touch was ensuring that the title of the show could be sung to the melody of the theme tune. He built a session band, including trumpeter Kenny Baker, trombonist Don Lusher, pianist Ronnie Price, guitarist Judd Procter, bassist Dave Richmond and drummer Alf Bigden, that could handle any brief. His best-remembered on-screen appearance was at the 1977 *Eurovision Song Contest*, where he took to the podium wearing a bowler hat, and conducted the British entry, 'Rock Bottom' by Lynsey De Paul and Mike Moran, with a rolled-up umbrella.

Behind the scenes, the 1977 contest was memorable for different reasons. The whole show had nearly been cancelled due to industrial action by cameramen. Alternatives were discussed, including recording the performances in each entrant's home country, but the dispute was eventually resolved and the show went ahead five weeks late on 7 May at the new Wembley Conference Centre. The broadcast was not without its problems, however. Location film for use between the acts was scrapped as unsatisfactory, leaving director Stewart Morris with no option but to let the cameras pan across the bemused, self-conscious audience. The event was won by France's Marie Myriam with 'L'Oiseau et l'Enfant', while 'Rock Bottom' – the lyrics being a pointed comment on the UK's industrial and financial woes – came second. At the end of the show, the credit roller refused to work, and production manager Marcus Plantin recalls a cameraman with a hand-held device falling 'head over arse' on Myriam's victory walk, 'so the shot started on her face and ended up on the ceiling'.[52] Morris must have sensed impending doom and cut away in time, as the viewers only saw the shot lurching briefly to the floor then righting itself, as the cameraman lost his footing walking backwards down the green room steps.

Although produced to the highest professional standard, disasters permitting, the *Eurovision Song Contest* was what critics referred to derisively as 'tits and tinsel' entertainment. It was this reputation for highly polished jollity that resulted in the BBC's first foray into satire, *That Was the Week That Was*, coming from the current affairs department rather than LE. For a few short years at the start of the swinging decade, the satire movement was an inexorable force. On 10 May 1961, *Beyond the Fringe* had opened at the Fortune Theatre in

London. With a minimalist set, no costumes and a cast of four recent university graduates, it killed off the West End tradition of revue (sketches and songs, all lavishly staged) single-handedly and almost instantly. Peter Cook's impersonation of Harold Macmillan became a cause célèbre, particularly when Macmillan came to see the show himself. Cook, rather than pulling punches, made the script even more barbed, with references to the prime minister spending his spare evenings sitting in a theatre 'listening to a group of sappy, urgent, vibrant young satirists, with a stupid great grin spread all over my silly old face'.[53]

Five months after the show's West End opening, on 5 October 1961, Cook opened The Establishment, a cabaret nightclub offering satire, jazz and dining. Twenty days after The Establishment opened for business, the first issue of *Private Eye* came out. Satire was talked about as though it was something new, rather than something as old as politics. Acres of newsprint were devoted to the phenomenon. One event in particular counted against the entertainment experts.

In July 1961, having sensed the tide, the BBC light entertainment group had responded by bringing over American satirist Mort Sahl for a one-off special with a celebrity audience. Unfortunately, the show had been judged a failure by the director general, Hugh Carleton Greene. He blamed LE for treating it like a variety show, with an introduction from Frank Muir and Denis Norden and a musical interlude from singer Georgia Brown and the John Dankworth Orchestra. Bill Cotton, as the show's producer, blamed Sahl for not tailoring his material to a British audience. Greene prevailed and declared that satire should be handled by the current affairs department.

When he took the job of BBC director general in 1960, it was clear that Greene – brother of the novelist Graham Greene – was a very different creature to his predecessors. His immediate predecessor, Sir Ian Jacob, had been a career soldier before joining the BBC – a fair man, but a disciplinarian and very much traditional authority. Greene shared the trade of journalism with William Haley who had been DG between 1944 and 1952, but Haley was another solemn and conservative figure, whereas Greene was not. Greene was the polar opposite of Lord Reith, but both stamped their own personalities and sensibilities on the organization, unlike many who have run the BBC. Reith's BBC was didactic and dictatorial. Under Greene, who knew the value of awkward questions, the BBC was no less rigorous, but less inclined to preach. Reith abhorred levity, Greene encouraged it – as long as it was well done and preferably possessed of a core of intelligence.

When it came to satire, Greene had experienced first-hand the political cabarets of Berlin in the thirties, when he had been working there for the *Daily Telegraph*. However, despite the support of Greene, it is unlikely that television would have been able or willing to transmit satire, had the satire boom happened any earlier. In 1944, as a wartime measure, the BBC had adopted a rule that forbade the broadcasting of any material on subjects due to be debated in Parliament within the next fourteen days. Unfortunately, many emergency measures taken in times of national crisis have a habit of becoming permanent fixtures.[54] In July 1955, the Postmaster General, Sir Charles Hill – known to wireless listeners as 'the radio doctor', thanks to his wartime medical broadcasts, but now a politician – made the rule formal and externally enforced, rather than self-imposed. When commercial television came along, Independent Television News argued that the rule applied only to the BBC and began testing its limits. The breaking point came during the Suez crisis in 1956, when prime minister Sir Anthony Eden and leader of the opposition Hugh Gaitskell were allowed on air to speak to the nation about a matter that the broadcasters could not report meaningfully. The absurd rule was finally broken in 1958 by Granada's coverage of the Rochdale by-election, and was not enforced subsequently.

The first satirical salvo on British television was fired by ATV on 29 September 1962 in the form of *On the Braden Beat* with Bernard Braden. To be fair, the show was more topical than satirical – part chat show, part sketch show, part miscellany of reactions to the week's events. Braden and his wife Barbara Kelly were Canadian actors who had arrived in Britain in the late forties and found almost instant favour on the airwaves, Kelly becoming a regular on *What's My Line*. *Breakfast with Braden* had begun on the BBC Home Service in January 1950; it was scripted by Muir and Norden, and broadcast on Saturday mornings at 8.15, an unusually early time for a comedy show. When it returned in October 1950 after a summer break, it had moved to Monday lunchtimes, being retitled, for some reason, *Bedtime with Braden*. Braden and Kelly were also early into television, first in 1951 with a BBC sitcom that laboured under the rather cumbersome title of *An Evening at Home with Bernard Braden and Barbara Kelly*, then in 1955 with a television transfer of the radio show, called *Bath-Night with Braden*.

Following *On the Braden Beat* came a contribution from Associated-Rediffusion – perhaps, the most conservative of all the commercial television companies – called *What the Public Wants*. It was the brainchild of Elkan Allan, who had been appointed A-R's head of entertainment the previous year. In many ways, Allan was an unlikely candidate for the job. He had begun his career as a journalist, making his name on the *Daily Express*, then still a colossus in Fleet Street. He moved into television on A-R's current affairs magazine *This Week*, where his contemporaries included Jeremy Isaacs and Cyril Bennett, both later to become significant television executives. Eventually, he progressed to become the programme's editor. In 1961, he received a summons from the company's general manager John McMillan with an offer of promotion:

> In 1961, I went to Vietnam and did *The Quiet War*, which was a major documentary. Just before I went, John McMillan said 'When you come back, would you like to be head of light entertainment?' I was surprised. I think it was because I had teenage children and had always been very aware of what was going on in the world of entertainment. I was always a very showbizzy kind of person. I said yes on one condition: that we drop the word light and just call it entertainment. Because it seemed to me to predispose whatever one did, if it were called light entertainment, to frivolity, and that wasn't necessarily what I wanted to do or John McMillan wanted to do.[55]

Despite Allan's background, *What the Public Wants*, featuring a cast of near-unknown revue performers, turned out not to be what the public wanted. *The Times* called it 'a feeble and irritating little show that suffers from the callow superciliousness of undergraduate revue'[56] and it lasted a mere four editions from its delayed debut on Thursday 1 November 1962 until its exit on 6 December. The main problem was the tight regulatory grip kept by the Independent Television Authority, which rendered the show's satirical attack toothless – especially the rule barring 'any offensive representation or reference to a living person'. (This part of the Television Act was repealed in 1963.) However, Allan acknowledged other faults: 'We had the wrong people. There were some good things in it – Tubby Hayes' band – but it didn't work.'[57]

The BBC's Royal Charter made it self-regulating, subject only to the scrutiny of the Board of Governors and the stipulations of the Charter itself. Any attempts at satire, if backed by the board of management, were on much firmer ground than an equivalent show at ITV. With the director general on your side, you were unassailable. This was the position that Ned Sherrin found himself in, when called upon to develop *That Was the Week That Was*. Sherrin had begun his career at ATV in Birmingham, before moving to the BBC, spending a short while as a very junior member of LE staff before heading to the television talks department. There he worked on the early evening magazine programme *Tonight*, under Welshman Donald Baverstock and Scot Alasdair Milne, both of whom were known for their phenomenal, and largely justified, self-belief. In 1961, Baverstock became assistant controller of programmes for the whole of BBC TV, and was approached by satirical ringleaders John Bird and Peter Cook about doing a show styled on their performances at Cook's Establishment club. Independently, Sherrin was casting around for ideas that would fit a late Saturday night slot. He paid a visit to the US to see the chat show giants in action, just as chat show pioneer Jack Paar was handing over to Johnny Carson on NBC's *Tonight Show*, but concluded that the format wouldn't work on British television. Instead, he turned his attention to the satire boom, and decided that

John Bird was the ideal host for a satirical show. Bird overcame his initial annoyance at having his own idea sold back to him, only to find that he was already committed to a US tour by The Establishment's company when Sherrin wanted to record the pilot. Instead, he suggested his then flatmate, Footlights contemporary David Frost, as a replacement host.

There was a small problem with the suggestion, in that Frost was working for a rival: namely Elkan Allan at Associated-Rediffusion. Upon leaving Cambridge, he had applied for one of the company's graduate traineeships, as a day job while he did his satirical comedy act at various nightspots. Unfortunately, he didn't make the final two,[58] much to Allan's amazement:

> I was absolutely knocked out with him and I said 'Obviously he's got to be one.' The head of drama and the third person said 'Oh no, we can't have him. He's much too ebullient. He'd be a headache.' I said 'I want him and if you don't take him on this scheme, I will take him on, on my departmental budget, because I think he's fantastic.' They said 'You're welcome to him.' So, he came and worked as a researcher for me. He was so bright, so clever, so funny. He was part of the satire thing, although the Fringe people hated him. They thought he was a real hanger-on. He did a one-man stand up at the Blue Angel, which I went to see, and thought he was terrific. So he came and worked for us.[59]

Frost's first outing in front of the camera was presenting one of Allan's brainwaves, a show about the latest dance craze, the Twist. It was enough of a success for Allan to plan two follow-ups: *Let's Twist in Paris*, then *Let's Twist on the Riviera*:

> So, David, I, and a film crew went down to Cannes where the Whisky A Go Go – the original discotheque – was, and unfortunately it just pissed with rain. If you go to the Riviera, you've got to have the weather. I said 'OK, nobody knows it's raining, let's pretend it's not. You do this with sunglasses and the summer suit.' We did the whole show in the rain and nobody ever knew. It was a good show, it worked. He was very good, did

it terribly well. Then of course, just when we were building him up, he elected to go to the BBC and work for Ned, and in fact broke his contract with Rediffusion.[60]

Frost's motivation wasn't economic. When the BBC's interest in him became apparent, Associated-Rediffusion offered him a four-year contract worth £18,000, not including appearance fees for shows. In contrast, the BBC were offering £650 for thirteen weeks of preparation, plus £135 per programme for presenting, if it made it to a series. 'I was convinced that TW3 [as That Was the Week That Was soon became known] had a future, albeit currently undefined,' Frost said thirty years later. 'TW3 was the sort of show I would have wanted to watch.'[61] As well as suggesting the host, Bird also provided the BBC satire show with its title, adapting the old 'That was Shell, that was' advertising slogan. The initial plan was to have Frost co-hosting with Guardian journalist Brian Redhead, linking the various sketches and musical items, and a pilot on these lines was made on 15 July 1962, with support from John Bird, Eleanor Bron and Jeremy Geidt from The Establishment. A second pilot was made on 29 September, without Redhead, and with the ambitious Frost showing an increasing inclination to regard himself as co-producer.

Only Frost, Bernard Levin (drafted in from the Spectator magazine to tackle relatively serious debates), and the cartoonist Timothy Birdsall, who drew marvellous works of satirical art live on air, as well as performing in sketches, were from a university background.[62] Of the show's repertory company, Willie Rushton had gone straight from Shrewsbury and National Service into cartooning and generally being wonderful, while Romford-born singer Millicent Martin had appeared on Tonight, performing topical songs, usually written by Sherrin and his long-term collaborator Caryl Brahms. Roy Kinnear and Lance Percival both came from the theatre, Kinnear having made a big impression in Keith Waterhouse and Willis Hall's revue England, Our England, and Kenneth Cope was appearing as Jed Stone in Coronation Street. Meanwhile, the writers were largely drawn from the mainstream press, rather than the ranks of conventional gagsmiths. Peter Tinniswood and David Nobbs had met as reporters on the *Sheffield Star*, the Peter Lewis–Peter Dobereiner partnership emanated from the *Daily Mail* and Michael Frayn was on the *Guardian*. The chief writer – with particular responsibility for co-writing Frost's material with the host himself – came from just outside the Fleet Street club, in the form of Christopher Booker, co-founder of *Private Eye*.

The scripts for sketches were usually in by Wednesday, but other material continued to arrive right up until the last minute, usually by taxi. The hectic pace meant that Sherrin soon decided to delegate some of his production responsibilities. Jack Duncan, a friend of Booker and Richard Ingrams – Booker's successor as *Eye* editor – from Oxford, came in to direct the sketch rehearsals. 'Ned realized that he couldn't cope with all the political stuff and spare the time to go down and do the sketches,' he recalls. 'I always thought that Willie had suggested me, but years ago, Booker told me it was him. So, I was chosen on a three-week contract.' Duncan's first move was to tame Frost:

> Frostie was in the sketches and really wanted to direct them all himself. I could see that this was going to lead nowhere so, wet and green as I was, I went to Ned and said 'I don't really want Frost in any more sketches, please. I'll do the sketches, Frost is a cabaret artist and a commentator. All the rest of them are actors, his style is completely different from theirs, he doesn't fit in any way. He doesn't want me there anyway.' So I got Frost banned from sketches. It was hectic, but brilliant – the best time in one's life.[63]

Many of the most memorable items from *TW3* were politically inspired, such as Booker and Frost's devastating *This Is Your Life* spoof dedicated to demolishing the useless home secretary Henry Brooke, and Gerald Kaufman's 'Silent Men of Westminster' item about MPs who never spoke in the Commons. The show also satirized the world of entertainment far more ruthlessly than an LE inside job would perhaps have dared. The first programme contained a Peter Cook-written send-up of *Jim's Inn*, one of the most popular ITV advertising magazines or 'admags', in which blatant plugs for products or services were inserted into a narrative drama or comedy show:

NIGE: Excuse me noticing it, but I didn't know you could run to a tie like that, Baz. It must have set you back all of 15 guineas.

BAZ: No, I'm rather pleased to see your eye lighting on this tie, because, in fact, it wasn't altogether as costly as that.

NIGE: How much was it?

BAZ: Three and sixpence, a matter of fact. I got it at Arthur Purvis, Marine Parade, Gorleston. It's a dacron tetralax masturpene in the new non-iron histamine luxipac.[64]

Jim's Inn was Associated-Rediffusion's production, featuring Jimmy Hanley as the landlord of a pub, while Southern had the benefit of Kenneth Horne in *Trader Horne*. These fixtures of the early commercial television landscape were to be outlawed in 1963, as part of the ITA's desire to make ITV as respectable as it was profitable.

That first *TW3* also featured a damning 'tribute' to Norrie Paramor, the EMI record producer behind the success of Cliff Richard and the Shadows. His tendency to put his own songs on B-sides (the royalty on a B-side being the same as the A-side that sold the disc), or give the publishing rights to his brother's company, were of particular note. Later in the run, a similar 'tribute' appeared, this time concerning *Oliver!* composer Lionel Bart, and the alarming similarities his tunes bore to older songs. In the finale, David Kernan sang Rodgers and Hart's 'Mountain Greenery' and Willie Rushton sang Hoagy Carmichael's 'Heart and Soul' as counterpoint to Millie Martin singing Bart's 'Fings Ain't Wot They Used To Be', Bart's song bearing an uncanny resemblance to both.

Another notable *TW3* item where LE met hard-edged satire was Herbert Kretzmer's still-powerful song about the revival of lynchings in the deep South, done in the style of the Black and White Minstrels, with vocal accompaniment from the real George Mitchell singers.[65]

Best remembered of all, though, was Keith Waterhouse and Willis Hall's evocation of an old-school comic – played by Roy Kinnear – entering the satirical ring with pun-laden references to Chancellor of the Exchequer Reginald Maudling, only to pull all his punches with the catchphrase 'No, but seriously, boys and girls, he's doing a grand job.'

This was in stark contrast to 6 April 1963, the night when a real old-school comic was enticed onto *TW3*, only to steal the show. By 1962, Frankie Howerd's career was in the doldrums, after a long run of success on the radio and on stage. In a fit of inspiration, Peter Cook persuaded him to take the unlikely step of performing at his Establishment club in September. Aided by a script from the combined might of Eric Sykes, Johnny Speight, Ray Galton and Alan Simpson, Howerd was a smash hit. It had been Speight's idea to play up the incongruity of the artist and the venue, painting Howerd as out of touch, so that the satirical punches had an even greater effect when they came. Ned Sherrin saw Howerd's resurrection, and sent associate producer Jack Duncan to sound him out on his normal turf:

> Ned sent me down to Eastbourne to watch Frankie on the end of the pier and it was a disaster, really. I thought he was brilliant, but the audience didn't. We went for a cup of tea and a sandwich afterwards in a really dreadful café, not even with the merits of a greasy spoon. People recognized him, and they deliberately made rude comments like 'Not a bad show, but the comedy was dreadful' as they passed by. I've never heard such nasty comments. He was really hurt. He was a delicate soul, as we know. I travelled back in the car with him and his pianist, who was also his driver. He was so depressed on the way back, and I didn't blame him, but I thought he was wonderful. I said to Ned 'He didn't go down well in Eastbourne, but I think he's terrific and we should have a go.' On that journey back, I got a measure of the sort of depression he felt about these mediocre people who sneered at his genius. He cared, he really, really cared.[66]

That care was apparent in the pains he took to ensure that his *TW3* booking made the Establishment success look like an out-of-town try-out. A fresh script was commissioned and Howerd was allotted an eight-minute slot.[67] On the night, Howerd's monologue ran for thirteen minutes, but nobody minded, for two reasons. Firstly, *TW3* was open-ended, being the last programme of the evening. Its length was dictated only by available material and overtime payments for the crew. (At the start of the second series, controller of programmes Stuart Hood tried to rein the show in by scheduling a serial based on *The Third Man* immediately afterwards. Sherrin and Frost conspired to give the plot away at the end of each *TW3* until it was axed.) Secondly, he was going down a storm. In Bernard Levin's discussion segment that week, his opponent had been society coiffeur 'Teasy-Weasy' Raymond, so Howerd claimed that the booking had come about after a chance encounter with Frost ('You know, the one who wears his hair back to front') under Raymond's driers. Then an insult for Sherrin ('Nice man. Underneath'), a reference to *Panorama* presenter Robin Day ('Such cruel glasses') and finally off into a monologue about the Budget. He had pitched the act perfectly, and that one appearance revitalized his career.

In addition to the open-ended nature of the show, an element of looseness was apparent in Sherrin's directing style. He made no attempts to disguise the mechanics of a television studio, with cameras and booms moving in and out of shot freely and the audience often fully visible. The sets for each item were basic and stylized, while for Frost's pieces to camera, the background was the bare studio wall. Other loosening influences were present, both for the performers and the audience. 'Being Talks, there was a wonderful piss-up before and after the show, which you wouldn't have got with Light Entertainment ... and the studio audience were served with the most appalling mulled wine, served by girls in black fishnet stockings,' recalled Willie Rushton.[68]

Although director general Hugh Greene thought satire on television a good idea, he lived in fear of one or more BBC governors resigning over the programme. This was despite the fact that the huffing and puffing from Postmaster General Reginald Bevins had come to nothing – the result of a personal note from Harold Macmillan urging him not to take action against the show since 'being laughed over . . . is better than to be ignored'.[69] The prospect of a general election made the decision easy. *TW3* would be 'rested' for election year. In reality, it never returned, although satire did, in the form of *Not So Much a Programme, More a Way of Life*, *BBC3* and *The Frost Report*. In the meantime, other genres of programming were in need of more urgent attention.

CHAPTER FIVE

'Can you see what it is yet?'

After the initial burst of *Six Five Special* and *Oh Boy!*, pop music on television had lost its way a little. None of the successor shows, such as the BBC's *Drumbeat* or ABC's *Dig This!*, caught the viewers' imagination in the same way. BBC Television managed one big hit pop show in the form of *Juke Box Jury*, a Saturday teatime fixture from 1959 to 1967, but it was a sedate panel game in which celebrities declared the week's new releases to be hits or misses under the control of the suave David Jacobs. In 1961, ABC producer Philip Jones took a step in the right direction, by combining the disc-grading system of *JBJ* with live performances from hit artists of the day. The result was *Thank Your Lucky Stars,* hosted from Birmingham by Radio Luxembourg disc jockey Keith Fordyce and his BBC Light Programme counterpart Brian Matthew. Following a trial run in the Midlands and North between April and June 1961, the show was networked that September.

The best-remembered part of *TYLS* was the 'Spin-A-Disc' segment, where a guest DJ would play the latest releases for three teenagers, who voted on them. Instead of *Juke Box Jury*'s simple yay or nay, the *Thank Your Lucky Stars* panel graded each release, with five points being the top score. So it was that a Black Country teenager called Janice Nicholls became a national television personality, known for her enthusiastic judgement on many releases: 'Oi'll give it foive.' In performance terms, the first networked show featured singer Eden Kane, born Richard Sarstedt, one of the three Sarstedt brothers to have a UK hit single. Also appearing in that debut transmission was actress Shani Wallis introducing 18-year-old Roy Tierney, whom she'd discovered singing in a coffee bar, as well as comic actors Harry Fowler and Mario Fabrizi introducing singer and comedian Kenny Lynch, followed by a burst of the then hip traditional jazz from Bobby Mickleburgh's Confederates. In November, Fordyce dropped out, leaving Matthew as sole host. By this time, the show was starting to attract enough big names to justify its title, including Cliff Richard and the Shadows, Petula Clark, 'Mr' Acker Bilk, Helen Shapiro and Billy Fury.

While serviceable, *Thank Your Lucky Stars* was a traditional variety show, only focused on pop bands. The next revolutionary step in pop music television came from an unlikely source. Associated-Rediffusion had been content to make excellent current affairs and drama programmes, and leave the entertainment to the rest of the ITV network. When Elkan Allan took over as head of entertainment in 1961, the job could have been viewed as a sinecure. The department had two big hit game shows, in the form of *Take Your Pick* and *Double Your Money*, to justify its existence, while ATV, ABC and Granada were all competing to get entertainment shows on screen. Allan decided against an easy life and began tackling the department's weaknesses:

> Quizzes and games pretty much took care of themselves. With *Take Your Pick* and *Double Your Money* going, there was actually nothing to be done with them. They theoretically came under me. I felt I had no knowledge of or expertise in situation comedy, so I recruited Sid Colin and he came in and did that as my right-hand man, as it were. I left that whole side to him. That left me with music, in which I was very interested.[1]

Initially, Allan was thinking in terms of a show for a regional opt-out slot, and he had a presenter already available in the form of Keith Fordyce. 'Keith Fordyce had a long-term contract [with Rediffusion], so I discussed with John [McMillan, programme controller] what else we could put him into,' Allan recalled. 'I said "Let's do a programme called *The Weekend Starts Here*, and let's have all the things, all the events and activities which young people can do in London that weekend." Then I thought that was a bit of a clumsy title, so I said "Let's call it *Ready Steady Go . . . The Weekend Starts Here.*"' The pilot was made at Associated-Rediffusion's Kingsway headquarters, and looked to be unspectacular until halfway through:

It had all kinds of elements in it. It had film, theatre, even, I think sport. Among the things was music. Concerts you could go to. We had Brian Poole and the Tremeloes, who were doing a concert at Brixton that weekend, in the studio and they were due to play twice – once at the start of the programme, once at the end. It had one commercial break in the middle. We set the studio in a conventional way with a stage and rows of seats. In the audience was my 14–15-year-old son, Andy, and his sister Mary. Anyway, when Brian Poole played his first number, one or two of the kids got up and did a little bit of dancing. We encouraged people to do what they wanted.

In the break, which could be as long as we wanted because it wasn't live, it was being recorded, Andy came bustling up to me and said 'Daddy, daddy, daddy, you've got to take the chairs away so that people can dance.' I said 'Jolly good idea' and ordered that the chairs be taken away. When Brian Poole did his second number, everybody danced and suddenly you could see what the programme should be. It shouldn't be film, stage and sport. It should just be music. And so we went on the air with a music programme and we were terribly lucky because we just caught the moment when the wave was forming on which the Beatles, the Kinks and the Small Faces were riding. It was extraordinary. We just caught that wave.[2]

The pilot was such a success that the show went straight onto the ITV network on 9 August 1963, with Fordyce at the helm and some assistance from a voice and face of youth. 'Keith is a tremendous professional, and he was able to hold the show together,' Allan explained, 'but it was obvious to me that what was needed was one, possibly two young presenters of the same age as the target audience. So we advertised for a researcher, but I had in mind all the time that this person would share with Keith the presenting and the interviewing.' The 2,000 applicants were whittled down to three on the final shortlist: Anne Nightingale, Michael Aldred and Cathy MacGowan. At the audition, Allan asked them to interview each other, advocating what they felt was most important for teenagers out of music, sex or fashion:

> Cathy immediately said fashion and we had this three-way audition conversation. They were all good, and I took on Cathy and Michael Aldred, who didn't last. Cathy was so strong, so good, so nice, so bright and clever, and so much of the audience [in terms of age and outlook] that she very quickly dominated that whole side of the show.[3]

Another strong influence on *RSG* was Allan's erstwhile secretary, Vicki Wickham. 'After dictating a memo to Vicki about the concept of the show, she put down her pencil and her notebook, and said "Elkan, I'm very sorry, but I've got to work on that show. I've got to. It's made for me." She became the rock on which the whole thing was based. It was she, I think, who went down to Eel Pie Island and heard this group whom no one had ever heard of. She came back on the Monday morning, and said "I saw this absolutely marvellous group, we've got to book them. They're called the Rolling Stones."'

Before long, musicians and cultural figures of that tumultuous time came to regard Television House on a Friday night as a social club. 'If swinging London had a centre, it was the green room at *Ready Steady Go*,' Allan recalled. 'Everybody came. David Hockney used to drop in. The Beatles dropped in whether they were in the show or not. Pretty well everybody was welcome and it was a wonderful thing. Poor old Rediffusion didn't know what had hit it.'

At the time that *RSG* took to the air, 'poor old Rediffusion' was still run by Thomas Brownrigg, a former naval captain who regarded the company as a ship. Time was measured in bells and rules were rules.

In 1964, Brownrigg retired, and the company was rebranded as Rediffusion London, complete with a sleek new corporate identity and a John Dankworth signature tune to replace its old march. Nonetheless, even hip, swinging, new-look Rediffusion must have emitted a shudder at one of Allan's more lavish stunts:

> We recruited the dancers by going round the clubs, and giving tickets to people who danced very well. I thought this was a bit elitist and unfair, so we announced on air, if you want to be a dancer on *Ready Steady Go*, be at Rediffusion at five o'clock next Tuesday. We had 10,000 people turn up and Kingsway was closed to traffic by the police. I had them come in the front door of Rediffusion and that's where the first loudspeaker was, they started dancing, and danced their way through the building and out the back. There was a back door which backed onto the LSE [London School of Economics]. By the time they were out the door, they'd either got a ticket or they didn't. It got us on the news.[4]

Part of the show's appeal was the way in which it didn't disguise the mechanics of television production, rather as *That Was the Week That Was* hadn't. 'Because of my documentary background, I said let's have a pop show that is openly and honestly in a television studio,' says Allan. 'Let's use the gantries and the spiral staircases. Let's see the cameras and be honest about it. Then, I still wasn't satisfied because of the innate phoniness of miming and so I said let's go the whole hog and have it all played live. It meant moving to Wembley because you couldn't do live in the little studio at Kingsway.'

At Shepherd's Bush, this activity had been watched with interest by Donald Baverstock, one of Grace Wyndham Goldie's golden boys in current affairs and now BBC1 controller. He asked head of variety Bill Cotton Junior whether the BBC shouldn't attempt a similar show. Cotton replied that, after years of US domination, enough of the top twenty was British to make it a possibility. Bands like the Beatles, the Rolling Stones and the Kinks made Britain the epicentre of the pop world. So it was that *Top of the Pops* began on New Year's Day 1964. There was no room at Television Centre, the Television Theatre or Lime Grove for the new show, the only available option being the Manchester television studio, a converted church at Dickenson Road, Rusholme. Sir Bill Cotton takes up the story:

> I said 'Fine, we'll do it there.' A lot of people said 'You can't do a pop programme, with all the imperatives that has, from a disused church in Manchester.' As I pointed out, we are an itinerant profession, we go where the work is. And they all turned up. The bands came from Liverpool and Manchester, but they were all living in London. And I said at the time that it would either run forever or be off in six weeks. It was the first time that you could actually say to a producer, in this case, Johnnie Stewart, 'I want to do a programme, and to be on that programme, you have to be in the top twenty, and there will be no other way of getting on it.' I knew how the charts worked. There were several charts, but in the end, we got one that represented all of them.[5]

Jimmy Savile presented the first show, which featured an appearance from the Beatles performing their latest single 'I Want to Hold Your Hand' – pre-recorded to prevent a roadblock in Rusholme. Savile was one of four regular presenters, the others being David Jacobs, Alan Freeman and Pete Murray. However, the presenters had to share the limelight with their producer, Johnnie Stewart, who appeared in the end credits of each show, in silhouette, with flopping quiff and jacket over his shoulder. Another producer made his mark at the front of the programme, albeit anonymously, as Jim Moir was responsible for the famous 'It's number one, it's *Top of the Pops*' announcement each week. In 1966, the show moved down from Manchester to studio G at Lime Grove, where it went from strength to strength.

A less fondly remembered series from Elkan Allan's time in charge of entertainment at Rediffusion was *Stars and Garters*, an attempt to bring the flavour of East End pub entertainment into the homes of viewers. 'That was a very interesting mistake,' Allan admitted. 'Dan Farson did for me a music hall documentary called *Time Gentlemen*

Please, about pub entertainers. It was terrific and brilliantly directed by Rollo Gamble. So we thought, I thought, let's do it every week. We will recreate a pub atmosphere in the studio and we will have one of the people from *Time Gentlemen Please*, Ray Martine, as a link man. It was a great failure. I never liked it. It was the opposite of what I was about. It was phoney and what we should have done was filmed in a pub.'[6]

The ideal choice would have been Dan Farson's own pub, the Waterman's Arms on the Isle of Dogs, and the decision not to use his facilities rankled. Allan suggests that the place was in such chaos, it made more sense to make it in the studio: 'He was ripped off by the barman, everybody, but it was a very jolly place. I used to go down there. But he was just screwed and, of course, he had his great weakness for pretty boys. He was always pissed.'[7]

Despite the problems, *Stars and Garters* ran for four series between 1963 and 1965, the final run being renamed *New Stars and Garters*. In place of Martine came actress Jill Browne from ATV hospital drama *Emergency Ward 10*, aided by Willie Rushton and his future wife, the Australian actress Arlene Dorgan. All three departed from the series in mid-run. Allan presented the departures as sackings, whereas Rushton insisted that all three had resigned and been double-crossed by Allan. The reasons given for the resignations were that all three had been told that they were the star of the show and that Keith Waterhouse, Willis Hall, Ray Galton and Alan Simpson were all on board as writers, which was not the case. The disagreement led to a page-long denunciation in *Private Eye*, of which Rushton was a founder, under the headline 'Ginger Judas'. Unfortunately, the article also suggested that Allan had been guilty of plagiarism, with regard to *Ready Steady Go* and several other Rediffusion shows. It went on, gleefully, to describe Allan as 'one of the most despised figures in television', before recounting a joke about Allan going to a 'fancy dress ball stark naked, covered in deodorant, in the role of an armpit'.[8] Allan sued:

Rediffusion had Lord Goodman as their libel lawyer. His eyes lit up, because *Private Eye* had been very nasty about him. He was well on the shit list. He said to me 'Well done, we can close the buggers down now. You'll get so much money for this.' I said 'I don't want to close them down, that would be a very wrong thing to do, in my opinion.' He was very upset with me. He said 'Well, you can do what you like, write your own apology and name any charity you like and I will guarantee that the apology goes in. That's what happened.[9]

Shortly after the disaster of *Stars and Garters*, Allan moved to become an executive producer (special projects), as Eric Maschwitz had been after his departure from the BBC. American musician/producer Buddy Bregman came in from the BBC to take over Rediffusion's LE programmes. Best known as an arranger and producer for the Verve label, particularly his work with Ella Fitzgerald, Bregman had joined the BBC in early 1964, after producing some successful TV specials in Europe. His impeccable contacts earned him the acceptance of his fellow producers, including Terry Henebery. 'He'd been brought in, this great whiz-kid from America,' Henebery says. 'Buddy got some great stuff going – he got all these artists coming in from America, these cabaret artists.'[10] Unfortunately for his reputation, there were other areas where the existing BBC staff were ahead of him:

We used to go down and have a right laugh watching him direct. He'd be smoking a pipe in the gallery, he'd have a score out and he'd be saying to the vision mixer 'And four,' and the vision mixer would say 'I can't take camera four.' He's doing it by audio, he's not looking at the monitors. He was accurate to the tee, but he wasn't watching the previews, the guys hadn't got the shots up. It was hysterical.[11]

One of the highlights of Bregman's time in charge of entertainment at Rediffusion was *Hippodrome*, a lavish variety series produced in the gigantic studio five at Wembley, which ran through the autumn of 1966. As a co-production with the US network CBS, the show was produced using two sets of cameras, one in 405-line monochrome for the UK viewers, another in 525-line colour for US transmission. The other advantage of US input was that the show could call on major stars from the other side of the Atlantic. One edition, featuring a troupe of footballing dogs among the turns, was hosted by the unlikely figure of Woody Allen.

Less glorious was Rediffusion's decision to poach singer Kathy Kirby from the BBC, where she had her own series, in a deal engineered by her manager, ex-bandleader Bert Ambrose. Sir Bill Cotton remembers how he found out that she was leaving:

> I got to hear of it on the last show that she did in a series. I thought we were going to do another series. The number one cameraman told me 'Well, that's the last we're going to see of her, then, Bill.' 'What do you mean?' 'She's going to Rediffusion. I've got a mate who's a cameraman there and her show's on their schedule.' So, I went into her dressing room, and the three of them [Kirby, Ambrose and her agent Sidney Grace] were standing there. I said 'Is it true that you're going to Rediffusion?' She looked at Sidney Grace, then she looked at Bert, and they looked at each other and then they looked down. I said 'Well, it's perfectly obvious that the answer's yes. Thanks very much,' and I walked out.[12]

In the event, the Rediffusion deal fell apart before the show could be made, and Kirby's old BBC slot had been filled. By the end of its time as an ITV franchise holder in 1968, Rediffusion had almost given up on LE, and was once again subcontracting its entertainment output, this time to David Frost's company, David Paradine Productions. This link brought in the Ronnie Corbett sitcom *No, That's Me Over Here* and the proto-Monty Python sketch series *At Last the 1948 Show*, starring John Cleese, Graham Chapman, Marty Feldman and Tim Brooke-Taylor, with 'the lovely' Aimi MacDonald.

★

While the ITV companies produced many expensive, lavish shows in their first few years, they had long been criticized for caring more about the bottom line than the 405 lines on the screen. In the early years, they had led a hand-to-mouth existence and there were many who confidently predicted the demise of one or all of the commercial contractors. By 1958, however, Associated-Rediffusion had turned the corner into profit, notching up £5.1 million before tax. Soon, the whole system was in rude health, as might be expected from a lightly regulated monopoly. Unwelcome attention had been drawn to this by Roy Thomson, the Canadian newspaper magnate behind Scottish Television, when he declared that an ITV franchise was 'a licence to print money'.

There were agonies about the way in which this profit was achieved. In particular, there seemed to be a reliance on relatively cheap American imports, such as the police series *Dragnet* and the situation comedy *I Love Lucy*, two of the biggest hits of early ITV. The criticisms received official backing when a government committee of inquiry into radio and television broadcasting, under the chairmanship of Sir Harry Pilkington of the Pilkington Brothers glass company, reported its findings in July 1962.[13] It bemoaned ITV's slender commitment to public service broadcasting and noted the massive profitability of the companies. As a result of the Pilkington Report, an 11 per cent levy on all net profits made by ITA franchisees was to be paid to the Exchequer. On the face of it, the government appeared to be admitting defeat and opting for a financial cut to keep quiet. In reality, the levy had very beneficial consequences for the quality of programming. It made sense to plough money back into programmes rather than letting it become taxable profit.

In contrast, the Pilkington Committee thought that the BBC was very much on the right track and recommended that the Corporation be given responsibility for a third television channel, using the newly-allocated ultra-high frequency band. The launch of BBC2 in April 1964 was to result in a further massive expansion in the BBC's programming capability and range, particularly in light entertainment. To meet the demand, production assistants and floor managers received long-awaited promotions to producer, while they were replaced in turn by the producers of the future.

From the outset, BBC2 was intended to be different to the other channels. The picture was to be better, the channel being the pioneer of the new higher-definition 625-line transmissions.[14] From 1967, it was to be the first European network to broadcast regularly in colour. Under the banner 'the Seven Faces of the Week', the programmes were to be scheduled around loose nightly themes: Mondays and Fridays were for family shows, Tuesday was set aside for educational fare, Wednesday for repeats and Thursday for minority programmes. Overall, they were meant to offer an intellectual alternative to the mainstream, crowd-pleasing fare on the existing channels. That's not to say that BBC2 did not aim to entertain. The bulk of its launch night on Monday 20 April 1964 was to be supplied by the light entertainment group: a performance by the surrealist musical comedy group the Alberts, a lavish production of *Kiss Me Kate*, then forty-five minutes of comedy. The key difference here was that the comedian featured was the Russian Arkady Raikin – and the show was to be conducted largely in his native language.

On the night, however, BBC2 proved different in a rather more unplanned way. When the BBC launched its television service in 1936, the occasion went off without a hitch. Similarly, the reopening of the service in 1946 had been flawless, as had the launch of commercial television in 1955. This time, however, a fire at Battersea Power Station deprived most of west London of electricity. Crucially, this included BBC Television Centre in Shepherd's Bush. Still based at Alexandra Palace, BBC News was unaffected, so viewers in the London area who had shelled out for a flash new 625-line set did get some sort of BBC2 broadcast – in the shape of newsreader Gerald Priestland explaining the situation and reading the news bulletins. By the time the fire was extinguished a couple of hours later, the decision had been taken by BBC2 controller Michael Peacock to delay the launch, including the fireworks display from Southend-on-Sea, until the following day, ditching the scheduled educational programmes. So it was that the first scheduled programme shown on BBC2 was *Play School*, broadcast at 11am on 21 April 1964 . Launch night itself began that evening at 7.20pm with presenter Denis Tuohy pointedly blowing out a candle and introducing the previous night's delights.

The only survivor from the original second night schedule was a concert by Duke Ellington's orchestra, forming the first edition of one of BBC2's best-remembered early programmes, *Jazz 625*. The series' producer, Terry Henebery, had joined from radio, as part of the new intake of producers gearing up for the increased workload:

> They were offering secondments to television, so I applied and went through the course at Woodstock Grove, the training establishment down in Shepherd's Bush. You spent [a] six weeks' intensive learning how to be a director, all the grammar, learning to do it the right way. To this day, I still think it's the best training anybody could have ever had, and nobody got it in any other part of the industry. In ITV, you tended to learn it all on the job.

The training course culminated in three practical exercises: directing a scene from a sitcom, illustrating three gramophone records and a free choice. For his free choice, Henebery called in a favour from his days at Aeolian Hall:

> You had a budget of 60 quid. I was ringing up all my contacts from radio, guys like the Alex Welsh band, and saying 'Look Alex, there's a probability that I'll get a series to do. Would you come and do this for threepence?' 'Yeah Tel, we'll do it.' So I did a *Jazz Club* with an audience at Riverside [a former film studio in Hammersmith, used by the BBC between 1954 and 1970]. That final exercise was recorded on 22 November 1963. Now, what happened on that day?

Apart from being the day that Aldous Huxley died, it was also the date of John F. Kennedy's assassination in Dallas. The cliché about Kennedy's death is that you never forget where you were when you heard the news. Henebery remembers well the shocked reaction at Riverside Studios:

> We'd done the rehearsal and somebody said 'Come and have a half of beer, Terry, don't get too tense.' When I got back, the crew were all in the

gallery, and suddenly up comes this 'Normal Service is Interrupted', a newsflash. The atmosphere . . . the hairs, if you had any, on the back of your neck stood up. That was my baptism of fire in many ways.[15]

Meanwhile, up at the BBC's Manchester studios, John Ammonds was producing a Harry Worth sitcom when the news came through, leading to an unlikely meeting of LE and current affairs:

We were recording a show that night in Dickenson Road. First we heard the news that he was badly injured, then that he was dead. And we thought 'Oh God, I hope the audience hasn't heard, because to do a comedy show after that, we'll be in trouble . . .' I don't think they'd heard. So we finished about 8.30, and the commissionaire called me to the front reception desk of the studio. It was Paul Fox, who was then head of current affairs. He said 'Look, we've got some tributes being done live. We've got the Prime Minister,' who was Alec Douglas-Home, and the leader of the Opposition was Harold Wilson. 'We've got him [Wilson] coming over with a very fast police escort from Chester to Manchester. Can you direct this into the network?' I said 'Well there's nobody else here.'

I told Harry he was coming. Wilson arrived at Dickenson Road and they shook hands. The first thing Wilson said was 'Have you got a private phone? I need to ring the Prime Minister and check what he's saying.' The only private phone I could think of in the place was in the kitchen, a little ante-room used for stocking the corned beef and soup. Can you imagine the Leader of the Opposition ringing the Prime Minister with all of this in front of him? This actually happened.

Harry had exactly the same type of Gannex raincoat that he had. [Wilson] went into the studio, and Harry said 'Do you mind if I come up to the gallery?' He was intrigued by the fact that we gave Harold Wilson the five minutes to go and wind-ups [visual cues from the floor manager] that he used to get. So we finished it, Harry came down the stairs with his Gannex coat, and Wilson said 'Thank you, Mr Worth, for bringing my coat.' Harry said 'Oh no, it's mine.' Wilson said 'Are you sure?' It could have come straight out of the show, this confusion routine.[16]

Once the director's course had been completed, the next step for a trainee was to spend some time as a production assistant on 'modest shows like *Juke Box Jury*, learning the craft', but Henebery's call to action as a producer came sooner than he expected. 'Bill Cotton called me in and said "Michael Peacock wants to do the culture end of things, which gets ignored by the one channel. Mike would like to do jazz. Can you come up with a format that would work?"' Henebery returned from a holiday in Portugal with a proposal for 'a formatted programme with interviews and profiles, but they said no, we don't have the money. They wanted to turn it around and get something on the screen quickly.'[17]

Instead, the new show was purely performance-based. The simple, effective presentation of the music – depicting the big-name jazz musicians of the day against a simple cyclorama backcloth, with a superb sound balance – confounded critics in Humphrey Burton's music and arts department. The decision to hand jazz to LE had caused ructions, with one music and arts producer fearing an onslaught of dancing girls and other vulgar distractions. The series was also aided by sympathetic compères: Steve Race at first, and later Humphrey Lyttelton, both musicians themselves. At Henebery's suggestion, it was Race who came up with the show's signature tune, based on the sixth, second and fifth notes of the scale.

At first, it seemed as though *Jazz 625* would be limited to reflecting the very best of the British scene. The first show after the Ducal fanfare had been an all-star jam session featuring George Chisholm, Kenny Baker, Tony Coe, Roy Willox, Laurie Holloway, Jack Fallon and Lennie Hastings; it was followed a week later by the Tubby Hayes Quintet with singer Betty Bennett. The reason for the lack of American artists was a long-standing disagreement between the Musicians' Union and the American Federation of Musicians. From the mid-thirties until 1956, no US musicians had been allowed to appear in the UK and vice versa. The deadlock had been broken by an exchange – a UK tour for Stan Kenton in return for a US trip for Ted Heath's band – but a decade on, the system was still firmly one-for-one. The breakthrough for *Jazz 625* came from agent and promoter Harold Davison, who was responsible for bringing most of the big names to Britain, as Henebery recalls:

> He said 'Would you be interested in Oscar Peterson showing up for it?' I said 'Yes, very, but what about the exchange?' He said 'No problem. He's Canadian, isn't he?' Now, I didn't know then that Oscar wasn't American. And it was the trio, the great trio with Ray Brown and Ed Thigpen. Harold said 'I've got the Dave Clark Five going out and doing *The Ed Sullivan Show*, so I've got exchange. As long as the unions are happy.' So, I had to go to Bill Cotton, my boss, and say 'We've got a marvellous breakthrough, Bill, but I'll need a bit more money on the budget, because it's not coming in at the same rate.' I think it was going to cost £1,000.[18]

At this time, the total budget allocation for a *Jazz 625*, including the cost of the (admittedly minimalist) set and the 35mm film or videotape[19] used to record the show was £800, so £1,000 on the artist alone was quite a leap. But in retrospect, it was great value, as Henebery remembers. 'This is 1964. £1,000 for Oscar Peterson and the trio to record an hour. Can you believe it? So Bill said "Is he any good?" I'll always remember Bill saying that to me. That began the avalanche of people coming in.' Among them was Erroll Garner, who did two editions of the show, perched as usual on a pair of telephone directories atop his piano stool to make up for his lack of height. Other stellar visitors included Clark Terry and Bob Brookmeyer – once in their own right and a second time as guests of John Dankworth – guitarist Wes Montgomery, pianist Bill Evans and ex-Ellingtonian saxophonist Ben Webster, who was making an appearance with Stan Tracey's trio, the house band at Ronnie Scott's club.

Woody Herman's big band also made an appearance. Memorable though their performance was, it was the preparations that stick in

Henebery's mind. 'I had to go to Bill Cotton and ask for some more funds when I was offered the Woody Herman band – that great band with Sal Nistico on tenor. I went to Bill, and he said "Has he still got a band?" I said "Very much; you want to hear it?"' It was agreed that Henebery would go to see the band in Scandinavia and talk about the plans for the show, popping in to see Mel Tormé in Copenhagen to discuss another programme. A flight to Stockholm and a long car journey to the Herman band's hotel brought the news that they were just heading out of town, with the next show a long way away. 'So, I'd gone all the way to Scandinavia to hear the band, and I didn't have the gall to say to anybody that I never heard a note played.' The recce for the show ended up being rather closer to home. 'I went down with the sound engineer, Len Shorey, and another member of my team to Portsmouth Guildhall, and they were booked to do two concerts on the same evening. The first house, there's hardly anybody in. Tubby Hayes and some of the guys had come down from London to hear the band. They start playing 'Blue Flame', the curtain went up and you were pinching yourself. When they did the show for us, it was fantastic.'[20]

The Television Theatre was a regular venue for *Jazz 625* recordings, but many editions were made as outside broadcasts at venues such as the Marquee club or the London Academy of Music and Dramatic Art. In 1966, the programme morphed into *Jazz Goes to College*, made entirely on location at seats of learning, as Henebery explains. 'My PA on that was Jim Moir. He'd been to university himself, at Nottingham, and he loved getting on the phone to the student unions and saying "Hello, this is the BBC here. We're thinking of recording in the Union, and bringing the Modern Jazz Quartet in." They'd say "We can't afford the bloody Modern Jazz Quartet." He'd say "No, no. We pay you a facility fee."'[21]

LE made many other memorable contributions to the early BBC2 schedules, not least its comedy flagship, *Not Only ... But Also ...*, which began its first fortnightly run on 9 January 1965. The first show was recorded as a one-off showcase for the comedic and musical talents of Dudley Moore, with his *Beyond the Fringe* colleague Peter Cook as a guest. However, a sketch took flight in which Cook and Moore sat at a pub table, wearing cloth caps and mufflers, as they traded unlikely tales of Hollywood stars banging on their windows, demanding sexual favours:

> Bloody Greta Garbo – stark naked save for a shortie nightie. She was hanging on to the window sill, and I could see her knuckles all white . . . saying 'Pieter, Pieter . . .' you know how these bloody Swedes go on.[22]

Michael Peacock, controller of BBC2, wanted a series, but only on the condition that Pete and Dud were to co-star.

Although a product of the comedy department, *Not Only . . . But Also . . .* was recognizably a variety show. Just as stage variety had become more star-led in the post-war years, so television variety had developed a sub-genre where a major performer or act – be they comedian or singer – would host, perform in sketches and introduce guests. In the US, the model for such a comedy programme had been Sid Caesar's *Your Show of Shows*, the breeding ground for writers like Mel Brooks and Neil Simon, while the musical template was set by the likes of *The Nat King Cole Show*.

Not Only . . . But Also . . . straddled music and comedy expertly. Peter Cook was a fount of comic invention, and while he was undoubtedly the dominant force, Dudley Moore was far from being a silent partner, either in writing or performance. Frequently, it was Moore's reaction to or summary of a Cook flight of fancy that got the biggest laugh. Moore's unique selling point was his fluent, joyous jazz piano playing, which could be featured either in its own right with his trio, or as the backing for guest singers like Marian Montgomery and Cilla Black. Not renowned as a jazz chanteuse, our Cilla – aided by Dud, with Pete McGurk on bass and Chris Karan on drums – made a pretty good fist of *Let There Be Love* in the first show of the second series.

★

BBC2 had been one result of the Pilkington Report. Another was the ITA's indication that more attention would be paid to programme quality when the programme franchises came up for renewal in 1967. There were some major changes in the ITV network map, as Yorkshire and Lancashire became separate regions, to be served by seven-day contractors, rather than one large region with separate weekday and weekend companies – namely Granada and ABC. Granada opted to remain in its north-western heartland, taking Lancashire and Cheshire, while a new company, Yorkshire Television, took over east of the Pennines. The Midlands, hitherto divided between ATV and ABC, was also to become a seven-day operation.

As well as the obvious kudos in broadcasting highbrow material, there was a sound social basis for the drive upmarket, with higher education having expanded massively during the sixties as the immediate post-war generation, the so-called 'baby boomers', reached school-leaving age. The old model of ITV had appealed to the lowest common denominator, which in the eyes of opinion formers in class-ridden Britain meant the working classes. However, the old divisions were becoming blurred as the whole country experienced greater affluence. The total personal income of UK citizens had grown from £10.9 million in 1954/5 to £15.1 million in 1959/60. Admittedly, this increase saw the gap between the north and the south widening slowly. In 1954/5, the London ITV area accounted for 29.1 per cent of that income, with the northern ITV region on 24.9 per cent, proportionately, far fewer northerners earned over £1,500 a year than their southern counterparts. Five years later, London's share had grown to 30.6 per cent, but the north had fallen back to 24.3 per cent. Migration may have had some effect: between the 1951 and 1961 censuses, the London population grew by 6.7 per cent, while the northern population grew by just 2.5 per cent. In contrast, the population in the area covered by Southern Television grew by 10 per cent over the same period, while the Anglia region's head count grew by 8.7 per cent, indicating a distinct southward bias.

The ITA had some justification, then, in forcing the ITV franchisees to aim higher, but many, including Lew Grade of ATV and John Spencer Wills of Rediffusion's parent company British Electric Traction, saw the ITA's intervention as needless tokenism. Others, including David Frost and BBC1 controller Michael Peacock, saw it as an opportunity to create the ideal ITV company. When Frost approached banker David Montagu for financial advice, the money man revealed that he was already involved with a bid for the new Yorkshire franchise with Aidan Crawley – who had been an MP for both the Labour and Conservative parties. Frost persuaded them both to come in with him in forming the London Television Consortium. This alliance applied for the London weekend contract, as did ABC and the incumbent, ATV.

With financial backing from, among others, Arnold Weinstock of electrical giant GEC and Donald Stokes of the Leyland Motor Corporation, as well as a management team including several former senior BBC executives, the London Television Consortium was a serious contender. The seriousness of its intent was obvious from its programme plans. The new applicant promised improved educational programmes and children's shows, both of which were the sort of noises the ITA wanted to hear, having been used to grudging provisions from some of the existing companies. The Consortium also professed 'a common belief that the quality of mass entertainment can be improved while retaining commercial viability'.[23]

When the contracts were announced on 12 June 1967, the London Television Consortium had won the London weekend franchise. After flirting with the idea of calling the new broadcaster Thames Television, they settled on the name London Weekend.[24] Flushed with confidence, managing director Michael Peacock restated the entertainment pledge rather more baldly: 'The present weekend programmes are bland, featureless, and tasteless ... You won't have to be a moron to get something out of London Weekend Television.'[25] This statement won the newcomer no friends within the ITV system, a tactical error given that London Weekend had to rely on the goodwill and expertise of the other companies when it came to scheduling.

Frank Muir moved from his job as head of comedy at the BBC to become the new company's first head of light entertainment. His main focus was to be comedy, while variety was handled by Tito Burns, a former jazz accordionist and ex-manager of Cliff Richard. The urbane, clever, witty Muir was much loved by his staff, the producers and the writers he shepherded, but there were tensions from above. Deputy managing director Dr Tom Margerison, whose background was scientific journalism rather than comedy or television administration, had decided that situation comedies should be forty-five minutes long. Muir demurred, suggesting that scripts would probably end up being heavily padded half hours, but Margerison prevailed. However, in the rush to get any decent programmes on air at all by August 1968, these were relatively small worries for Muir.

London Weekend's victory had ramifications for the London weekday operation. As well as applying for London weekends, ABC had gone for the Midlands, but been beaten by ATV. The ITA realized, however, that ABC was a distinguished contributor to the ITV network, and that a way should be found to keep it in the family. The answer was, potentially, the worst of all possible worlds. Rediffusion had reapplied for the London weekday franchise, but at the interview stage, there was a disagreement between John Spencer Wills of parent company British Electric Traction and the ITA. Wills' argument was that Rediffusion did not need to prove its worth. The ITA responded by instructing Rediffusion to join with ABC and form a new company to fulfil the contract, ABC to be the senior partners, with 51 per cent of the shares. However, out of this combination of revenge and fudging came one of the most important programme-making companies in the history of British television – Thames. The new operation settled in at the ABC studios in Teddington, with a presence in the old Rediffusion building on Kingsway, while its Euston Road headquarters were being built. In actual operational terms, Rediffusion became almost a sleeping partner in the new company, and the Thames board was ABC-dominated, with Sir Philip Warter as chairman, Howard Thomas as managing director and Brian Tesler as programme controller.

Rediffusion's abandoned Wembley studios became the interim home of London Weekend, while it was waiting for its state-of-the-art colour studio centre to be built on the south bank of the Thames near Waterloo station. There being no real office space at Wembley, an unprepossessing tower block in nearby Stonebridge Park was taken over for modern open-plan offices, and swiftly renamed 'the Leaning Tower of Neasden' by its inhabitants.

London Weekend was to make full use of its founding father, David Frost, on screen. As well as hosting satirical comedy for the BBC in the form of *The Frost Report*, he had been presenting *The Frost Programme* for Rediffusion, a show that could go from pure light entertainment to heavyweight current affairs in the pan of a camera or the length of a commercial break. This was the show on which Frost conducted a masterful demolition of insurance fraudster Emil Savundra. Not yet 30 years old, Frost was already incredibly well-connected – a quality embodied in his famous stunt of inviting the Prime Minister and other opinion formers to breakfast at the Connaught hotel. The other members of his production team at Rediffusion were similarly on the inside track, as the show's director William G. Stewart recalls:

We had hugely impressive people like Tony Jay, Clive Irving, Peter Baker (who had been deputy editor of the *Daily Express*), and writers like John Cleese, Barry Cryer and Neil Shand. So we had a great team in all directions – entertainment and serious journalism. We sort of acknowledged that there were five people in the world that we could not get on the telephone through somebody in that room: the Queen, the President of the United States, De Gaulle, Ho Chi Minh and Krushchev. Anybody else, somebody would know somebody. I remember listening to him [Frost] on the phone one day and he was saying 'Well ask her. We'd love to have you on the show. Ring me back as soon as you can. How soon can you get her? Ten minutes?' I asked 'Who was that?' He said 'Tony Armstrong-Jones. If he goes on television, he has to ask the Queen's permission.'[26]

While others might have cavilled at the fusion of gravitas and frivitas, Frost saw it as all part of the same business. To him, according to Stewart, 'it's all about communication'. Sometimes, however, the gear changes were harder to achieve, as Stewart discovered in late 1967 on a Rediffusion *Frost Programme*:

We were doing a serious interview up to the commercial break, and then we'd come back with an entertainment item. In this case it was Shirley Bassey. We came to the break and I saw Shirley Bassey on all the monitors. We were live and I heard my PA say 'Two minutes, studio, commercial break.' So I sat back. Frost came in. He said 'Bill, tell Shirley we're going on with the interview after the break. Will she come back tomorrow?' I thought 'Oh God.' I looked up and thought 'She's taken hours to get to look like that.' I leaned forward to the microphone, quietly said to the floor manager, David Yallop, 'Will you explain to Shirley that we're going on with the interview after the break? I'll explain it later. We'll be very happy to have her back tomorrow.' I heard a very quiet voice, I knew what it was. It was a hand over the microphone: 'I'm not telling her.' I said 'David, do as you're told. You're the floor manager. Just go up to her, say it nicely and I'll explain it afterwards.'

So Geoffrey Hughes, who was the producer, sitting behind me, said 'Bill, you go down and tell her.' I was directing. I heard my PA say 'One minute, studio.' I ran out, ran down the steps, to the bottom of the gantry, walked over to Shirley Bassey and said 'Shirley'. She looked at me and said 'You don't have to tell me. You don't want me, do you?' and she turned to walk away. I could have left it alone, but I suddenly heard myself say 'We can't leave a serious interview like that at the commercial break and come back to a girl singer,' and as I said the words 'girl singer' she looked over her shoulder. I'd just called Shirley Bassey a girl singer. I was sick. I thought 'What have I done?' She was absolutely wonderful about it afterwards. She said 'Of course I'll come back tomorrow.'[27]

At LWT, the matter was addressed by having Frost present three distinctly different shows a week. *Frost on Friday* was to be the serious current affairs show, or as Julian Critchley put it in *The Times*, "'actuality-Frost"; the fearless inquisitor'.[28] *Frost on Saturday* would take the lighter end of the *Frost Programme* repertoire, while *Frost on Sunday* would be all-out comedy and variety. The launch night, on Friday 2 August 1968, was to kick off with *We Have Ways Of Making You Laugh*, a live comedy show hosted by Muir himself, who had taken the job reluctantly when pressed by producer Humphrey Barclay. After that, LWT's idea of weekend entertainment differed wildly from that of its predecessor, ATV. On the station's second night, a production of Stravinsky's *Soldier's Tale* was mounted in the *Saturday Special* slot, up against *Match of the Day* on BBC1. Tellingly, in the Midlands, ATV did not take the LWT production, instead scheduling a showing of the western *Elmer Gantry*, just as it had opted out of showing the first *We Have Ways Of Making You Laugh*, in favour of *Strategic Air Command*, starring James Stewart.

As it transpired, nobody transmitted the first *We Have Ways Of Making You Laugh*. Ongoing industrial action over a pay and working hours settlement throughout the ITV regions meant that screens went blank after only fifteen seconds. The performers were allowed to remain oblivious and carry on, in the hope that sound and vision would be restored, but it never happened. The first *Frost on Friday* managed to make it on-air, complete with novelist John Braine bemoaning the erosion of freedom, and *Frost on Saturday* went ahead as planned, being a pre-recorded interview with Bob Hope. The first weekend's *Frost on Sunday* was another matter, though, being all-live. It became clear that the studio would not be ready in time, so the show went ahead from the *World of Sport* studio with a crew composed entirely of management. Programme controller Cyril Bennett was acting as floor manager, while Michael Peacock was in the gallery, calling the cameras, leading Frank Muir to comment that 'the managing director is managing to direct'.

From the following Monday, 5 August, across the whole of the ITV network, 1,000 technicians were on strike, 800 had been dismissed and a further 1,200 had been locked out by television bosses. For the next fortnight, an emergency service with no regional variations was put into action, using recorded programmes and films, played out from the abandoned ATV London switching centre in Foley Street and the Thames studios at Teddington.[29]

Unfortunately, when normal service resumed, London Weekend's programmes failed to gain the audiences that the advertisers were used to. The doubters had predicted that high minds would result in low ratings, and so it proved. The ratings flop resulted in a sharp decline in advertising revenue for LWT, in favour of its weekday rival Thames. At one point, speculation abounded about the new company being merged with Thames or ATV, but the ITA had staked too much on the newcomer to let that happen. Fortunately it wasn't all gloom, as, in entertainment, there had been some programming successes, most notably the situation comedies *On the Buses* and *Please Sir*, though they weren't quite enough. Reviewing LWT's first year on air, Julian Critchley observed that 'London Weekend has suffered from too wide a gap between promise and performance' and that its executives had 'discovered only too quickly that the traditions of public service broadcasting could not survive in the different atmosphere of commercial telly . . . the weekend is a time not for stimulation but for titillation. Sandie Shaw and not Stravinsky.'[30] Just over a month later, on 18 September 1969, Michael Peacock was dismissed by the London Weekend board. The following day, six senior executives resigned in support of Peacock, among them Frank Muir. In November, Cyril Bennett followed, to be succeeded by his former Rediffusion colleague Stella Richman, who had built her reputation producing drama, before becoming one of British television's first female senior executives. It was Richman who appointed Barry Took to be LWT's head of light entertainment, taking up the post in February 1970.

Like his predecessor, Took had a strong pedigree as a comedy writer – most notably on Kenneth Horne's hit radio series *Round the Horne* – and a fair bit of experience as a performer before heading over to the other side of the desk. Took realized that the output had to be as populist as possible. One of his inheritances was the sitcom *Doctor in the House*, which he described as 'slightly rocky'.[31] His solution was simple. 'In a phrase that I feel was full of delicacy, nuance and a deep understanding of the psyches of all concerned I said, "I don't want a load of poofs running around a hospital, I want stories about old ladies with bladder trouble." And that's what I got, and the ratings soared,' he recalled in his autobiography.[32]

Stella Richman had also enticed Terry Henebery over from the BBC to be an executive producer in light entertainment, but almost instantly he wondered if he'd made the right move:

> It wasn't the happiest place. We were told at one point that we all had to be at our desks that day because the ITA were coming round to have a look. So everybody had to be talking gobbledegook down phones, saying 'Yes, book him, book him.' Dead phones. As long as we appeared to be busy and industrious. Of course, they nearly lost their franchise during the time I was there. Nothing to do with me, guv, as they say.[33]

LWT should have been coining it, but just a few years into its franchise, money was tight, as advertisers continued to spend their money elsewhere. Terry Henebery had been brought in to mount big, prestige shows, including a programme on Richard Rodgers that involved a trip to America, but the company now realized it could not afford them:

> I had a three-year contract, and fifteen months into that, Stella Richman gets fired, overnight. Cyril Bennett's brought in. I was called into Cyril's office, and he said 'Look, we know you've been brought in to do a certain thing. We're not going to be [doing it]. We've got to survive here. The sort of programmes that you were brought in to do by my predecessor, Stella, aren't going to happen. You can sit around and play poker dice for the next year and a half or whatever it is you've got left, or we can come to a settlement on your contract.' So, I got a lawyer onto it, we got a settlement, and I came out into the jungle.[34]

★

While London Weekend was going through its growing pains, BBC1 was developing its variety output, most notably in singer-led shows. Cilla Black, Val Doonican, Dusty Springfield and Lulu all began series of their own in the late sixties. Although videotape had been in use since 1958, many of these shows were still transmitted live, requiring fearsome concentration from the performers and the crew. Paul Smith, then a floor assistant, as the 'call boys' had become known, recalls 'techniques I learned that are now completely and utterly dead. Striking things and putting them back, and getting them out on a live show. The artist is set up with hand mike on the stool, 'thank you very much', they'd cut to a close-up. You'd wait for the close-up. And that was your cue, in you go. The sound man goes in from one side, takes the mike, AFM from the other side, takes the stool. Back to the wide shot and they've disappeared. You were watching all the time. You'd crawl across the floor, putting things in and out because it was all live. If I were directing a show now and I said "We'll get to the close-up, go in, set the mike," they'd ask what I was talking about. I'd have to go through it slowly.'[35]

The formats for the singer-based shows was usually fairly simple. The star would sing a combination of their hit songs, standard numbers and new tunes. There would be a guest star, who, if a singer, would do a couple of numbers on their own before duetting with the person whose name was on the title sequence. Then it was time for a closing number from the star of the show. The guest bookings could be interesting. On one September 1966 edition of *Dusty*, produced by former designer Stanley Dorfman, Woody Allen treated Thursday night BBC1 viewers to some of his stand-up act. On another, in August 1967, Warren Mitchell appeared as Alf Garnett, insulting pop singers of the day and appearing in a Johnny Speight-written sketch featuring theatrical anarchist Ken Campbell as an inept magician. As marvellous a singer as she was, working with the temperamental Springfield could be a trying experience. On one show, several aborted takes in front of an audience resulted in her walking out of the studio in high dudgeon. Thinking on his feet, the floor manager shouted after her 'Put the kettle on, love. We're coming with you.' She turned around, laughing. The ice had been broken, and she went on to give the performance that had eluded her, but many around fully expected her to attack the floor manager physically.

Lulu's late-sixties television outings are remembered primarily for the occasion when the Jimi Hendrix Experience were booked to appear on the 4 January 1969 edition of *Happening for Lulu*, possibly the most of-its-time title ever given to any television programme. The band played a blistering version of 'Voodoo Chile', before handing back to Lulu, who introduced the next number, 'Hey Joe'. However, to the amazement of all in the studio and at home, Hendrix stopped playing his own hit song midway through and announced 'We'd like to stop playing this rubbish and dedicate a song to the Cream,' who had split up the previous November. With that, he launched into a ragged, but heartfelt instrumental version of 'Sunshine of Your Love', during which he turned to Mitch Mitchell and said 'We're off the air now.' They weren't. Director Stanley Dorfman stayed with the action, knowing it to be a proper happening for Lulu. Thanks to an enterprising engineer, this sequence is all that survives of the entire thirteen-part series.

Cilla Black had asked expressly for Michael Hurll as her producer after receiving 'the bollocking of her life' from him when she had turned up late for a *Billy Cotton Band Show*.[36] Far from being upset, she was impressed with his forcefulness, as well as his loyalty to the show and its star. Her faith in Hurll was fully repaid as he dreamed up stunts that ensured the show would not be a mere case of 'This is ... that was ... thank you ... you're just wonderful.' Alongside the songs, comedy sketches and guests, outside broadcast units were sent to viewers' houses so that Cilla could surprise them in mid-show. The show capitalized on her folksy Scouse charm and her easy way with the viewers. Sir Bill Cotton remembers how naturally it came to Cilla, just as it hadn't with Kathy Kirby: 'I had spent a long time telling her that it wasn't just singing a song, it was talking to the audience. If you want to see what I mean, look at Cilla Black. She can't bloody sing, but on the other hand, she can talk to the audience. The audience want to hear you talking to them, if you're doing that type of show.'[37]

Sometimes, however, the outside broadcast crews would descend on rather grander premises than a viewer's humble abode, as Jim Moir – then a fledgling producer working with Hurll – recalls:

I was at the Royal Albert Hall. Cilla left the Television Theatre during a live show, got on the back of a motorbike, went to the Commonwealth Institute, where she switched to a car, and from the Commonwealth Institute drove to the Royal Albert Hall, to walk in, interrupt a concert and sing a song. It was amazing and I've never had adrenalin like it, because I was worried she wouldn't make it in time. The simple command from Television Theatre: 'On you, Albert Hall.' I directed this sequence, not more than ten minutes, including the 'Largo al Factotum', and it was just fantastic. It took me about forty-eight hours to get the adrenalin out of my system. That was because Hurll took the chance, but it wasn't a chance. It was a planned event. Of course, he had backup, but had it gone awry, it would have been very noticeable.[38]

Moir cites Hurll and Stewart Morris as two of the great risk-taking producers in light entertainment, recalling one of Morris's stunts with particular relish, in which he 'ran Susan Maughan down the River Thames on one of those aqua cars, driving up the bank into Riverside 2. These are top men. All to bring a spectacle to the audience.'[39] Morris also pushed the envelope in his production of BBC1's *The Rolf Harris Show*, a weekly date with the affable Australian entertainer and artist. Moir recalls one edition, in which the stage of the Golders Green Hippodrome (which was used extensively as a studio in 1968 and 1969, while the Television Theatre was being converted to colour operation) was stuffed with 'lions, tigers and water features'. Moir notes that Morris pulled the whole spectacle together in record time, all being 'done as a set and strike on the pre-record day, which alone should have been three days in the studio somewhere else'. Unsurprisingly, Morris remembers it pretty well too:

[For] the Moulin Rouge [set], we erected a giant swimming pool, and health and safety went crazy. I said 'Don't worry, the fire brigade will come in and suck that water out very quickly,' and they did. What they were really worried about was that we had a tiger, a full-grown live tiger, which was fixed to the stage with bolts and things, but not so you could see. The trouble was that I wanted to have a couple of girls sitting with it, and he used to get a bit friendly, so that didn't work. Some idiot said 'You'll have to have a marksman there, in case the animal needs to be shot.' I said 'Are you serious? You're going to have somebody with a live rifle in a building with an audience and thirty-one people on the stage? That's ridiculous. We'll sedate the tiger.' So we did. And on the rehearsal it just looked like it slept. I sent quickly to Egton House [where the BBC gramophone library was situated] and got a disc of tigers roaring and thought if I played it, it might at least put its ears up. And it did. I got into trouble for that. Never mind. The things we used to do, Jesus.[40]

The Rolf Harris Show was a fixture in the schedules on Saturday nights – traditionally, variety's biggest night on screen – from 1967 to 1971. Harris was already well known for hit records like 'Tie Me Kangaroo Down, Sport' and 'Sun Arise', but other talents were to come to the fore in the series. Morris recalls 'a lot of sleepless nights thinking "How do I make this?" They said to me this has got to be seven o'clock on Saturday night, our main LE spot, so you've got to do a show that is not a children's show. I already knew he could paint. I didn't know then that he'd already exhibited at the Royal Academy. I didn't realize his real talent. And that's when this idea came up.' This idea being that Harris would produce a giant painting live on air during each show. Thus it was that a whole generation spent their Saturday teatimes watching an Australian gent humming to himself and daubing a huge canvas with a thick brush, occasionally breaking off to ask the audience 'Can you see what it is yet?'

Val Doonican's shows, which were a fixture of the schedules for over twenty years, were far more sedate affairs, Doonican being very much an Irish version of US crooner Perry Como. If Doonican rocked, it was, as one of his album titles reminded us, 'but gently'. Indeed, Doonican's longest serving producer, Yvonne Littlewood, had worked on all of Como's shows for the BBC, whether as production assistant or producer in her own right. Doonican's early series, however, were produced by John Ammonds in the converted church in Manchester.

Somewhere between Doonican and Dusty in terms of attitude came artists like Shirley Bassey, who made a number of spectaculars for the BBC during the seventies. Stewart Morris produced them and can vouch for the power of the Bassey pipes: 'For one of her specials, I stood her on the top of Cardiff Castle, singing the Welsh national anthem. I'm in a helicopter with no doors on it, about 50 feet away, filming her and the castle in the background. I've got a jet engine behind me, and I could hear her singing.' Having conquered Cardiff Castle, Morris then sent Bassey out to film a sequence on a North Sea oil rig, and while he could still hear her some distance away, this time, she wasn't singing:

The helicopter pilot said 'We should turn back. I can't land if there's more than, say, a 10-knot wind, and it's 15.' I said 'You tell her.' He said 'I'll try and land it.' Anyway, we got on it. I saw this lift, like a bosun's chair, and I said 'Shirl, you've got to do part of the song in this lift. I'm going to just lift it slightly off the deck and with the angle of the camera, I'll shoot you against the sea, so that no one will know that you're still on the deck.' She wouldn't have it, but she fancied the captain and I said 'If I get the captain to go in the rig with you, will you do it?' She said 'Yes.' So I had a quiet word with the captain and the crane driver, and I had them all on my talkback. And as soon as she's into the song, I gave the signal, and she was lifted up and swung out over the sea. And we did the biggest edit job in matching the effing and blinding to the song. She never sang a word of the song. The language coming out of her was unbelievable. She came back, landed, and said 'You dangerous bastard.' But it looked good on the end product.[41]

The show Morris made with a clean-living group of talented siblings was a similarly taxing project for different reasons:

I persuaded the Osmond family to come, and Robin Nash directed it. I put them in a furniture van and took the van into the scene dock of the [BBC Television] Theatre to get them in. There were unbelievable crowds all the way around the Theatre down the side. There was no way we could have got them in, so eight o'clock in the morning, the furniture van picked them up – we'd fitted it out with sofas and Coca-Cola, so the mother and the five of them would get in and be delivered into the scene dock. Before the camera crew came in, they were rehearsing, and the mother, who had the most phenomenal perfect-pitch ear, would call out 'that's a flattened ninth', if one of them sang a bum note. She sat there, knitting. So much talent among all of them.[42]

CHAPTER SIX

Saturday night's all right for fighting

The fifties and sixties had been a rich time for television variety, but in the seventies the genre came of age. In 1970, just under 16 million television licences were issued, 6 million more than a decade earlier. Over the following decade, the rate of growth slowed, with 18.3 million licences in 1980. From being the luxury of a privileged few, television had become almost as much of a necessity as gas, electricity and water. The potential audience for television at any one time was around two-thirds of the whole UK population. With only three channels to choose from, and BBC1 and ITV competing vigorously, some shows, particularly seasonal specials, almost managed to realize that potential.

The seventies also saw the chat show coming to prominence. Chat shows had been a cornerstone of entertainment television in the US almost from the start, but the genre did not take hold in Britain until the sixties. One of the main reasons for this was the smaller pool of potential guests – between them, New York and Hollywood could supply enough talking heads with product to shift to keep any number of shows, from Jack Paar and Johnny Carson downwards, jabbering five nights a week. In Britain, the perception seemed to be that it was only a matter of time before you'd get through everyone and the host would be left twiddling his thumbs. Eventually, at ABC, Brian Tesler decided to wade in. First of all, he had been given the task of beefing up the ITV network's sports coverage. 'I wanted to call it *Wide World of Sport*,' he explains, 'but then I realized it was hardly going to be wide, because the BBC had all the contracts. It was going to be very narrow. So we just called it *World of Sport*. I needed a good front man, and the only one I could think of that I wanted was Eamonn Andrews, who was doing the Saturday afternoon radio sport.' Tesler also thought that Andrews – veteran of *This Is Your Life* and *Crackerjack* – would be ideal for a chat show. The pair shared an agent, Teddy Sommerfield, but the negotiations were far from uncomplicated:

> It was all done very secretively. I drove up to a square – Portman Square, I think it was – and I went into the back of a blacked-out Mercedes. Teddy would be sitting there and we would discuss the contract. At the end of the discussions, I would get out and go back to my car, never to be seen to be doing this. Eamonn liked the idea, because like me he was a hardboiled American fiction fan. He wanted to do two more shows. He wanted to do a children's show. I said 'He can't, we don't do children's shows, but I've got something I do want him to do. Our version of *The Jack Paar Show*, a Sunday night, live chat show,' and he was very interested.[1]

The first *Eamonn Andrews Show* went out on Sunday 4 October 1964. Many didn't share Tesler's faith in Andrews as a chat show host. In the radio comedy *Round the Horne*, he was satirized as Seamus Android, portrayed by Bill Pertwee as the height of conversational ineptitude and blank incomprehension. In fact, Andrews made a decent fist of the job, more moderator than inquisitor, and very much in the self-effacing Johnny Carson mould. For one night in May 1966, the show came from the Piccadilly Hotel in Manchester, to mark the first decade of independent television in the north of England. The guest list was A1: on the stage were Harry H. Corbett, Billie Whitelaw and Hallé Orchestra conductor Sir John Barbirolli, all of them with strong Mancunian links, while humorist Peter Moloney represented Liverpool, with musical interludes from Gerry Marsden (*sans* Pacemakers) and Jackie Trent. The audience was no less star-studded, including both Manchester City manager Joe Mercer and his United rival Sir Matt Busby. The highlight of the conversation came when Barbirolli asked

Corbett, who had been born in Burma, raised in Manchester, and was best known for playing a Londoner, 'Are you a proper cockney like me or a fake?'[2]

BBC Television waited until 1967 before making its entry into the world of chat. Bill Cotton, as head of variety, had been mulling the idea over for some time, but was at a loss for a suitable host, until his mother suggested a pirate radio disc jockey she had seen on a Southern TV regional show, a young man called Simon Dee. Born Carl Henty-Dodd in Manchester in 1935, he had been educated at Shrewsbury, a couple of years above the *Private Eye* nucleus of Willie Rushton, Richard Ingrams, Christopher Booker and Paul Foot. Instead of turning to satire or investigative journalism, Henty-Dodd worked as a photographer, a vacuum cleaner salesman and an actor before finding his niche at the launch of Radio Caroline in 1964. Adopting a snappier stage name and showing a distinct love of Tamla Motown music, he soon became a hit with listeners to the watery wireless. However, after a year, he came ashore, to work as a freelance for the BBC Light Programme and Radio Luxembourg, the first of the pirates to go 'legit'.

On closer inspection, Cotton found that his mother's hunch had been right. 'He was . . . good-looking, a snappy dresser . . . very articulate . . . he seemed to fit the bill,' he recalls in his memoirs.[3] The title of the show was to be *Dee Time*, reflecting its early evening placement on Tuesdays and Thursdays, and the original plan was for the show to be co-produced by Terry Henebery – still at this time a BBC producer – and Johnnie Stewart. As with Stewart's *Top of the Pops*, the only place available for the launch of the new show was the converted church in Manchester, and it was there that a pilot was recorded on 31 January 1967. Stewart's connection to the production was, however, brief, as Henebery recalls:

It was largely based on the idea of the *Johnny Carson* show in America. We worked it so that there would be a producer in the box and another producer alongside the girl on the Autocue control and camera 4, the dedicated camera for the links, which had got an Autocue head on it. So

Johnnie was up in the box, I was going to stay on the floor and Syd Lotterby, who has gone on to win more BAFTA awards for comedy than I've had hot dinners, was the director. As we're getting ready to go, the floor manager puts the word [out]: 'Where's Johnnie Stewart? We're ready to go. Has anybody seen him?' I said 'I don't know.' Johnnie had suddenly got into his mind that he didn't want to do it. He didn't want to take the whole gig on at all, so I carried on. He was just outside the control room. They said 'Aren't you going in?' He said 'No, Terry's on the floor.'[4]

Perhaps unsurprisingly in the circumstances, 'it wasn't a very good pilot', although Henebery remembers that Dee had to share some of the blame. 'Bill Cotton came up for the pilot, and afterwards I was called in to Bill and Tom [Sloan]. They said "The situation is that we're going to do another pilot. Simon Dee's been given the hard word. He's got to work harder, we're going to invest in it. We'll do one more pilot up in Manchester, and if it's all right, we'll transmit that as programme one and do a live one on the Thursday. You're going to be in charge, and you'll have our total backing."'[5]

Henebery also had the support of a first-rate production team. The (fresh from a tour of duty *On the Braden Beat*), Joe Steeples and Michael Wale, while the production assistants were Roger Ordish and David O'Clee (both on attachment from BBC Radio) and Jim Moir. 'There was a flight [from Manchester to London] – almost half of it was filled with people to do with the Simon Dee show,' Ordish recalls. 'It was bringing the guests back so they could get back to London that night, and if it was the second show of the week, we were all piling back on there as well. We used to spend four nights in Manchester and three nights in London.'[6]

The first show, recorded on 27 March 1967 and transmitted on 4 April, was packed with so many big names that success was practically guaranteed. In a music-heavy line-up, viewers saw and heard Cat Stevens performing 'I'm Gonna Get Me a Gun', while the Jimi Hendrix Experience were present with 'Purple Haze'. As if that wasn't enough, Kiki Dee did 'I'm Going Out the Same Way I Came In', Lance Percival gave the nation 'The Maharajah of Brum' and Libby Morris sang 'I Could Fall in Love and Everybody Says Don't', all backed by the BBC Northern Dance Orchestra in 'house band' mode under Bernard Herrmann.

Not surprisingly, *Dee Time* took off. From the launch, the show had a memorable set of closing credits, featuring Dee playing up his playboy image to the full, picking up a dolly bird in a Jaguar E-type and speeding her down a spiral ramp. The effect was nearly achieved at great human cost, as Jim Moir recalls: 'I was on the back of the film car, which was a Land Rover thing. I sat with the cameraman, holding the basher, trying to illuminate his face. Honest to God, as we were coming down the ramp we nearly had our heads taken off by the overhanging concrete beams.'[7] As it was, minor injuries had to suffice. 'The shot of the girl jumping into the white E-type – it's not ecstasy, she's shrieking in agony,' Terry Henebery observes. 'Because I said to her on about take three "When Dee comes screaming up, it's no good trying to open the door and get in, we haven't got the time. Can you jump in over the door?" So she did and at the point when she jumped in, and was just about to put her bum on the seat, he let the clutch out – Boom! – and she caught her leg on the scuttle. So she's shrieking in agony, and we're lucky we didn't get sued by the agency.'[8]

In addition, Dee overcame his initial teething troubles to become an engaging interviewer, but there were occasions when his mettle was tested severely. Henebery remembers with particular fondness an appearance by the team from the hit radio comedy *I'm Sorry I'll Read That Again*, enlivened by Neil Shand's suggestion that Harry, the driver who ferried the stars to the studio, should join them on screen. Nobody told the host. 'Dee's face was a picture,' says the producer. 'He's looking at me, because it's live, the band are shrieking. Harry sits there, gets a paper out and starts to read it, he gets a sandwich out, he takes his shoes off. All the time, Dee is saying "Who is he?" and they're saying "Nothing to do with us," and you can't do anything, because it's live. The rider to this is that the son he had never seen in years saw him on the screen, and they got together.'[9]

After proving itself on Tuesdays and Thursdays, *Dee Time* moved to kick off the Saturday night schedule from 23 September 1967. At the same time, the show moved from Manchester to studio G at Lime Grove, where the show acquired an introduction as distinctive as its closing credits. The sports programme *Grandstand* was being transmitted from studio H next door, with Len Marten as the voice of the football results. 'We said "Len, would you like a few more bob? Come in and just do the voiceover for the beginning of our show." So he did the "Siiiiiiiiiiiiiiiiiimon Dee!"'[10]

The high spot of the show's first year was to be a live broadcast from the Montreux Television Festival, but the achievement was muted somewhat by Henebery's involvement in a serious car accident on a Swiss motorway the day after, requiring several months' recuperation.[11] Colin Charman moved over from directing the show to become producer for four months until Roger Ordish took over in September 1968. A typical piece of BBC bureaucracy meant that Ordish had to change radically the way the show was produced. 'I wasn't actually of producer rank, I was only an assistant producer, and Tom Sloan said "I can't ask a fully fledged producer to come in and direct for you, because you're so junior. You'll have to direct it yourself." Which is quite ridiculous. I replaced two people and I was replaced by two people. I did, I have to confess, lose control of what was happening. You were doing pop groups, live, and things like that.'[12]

Ordish's baptism of fire came on 21 September 1968, his second show as producer/director: 'I said to one of the researchers that Sammy Davis Junior was in town and that there was a good chance of getting him, but he was considered to be terribly unreliable. I said to the researcher "Just stick with him, go find him, stay with him and bring him to the studio."'[13] The fears were justified, as Davis gave his chaperone the slip, with the result that the show went on air with no sign of its star guest. Midway through the programme, a whisper reached the production gallery that Sammy was in the building. What followed was a textbook example of how to snatch victory from the jaws of defeat, only to be defeated anyway by events:

The musical director Max Harris, a marvellous man and a very clever arranger, came to speak to me directly, while I was trying to direct the show. 'Erm, Sammy Davis has come into the orchestra area, and he's distributing some music that he wants us to play, because he wants to sing a song.' I said 'Well that's great, but you've not rehearsed it.' He said 'Well the trouble is, his arrangement includes fourteen strings and we haven't got any strings, as you know.' That [sight-reading ability] showed you the absolute brilliance of British musicians at that time. The very best people were earning a fortune, but they were always, always playing. When they had to reproduce the backing track for something that was on *Top of the Pops*, probably it was they who had done it in the first place. [Trombonist] Don Lusher definitely. The crazy drummer, Ronnie Verrell. They somehow botched this thing up for Sammy Davis Junior to sing. The lighting guy said 'Where's he going to stand?' [He was] just turning everything on. Sammy Davis was giving out the time – 'It's like this.'[14]

Posterity has not been kind to *Dee Time*, with only two complete shows and a handful of clips surviving, but thankfully Davis's complete, unrehearsed performance of 'This Guy's in Love with You' does exist, and it is truly electrifying stuff. In his introduction, Davis levels with the audience about the unusual circumstances:

This is completely live and ad-lib. The music was brought by my arranger George Rhodes, who, because of the union problems, is not allowed to conduct, but the band is more than the kind of band that I would love to work with all the time. So, I thank the cats, and I know it's off the wall, man. It starts with the bass. I will give you 'One, two . . .' and you will start. All right? It's all live and it's all happening folks. In colour, but you can't see it.[15]

At the end, Dee comes on with a look of obvious delight and relief across his face, shakes Davis's hand and kisses him on the forehead, unaware that the 15 million BBC1 viewers had missed most of this magic moment. In the box, Ordish's mood, which had gone from panic to joy as Davis pulled it out of the hat, suddenly turned to horror: 'We got to the end of verse one and the bloody presentation took us off the air because we were over-running, and put on a trailer about some boring thing like *Doctor Who*.'[16]

Ordish produced and directed the show single-handed until May 1969, when Richard Drewett took over as producer, with Jim Moir directing. Throughout the run, the show was in rivalry with *Eamonn Andrews* at ABC, particularly for the top international stars. There was a ceiling fee of £250 for *Dee Time* for an interview and a performance, with 100 guineas for an interview alone. There were other issues and controversies, such as the odd lawsuit, including one from pop publicist Tony Brainsby and Brian Michael Levy concerning remarks made by a female singer on the show, and another from an *Evening Standard* journalist accused by Max Bygraves, after a bad review, of being too tired to do his job.

Dee's tenure at the BBC came to an end in December 1969, after an approach from London Weekend's head of variety Tito Burns, offering a £100,000, two-year contract. Even if he had been able to match the LWT offer, Bill Cotton would almost certainly not have been inclined to do so. His regular clashes with Dee had used up whatever goodwill he felt towards the star, and Cotton was far from alone.

Unfortunately for Dee, LWT already had a chat show, and it was hosted by one of the directors of the company. As such, David Frost frequently pulled rank when it came to booking guests. Dee's subordinate status meant that his requests met with even more opposition than they had at the BBC. 'Stella Richman was running London Weekend,' says Sir Bill Cotton. 'She phoned me up and offered me a job. I said "No, thank you." She said "So, will you tell me how to handle Simon Dee?" I said "Well, just turn down anything he suggests, because it'll be stuff I've stopped him doing over the last three years." He wanted to conduct the band, book the show.'[17] Worst of all for Dee, he had to do without the support of the person who had hired him. Tito Burns had resigned from the company, between the signing of the Dee contract in October 1969 and the start of the series in January 1970, as part of the mass exodus of senior executives following the boardroom putsch that ousted managing director Michael Peacock. At the end of the run in July 1970, Dee was quietly dropped by LWT, and his career never recovered from the blow. 'There was a time in the second year when he was a very powerful force on British television and he could have gone anywhere. But he was just a bloody fool,' says Cotton.[18]

★

After Dee's defection, it was a couple of years before the BBC established another hit chat show. In the interregnum, various experiments were tried, including one show hosted by the unlikely figure of Derek Nimmo, a major sitcom star at that time with *All Gas and Gaiters*. The show, called *If It's Saturday, It Must Be Nimmo*, ran in the *Dee Time* slot from October 1970, and used Richard Drewett as producer and Roger Ordish as director, both from *Dee Time*. Nimmo's engagement was contractual, as Ordish explains: 'They'd said "We'll give you thirty-two shows," and he'd said "No I want forty-eight shows." So they'd say "All right, thirty-six shows." They'd got him for more shows than they wanted him, and they hadn't got the scripts. So we did a chat show. It was wonderful, I loved doing it.'[19]

A far less joyful experience all round was Peter Cook's stab at the genre, *Where Do I Sit?*, which began on BBC2 in February 1971. If nothing else, this show proved that the perfect chat show guest – and, as an interviewee, Cook was never anything less than superb value – could be the world's worst chat show host. Cook didn't prepare for the interviews, and had made the mistake of insisting on being allowed to sing a song in each show, despite having a singing voice as limited as his comedic brain wasn't. On top of all this, the producer, Ian MacNaughton, was better known for his work on wild, surreal comedy shows such as Spike Milligan's *Q5* and *Monty Python's Flying Circus* than for his ability to keep a chat show on the rails. Reviewing the first show for *The Times*, Chris Dunkley deplored the 'endless weak jokes about the technical trivialities of television production', including frequent shots of MacNaughton in the production gallery, telling Cook what to do next. Dunkley went on to describe Cook's interview with US humorist S.J. Perelman as 'pathetic', and summed up the whole show as 'dismally embarrassing . . . a sad disappointment'.[20]

The viewing public and, crucially, Bill Cotton agreed with Dunkley. *Where Do I Sit?* lasted just three editions. 'I wanted to take it off after the first show,' Sir Bill explains. 'I was very fond of Peter. He tried to sue us, but it came out, in a meeting with the lawyers, that he'd spent the money, so we came to an agreement. I said to him "I wish you'd told me that before all this. Money I can deal with. Bad shows are far more difficult." In America, if it wasn't going well, you just went to a commercial, changed it all around and started again. At the BBC, you couldn't do that. You had to actually build the show so that it worked.'[21]

The job of building such a show for the late night Saturday BBC1 schedule was given to producer Richard Drewett and Michael Parkinson. A former *Manchester Guardian* and *Daily Express* journalist, Parkinson had moved into television via Granada's regional news show *Scene at Six-Thirty*, before graduating on to Granada's *Cinema* series, where his interviews brought him wider attention. Sir Bill Cotton remembers 'Tony Preston, the assistant head of variety at the time, brought him in to have a drink with me, because he'd been in to see him. Within twenty minutes, I realized that he was as star-struck as I was. I can't say at the time I actually thought of all the good things that he brought, [but] I did know that performers would get a decent break with him, and he'd ask questions and listen to the answers. He'd get them to talk.'[22]

Parkinson had worked for the BBC before, but this made Cotton's job harder rather than easier. BBC1 controller Paul Fox was reluctant. 'As head of current affairs, he had used him on *24 Hours* and said he was idle. He's a good journalist, Parky, but he has his subjects. They were controversial, some of the questions. Probing, but there was no point-scoring. There was very little trying to make himself important. Now, they [chat show hosts] treat it just like their show – you're on here to make me look good.'[23]

The first edition of *Parkinson* went out on BBC1 on 19 June 1971, featuring interviews with Terry-Thomas and tennis player Arthur Ashe as well as a Frost-style confrontation with royal photographer Ray Bellisario. It wasn't the polished experience the show soon became and Barry Norman's *Times* review described the Bellisario encounter as 'an awful mistake'. The first twelve-week run had included an interview with John Lennon, then at the height of his battle with US Immigration, but the biggest catch of all had been Orson Welles. Unsurprisingly, with such heavyweights (in every sense) appearing, the show had been a success, and the decision was taken to bring it back very quickly, resuming on 10 October, after only a five-week break. The show soon achieved a momentum. In only the second show of the run, Parkinson met the boxer Muhammad Ali in a now legendarily charged encounter.

The start of the second series had not gone entirely as intended, though. John Fisher, who was with the show from the start to its final series in 1982, first as a researcher, then from 1977 as its producer, recalls the horror story. 'Paul Fox turned around and said "I think it would be good to start the new batch by repeating the Orson Welles." They looked and it had been wiped. Within weeks. "Don't worry" says Paul Fox, "I'll give you the money to do it again." Poor Richard has to explain that it's not quite the same. One, you're catching the spontaneity of a moment. Two, you're talking about Orson Welles. It might have suited him to do it in the summer, but he might not want to come back.' Nonetheless, Fox told Drewett that the offer would stand, and in 1973, the opportunity arose again, as Fisher relates:

At that point, Welles was working in Madrid. He said he could fly over one Sunday, and the deal was done. The fee, I'm sure, was £2,000, which was crazy money, plus expenses. We were due to be recording at half past three, four o'clock, so we were sitting in the office at Television Centre on the Sunday morning. Parky had worked the questions out and the challenge had been not replicating what had been done the previous time, doing a definitive interview with Welles, trying to bypass what we'd already talked about.

215

At about quarter to ten, the phone rings. It was Welles' representative calling from Madrid. 'Mr Welles has two demands and he's not stepping on the plane unless you can put them into action. One, because of his size, he wants three seats removed from the aeroplane, and the money has to be available in sterling on the tarmac at Heathrow as he steps off the plane.' Tony James, an amazing man who was the fixer of light entertainment, said 'Can you give me a number to call you back? Leave it with me.' He got onto the airline. He somehow schmoozed them. We had a wonderful connection, a man called Pat Furlong, who ran the BBC shipping office at Heathrow. He looked after the lah-dis, as we called them [lah-di-dahs = stars], as they came through, as well as more mundane things such as making sure that Alastair Cooke's tape arrived on time every Friday. Thanks to Pat Furlong and Tony, the money was available for him.[24]

I'll never forget being in reception with Richard when this Old Testament prophet ballooned in, with the cape of a million sherry adverts. He didn't have a cane, he had a staff. He was walking with great difficulty. We'd already been told he wouldn't be able to go up to hospitality on the first floor. If we wanted to give him hospitality, it had to be in his dressing room. It was a typical BBC dressing room, very long and narrow. So we set up a small drinks table in there, for after the show. He literally filled half that room. I've never been in the presence of anybody whose personality drained you so physically. He was charming and voluble but you came away thinking 'Jesus'. He had more charisma than anybody I've ever met.[25]

Considering some of the legends who parked themselves in front of Parky and his team during the show's eleven-year run, Fisher's description of Welles carries real weight, but the sherry-advertising film genius had competition. Welles had staked out his territory by arranging for the hospitality to be in his dressing room, but, according to Fisher, there were two guests who almost matched him for charisma. 'One was Richard Burton, the other was Tommy Cooper. I remember doing a show with Eric and Ernie. Everybody was gathered around Eric

Morecambe, listening, and he said "You're listening to me now, but if Tommy came in, everybody would go." He had this magnetism.'[26]

During the run-up to the show, it was usual for the researchers or producer to have meetings and lunches with the guests, to discuss their appearance on the show. For Fisher, though, the veteran wisecracker George Burns stood out as 'the only celebrity who asked me to have lunch with him after the show'. On his second appearance on the show, the first having been with Walter Matthau at the time of the release of *The Sunshine Boys,* Burns had picked up on Fisher's deep interest in the history of entertainment, particularly in magic:

He'd toured with a great American vaudeville magician called Nate Leipzig, and there was a card trick he used to do, which Nate Leipzig had taught him. It was a comedy thing. I said 'Will you please do that on the show?' Halfway through the interview, talking to Parky, he said 'There's a trick I'd like to do for that boy, what's his name? John Fisher.' Afterwards, just as he was about to go, he said 'What are you doing tomorrow? Come and have some lunch at the Dorchester.'

I turned up and it was just George and his manager, a wonderful man called Irving Fine, who had also been the manager for Jack Benny. He asked 'What do you want to know, kid?' So there I am, asking 'What was Jolson really like? What was the strangest act you ever worked with?' He was paying – there was no way he was going to let me pay, which I could easily have done on a BBC expenses account. He said 'If you're not doing anything, come up to the suite. We can carry on talking.' I'm not going to say I've got another appointment, I'm in the presence of this legend. We got to the suite and he said 'I've just got to apologize about one thing. I'm expecting somebody to come up from the foyer. I've just got to do a couple of minutes' business with them. They could come any time. You just stay here. Irving will get you a drink. I want to talk with you.' We carry on, he's regaling me with anecdotes. He says 'Ah, there's the knock at the door.' He goes to answer it, but there's nobody there. I'm not surprised by that, because I didn't hear a knock. He came back, another five minutes and 'There it is . . . must be my hearing.' We carry on, and then there is a knock, and Irving says 'I'll get it.' Irving opens the door and it's George Burns. He stands there and he says 'I just thought you'd like a little magic.' He'd conditioned me to expect the knocks. I hadn't paid any notice to the fact that he'd just gone into the next room to grab a cigar or whatever it was, but no sooner had he gone, he'd skedaddled through the far door, and along the corridor, in split seconds.[27]

Not all of the guests will be remembered for their charm. Most notorious was the night in November 1976 when Rod Hull and Emu began wrestling with Parkinson, prompting fellow guest Billy Connolly to comment that if he were attacked he'd break the bird's neck and Hull's arm. The surprises were usually more pleasant, though, particularly those of a musical nature. Just as the show promoted unlikely combinations in discussion, *Parkinson* was also responsible for some inspired musical groupings, often aided by organist Harry Stoneham's endlessly versatile house band. Fisher remembers that 'on one show, we had Placido Domingo, Cliff Richard and Sammy Cahn. The last fifteen minutes – we only had half an hour to rehearse this – was just Cliff Richard and Placido Domingo at Sammy Cahn's piano, singing his songs.' An earlier piece of alchemy had fused the classical world with jazz at a time when the term 'crossover' had yet to be invented:

It came to our very first Christmas [Fisher explains] and we'd been trying throughout the year, 1971, to get Yehudi Menuhin on the show, but he'd always refused. Stephane Grappelli had a bit of a resurgence in Paris. I said, flippantly, because I was still relatively junior in this business, wouldn't it be funny if we could get Stephane Grappelli and Yehudi Menuhin on the same show? To Richard [Drewett]'s credit, he picked up on it and said 'That's not such a bad idea. I wonder whether Menuhin admires Grappelli?' Of course, he did. And it was because of Grappelli that Menuhin came on. We did that show on a Sunday morning, probably because we were pre-recording for Christmas, and I remember going out to the airport at some unearthly hour, seven o'clock or something, to meet Grappelli – a sweet man with a twinkly sense of humour – for the first time and take the car journey with him across to Highgate, to Menuhin's pad, where they rehearsed. To be able to introduce those two people. They'd never met. They came on the show as a double, two, maybe three more times after that, and did many albums together.[28]

There was a similarly memorable, if not as long-lasting, pairing in a 1980 show that brought harmonica-playing anecdote factory Larry Adler and violin soloist Yithzak Perlman together for a sublime and all but impromptu version of 'Summertime'. On a show near the end of the run in 1982, however, a truly off-the-cuff moment occurred, and it involved a man who seemed to be making a habit of wandering into BBC studios while chat shows were in progress. The booked guests were all-round entertainer Roy Castle, mischievous DJ Kenny Everett and the irascible bandleader and drummer Buddy Rich. Whereas many shows despatched each guest at the end of their allotted time, on *Parkinson*, the guests stayed around and joined in the discussions. On this occasion, Parkinson's law of guest interaction was in full force. Rich was obviously delighted by Castle's story of an inept pit band drummer who didn't know the difference between his bass drum pedal and his hi-hat. Then, after asserting that he can beat a rhythm out of anything, Rich was challenged by Castle to play a handful of change and a pair of £5 notes. When Castle responded with a spot of tap dancing, the show was already firing on all cylinders.

However, with Rich's face in close-up, some off-camera action causes the entire audience to gasp, and it becomes clear that something great is about to get even better. Just what becomes clear in the next shot, a cutaway to Sammy Davis Junior, wandering nonchalantly onto the set. Rich walks past him playfully before grabbing the singer from behind in a bear hug. Davis, who claims he is in town 'to find out what's going on with Richard [Burton] and Elizabeth [Taylor]',[29] had rung the *Parkinson* production team on the morning of the show, and asked if he could come and say hello to Rich, his friend since their days in vaudeville as child performers. Davis announces that he knows

Castle well, and that he admires Everett, but doesn't yet know him properly. Everett repays the compliment by attempting to tap dance in his plimsolls – causing Davis and Rich to collapse in delighted convulsions behind him. The old-timers reminisce about their first encounter, before Parkinson persuades Davis to busk a number with the rhythm section of Rich's big band ('Almost Like Being in Love', in B flat, it transpires). The warmth of the occasion is almost palpable, one of those moments when television can truly be described as magical.

Unfortunately, there were occasions when the musical guests exuded a distinct chill. In particular, the camp pianist Liberace refused to play along, until the host suggested that a good old-fashioned stitch-up would achieve the required result, as Fisher, still at this point the junior of the team, recalls:

I go along to the hotel and sit with Lee [as Liberace liked to be known] and his manager Seymour Heller, who was known in Hollywood circles as the 'Silver Fox'. If we had a performer on the show, we'd always request that they'd do their party piece. With Jack Benny, he played a number on the fiddle. Even if it was something they weren't known for. Jimmy Stewart played accordion on one show. So, I ask: 'Now, Mr Liberace . . .' 'Call me Lee.' '. . . you will play something for us?' At which point Seymour Heller came in and said 'In no way is Mr Liberace playing anything. He is here in this country on your show in his capacity as an author.' Lee was simpering on the sofa, but there was no arguing. You didn't argue with Heller.

I came back dejected, because I had failed. It was my job to persuade people to do these things. Parky said 'Well, if we confront him with that on air, he can't refuse, can he?' We all said 'Yes, but it's easier said than done. It's not like pulling out a pack of cards for a magician.' We realized we were in the big studio – TC1 – that day, so we had a lot of wasted space. You had our set, Parky's chair area, Harry Stoneham and the boys [in the house band], then the audience. But then you had this corridor area, a black hole. We found out what piano he played, so he couldn't refuse because it wasn't what he was contracted to play, and got a full-size concert grand in. We put it in this area, and we covered it all over with black cloth on flies. We come to the show, Parky was doing the interview, and at the end he says 'Thank you Lee, but we can't possibly let you go without playing for us.' Liberace replies 'I'd love to, but we haven't got the piano.' At which point, the black cyc[lorama – as the backcloth covering the studio wall was known] went back, the black cloth went up, and there, in the spotlight, was this piano. At which point, Seymour Heller, who was on the floor, came over and got me by the lapels, saying 'You are going to pay for this. You are going to pay for this.' Meanwhile his only client has been ambushed and is having to fake sincerity like he never had before – 'Is there any tune I can remember?' But he did it, he played, and he got a resounding ovation from the audience.[30]

In America, chat shows were nightly, whereas *Parkinson* was weekly. By 1978, Bill Cotton – by now BBC1 controller – thought it was worth trying five shows a week. The only obstacle was the seemingly immovable feast that was the nightly current affairs show *24 Hours*, but when BBC2 controller Brian Wenham agreed to take that over, the scene was set for *Parkinson* five nights a week. Cotton had, however, reckoned without the snobbery of the BBC governors, who tended not to rate what they saw as vulgar entertainment programmes too highly. They vetoed the plan, leaving Cotton with five slots to fill. He was allowed one midweek *Parkinson*, which he placed on Wednesday nights.

Just over a year after Parkinson's chat show had taken to the nation's screens, London Weekend Television presented ITV's rival offering. If Michael Parkinson was yin, Russell Harty was yang. Parky was a Yorkshireman, Harty a proud Lancastrian, the son of a Blackburn greengrocer. Parkinson went straight from school to journalism with two O levels to his name, while Harty went to Oxford, before becoming a schoolteacher at Giggleswick, where one of his pupils was future *Countdown* host Richard Whiteley. Parky was and is gruffly masculine, Harty was gossipy and camp. Nonetheless, the rivalry between Parkinson and Harty was a warm, friendly one. They guested on each other's shows and when Harty died prematurely in 1988, Parkinson spoke at his funeral. Perhaps the main difference between the pair was that Parkinson, while he could be tough when required, was fundamentally reverent, especially when faced with the heroes he'd seen as a boy at the Barnsley Gaumont, while Harty was anything but. Alan Bennett, whom he met at Oxford, summed up his friend's chutzpah at his memorial service: 'He had learned then, by the age of twenty ... that there was nothing that could not be said and no one to whom one could not say it.'[31]

Harty had begun his media career relatively late, joining BBC Radio as a producer in 1967, at the age of 33, moving to London Weekend Television in 1970 to work on Humphrey Burton's arts magazine programme *Aquarius*, where his talent was noticed. On 21 October 1972, *Russell Harty Plus,* his first chat show, went out, with a guest list including actor Michael York and actresses Phyllida Law and Hylda Baker. His first 'Emu' moment came in the eleventh show of the first run, in January 1973, when interviewing the Who. Pete Townshend got the encounter off to a flying start by knocking over his amplifier stack, leading Harty to ask whether the item belonged to him or LWT. Harty then had a nightmare of a time trying to get a word in edgeways, as all four members of the band talked across each other, while Keith Moon played claves, staged a mock walkout and bit Townshend's knee. However, even this was eclipsed in November 1980, during Harty's first series for BBC2 after moving from LWT, when singer Grace Jones began slapping Harty around the head because he turned fractionally away from her to speak to another guest. In later BBC shows, Harty appeared unannounced on viewers' doorsteps and invited himself in for a cup of tea and a natter. When they worked, these encounters were as illuminating as any celebrity interview, Harty being warm and natural. Unfortunately, one punter wounded Harty as much as Grace Jones did by admitting she had no idea who he was.

Harty's last work at London Weekend had been *Saturday Night People*, co-hosted with *Observer* TV critic Clive James and Janet Street-Porter. The experiment was interesting, but flawed in that each of the triumvirate was bound to regard themselves as the star of the show, and would invariably attempt to pull it in their own direction. James's wit and his grasp of both high and low culture would, in time, make him a perfect chat show host at both LWT and the BBC. Harty remained a favourite with both BBC2 viewers and impressionists up to his death.

With Harty covering the BBC2 end of chat, Terry Wogan was preparing to take over the BBC1 baton from Michael Parkinson. Parky had become one of the founding directors of TV-am, the successful applicant for the new breakfast television franchise awarded by the Independent Broadcasting Authority, as the ITA had become in 1972. The whimsical Irish disc jockey began with a trial run on Tuesday nights in May 1982, before moving to the hallowed Saturday night slot in January 1983. 'The try-out happened while the Falklands War was on,' says producer Marcus Plantin. 'It worked very well on a Tuesday. The Tuesday show was a lot more dangerous than the Saturday show.' Plantin notes one crucial difference between Wogan and his predecessor. 'The difference, and Terry's quite honest about it, is that he's not a journalist. He'll listen, but he won't probably absorb and ask questions spontaneously. So, it has to be constructed and it was an edit job. Nothing wrong with that. We used to run everything long and pick the best bits. Put them together, hopefully seamlessly.'[32]

When Michael Grade came in as controller of BBC1 in 1984, he decided to build a weekday schedule to run from February 1985, underpinned by *Wogan* live from the Television Theatre on Monday, Wednesday and Friday, with the new soap opera *EastEnders* on Tuesday and Thursday. Plantin was in the frame for the job of producing the thrice-weekly show, but was saved by overtures from his old mentor Alan Boyd at London Weekend. 'The money was a lot better, and I didn't really want to do three days a week of *Wogan* as a live show, because I didn't believe in it,' Plantin says. 'As much as I love Terry, and I've got a lot of time for him, he's best when he's recut.' For all its faults, *Wogan* lasted for seven years before giving way to the Spanish-set soap opera *Eldorado*.

★

As chat shows became a more important element of the television variety schedules, the game show was also coming of age, with the BBC accepting that it would have to tackle ITV head on. For years, ITV alone had doled out cash and prizes, while the BBC had clung to the relative gentility of panel games. These were the televisual equivalent of the Victorian parlour game, in which the only reward was the approval of the host and audience, not to mention the sense of a job well and wittily done. With shows like *The Generation Game*, the BBC entered the game show arena fully.

The reason for the shift was that ratings, which had always been important, had become crucial, as the BBC came under increasing pressure to justify its right to the licence fee. Politically, the Corporation did itself no favours in 1971 with the transmission of *Yesterday's Men*, an unflattering documentary about the Labour Party in sudden and reluctant opposition. The relationship between the BBC and politicians would become increasingly adversarial over the next twenty years.

The development of the game show also reflected social changes. Just as BBC2 was a response to post-war improvements in education, game shows reflected a new, acquisitive, consumerist outlook, possibly a delayed reaction to the years of austerity and rationing. After so much make do and mend, the nation was asserting its right to amass as many candelabras and cuddly toys as it could get hold of. When Rediffusion lost its franchise in 1968, two of the game show stalwarts of the commercial television schedules went with it, namely *Double Your Money* and *Take Your Pick*. In their stead came other shows, not least of which was ATV's *The Golden Shot*.

The format came from Germany, where it was known as *Der goldene Schuss*. The McGuffin was a crossbow attached to the front of a television camera, operated by a blindfolded cameraman, who was receiving instructions on his aim at a novelty target from a viewer at home over the telephone. As such it had to be a live show, and it should have been a thrilling proposition, but *The Golden Shot* was not an immediate success. When it began in a prime Saturday night slot in July 1967, it was a ratings disaster. Although strong competition from BBC1, in the form of the *Black and White Minstrel Show* and *Billy Cotton's Music Hall*, was the main cause of the early disappointment, it had too many rounds and the choice of host did not help matters. Bob Monkhouse was the front-runner for the job, and wildly enthusiastic about the idea, but Lew Grade decided to offer it instead to Canadian singer Jackie Rae, former host of Granada's musical quiz *Spot the Tune*, who failed to stamp his personality on the show. Rae had impressed Grade when he played a game show host in a *Charlie Drake Show*, but although Rae could play a game show host perfectly well when scripted, he had none of the necessary ability to think on his feet and steer an unpredictable show to a satisfactory conclusion. And with live weapons in the studio, *The Golden Shot* was certainly unpredictable.

When Monkhouse was booked for a guest spot one week early in the show's run, he saw his chance. Instead of the crossbow, he arranged a cannon, from which a stooge was to be fired, as well as some other outlandish props, including a soundproofed booth that turned out to be a working shower. Suitably equipped, Monkhouse sent the show up something rotten, upstaging Jackie Rae. Producer Colin Clews advised Monkhouse that Grade and Bill Ward had given up on the show and stopped watching, so Monkhouse arranged for a telerecording to be made and ensured that the senior executives saw what he could do. The result was that Monkhouse took over from Rae and took firm control of the show.

At his suggestion, the number of rounds was reduced, to make proceedings rather less breathless and give guest stars a chance to shine. Originally named Heinz, in honour of the German original, the factotum who loaded the crossbow was given the more homely name of Bernie, leading to the alliterative and still fondly remembered catchphrase 'Bernie, the bolt'. Each edition was to have a theme, with the targets fashioned to correspond with the subject of the week. An early success was a music hall-themed show, with turns from variety veterans like comedian Sandy Powell, sentimental singer Randolph Sutton and male impersonator Hetty King, who had been Frankie Vaughan's mentor.

The changes improved the ratings drastically, and the final push came when the show moved to Sunday afternoons. Monkhouse has suggested that the rescheduling came about after Lew Grade's nephew Michael, then a show business agent, remarked to his uncle that cinemas were full on Sunday afternoons because there was nothing on television. There may be some truth in this, but the lead is more likely to have come from ATV's rival ABC, which shifted the show to Sunday teatimes in the Midlands and North after just a couple of months on air, with favourable results. From January 1968, the rest of the network followed suit.

Monkhouse's tenure on the show came to an abrupt end in 1972, when Francis Essex – who had returned from Scottish Television to become the controller of programmes at ATV – got wind of an apparent misdemeanour. One week on the show, Wilkinson Sword shaving products were the runner-up prize. Shortly beforehand, Monkhouse had been seen lunching with an advertising executive connected to Wilkinson Sword, at which a brown envelope was handed over. When this was reported back to Francis Essex, the assumption was that Monkhouse was taking cash bribes to feature Wilkinson Sword products. In fact, the contents of the parcel had been a rare and mildly salacious comic novel that the executive thought Monkhouse might enjoy. Nonetheless, Essex was unhappy with the host's relationship with an advertiser and sacked Monkhouse, replacing him with Norman Vaughan.

Unfortunately, in Monkhouse's words, Vaughan took to the show 'like a cat to water'.[32] Vaughan likened the experience to trying to be funny while directing traffic, and his discomfort showed. Eventually, much to his relief, ATV released the affable Vaughan from his contract, but his successor was even more out of his depth. Charlie Williams was a Yorkshire-born professional footballer turned comic. He was also black, and won no points with the emancipation lobby through his willingness to tell racist jokes. Like Rae, he proved unable to keep the show on the rails, and after six months, he was given the boot. Realizing that he had dismissed the perfect host over something trivial, Essex asked Monkhouse back. Monkhouse agreed on condition that he would be allowed to take on ATV's anglicization of the *Hollywood Squares* quiz, in which contestants tried to work out whether celebrities, sitting in a 3x3 noughts and crosses grid, were answering questions truthfully. There is a lot of snobbery about quiz shows, but the fact remains that hosting one well takes a great deal of skill, which Monkhouse had in spades. He regarded the quiz show as an utterly valid form of entertainment, and never looked down on what he was doing. He also loved the mechanics of the shows he presented, whereas all the other *Golden Shot* hosts looked like they wished they were doing something/anything else.

One of the few comedians at the time who matched Monkhouse as a game show ringmaster was Bruce Forsyth, with years of hair-raising live experience on the 'Beat the Clock' segment of *Sunday Night at the London Palladium*. After finally leaving *SNAP* in 1964, his career had somewhat been in the doldrums. He had appeared intermittently in his own shows for ABC, but a long and bitter battle with his agent Miff Ferrie had got in the way of bookings. Traditionally regarded as an ITV performer, the next big step in his career was to be with the BBC.

Bill Cotton Junior, newly elevated to head of light entertainment following the death of Tom Sloan in May 1970, visited the Dutch television service to give a talk. In return, his hosts showed him their hit game show *Één van de Acht* ('One Out Of Eight'), in which eight families competed to accomplish tasks set for them by experts. This aspect of the set-up was a win-win situation. If a task was completed well, the viewers could enjoy the vicarious satisfaction of a fellow ordinary punter having mastered a craft in minutes. If a task went disastrously, the viewers commiserated and empathized with the poor soul on screen. It was a people show. At the end, the winners were shown a series of prizes on a conveyer belt, and went home with every one of them that they could remember.

Cotton thought it was a great format, and knew instantly that he wanted Forsyth for the job. Indeed, in Cotton's mind, the man and the show were inextricably intertwined. 'I actually called it *The Bruce Forsyth Show* to start with, but then I thought, no I won't do that, in case he buggers off,' Sir Bill admits. 'I thought the format could work with somebody else, although at the time, I couldn't imagine doing it with anybody else.'[34] Instead, Cotton called it *Bruce Forsyth and The Generation Game*. Forsyth had been trying to convince Cotton to let him do a chat show, but once he saw the tape of the Dutch show, he was sold.

For the production of the new show, Cotton turned to a pair of his bright young producers from the mid-sixties intake, Colin Charman and Jim Moir. Moir recalls that, while the format was basically sound, he soon realized that he would need to make some fundamental changes:

> I was shown a short extract of the tape, we were then sent to Holland, to Vara Television in Hilversum where we realized that *Één van de Acht* was two hours long. Typical continental Saturday night television: these games interspersed with the Anne Ziegler and Webster Booth of Holland, oompah bands, dancers, a great big variety show with this running through it. I remember meeting with the Dutch producers, with whom we got on extremely well, and who were very flattered that the BBC was interested in *Één van de Acht*. I said 'It's two hours here, of course it'll be shorter at home.' 'Oh, how long's that?' 'Forty-five minutes.' The meal stopped. They were affronted, how could it be done in forty-five minutes? I said 'Well, it will be.' What we extracted from their show were the conveyer belt, which was revolutionary, and some of the wacky games that they had, which were really attempts at an expertise. I particularly remember the Punch and Judy man, putting the people behind to do that. It was a very, very great success and Bruce Forsyth hit the ground running. He was the perfect host.[35]

His suitability manifested itself in the way he kept such a fast-moving and unpredictable show firmly on the rails, and in the gently mocking way he dealt with the contestants, particularly his grimaces to camera when one of them said or did anything daft. A pilot was made and judged to be adequate but rough in places. Unfortunately, the first recording – just two days before the series was due to make its on-air debut – turned out to be over-complicated and slow, so the decision was taken to edit the pilot hurriedly for transmission. Unaware of the backstage dramas, viewers liked what they saw. Although pre-recorded, the show didn't follow neat, tidy, pre-rehearsed lines, so the host and the director had to treat the show effectively as live, as Roger Ordish, who directed some of the early editions, recalls:

Although it wasn't live, the direction aspect of it needed to be live. You had much less equipment than people nowadays. I think we had four cameras. You have four people doing something with a piece of pottery, you've got to have one on Bruce, and you need to see one on everything that's going on, so the cameramen really were brilliant. You know they're only seeing what's on their screen, so how can they know that they have to be over that way? They really needed to be directed. You had to see what Bruce was doing, and then you'd hear Bruce's voice, saying 'Oh dear,' and you'd think 'Oh what's he talking about? I can't see what he's talking about.' But the real adrenalin of doing it was tremendous.

It was so exciting doing it. I loved working with Bruce Forsyth. He's absolutely brilliant. My favourite Bruce line, which always sticks in my mind, I think it was the good old classic, the pottery, or a variant on that which had something that didn't work. Bruce was looking at this man's product on the turntable and saying 'Oh dear. What went wrong?' The man said 'Yes, I'm afraid it is a bit puckered,' and Bruce said 'Well and truly puckered.' A lovely moment.[36]

CHAPTER SEVEN

My auntie's
got a Whistler

The normal procedure for a light entertainment star had been to establish themselves at the BBC, before departing to ITV for more money, but Forsyth wasn't the first to reverse the trend. In 1968, Eric Morecambe and Ernie Wise had left ATV for the BBC. The official reason given was that they wanted to make shows in colour, and BBC2 already had the ability, whereas ATV was not due to transmit in colour until November 1969. In fact, the last ATV series had been made simultaneously in colour for America and monochrome for the domestic market, and Sir Bill Cotton was in no doubt about the real motivation: 'It was money. He [Lew Grade] wouldn't meet their demand.' Grade had offered them £39,000 for thirty-nine twenty-five-minute shows, but his nephew Michael, working as Eric and Ernie's agent, put professional matters ahead of family ties and offered them to Cotton, as Sir Bill recalls:

> They were an unknown commodity to a degree. They'd done very well for ATV, but they weren't enormous stars. I made an offer that was right at the top of the BBC's scale. Artists' bookings said 'You can't pay that amount of money, that just puts everything out of kilter. You'll get everybody saying, well if they get that money, why don't I get that money?' Well, I said, 'Line them up and I'll tell them why they don't. If anybody wants to come to me and say we want the same money as Morecambe and Wise, I'll say you be as good as them, you'll get it, I promise you. No question, you might even get more.'[1]

Cotton got his way by rationalizing that it was a three-year contract, and while the price may have seemed steep at the start, his confidence in Morecambe and Wise's talent was such that it would make it seem like a bargain by the end. The idea of spreading the cost over BBC1 and BBC2 also helped justify the finances, as John Ammonds, the producer from their radio days in Manchester who had been selected to take on the new series, explains. 'Lew Grade could never guarantee repeats because of the regional structure. We were on BBC2 in colour, then BBC1, which wasn't in colour, for which you get a double fee. So it was twice the money. That was a major thing. The big audience was when it got onto BBC1.'

As well as reuniting Eric and Ernie with Ammonds, Cotton had secured the scriptwriting services of Dick Hills and Sid Green, but the producer found them less than ideal, despite their track record with Eric and Ernie. 'They thought they could do anything, that was the trouble. They did write some good stuff, but they didn't write good stuff all the time. Also they were doing half-hour shows on commercial with two guest stars. So they didn't have much left to write.'[2] Nonetheless, the first recordings went ahead in early August 1968, to be transmitted on BBC2 in colour a month later. The series went down well with viewers and executives, and hopes were high for a second series building on the success, but it nearly didn't happen. On 7 November 1968, driving back from an engagement at Batley Variety Club to his Leeds hotel, Eric Morecambe suffered a severe heart attack.

He survived, and slowly it became apparent that he would eventually be fit to resume work, but as preparations were being made for a shorter second series, this time of forty-five-minute shows, the production hit another setback. Over lunch with Hills and Green's agent, Roger Hancock, Bill Cotton was taken aback to hear Hancock demand executive producer status for the writers as a condition for continued involvement. Morecambe and Wise's contract stipulated that Hills and Green should be the writers, so Hancock must have felt that their position was strong, but Cotton refused on a point of principle. 'I said "That is not negotiable. I am not having a couple of writers decide."

We were only on the avocado when he threw this bombshell, and I said "Well, now what do we talk about?" We chatted away, and he said "Are you sure?", I said I was positive. He said "Well what are you going to do?" I said "I have no idea, but something will turn up."[3]

What turned up was Eddie Braben, a dry, whimsical, former fruit and veg salesman from Liverpool, who had been making a respectable name for himself writing for the wild-haired laird of Knotty Ash, Ken Dodd. Cotton heard from Michael Hurll that Braben had decided to leave Dodd. Morecambe, Wise and Ammonds were all thrilled to hear that Braben might be available. Ammonds approved particularly because he knew Braben's approach to be more disciplined and diligent than that of Hills and Green, who would come in with ideas that they would develop with Eric, Ernie and whichever producer was in charge. In contrast, Braben was a self-contained gag machine, sending complete scripts from his Merseyside home. Ammonds observes that the writer had a lot in common with the performers:

> Like Eric and Ernie, he'd left school at 14. Eric said he didn't get as far as long division. Eddie's stuff was brilliant. We did some pretty heavy editing, Eric, Ernie and myself, but we couldn't have managed without Eddie, because he was such a marvellous gag man. He had this wonderful, Liverpudlian weird type of comedy. In one show, Eric had a trombone, Ernie was sitting alongside, and Eric was reminiscing about Mr Hardcastle, the bandmaster at the works. His one big ambition was to go down to London to the Albert Hall and see the finals of the brass band contest. Ernie said 'Well, did he make it?' Eric said 'Well he did get to the Albert Hall, but he went on the wrong night and Henry Cooper knocked him out in the first round.' That to me is classic Eddie Braben comedy.[4]

Braben also shifted the dynamic of the partnership slightly. At ATV, Ernie had been more of a conventional straight man, a relatively suave chap who had to deal with interruptions, digressions and diversions from his bespectacled friend, a miscreant child in a man's body. Braben's masterstroke was to give Ernie his own distinct comic persona – a vain, pompous, astonishingly prolific playwright with a taste for anachronistic historical epics, and a touching, but misguided, belief in his own abilities. The writer drew on the long friendship between the performers, and made it clear that while Morecambe was allowed to make fun of his companion, he wouldn't let anyone else get away with it. Braben supplied them with a back story which turned out to be a patchwork of their upbringings and his own, with references to Milverton Street School and a local temptress called Ada Bailey. He also supplied them with a life on screen, by setting sketches in the fictional flat that they shared, introducing an element of situation comedy into a variety format.

Guests were always a vital part of any variety show, and with Braben, Eric and Ernie continued and developed their policy of gentle mockery towards anyone who dared to appear on the show. This is almost certainly a key to their massive popularity. As a nation, the British can't bear anyone who's too full of themselves, as celebrities often can be. When Morecambe and Wise insulted a star, they did so with the full support of their audience, and the stars did their images no harm by taking it on the chin. And, as the show became increasingly popular, ever more illustrious figures lined up to be insulted. The turning point was their 1971 Christmas special. That was the show in which Shirley Bassey lost her shoes while singing her big number, only to have them replaced with the hobnailed boots of Eric and Ernie, dressed as a pair of brown-coated scene hands. It was also the show where Glenda Jackson was serenaded by Frank Bough, Cliff Michelmore, Patrick Moore, Michael Parkinson and Eddie Waring. As if those weren't riches enough, it was also the show in which Eric attempted to play Grieg's *Piano Concerto* under the baton of 'Andrew Preview'.

Throughout their career, Morecambe and Wise were never shy of reusing successful material, and this sketch was a revisitation of a routine written by Hills and Green back in the ATV days, but with several important differences.[5] The 'all the right notes, not necessarily in the right order' line is present in the original, as is the gag about the introduction being about a yard too short, but the presence of

André Previn as Andrew Preview takes the 1971 remake to a new level. It had been Ammonds's idea to enlist the conductor, after he saw him in a show made by John Culshaw for the music and arts department. Ammonds found Culshaw in an editing suite and asked whether he thought Previn would be game. Culshaw replied that he and Previn were lunching the next day, so he'd ask:

> True to his word, he rang me the following day, said André was very interested and gave me his number. I rang him, said I produced Morecambe and Wise and he said 'Before we go any further, you've got a great show there.' I said 'Thanks very much. I'm glad you said that because I want you to be on it.' He said he'd do it, so I asked him 'Can I call your agent and tell them you're interested?' He said 'Better than that. Ring my agent and tell them I'll definitely do it.'[6]

There was one small sticking point. Morecambe and Wise were hard workers, and were used to having their guests for a full week of rehearsal, but Previn's globe-trotting schedule allowed for a maximum of three days. Always a worrier, Eric Morecambe was concerned that it wouldn't be enough, but Ammonds replied that a few pages of dialogue wouldn't phase a man who carried whole symphonies around in his head. At the first read-through, Previn was spot on. 'The first time we did it, I cried laughing,' recalls Ammonds. 'We did it for about two or three hours, and every time he did it, it got funnier and funnier.' Unfortunately, on returning to his office, Ammonds found he had a message from Previn's agent explaining that the conductor had to pay a sudden visit to his ill mother in America, and that he wouldn't be back until the night before the show. Ammonds had no doubt that Previn would pull it off. His main concern was Morecambe:

> I thought 'Christ, how do I explain this to Eric, who's jibbing at three days?' I told Eric the next morning, and he said 'Sod him, we don't want him.' I said 'Whoa, you saw how good he was. We can rehearse, we'll be all right. I'll book a room at the Centre with a piano and we'll rehearse.

He lands at 5pm, I'll get a car to get him to the Centre for 6pm, and we'll rehearse until 10.' That's exactly what we did and every time we did it, I cried laughing. Eventually, André went, Ernie went and I was left with Eric. He said 'John, this is not going to be as funny as you think it is.' I just shrugged my shoulders because the following night with the audience, it went through the roof. He was marvellous.[7]

Over a drink many years later, Morecambe brought the subject up and told Ammonds 'John, I've never been more wrong. It's the funniest thing we've ever done.' As Ammonds admits, 'Some younger producers would have wilted – once he'd said "Sod him, we don't want him," that would have been it, but I knew it was going to be a gem.' It made Previn a celebrity among people who would never have listened to classical music if their lives depended on it, but the greatest accolade came from the landlord of his local pub. As Previn told Ammonds, 'When I'd been on *Morecambe and Wise*, they gave me my own tankard.'[8]

Producing such a high-ratings show was a high-pressure job, but Ammonds thrived on it, helped by a marked lack of interference from above. 'That was the joy of it really. I was absolutely in control. One year, I was editing until midnight on Christmas Eve. I was down in the dungeons at Television Centre and I thought to myself "Here am I – it's going to play to 24 million tomorrow night, and I'm the one man responsible for what goes in and what doesn't." On the money I was getting it was even more ridiculous.'[9] Nonetheless, in 1974, Ammonds decided to move on. He had concerns that Eddie Braben was being overworked, but Eric Morecambe brushed off suggestions that other writers join the team. Ammonds also found himself being spread too thin, taking on responsibility for impressionist Mike Yarwood's shows. Fortunately, the ideal replacement was already part of the family, in the form of Ernest Maxin, who had been lending the shows his choreographic expertise when not producing the *Black and White Minstrel Show*.

Under Maxin, *The Morecambe and Wise Show* experienced a subtle shift. Ammonds was a ruthless script editor and an expert in directing the written word. Raised on a diet of Hollywood musicals, Maxin's forte was in visual comedy and the big showpieces: 'They used to call me "Mr MGM" – Maxin Goldberg Maxin.'[10] The MGM influence was obvious in the 1976 and 1977 Christmas specials. The former featured both the famous *Singing in the Rain* send-up, with Ernie as Gene Kelly and Eric as the deluged cop, and Angela Rippon's celebrated emergence from behind the news desk. Inspired by Rippon's example, others wanted to get in on the act. Maxin recalls: 'One of the newscasters, I think it was Richard Baker, put his head round my office and said "Do you think you can use me in a show?" He's a musician, and I said "Yes, I'll have a think about it." Then later that day, Michael Aspel put his head around my door, and I thought "Hang on, I'll use them all together."' So it was that the following year's show featured a stunning pastiche of *South Pacific*, with Aspel, Baker, film reviewers Philip Jenkinson and Barry Norman, Michael Parkinson, Eddie Waring from *It's a Knockout*, and Baker's fellow newsreaders Richard Whitmore and Peter Woods in sailor suits. This unlikely chorus sang *There Is Nothing Like a Dame* and appeared to turn cartwheels and somersaults, thanks to a few professional acrobats and some clever editing. Maxin notes that the routine gave Morecambe the jitters, just as Andrew Preview's appearance had six years earlier:

When we got to rehearsals, I hadn't actually realized that I couldn't get them all there at the same time, because they were all on different duties. Eric was very poorly – this was just before his second heart attack. His lips went blue, he went to the piano in the rehearsal room, leaned on it and said 'This will never work. I can't see it working.' I couldn't convince him, but Ernie put his arm around him and said 'Look, if it doesn't work, we don't use it.' If it hadn't been for Ernie, that number wouldn't have gone on.

We shot the whole thing in fifteen minutes, and finished at about eight o'clock. Eric was so worried. Ernie wasn't worried at all. Eric asked if he could come and watch the edit, and I said come back at about 11. I saw it run through, and it looked great. He came in, ashen white. He said 'Well?' I said 'The best thing to do, you come and sit beside me and we'll run the thing.' I watched his face. I could see the reflection in the screen. He was sitting back. As it went on he began to lean forward, and at the end the tears were running down his face. He said 'Bloody hellfire, Ernest, it works,' put his arms around me, and gave me a hug.

How we did it was, you'd see Frank Bough in a mid shot to establish him there. Stop, cut to a long shot, see the acrobat do the trick. Then you come out of it like you've just done the trick, put the three together. Some of the public thought it was real. Richard Baker came into my office and said 'I'm in trouble. I've been invited to open a fête and do my acrobatic trick. What can I do? I can't give the game away.'[11]

That show pulled in an audience of 28 million viewers and meant that the pair ended their BBC career on a massive high, for in 1978, they succumbed to overtures from Philip Jones at Thames to rejoin commercial television's star armada. The move came just as Bill Cotton Junior was stepping up to become the controller of BBC1, after eight years in charge of light entertainment.

When John Ammonds left Morecambe and Wise, his main commitment had been to Mike Yarwood, whom he describes as 'the most nervous performer I think I've ever encountered, except Frankie Howerd'.[12] He was also that greatest of show business clichés, a shy man driven to perform. Born and raised in Stockport, Yarwood had come up on the pub and club circuit around Manchester in the early sixties, and gained a considerable reputation as an impressionist. One of his earliest triumphs had been an uncanny ability to mimic both Harry H. Corbett and Wilfrid Brambell in their roles as Steptoe and Son. With the help of his friend Royston Mayoh, a producer at ABC's Didsbury studios, he made his first appearances on television as an impressionist, but it was when he appeared on *Sunday Night at the London Palladium* in 1964 that he became a national name. A BBC2 series called *Three of a Kind* followed in 1967 (the other two were comedian Ray Fell and singer Lulu), then two series for ATV. He returned to the BBC for *Look – Mike Yarwood!* (produced in tandem with his radio series, *Listen – Mike Yarwood!*) in 1971, beginning the run that, with *Mike Yarwood in Persons* from 1976 onwards, was to make him a superstar.

Although too gentle in his humour to be regarded as a real satirist, Yarwood's stock-in-trade was the political figures of the day, in particular Labour prime minister Harold Wilson and his eyebrow-heavy Chancellor of the Exchequer, Denis Healey. As important as his considerable voice skills was his ability to change between characters in the fraction of a second it takes to cut between cameras. Clever angles and direction meant that he could have conversations with himself as two different characters. The apex of this was singing 'My Way', with a line from each of his best-known impersonations. Much of his material relied on placing august governmental figures in incongruous situations, such as depicting Edward Heath on *Top of the Pops*, singing the Rod Stewart hit 'Sailing', a reference to his maritime proclivities. Away from politics, Yarwood also did a devastating Hughie Green, who spent many years working with Yarwood's old associate Royston Mayoh. He was also, with Stanley Baxter, at the forefront of using television technology to play multiple characters.

Unfortunately, the election of Margaret Thatcher as prime minister in 1979 rendered many of Yarwood's signature take-offs redundant. Janet Brown was drafted in to play the Iron Lady, but Yarwood never quite recovered. He followed Morecambe and Wise to Thames in 1982, and remained popular without ever quite recapturing his preeminence. Even with advances in technology, his shows remained among the most labour-intensive in television. At Thames, his 1985 Christmas special was scheduled for five days in the studio at Teddington, after three weeks of rehearsal and other shooting. This was to be followed by a week of editing before transmission, a short lead time for such a complex production, as director/producer Philip Casson observed. 'We've got to put it together, dub it and track it, so that it goes out by December 23. But it's only late in so much as it's close to the air date.' Casson also indicated that most of the studio time was spent waiting for Yarwood to emerge from costume and make-up: 'The time has nothing to do with how long it actually takes to shoot it.'[13]

He added the Prince of Wales to his repertoire, aided by actress Suzanne Danielle as an almost-mute Diana, but Yarwood was not sufficiently able to move with the times. As late as 1984, he was still doing Harold and Albert Steptoe, ten years after the last episode of the sitcom had been screened. He was also battling alcoholism, caused by drinking to calm his considerable nervousness. His last Thames show was in 1987, after which he slipped into semi-retirement.

Performers like Morecambe and Wise had worked their way up from the variety theatres to television, so the demise of the variety halls had robbed up-and-coming performers of a vital training ground. Most new artists had once learned their craft on the lower-rent halls, the 'number twos', and these had been among the first to close, many disappearing in the years immediately after the Second World War. When the top-line venues, the 'number ones', followed in their wake, it seemed like there was nowhere for performers to go. Talent shows had existed for as long as television – ATV had Carroll Levis' *Discoveries*, while Hughie Green's famous *Opportunity Knocks* ran for seventeen years from 1961 – but the chances of an untried performer getting straight on screen were small, the chances of that performer being a hit were infinitesimal, and the wrong type of exposure was potentially fatal to a career. The answer came from the north, where, in many respects, live entertainment had remained close to its music hall roots. Each town may have had its variety theatres, but it also had working men's clubs and social clubs, where acts were booked for the enjoyment of those who went to drink, an echo of the early music hall days. It was in these venues that the likes of Yarwood served their apprenticeships.

Bernie Clifton had begun his show business career in the late fifties as a singer, working with the band at his local Co-op dance hall in St Helen's ('The very dance hall I was thrown out of for riding the doorman's bike around the dance floor'). When he was called up for National Service he kept his hand in with weekend gigs in pubs and clubs, and found himself in a very fortunate position. 'I was stationed at RAF Lindholm near Doncaster,' he explains. 'At the time, that was the new entertainment centre of the north. The theatres were closing, the clubs were opening, and Doncaster and Sheffield were where it was at.' It was during this time that he began adding comedy to the musical element of his act:

In St Helens as a fifteen-year-old, we had this weird, funny sense of humour. We'd go to the pictures on a Sunday, and instead of watching the film, we'd start this thing called the 'ten o'clock rally'. As the cinema clock got to ten o'clock, we would all have secreted on our person some form of noise-making machine – a bicycle bell, a rattle, a mouth organ, a kazoo or a Jew's harp. Anything you could put in your pocket. We used to ruin the film. I don't know if it was so much [being] Catholic, it was bred on those little side streets, those little rows and rows of terraced houses. If you didn't do something, you'd go mad.

When I was doing the pubs and clubs, I insulated myself from the deaths by becoming an entertainer. It would depend where I was. I'd try a few gags out if the audience were nice, and if they liked it, I'd try more. On it went. The following week, if I was down the road five miles and they were a tough audience, I wouldn't do any gags, which really confused the small following I had. Off stage, I was Harry Secombe, Peter Sellers, Spike Milligan, but on stage I was shy. There's a difference between being funny in a bar with the lads, and doing it on stage. I've still got my [business] card. I was a 'vocal entertainer'. On the cards it says 'Entertainment guaranteed. Own transport'. Which is a bizarre thing to say on a card, but very important. If you had your own transport, it would mean that you could do the last spot after the bingo and not get the 9.30 bus from the pit village back into Doncaster.[14]

During the sixties, the smaller clubs and pubs in the north were joined by a new breed of club, vast venues offering reasonably priced drinks, a full menu, the chance to gamble and see some top-class entertainers at work. The pioneer was the Greasbrough Social Club, near Rotherham in South Yorkshire, which had been established in 1920 as the United Army, Navy and Airmen's Club. By 1957, it had 200 more members than could be accommodated in its 300-capacity wooden premises, so a new £36,000 club, with a concert room holding 450, was built opposite. The entertainment on offer proved so popular that the membership list soon grew to four times the club's capacity.

The best known of all these super-clubs opened on Easter Sunday 1967 in Batley, West Yorkshire, on the site of a former sewage works. The entrepreneur behind the scheme was Jimmy Corrigan, the son of a travelling showman. Corrigan had been a bingo caller at his family's fairgrounds in his youth, so when bingo halls were legalized, he recognized the opportunity and began building a chain, twenty-three strong at its peak. Anxious to diversify, the success of Greasbrough had prompted Corrigan's next move, and when he saw the derelict site in November 1966, he moved quickly. With a £60,000 loan from Scottish and Newcastle Breweries, the building proceeded at breakneck pace, with floodlights being installed on site to allow workmen to work until midnight.

The publicity for the opening night promised 'seating for 1,500', 'a full two-hour show', 'light catering' and 'drinks at normal prices', not to mention the luxury of air conditioning. The choice of the Irish singing group the Bachelors as the opening attraction reflected the Corrigan family's background, as did the arrival of Val Doonican for the second week. After that, Kathy Kirby and Kenny Ball shared top billing for a week, then it was Jimmy Tarbuck's turn, followed by Bob Monkhouse and Lonnie Donegan, then – just two months before her tragic death – the Hollywood starlet Jayne Mansfield. Batley Variety Club was a roaring success from the start, and in time, everyone who was anyone in entertainment performed at the club.

In 1968, the newly established ITV company Yorkshire Television highlighted the growth of Batley as an entertainment hotspot by sending an outside broadcast crew to record a variety show pilot at

Seriously, they're doing a grand job: *That Was the Week That Was*, 1963

The George Mitchell Minstrels on record, 1964

The weekend starts here with Dusty Springfield on *Ready Steady Go!*, 1964

BBC2 starts here with Duke Ellington on *Jazz 625*, 1964

Right: Shirley Bassey and Tommy Trinder share a joke, circa 1957

Below: Bruce Forsyth and Sammy Davis Junior share an LWT variety spectacular, 1980

Left: Rolf Harris, British television's original Mr Saturday Night

Below: Michael Parkinson, inheritor of the Saturday night crown, raising a glass on a motor boat with bandleader Harry Stoneham

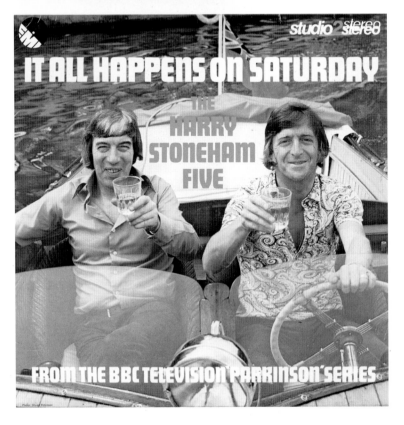

the club, hosted by singer Ronnie Hilton. Unfortunately, a lack of available programmes meant that the pilot went out hurriedly in an unfinished edit, which soured relations between Corrigan and Yorkshire. Barney Colehan, the BBC's northern region TV light entertainment producer, had put northern clubs on television in the outside broadcast series *Club Night*, but the job of representing this new arena of entertainment fully on screen fell to Johnnie Hamp, head of light entertainment at Granada in Manchester. Raised in Carshalton, Surrey, Hamp had begun his show business career as a performer, doing a Danny Kaye-inspired mime act in a touring show put together by Bryan Michie, the ex-BBC radio producer who had discovered Morecambe and Wise. The first show on the tour had been at the ornate, gothic Granada in Woolwich and when he had completed his National Service in the RAF, he approached the company for a job. After working as assistant manager at various Granada 'theatres' (as Sidney Bernstein insisted on his cavernous, lavishly decorated cinemas being called), he went to head office in Golden Square as the publicity manager's assistant, being promoted to the top job when the incumbent died. He also began putting together live shows for the circuit, before moving over to the company's London-based television operation at the Chelsea Palace in 1960.

> I was doing things like *Spot the Tune* with Marion Ryan, *Criss Cross Quiz* with Barbara Kelly and a show with Bob Holness called *Take a Letter* [Hamp recalls]. Granada did a lot of quiz shows at that time. Then I went up to Manchester, specifically to produce light entertainment. Granada was very much a drama and current affairs organization. There wasn't a light entertainment department at all, but I tried to make a few big shows. When blues musicians like Muddy Waters were touring over here, I put together a show called *I Hear the Blues*. The last show I remember doing at Chelsea was *The Bacharach Sound* in 1965.[15]

Whereas the BBC tradition had been for producers to be directors as well, Hamp was less a technician and more of an old-fashioned impresario. 'I always thought that the producer's job was to put the show together,' he rationalizes. One of his best-known early productions was a one-off stand-up comedy special in 1965 starring Woody Allen, who was then hardly known outside Greenwich Village. 'He was making *What's New Pussycat* at the time, and I went across to Paris to see if he'd be interested in making a one-off show. He was quite insistent about plugging his new LP, and I said "I'm not going to let you just plug the LP. At least we can turn it into a gag."'[16] Hamp replaced the vinyl LP in the sleeve with a fragile 78 rpm disc, which Allen dropped and smashed.

Such specials aside, a significant outlet for Hamp's work in the mid-sixties was the regional news magazine *Scene at Six-Thirty*, hosted variously by Mike Scott, Gay Byrne and an up-and-coming reporter from Barnsley called Michael Parkinson. Although nominally a current affairs show, it featured entertainment guests every night of the week. Elsewhere in Manchester, the BBC was making *Top of the Pops*, but Hamp was able to get the best new bands into the *Scene at Six-Thirty* studio before their record had hit the charts, stealing a march on the opposition. One of those bands was the Beatles: 'We were in the right place at the right time,' Hamp confesses. 'It was a regional show, but it was a big region, because we covered Yorkshire as well at the time, and we were often in the top ten.'[17]

The competition between ATV and ABC, and later ATV, Thames, Yorkshire and London Weekend Television, had always meant that Granada tended to enter the light entertainment melee only when it could offer something distinctive and different. The burgeoning club scene gave Granada that in spades. 'I went to a lot of clubs to see the top of the bill, and I always found that there was a pretty good comic as compère,' Hamp says, as he recalls the inspiration for *The Comedians*, one of Granada's big entertainment successes of the seventies. He gathered some of the best club comics, including former dance band crooner-turned-club owner Bernard Manning, the great if relentless Frank Carson, ex-professional footballer Charlie Williams and former teacher Jim Bowen, and recorded them doing their acts, or, in Manning's case, the cleaner end of it, in front of a studio audience. Hamp's stroke of genius was to take only the very best gags and to use the new technology of videotape editing to create a quick-fire comedic assault. Hamp estimates that 80 per cent of the material recorded was never used. Even though videotape editing had come on a little from the early days of physically cutting the tape with a razor blade, 'it was still cumbersome – we were working with two-inch tape. If there was a joke an hour and ten minutes in, it took about six minutes to wind through, and then you might find that you didn't want it anyway.'[18]

There was scepticism about whether the show would take off. Even Frank Carson thought it would never work. It worked. Fast-moving in a way that had not been seen on British television before, *The Comedians* would become a massive hit and made stars of the comics it featured, sending their club earning potential skywards and propelling some into their own television shows. It was to run for eleven series between 1971 and 1992. Bernard Manning, who had been dismissed by many at Granada as just a blue comic until Hamp showed them how clean he could work, was to become a central figure in Hamp's next big hit show.

The Wheeltappers and Shunters Social Club, which began in 1974, wore its clubland influences proudly on its sleeve. It had begun as part of the stage version of *The Comedians* that Hamp put on in Blackpool and at the London Palladium. The segment proved so successful that Hamp realized it could be a potential format. 'Shows never turn out as expected, but this one worked out exactly as I'd written it,' notes Hamp.[19] The idea was to feature up-and-coming turns, which included comedy double act Cannon and Ball and magician Paul Daniels, alongside established turns in a fictitious northern working men's club setting, linked by compère/singer Manning and the clueless, ignorant chairman of the committee, played by *Comedians* favourite Colin Crompton. Viewed from a modern perspective, the idea that big stars like Buddy Greco, Tessie O'Shea, Howard Keel, Bill Haley and Roy Orbison would play such a venue seems to be a big joke, but in reality, it wasn't so far from the truth, with the likes of Louis Armstrong playing Batley. No star, no matter how elevated, was safe from Manning's knocking introductions. He introduced the Irish singing group the Bachelors by saying 'They've been here three or four times before. They come here every week for £10. I know very well they can't afford to pay us.'[20] Crompton's deliberately ill-informed interruptions (mostly written by Crompton himself, with occasional help from Neil Shand) were also a constant, heralded by the clang of the fire bell he kept on his desk. 'Just notice, anybody going on the Territorial Army weekend, reveille is at six o'clock. If you don't like this Italian food, take some butties,' was one early example.[21]

Where *Stars and Garters* had tried and failed to recreate the atmosphere of an East London pub in a television studio ten years earlier, the *Wheeltappers and Shunters* got the mood absolutely right in a similarly artificial setting. The atmosphere was almost palpable, the illusion was perfect. The audience were all in the mood, as well they might be with twelve acts per show and unlimited free beer on offer. 'Normally you issue 500 tickets to get 200 people in, but not for the *Wheeltappers*,' Hamp notes. The cameras were well hidden, and the studio audience were lulled into forgetting that they were on television by an absence of the procedures that usually characterize television recordings. 'We never had a countdown, we just used to start it,' Hamp recalls. 'Bernard would sing a song. We didn't make a big thing of it.' The net result was that Hamp 'used to get phone calls trying to book a table. Tim Farmer [the show's designer] should have won an award.'[22]

David Liddiment, later to become Hamp's successor, but then a junior member of the Granada programme trail-making staff, expresses great admiration for the way the show was made.

What was clever about the *Wheeltappers and Shunters* [was that] when you went into studio 6 for a recording of the *Wheeltappers* you were not in studio 6. You were in a club. It was four walls, it ran uninterrupted, they never stopped. If something went wrong, Bernard would come on, do a bit of banter with Colin, the show never stopped. He gave an audience an evening's entertainment, the same with *The Comedians*.[23]

The *Wheeltappers and Shunters* served its last pint in July 1977, but the idea of showcasing new acts without forcing them to compete in a talent show carried on. One later series developed by Johnnie Hamp was *Fully Licensed for Singing and Dancing*, which ran on Friday nights in 1979 and 1980. Instead of recreating the club atmosphere in the studio, outside broadcast cameras went to the north's cabaret nightspots and recorded acts on their home turf. The results were then linked by gentle Irish comedian Roy Walker, another *Comedians* discovery. This was followed in 1981 by *The Video Entertainers*, for which Hamp went in front of the cameras himself, at the instigation of Granada managing director David Plowright, to introduce the acts in front of a set featuring a television and one of those new-fangled video cassette recorders (a top loader with 'piano keys') such as could be obtained from Granada's own TV rental shops.[24]

Johnnie Hamp's unpretentious, but deceptively clever television programmes in the seventies and eighties captured a microcosm of the era's entertainment world, from the strangest spesh acts to the bill-topping Hollywood stars. Away from television and the clubs, the best performers were guaranteed bookings in the highly successful summer shows that each major seaside town offered. Blackpool was the Mecca, with three theatrically equipped piers, several large theatres on land, the famous Tower ballroom and circus, and a plethora of smaller bars, each of which could usually support an electric organist, a drummer and a singer/comedian, not to mention the Pleasure Beach at the south end of the 'Golden Mile' for the children. At the resort's peak in the forties and fifties, there was barely enough space left on the beach for the famous donkey rides, largely because whole factories would close for a uniform holiday period, rather than organizing staggered leave.

Before she became a theatrical agent, Blackpool native Jan Kennedy was a singer, known as Jan Currey. 'The sixties was when it was at its height,' she asserts, and she should know, having been crowned Blackpool's 'girl of the year' in 1965. 'I remember doing a tour of all the theatres in my capacity as girl of the year. At the ABC, we had Marty Wilde, at the Opera House, we had the Black and White Minstrels, at the North Pier we had Gerry and the Pacemakers and at the South Pier, I think we had Freddie and the Dreamers. In every major theatre, there was a major show. And on a Friday night, they used to queue round the block for tickets to the show. On Friday they used to arrive to go to the guest houses and hotels, the wife used to go and unpack, and the husband went to queue for theatre tickets. That's how it was. You couldn't walk on the promenade, you couldn't get a place on the beach.'[25]

Other resorts were just as busy. East Londoners had Southend-on-Sea, with the longest pier in Britain and the sprawling Kursaal complex offering almost every amusement known to man. South Londoners had Margate; Midlanders favoured Great Yarmouth in Norfolk, with its two thriving pier theatres – the Wellington and the Britannia – and Jack Jay's famous Windmill Theatre, complete with a working, illuminated windmill on its tall, elegant 1908 facade. In the days before cheap air travel, British holidaymakers seeking fun rather than elevation were so spoilt for choice with the likes of Bournemouth, Eastbourne, Worthing, Weston-super-Mare, Scarborough, Lowestoft and Morecambe that they could have visited a different resort each year without repeating themselves once during their children's formative years. In reality, tribal loyalties and transport tended to keep the punters visiting the same towns year after year, and, once they'd found one they liked, usually the same guest house each year too.

For those who favoured familiarity over the unknown on their summer break, holiday camps were ideal, funfair proprietor Billy Butlin having opened the first at Skegness in 1936. In the early twentieth century, standardization had been an important factor in industry and business. This was not in the sense of levelling down to a low common denominator, so much as producing objects or services to a consistently high standard at the lowest cost. At a holiday camp, everything the average working-class holidaymaker could possibly want in terms of food, drink and entertainment was available on site. After the Second World War, Butlin's success enabled him to expand further, until he ran a total of nine camps, including Clacton, Pwllheli and Bognor Regis. In 1946, Fred Pontin had opened a rival firm, beginning with a camp in Somerset.

Into the seventies, domestic resorts and holiday camps remained in rude health, but gradually, the rise of cheap flights and package tour operators ate into their market. Resorts like Great Yarmouth did a passable impersonation of booming and bustling into the late eighties, but smaller resorts had begun their retrenchment earlier. Only Blackpool remained, and remains, largely oblivious to trends in holidaymaking.

The glory days of clubland came to an end rather more abruptly, beginning with the introduction of the 1968 Gaming Act, which insisted on a complete separation between gambling and entertainment. Clubs could offer both, but each had to have a separate entrance, and it was no longer possible to see the stage from the casino area. Later legislation denying many clubs gaming licences of any kind finished the job off. 'Most of them were run with gambling at the side,' says Jan Kennedy. 'The Cresta club, Solihull; Batley Variety Club; Wakefield Theatre Club. The gambling licences paid for the entertainment, as they do at Las Vegas and other major entertainment resorts. So the demise of the variety club entertainment really slipped back with the licensing laws. The variety clubs in that sense of the word really started to go downhill from that moment, which was a great shame. The working men's clubs carried on.'[26] Batley Variety Club soldiered on in greatly reduced circumstances until July 1978, reopening that September as West Yorkshire's answer to Studio 54, a discotheque called Crumpet.

★

Despite all of the innovations that had taken place in variety formats, the demise of *Sunday Night at the London Palladium* in 1967 and the closure of many of the traditional outlets for live variety, the traditional act shows were still going strong on television. *International Cabaret* had been part of BBC2's programme roster from its first weekend on-air, but its ancestry went back much further, a show with an identical title having gone out from Alexandra Palace in pre-war days. Indeed, the core purpose of the show in the sixties was nearly identical to its 1937 counterpart – presenting the best European performers, particularly speciality acts, to a British audience. There were also similarities with *Café Continental*, which had been pensioned off in 1955 when producer Henry Caldwell left for commercial television. On both shows, the studio was laid out as a cabaret club, with the audience at tables. In the case of *International Cabaret*, the audience at the Television Theatre had the benefit of free cigarettes, supplied as fully practical props at the request of producer Stewart Morris.

In July 1966, Kenneth Williams took over as compère. He replaced the usual slick, respectful introductions that acts and viewers had come to expect with rambling monologues about the various indignities he had been forced to endure in rehearsals. After expounding at length about fictional run-ins with the make-up and lighting staff, who found it impossible to make him any better looking, and chiding the audience for an insufficient response by reminding them that it was a variety show not a séance, he would then introduce the acts as if it were an afterthought. It was a clever stroke, contrasting physically strenuous performances with a host who seemed utterly indifferent to the whole shebang. Always his own harshest critic, Williams thought that he'd fallen flat on his first show, and it wasn't until he saw a playback a couple of days later that he realized that it had gone very well indeed. Sufficiently bolstered, Williams made the series his own. Stewart Morris remembers him as 'the most directable guy . . . such a funny man, but personally so unhappy. [He had] a great brain. He and John Law used to sit together in that little office and knock it [the script] out. Bless him, he was always word perfect.'[27]

Meanwhile, Stewart Morris was traversing Europe making sure that Williams and Law had acts to write introductions for, however idiosyncratic:

I used to spend the summer, basically, touring Europe looking for acts, especially spesh acts, very hard to find, but they were around. One was a girl who came on with a machine that looked like a pinball machine and it had a little dummy artist [gestures to indicate a diminutive figure] that high who would paint on the upright surface at the back. It was quite amazing. I think she really just talked to it. I don't think she played any great part. But inside that was a man. Folded up with his arm up the back, drawing blind. He had to be let out within moments of the end of the act, otherwise he'd be dead. He couldn't breathe. He used to get out and it used to take minutes to revive him because he was folded and couldn't unfold. He was locked in position.

I think the greatest spesh act I ever worked with was Italian – an opera singer, and his partner was a waiter. The opera singer used to come on in white tie and tails, and then came the irritations of the waiter, this little guy. The way I did it, I got him to serve drinks around the tables before the act so they'd seen him working, and when he dropped a cup, then a tray of cutlery, it was all set up. It worked perfectly, falling over, dropping the tray. In the end he'd get up there and do pirouettes – ballet – on the stage. Then the opera singer would lift him up and he would still be singing the aria. A brilliant act and also the most expensive act I ever used, and I had to wait a long time to get them.[28]

Morris has similarly fond memories of an equestrian trio called Les Cascadeurs, whom he used in the winning 1977 BBC entry for the Golden Sea Swallow prize at the television festival in Knokke:

As the producer/director, you had to do the show as live, you were not allowed to edit it or stop, and if you did, that was going to be transmitted. I took Rolf Harris, Bonnie Tyler and this spesh act that I'd seen at the Lido in Paris. A wonderful French agent called Carmen Bajot took me there. Part of the act, a man canters onto this tiny stage, and the horse falls, literally goes right over and throws him. Lands by my feet, for Christ's sake. The horse is whinnying, feet thrashing and I'm about to leave. I said 'Carmen, we cannot ever do this on television, it's too bloody dangerous,' and she said 'Stewart, I'm going to bring you back tomorrow and you will see the horse fall in precisely the same place,' and I did go back because I didn't believe it. We did the show in the ballroom in the casino on the first floor. There was no lift so I said to the casino manager 'We've got no alternative. We've got to go up the grand staircase.' And that's what we did, rode the three horses up the staircase, into the ballroom and into a room we'd converted into a mini stable. When we did the act, the guy did the fall and they had the old travolator, so the horse would go on it, having picked up Bonnie Tyler, and was cantering off into the night. I'm afraid the opposition didn't have anything like that. Great entertainment, great showmanship.[29]

Over at ATV, a mid-seventies revival of the *Palladium* show, with Ted Rogers as host, had foundered, but in 1977, a new variety show from the company hit the airwaves to great and instant acclaim. Instead of using an established comedian as host, ATV took a risk on a newcomer. Moreover, he was a frog, and his leading lady was a pig. Over the next five years, *The Muppet Show* would attract star guests as diverse as John Cleese and Julie Andrews – on whose special the Henson puppets had first come to Lew Grade's attention. One of the most memorable visitors to *The Muppet Show* set at Elstree was drummer Buddy Rich, enlisted at the suggestion of musical director Jack Parnell. 'I remember going to Jim Henson saying "Hey, you ought to get the greatest drummer in the world – Buddy Rich,"' Parnell remembers. 'He said "Who? Never heard of him." I think he was kidding me. I said "He's the greatest thing you ever heard." He said "All right then," and we got him, just like that.'[30] Rich was to take on the infamous Muppet drummer Animal, whose percussive noises were in reality supplied by Parnell's successor in the Ted Heath band, the great Ronnie Verrell.

Henson had developed the puppets originally for the US children's show *Sesame Street*, but had been trying to take them to a wider audience. With the exception of some appearances on *Saturday Night Live* in its early days, Henson had not been able to interest any American networks in his creation. The impasse was broken when they came to Elstree to appear in a Julie Andrews special for ATV. Lew Grade 'was tremendously taken' with what he saw and told Henson that the Muppets could have a series of their own, a series that Grade then sold back to the US network CBS.[31]

★

'Spesh' acts apart, the seventies also saw the final flowering of performers who had come up through the variety ranks in the traditional way, having entered the business while there was still a circuit to speak of. All were of a standard befitting their experience, but a couple stood out from the rest, such that they are still fondly remembered, years after their death. One was Tommy Cooper. Like many comedians born during the reign of King George V, Cooper found his performing feet in the services, although his earliest shows as a conjuror had been for the benefit of his colleagues at the British Power Boat Company in Hythe, near Southampton, where he had been an apprentice before the Second World War. It had been there, when a trick involving an egg on a piece of elastic went wrong but got laughs, that Cooper first glimpsed the comic possibilities of magic by misadventure.

He seems to have spent most of his wartime service in the Royal Horse Guards as a protected species, beyond the rigours of conventional military discipline, aided by his status as the camp clown. Given to performing in a pith helmet, he adopted his trademark fez when working with a Combined Services Entertainment unit in the Middle East. Someone appeared to have taken the pith, so he purloined a waiter's headgear and a comic legend was born. After demob, he worked at the Windmill Theatre, and appeared on television, including a spot in the first variety show to come from the BBC studios at Lime Grove, in December 1950, but the new medium seemed unsure how to handle his obvious talent. Indeed, it wasn't until the late sixties that Cooper was presented to his best advantage on television, by which time he was already a national treasure through his ceaseless live work in theatre and cabaret and further guest appearances on TV variety shows.

The first of television's unsuccessful attempts to harness this force of nature was *It's Magic* produced by Graeme Muir for the BBC in 1952. Only one series was made, and it wasn't until 1957 that anyone tried to repeat the experience, when Associated-Rediffusion made one series with him. Then followed a one-off *Saturday Spectacular* for ATV, and a series called *Cooper's Capers* in 1958. Once again, the trail ran cold, this time for eight years. Cooper had made several memorable guest appearances on the *Billy Cotton Band Show*, and Bill Cotton Junior, as BBC TV's head of variety, had wanted to sign Cooper for a series. There was then an internal kerfuffle over whether the Cooper show should be made by the variety department or Frank Muir's comedy department. When the comedy department won, but decided to make a pilot before proceeding to a series, Cooper's agent Miff Ferrie took his client to ABC at Teddington.

Unfortunately, the first ABC outing was as unsatisfactory as his previous television shows. Ferrie had a tendency to regard himself as a comedy expert, despite being, in writer David Nobbs' estimation, 'about as funny as Liverpool Street station',[32] and consequently he often interfered with the creative process to disastrous effect. The show's format – the credit or blame for which was taken by Ferrie – was an odd mishmash of a variety show and a cod current affairs programme, under the title *Cooperama*. There were the usual speciality acts and musical guests – one surviving show features a pair of acrobats in the first half and jazz clarinettist Acker Bilk in the second. However, instead of being allowed to front the programme himself, Cooper was interviewed about his life and exploits, some genuine, some fictitious, which would then be illustrated with sketches in flashback. The original plan had been to enlist a genuine heavyweight interviewer, but when none proved available, actor Derek Bond was booked. Bond had some experience as a genuine interviewer on the BBC's *Tonight* programme, but was less than ideal when playing one from a script.

Happily, ABC's second attempt – *Life with Cooper*, beginning in 1966

– hit the mark. Out went the interviewer, leaving Cooper to speak to the audience directly in stand-up mode, and out went the guests, leaving a good, tight sketch show. It was to be the blueprint for all Cooper's subsequent television shows.

Les Dawson was another performer who, like Cooper, was in a league of his own. On a very superficial level, Dawson was just another northern comic, telling mother-in-law jokes. In fact, Dawson was a craftsman, honing his material carefully, choosing each word very deliberately for the maximum effect. His mother-in-law jokes were eloquent, often showing him to be the frustrated novelist that he, for many years, was. He was a master of bathos, his florid descriptions building the audience up perfectly for a vulgar punchline. A prime example was a lyrical monologue about sitting, taking in the beauty of the night sky, that ends with Dawson realizing that he needs to put a new roof on his outside lavatory.

Tough audiences in rough areas warmed to him because of his lack of false jollity, and because they recognized one of their own. He had been born in 1931 in Collyhurst, one of the poorest parts of Manchester. Before achieving success as a comic, he had been a Hoover salesman, an apprentice electrician of stunning ineptitude, a National Serviceman and the pianist in a Parisian brothel. His was the comedy of misery and resignation. 'Good evening, fun hunters' was a regular opening line to his act, delivered with heavy irony. When he made his first major television appearance in the sixties, he explained the dressing room hierarchy – top acts on the ground floor, lesser acts on the first floor, and so on. Then came the killer punchline: 'To give you some idea what they think of me, my room's full of falcon droppings, and the mice have blackouts.'[33]

He had good reason for his pessimism, as his career received many setbacks before he hit the big time. In the fifties, he had become a protégé of comedian Max Wall. One night, when singer Edmund Hockridge dropped out of Wall's television show, Dawson was asked to step in. At the eleventh hour, Hockridge changed his mind, leaving Dawson to watch the show alone in a pub. In any case, his connection to Wall soon became worthless, as the elder comedian was hit by scandal following his decision to leave his wife for a younger woman, something that would barely register as a misdemeanour nowadays. It got worse. On the night that a representative of the Delfont agency was due to see Dawson performing at a Liverpool club, the venue burned to the ground. He made several television appearances, including a run of bookings on *Big Night Out* with Mike and Bernie Winters, but he seemed to be permanently stalled until he auditioned successfully for *Opportunity Knocks*, Hughie Green's long-running talent show. He was a smash hit, and this led to a booking on the untransmitted pilot for *Blackpool Night Out*. Given Dawson's known tendency to find the cloud in every silver lining, we can be sure that he was telling the truth when he said in his first volume of memoirs 'in show business parlance, that night I "murdered" them'. A couple of bookings on the actual series followed, and Dawson stormed it every time. He had arrived.

Throughout the second half of the sixties, his profile in the clubs and theatres was high, and he was eagerly booked for regular guest appearances on other people's TV shows, but it wasn't until 1969 that he got the chance to shine in his own star vehicle. Yorkshire Television's first head of light entertainment had been veteran gag writer Sid Colin, but he soon decided that executive life wasn't for him, and so his deputy, *That Was the Week That Was* alumnus Jack Duncan, took over. It was Duncan who approached Dawson, during a Christmas show at Leeds Grand, to make his own show for Yorkshire. A chance remark from a dancer gave the show its title, *Sez Les*, and the first series began in April 1969.

The university-educated Duncan and the elementary school-educated Dawson had more in common than was immediately apparent. Both were jazz fans, so when Dawson suggested using the Syd Lawrence Orchestra as the show's house band, Duncan was only too willing. Dawson wanted to be recognized as a serious novelist, while Duncan worked rather reluctantly in LE, feeling that his natural home would have been in drama or documentaries. 'When Sid left, Donald Baverstock asked me to do the job. Well, I had a family to bring up, it was more money, but I didn't want to be stuck in LE, because I wasn't any good at it,' he claims. 'My background at Oxford was serious, heavy stuff. Marlowe, *Tamburlaine the Great*, *Faustus*. I was never known for being a funny man at all.'[34] In this assessment, Duncan does himself a great disservice. He might have been even better in drama, but this is the man who commissioned *Rising Damp*. Certainly Dawson thought highly of Duncan's abilities as a comedy and variety executive. Writing some years after Duncan had abandoned television to run his own bookshop, Dawson declared 'if I had my way he'd be back in the studios. He had ideas and was never afraid to stand by them'.[35]

Although it was almost exactly contemporaneous with the innovative *Monty Python's Flying Circus*, and indeed some late shows in the run featured John Cleese as a supporting player, *Sez Les* was not in the business of pushing back boundaries. It was a traditional variety-oriented, sketch-based comedy show with musical guests. Where it scored was in having great scripts, sympathetic production and a star who was absolutely ready to seize his big chance. Of the writing duties, Dawson wrote his own monologues, while the bulk of the sketches were penned by David Nobbs – also the show's script editor – and Barry Cryer. In his autobiography, Nobbs remembered an audacious quickie written by Cryer with great fondness:

> Les, in a filthy raincoat, enters a posh bookshop, asks 'Got any dirty books?' John [Cleese] looks at him in disgust and disdain, a whole variety of scornful looks which we timed at fifty-four seconds, then says 'Yeah, what kind of thing are you looking for?' Try that without the pause. There's no joke at all. The pause was the joke. Eat your heart out, Harold Pinter.[36]

It was during the *Sez Les* years that Dawson developed the characters with which he would become most closely identified: bespectacled sex maniac Cosmo Smallpiece and the gossipy old dears Cissie and Ada, played by Dawson and the always reliable comic actor Roy Barraclough. Dawson's Ada – named in honour of his real-life mother-in-law – is particularly noteworthy, being an obvious homage to Norman Evans's 'Over the Garden Wall' act of thirty years earlier. Dawson and Evans had mobility of features in common, and the mannerism by which Ada pushed up one of her breasts while talking was an echo of the older comedian's act. Dawson also became known for horrendously out-of-tune piano playing, all the time exhorting the audience to sing along, apparently oblivious to the fact that singing along with such a discordant racket would be impossible for all but the most tone-deaf.

In 1977, after eight years and sixty-eight shows with Yorkshire, the BBC enticed Dawson over to become one of the stars in its light entertainment firmament. His first series was a straight-ahead variety show in which he was paired with singer Lulu and producer John Ammonds. Alternating fortnightly through the spring of 1978 with the wildly popular *Mike Yarwood in Persons*, *The Les Dawson Show* was an unexpected flop, and Dawson began to wonder if he had made the right move. The follow-up series, *The Dawson Watch,* produced by Peter Whitmore, was more formatted – tackling a different subject each week in comic form – and more successful. Dawson also kept his profile up with guest appearances on other BBC shows, including a memorable spot on Shirley Bassey's 1979 BBC1 series, in which he reduced the normally composed Bassey to genuine tears of laughter with his musical antics.

In 1981, a return to the variety melee, with Ernest Maxin as producer, proved to be a hit. In the absence of Lulu, Maxin came up with Kids International, a multi-racial troupe of child performers. 'I wanted to break down the racial hatred that was going on in this country,' says Maxin. 'The Brixton riots [had happened], the press were exaggerating. Being Jewish, I had a lot of that when I was a young boy. I decided to get a United Nations of children together between the ages of 6 and 11. I wanted about 30, so I auditioned 1,000 children of all different races, [from] within the home counties radius. There was a classical boy pianist, a black boy, and I taught him to play jazz. There was a little black boy who was 8 and a half, I taught him to dance like Sammy Davis and Fred Astaire. We had Japanese children, Arab, Israeli, Chinese,

Indian – a complete cross-section. I put them in the show with Les, and they were so successful that Norman Murray, who was Les's agent, said "For the next series, we've got to take them out. They're getting too successful." I was getting thousands of letters into my office in dustbin liners.'[37] Kids International went on to make their own special in May 1982, but their career was finally curtailed by the problem that had brought an end to Maxin's own career as a child performer. As they grew up, they stopped being cute.

Their replacements had no such built-in obsoleteness, indeed their appeal depended entirely on their maturity. Dawson had appeared in a stage show with the traditional complement of stick-thin dancers, and had decided to do his bit for equal opportunities by employing a dance troupe composed of larger ladies of a certain age. Some involved with the production were unsure that the Roly Polys would work, but in the event, they took off in a way that surprised even Dawson.

Throughout his life, Dawson had been overweight, a smoker, a heavy drinker and a worrier. The death of his first wife, in 1986, had put an almost unbearable strain on him, and he had eased off on his career to be with her through her illness. He took over *Blankety Blank* from Terry Wogan in 1984, the production-line recording methods requiring far less effort than his usual shows. In 1989, he also took over *Opportunity Knocks*, which he had won in the ABC days. The show had been revived in 1987 by the BBC, with Bob Monkhouse at the helm, and the voting now done by telephone rather than by post. Hughie Green was nowhere to be seen, however, despite owning the format. 'We paid him £5,000 a week on the condition he didn't come near the studio,' producer Stewart Morris explains. 'All he wanted to do was knock everything.'[38]

Monkhouse's departure was financially motivated. 'The BBC paid him nothing, flumpence,' Morris relates. 'He got a decent offer from ITV and off he went, very sensibly.' Dawson came in for two series, but his lugubrious presentation was a world apart from Green's winking, smirking declarations that everything and everyone was wonderful. Morris remembers that despite being 'lazy' when it came to rehearsal, Dawson was 'an absolute delight to work with. He'd sit me down in his dressing room with a little glass of something and I'd say Les, you have to run through the material, I've got to hear it first, because if there's something in there that I know I've got to cut out, I'd rather you know now. He'd have me crying with laughter, absolutely in tears. What a lovely guy.'[39]

1989 also saw Dawson marrying for a second time, but the happiness was cut short on 10 June 1993, when he succumbed to a heart attack. Dawson had somehow managed to remain unique while also being part of a proud lineage of lugubrious, pessimistic comics and a perfect example of a particularly northern type of humour. When he passed on, an important piece of variety history died with him.

Like Dawson, Ken Dodd has always taken the business of laughter very seriously. The wild-haired Liverpudlian comic has a knowledge of variety's heritage equalled, among performers, only by that of Roy Hudd. John Fisher, who became a respected TV executive and comedy historian, can testify to the power of Dodd's recall. While still a student at Oxford in the 1960s, he met Dodd when the comedian was at the city's New Theatre: 'He was absolutely wonderful. I sat with him and chatted about the old time comics, magic and spesh acts'[40]. Several years later, when Fisher was working at the BBC's Manchester television studios, the pair met again, and 'he remembered me as somebody who'd been in his dressing room at Oxford. There's no reason why he should have done. A great man'.

Always a highly individual performer, with his electric-shock coiffure, protruding teeth and tales of the Knotty Ash jam butty mines, Dodd now stands alone as the torch-bearer for live variety. Now in his ninth decade, he continues touring the nation's theatres, selling out wherever he goes, and keeping the audiences entertained until after the last buses have run. While *The Ken Dodd Happiness Show* also contains several other supporting acts and the Diddy Men, the bulk of the stage time – often three hours of a marathon five-hour performance – is occupied by the star.

Although he is far more than just a catchphrase merchant, several lines have become closely associated with Doddy, not least 'How tickled

I am' and his regular declarations that everything is 'tattifalarious'. If the mother-in-law joke was Dawson's calling card, Dodd's equivalent is the 'What a wonderful day for . . .' gag, in which all manner of daft, cheeky, inappropriate activity is suggested. 'What a wonderful day for going up to the Kremlin,' runs one, 'and asking "Is Len in?".' He also corrupts clichés and quotes beautifully, for example, 'If music is the food of love, give us a tune on your sausage roll.'

He began his professional career with an engagement at the Empire, Nottingham in 1954; by 1958, he was topping the bill in summer season at Blackpool. One of Dodd's earliest influences had been Suzette Tarri, a comedienne with a mildly risqué Cockney charwoman act. When, some years after her death in 1955, John Fisher saw pictures of Tarri in action, he noted that her main prop was a feather duster, which Doddy appropriated as the famous tickling stick.

Dodd's crowning achievement was his record-breaking run at the London Palladium in 1965, in *Doddy's Here*, with the vocal trio, the Kaye Sisters, and comedy beat group, the Barron Knights. *The Times'* reviewer observed that while 'in his way, an engaging comic', Dodd was guilty of self-indulgence and dishing up 'the corniest patter about kippers and nightshirts' along with 'gags one thought dead with the thirties.'[41] The audiences had no such reservations and kept the show running from 17 April to 11 December, when it had to make way for the Palladium's annual pantomime.

The low point of Dodd's career came in 1989, when he went through a well-publicised trial for tax evasion. With the support of George Carman QC and some well-chosen replies to the prosecutors' cross-questioning, Dodd was acquitted. Although harrowing at the time, the experience has since been mined extensively by Dodd for comic purposes – such as the claim that he pioneered income tax self-assessment. Even if the verdict had gone against him, however, it's unlikely that it would have dented his massive popularity. 'No performer has more time for his public than Ken Dodd,' says John Fisher, and the affection is fully reciprocated.

CHAPTER EIGHT

'Let's get the network together'

While the BBC had been establishing its dominance over light entertainment, London Weekend Television had been fighting for survival. Following a bruising on-air encounter with David Frost in October 1969, Rupert Murdoch vowed to take over LWT, and, within a year, had a controlling interest in the company and a seat on the board. Perhaps predictably, Murdoch's hands-on management style and his championing of downmarket populist programming went down like a sausage roll at a bar mitzvah, both at the Leaning Tower of Neasden and with the ITA. However, his money was welcomed and, in the words of LWT's historian David Docherty, his brief, tempestuous tenure 'flattened the ground, cleared out the dead wood, and prepared the company for rebuilding'.[1] The man chosen to rebuild LWT was John Freeman; he had been David Frost's original first choice in 1968 and became chairman and chief executive in March 1971. In his long and distinguished career, Freeman had been a Labour MP, editor of the *New Statesman*, the unseen interviewer in the BBC's legendary *Face to Face* series and the British Ambassador to Washington. Running LWT called on the journalistic and political skills that he had accumulated in all of those roles.

Although Freeman's leadership skills were critical to LWT's recovery, the contribution made by programme controller Cyril Bennett must not be underestimated, particularly in the field of light entertainment.

Bennett's background was originally in journalism and current affairs, but he had more than a touch of show business about him. Stanley Baxter recalled his endearing tendency to lapse into Groucho Marx impersonations if discussions got too heavy. His one weakness was a desire to milk a successful show once it had been established. Bennett was responsible for the appointment of Michael Grade as head of light entertainment. Grade proved surprisingly unsuited to the role, despite his family pedigree, but justified Bennett's faith when he took over as programme controller himself after Bennett's premature death in 1976.

Morale at LWT was undoubtedly boosted in June 1972, when the company finally moved into its new purpose-built office and studio centre on the south bank of the Thames. Apart from the massive studio 5, the old Rediffusion complex at Wembley had not been ideal for modern colour production. Most of the original film studios there had very low ceilings by industry standards. At Kent House, producers could stretch out, and even better, their offices were on the same site, with panoramic views of central London.

Among those producers were a pair of new appointees who helped revitalize LWT's light entertainment output. One was Jon Scoffield, a former designer who had earned his spurs at ATV, and the other was David Bell, who had made his professional name north of the border at BBC Scotland and Scottish Television. Scoffield's main contribution to the programme roster was *Who Do You Do?*, a compendium of the best impressionists at work in the UK at the time. With a gold-standard writing team including the dry wit Dick Vosburgh and the one-liner king Barry Cryer, it ran for five series and three specials between 1972 and 1976. The show enabled impressionist Freddie Starr to consolidate his success after a breakthrough appearance at the 1970 *Royal Variety Performance*, where his Mick Jagger impersonation went down a storm. Unfortunately, the erratic personality traits he later became famed for were already present. After a series of explosions, he went on a charm offensive, and the 'nice' Freddie scared the crew and writers more than his natural, tempestuous side had ever done. Other performers who impressed were Peter Goodwright and Roger Kitter, as well as Janet

Brown, already a television veteran with credits going back to the early Lime Grove days, and the completely unrelated newcomer Faith Brown.

The next career step for both Browns came courtesy of the Conservative Party, which had, in 1975, elected Margaret Thatcher as its leader. Both added the Leaderene to their repertoire and flourished. Janet Brown was rewarded with regular guest spots on Mike Yarwood's BBC shows, saving him the trouble of dragging up, while Faith Brown was given an LWT special, *The Faith Brown Awards*, in 1978. An audience of 9.8 million suggested that she was worth a series. The job of bringing it to the screen was given to John Kaye Cooper, who had done the special and was one of LWT's most promising and technically adept young producer/directors. 'Michael Grade said "Let's do *The Faith Brown Chat Show* – chatting with herself,"' Cooper recalls. 'It was probably the biggest disaster I was ever involved in.'[2]

To be fair, *The Faith Brown Chat Show* was a complex affair that would have given many a far more experienced performer kittens. It used split-screen technology to show the real Faith Brown interviewing herself as various personalities, including Barbra Streisand and Kate Bush. Kaye Cooper recalls the strain that the performer and crew found themselves under:

She was talented, but she didn't have a lot of self-confidence really. We were stretching her a lot, because clearly we wanted someone who did more than about six or seven impressions. We needed a somebody with a much wider range. When the camera was put on her, she wanted to give this performance, and even though she was being herself, you got shades of all these people that she did. An awful mid-Atlantic voice came out. I remember sitting on the set with her, literally with the cameras rolling, getting her to do it line by line, because it was split screen. I had locked-off cameras on her, doing the two-shot where she's talking to herself as Barbra Streisand, and she couldn't get the lines right. It was taking forever to make the show.

Unfortunately, I don't think Faith ever really recovered from that. It was her big chance. She was a lovely lady and I felt at the time that we pushed her too far. *The Faith Brown Awards* had been all her best impressions, carefully put together over a period of time. I feel we should, six months later, have done another special with her. We were trying to move her into Mike Yarwood territory far too fast and I don't think she was ready for it. She did very well in the clubs later.[3]

John Kaye Cooper owed his first break into television to producer David Bell and comedy actor Stanley Baxter, whom he met when working as an assistant stage manager at the Glasgow Alhambra in 1966. Baxter was appearing as the panto dame in *Cinderella*, and the show included a music hall staple, the slapstick wallpapering routine made famous by Albert Burdon. Kaye Cooper had begun his career at the Grand Theatre in Leeds, where he learned from an old stagehand the perfect recipe for the paste, or 'slosh' (the key being a certain amount of glycerine). Soon, he became the only one that Baxter would trust to make it. 'He did a very good job mixing the slosh, but he had very sensitive eyes,' Baxter observes. 'I used to feel so sorry for him. He'd be down in the basement with this big electric mixer, his eyes getting redder and redder. He was going to make it [because] the ambition was burning out of the pores. I said to David Bell "This guy's shit hot and he's desperate to get into television, you've been at STV and now you're at the BBC. If we both write a letter of recommendation to STV, do you think we can get him in?"'[4] Kaye Cooper began as a trainee cameraman, moving on to become a floor manager, then graduating to Thames Television and then LWT.

One of Kaye Cooper's first productions at LWT was a spectacular involving two child stars, singer Lena Zavaroni and actress and dancer Bonnie Langford. Both had come to prominence by winning *Opportunity Knocks*. Among the mixed reviews for *Lena and Bonnie* was one from Richard Afton, by now the hatchet-man television critic of the *Evening News*, in which 'he was savage about Bonnie Langford and glowing about Lena Zavaroni. It was only years later that I realized why. He was a big friend of Philip and Dorothy Solomon [Zavaroni's managers]. He'd been primed to say it.'[5]

Kaye Cooper was also tasked with salvaging something from *Freddie Starr's Saturday Madhouse*. 'It was quite a nice idea, but it wasn't working,' he explains. 'It was set in a house where the doors led to a chip shop, a chemist and a disco, where the sketches were done. A series was done, but it was quite hard work getting there.' Kaye Cooper was detailed to take over the project, enlisting Russ Abbot from the comedy group the Black Abbots as the central figure, replacing Freddie Starr. Portly actress Bella Emberg survived from the previous show, while in came Susie Blake, Sherrie Hewson, Jeffrey Holland and a gangling, manic young impressionist called Michael Barrymore, who had been brought to Kaye Cooper's attention by musical director Alyn Ainsworth. 'I went down to Blazers [a Windsor cabaret venue]. Nobody knew I was there. I went to see this odd, amazing act of this man who did half the act upside down with his legs in the air. I invited him to lunch in the dining room at LWT. I recognized the insecurity even then, all that came out in that meal that day. Virtually his life story. I needed someone a little crazy who could do odd characters, and he could do almost anybody.'[6]

The concept of using videotape technology to enable one comedian to play several roles at once, as Kaye Cooper had with Faith Brown, had been developed and refined by Kaye Cooper's original sponsor, the character comedy specialist and Hollywood parody expert Stanley Baxter. Baxter had been brought over from the BBC to LWT in 1972 by his old friend and supporter, the producer/director David Bell. 'I'd met him [Bell] when he was a trainee cameraman at STV,' Baxter remembers. 'He went from [that] to floor manager, then [he was] whipped away to the BBC to become a director, and he never looked back.'[7] Baxter's painstaking, parodic shows, aided by razor-sharp scripts from Ken Hoare, were to become the gold standard in LWT's light entertainment for more than a decade. The Baxter–Hoare–Bell association began in October 1972 with a series of four programmes under the title *The Stanley Baxter Picture Show*, but the massive amount of work required for each edition – nineteen days in the studio being quoted for one Baxter show – meant that it made more sense to concentrate on one-off specials.

Bell's signature style as a producer was for glossy, expansive shows with big production numbers. 'David was head of shiny floors and immaculately glamorous things,' recalls former colleague Alan Boyd.[8] A large part of what made Bell and Baxter a perfect creative partnership was their shared affinity for the glory days of Hollywood. 'He had the same preoccupations with these marvellous musicals,' the comedian recalls. 'To escape from the "dreichness" – there's a good Scots word for you – of Glasgow in midwinter, into this wonderful world of *Top Hat* was just magical. It so influenced me that I spent half my life after that trying to recreate some of it, but always with a comedy peg.' Indeed, no Baxter show was complete without a Hollywood pastiche, in which he played the glamorous females too. 'I did both Fred Astaire and Ginger Rogers. I always preferred doing males to females for obvious reasons. There's greater verisimilitude. A man of five feet ten and a half can only be a joke in drag.'[9]

The Baxter shows also spoofed less glamorous forms of broadcasting. One particularly memorable sketch in his 1973 Christmas special was a mock documentary about the making of a religious programme with a trendy director who declares it permissible to talk about anything but religion, in an accent pitched somewhere between LA and the Gorbals. 'There were a lot of people around then, trying to sound mid-Atlantic, but you could hear the Scots coming through all the time,' he observes[10] – the main secret Scot who springs to mind being Radio 1 DJ Stuart Henry. Naturally, he played every part: the director, the interviewer, the timid vicar with the toupee ('Stu, we've got a little fakey we didn't know about'), the floor manager and for good measure, the voice-over. The poor, innocent churchman is informed that the programme has to be non-sectarian ('You mean like Jess Yates?' 'Please, not while I'm eating'), and also that the studio was set up for a Jimmy Tarbuck special, making it impossible to rejig the lighting for a mere godslot show. As well as containing Baxter's taboo-busting impersonation of the Queen (thinly disguised as the 'Duchess of Brendagh', a reference to Brenda, the below-stairs staff's nickname for Her Majesty, also adopted by *Private Eye*), the 1973

Christmas show featured a superb parody of the BBC news magazine *Nationwide*. In the original programme, it was customary to take contributions from various regional studios. In the sketch, Baxter played all of the regional representatives, speaking not a single intelligible syllable, but remaining perfectly meaningful and understandable, purely through the music of the accents.

The high quality of the Baxter shows came at a price, and the LWT bean counters occasionally upbraided David Bell for allowing such extravagance. He always had a ready reply: 'It's not your money, dear.' Fortunately, the financial structure of ITV, with its post-Pilkington government levy on profits, meant that it made sense for the companies to spend as much as possible on the programmes before even thinking about satisfying the shareholders, so, when times were good, Bell was not merely indulged, but encouraged.

In 1976, *Stanley Baxter's Christmas Box* used two charladies cleaning the videotape suite at BBC Television Centre as a clever linking device for various parodies of seasonal viewing: 'Look what they're putting out over Christmas. *Cilla Black Goes to Las Vegas, Shirley Bassey Goes to Pieces, I'm Dreaming of a Black Boxing Day: the Muhammad Ali Special* – they're all recordings. It's a fraud.'[11] However, the crowning achievement of Baxter's time at London Weekend was probably 1979's *Stanley Baxter on Television*, a sharp, satirical response to Lord Annan's Report on Broadcasting which was intended as a late-seventies equivalent of the Pilkington Report. The show – produced by John Kaye Cooper, Bell having become a senior executive – opened with Baxter as a civil servant answering the telephone: 'Good morning, Prime Minister ... Oh, I agree, it's dead boring. Not a laugh in it.'[12] It then launched into a fraught meeting between Lord Grade (as Lew had become in Harold Wilson's infamous 'Lavender List' of honours in 1976) and Miss Piggy of *The Muppet Show*, before going on to show how Sir John Gielgud might have presented *The Generation Game*.

Bell was openly gay at a time when it was only just legal to be so, and many who worked with him remember his camp, caustic wit with great affection. In the mid-seventies, Kaye Cooper was producing drama at Yorkshire Television when the call came from his old mentor. 'I got the call out of the blue one day from David, and I can remember the lines now. He said "Hello dear. How are ye? What are you doing with all those drama queens in Yorkshire? Come down here with us LE queens [at LWT] and work on some shows."'[13]

Marcus Plantin, who joined LWT in 1985, adds 'A lot of people say "Oh, Limp-Wristed Television" and all that, but it was a rather more open atmosphere than the BBC [which had] Johnny Downes, John Street and a lot of people in blazers and regimental ties. It hadn't loosened up, whereas at LWT, Mike Mansfield had been there, a very big camp personality. David [Bell], Humphrey Barclay. It just made the place flamboyant – that's the best word. It was a company with panache and style.'[14] Stanley Baxter counters by saying 'You could call it equally Jewish television. Cyril Bennett was a wonderful guy – Jewish. Michael Grade – Jewish. Cyril and Michael were the ones who kept giving me a green light when the complaints came in [from the accountants]. "You know what this is costing?" "This is our flagship. Cut something else."'[15]

★

When Baxter arrived at LWT in 1972, Brian Tesler – who was to guide LWT from the late seventies to the mid-nineties – was director of programmes at Thames Television, and the next in line for managing director. Tesler's tenure at Thames had been a markedly successful one, building on the best elements of ABC and Rediffusion:

> I had to merge the two programme departments. It was obvious to me that in features and current affairs I had to have Jeremy Isaacs from Rediffusion. Grahame Turner and Rediffusion's OB unit were the best in the business. ABC didn't make children's programmes, so it had to be Lewis Rudd from Rediffusion, who ran a very good department. At ABC, Philip Jones was the best light entertainment man in the business, and his department was great, and I thought Lloyd Shirley was marvellous as head of drama for ABC. So, in actual fact, of those

departments, there were only two that came from ABC. Two of the most important, of course.[16]

With LWT and ATV providing the lion's share of the ITV network's variety after August 1968, Jones was able to concentrate on building up the situation comedy roster at Thames. An early hit was *Father Dear Father,* starring Patrick Cargill as a widower trying to bring up two teenage daughters. *Bless This House* was also popular, starring Sid James as another father trying to understand his children. Both were produced by William G. Stewart, who had won his sitcom directing spurs at the BBC on Eric Sykes' shows. Later on came *Man about the House*, written by Johnnie Mortimer and Brian Cooke and produced by ABC alumnus Peter Frazer-Jones, in which a chef shared a flat platonically with two young girls-about-town. The new company kept up ABC's support of Tommy Cooper, a relationship that was to bear ever more fruit, and brought Benny Hill into the fold.

Hill had had a long association with the BBC and a brief flirtation with ATV, but it was at Thames that he was to do his best-remembered, if not necessarily his best work. On the evidence of the few surviving recordings, his early-sixties BBC shows are almost on a par with the work of Stanley Baxter or Ronnie Barker in terms of complexity and inventiveness. One, set at a wedding, shows the bride's mother's unflattering view of the groom in flashback, and the groom's mother's reciprocal view of the bride. Hill plays several parts beautifully, and the twist at the end is a corker. In contrast, the Thames shows featured the broadest of broad comedy – still very funny at their best, but nowhere near as subtle. Chief among his recurring characters at Thames was the beret-wearing simpleton Fred Scuttle, who turned up in each show as the proprietor of various unlikely schemes including a health farm. In one show, Scuttle was claimed to be responsible for the smooth running of the Thames studios. Henry McGee, playing an interviewer, asked who Scuttle's favourite comedian was, to which he replied 'Oh, without a doubt, sir, Mike Spilligan. Spike Milligan. Sorry. I've had my nose fixed, and now my mouth won't work. Good job it wasn't Marty Feldman.'

Although Jones was to become Hill's great patron, the comedian came to the company through a previous association with Tesler:

Benny, in between BBC contracts, had done some shows for ATV. I did the first of them [at ATV], it wasn't a good show, and I was very unhappy with it. It really was a reworking of old material that he'd done at the BBC. It was a hack job. He went back to the BBC and became again a smash, but I'd heard he was unhappy with his director, a sweet, very nice man called Ken Carter. I got a phone call from Richard Stone, Benny's agent, saying 'Benny is thinking of leaving the BBC. He wants a change of director. But he's also aware that the show he did with you wasn't very good and he's always felt a bit bad about that. So we'd like to give you first chance, but it depends on who's going to be the director, who's going to be in charge.' I said 'Well the best guy in the business, Philip Jones.' 'Right, we'll have a meeting, Philip, Benny and me.' So they had a meeting, and it went well, and he said 'Yes, we'll come to terms.' That was the happiest of all possible marriages. Philip, nice guy that he was, put good people with Benny, [but] he was always there if anything went wrong. You can see it in several of the tapes. Anything goes wrong, Benny suddenly goes 'Philip!' Philip was always there to nursemaid him.[17]

Thames had inherited ABC's talent show *Opportunity Knocks*, along with its host Hughie Green, but not his Rediffusion quiz show, *Double Your Money*, which had been put down humanely when the new franchises began. Eamonn Andrews was also a big name for Thames, one who was to remain loyal to the company for the rest of his life. His main responsibility was to present the early evening regional magazine programme *Today*, but he had also revived *This Is Your Life* with great success. The show had made its British debut on the BBC on 29 July 1955 at 7.45pm. It had grown out of an American radio game show, *Truth or Consequences*, hosted by Ralph Edwards, who had taken the idea to US television in 1952. The idea was simple: a person of note – sometimes a conventional celebrity, sometimes a worthier candidate, like a war hero – was caught unawares and presented with a potted biography. Friends, family and associates would make grand entrances in order to pay fulsome tribute to the subject of the show. What turned an interesting idea into ratings gold was the surprise element. As the show was live and the subject was to be oblivious to the honour until the last possible moment, viewers had no idea who the show was going to be about, and so millions watched the opening of the show each week, at the very least, with bosses hoping fervently that many of them would stay the course not just for the rest of the show, but for the whole evening's viewing.[18]

Andrews, who had risen to fame on the BBC presenting *What's My Line*, had seen the American version during a trip to commentate on a boxing match in San Francisco, and become convinced it was a winner. Ronnie Waldman, the BBC's then head of light entertainment, agreed with him, and paired him once again with *What's My Line* producer T. Leslie Jackson to bring the show to British viewers. The first subject was to have been ace footballer Stanley Matthews, but the press got wind of this and reported the fact several days before the show was due to launch. 'I therefore had to cancel it,' remembered Jackson. 'I had then until Sunday to get a new programme together. The only person whose life I knew anything about was Eamonn Andrews.'[19] Andrews was told there was a change of plan, but not the full details. He went to the studio apparently believing that the first show was to be about the boxer Freddie Mills. Ralph Edwards had come over from the US, ostensibly to hand over the famous book containing the host's script to Andrews at the start of the show. When Andrews saw the name on the front, it was his.

Although each show was planned meticulously, it wasn't always a smooth run. On 6 February 1961, Tottenham Hotspur footballer Danny Blanchflower became the first person to decline the honour, reputedly calling the programme 'an invasion of privacy' and declaring that he was not going to be 'press-ganged into anything'. As this was an occasion when the surprise was to be recorded slightly in advance of the live transmission, a reserve programme was transmitted.[20] Blanchflower refused a second attempt three months later. In October of the same year, a technical fault on one edition of the show led to the director's talkback going out live on air as the pick-up was being transmitted from film. Viewers heard Yvonne Littlewood 'yelling "Sound on film, where's the sound gone? . . . Oh Christ, not again."'[21] Ever the diplomat, Eric Maschwitz had defended Littlewood at the programme review board, suggesting that she was merely 'asking for help from above'.[22]

When Eamonn Andrews left the BBC in 1964, to begin his own chat show and *World of Sport* for ABC, the show came to an end, declining ratings suggesting that it had run its natural course, but the Thames revival proved otherwise. With *World of Sport* being handled by London Weekend from August 1968 onwards, Andrews began looking for other shows he could present for Thames. Brian Tesler explains: 'He came to me and said "This is what I'd like to do," and handed me a little piece of paper with *This Is Your Life* on it, and inserted between "your" and "life", [the word] "colourful", bless his heart, because colour was just coming in. He wanted to revive *This Is Your Life*, and he persuaded me that it would be a good idea, that there was a lot of mileage left in it.'[23]

Although Andrews' suggested title modification wasn't adopted, the revived show returned to the airwaves on 19 November 1969, in the first week of colour broadcasting on ITV, with an edition devoted to the singer and comedian Des O'Connor. Andrews was right about the mileage left in the show. The show's second lease of life lasted thirty-four years, and the format may yet return. Throughout its entire history, it remained substantially unchanged, with the earliest surviving editions being recognizably the same show as the last. Ever present was the pleasant twist at the end of the show. Sometimes it would be the arrival of a relative from abroad who had earlier been heard or seen only in a recorded greeting. Other times, it would be the opportunity to fulfil a lifelong ambition. When, in January 1959, bandleader Ted Heath was the show's subject, his wish to conduct a brass band was taken care of courtesy of Foden's Motor Works Band trooping on under the end credits. Following Andrews' death in 1987, his place was taken by Michael Aspel, who had much in common with his predecessor. Both had hosted the BBC children's variety show *Crackerjack* for many years, and Aspel had also made his own mark on the world of chat in the eighties, with *Aspel and Company* for LWT. Both managed to be gentle, warm, unthreatening personalities, without being truly bland. Indeed, Aspel's entire career has been marked by his subtle wit.

★

Brian Tesler had been the first choice to take over from Howard Thomas as managing director of Thames when Thomas became chairman, but there was a snag. Tesler had leased his services to Thames'S through his own company. John Read, chairman of Thames's majority shareholder EMI, wanted Tesler to sign directly and also to cut his agent Teddy Sommerfield out of the negotiations. Tesler was not keen to abandon the arrangement he had worked under since ATV days nor to abandon his agent and friend, and so sales director George Cooper was appointed. Tesler would have been happy to remain as Cooper's director of programmes, but for an approach from film producer Robert Clark, a former ABC board member who was now affiliated with LWT:

He said 'I don't want to know how it happened. I just want to know one thing. Are you under contract to Thames?' I said 'Well, actually, no, my contract as director of programmes has expired and no one has said anything to me.' He said 'Fine, you're free. The second thing – would you like to come and talk to John Freeman about a position here?' 'What sort of position?' 'His deputy.' I was a great admirer of John Freeman, so I went to see him. I picked him up, and we walked round Kew Gardens for about an hour, discussing television. We'd obviously come across each other sitting at the same industry tables, so we knew each other very well. He said 'I'd like you to come across here as my deputy, and if it all works out, in two years' time, I'll step down as managing director, remain as chairman, and you become managing director. If it doesn't work out, tough.' I said 'Yes, fine.' So I joined LWT. I said goodbye to Howard and everybody else. I think Howard kicked himself for not signing me up, but he was becoming chairman and it just slipped his mind.[24]

Although London Weekend had made considerable strides by 1974, when Tesler joined, he knew the company still had some way to go. 'It was in a fairly bad way,' he asserts. 'Its programme structure was somehow not right.' Many within the company viewed him with suspicion, believing that programme controller Cyril Bennett should have been offered the job, but Tesler is convinced that Bennett 'was a lovely man and a good friend, but he would not have been right as managing director'.[25] In particular, his tendency to keep departments separate and deal directly with their heads caused problems. In November 1976, Tesler called a conference at Selsdon Park to discuss the company's future direction, at which current affairs head John Birt famously realized that he had never had lunch with most of the other people at the table. The conference ended positively, but the whole event was overshadowed by Bennett's death in a fall from the balcony of his Chelsea flat. Many within the company believed that Tesler was trying to ease Bennett out. In fact, Tesler had already begun the process of renewing Bennett's contract. To this day, no one knows for sure if it was suicide or an accident.

While the company was coping with its grief, Tesler had to think about who would succeed Bennett as director of programmes. The man he chose had not only learned much of what he knew from Bennett, but also shared his mentor's ebullience and humour. 'It was clear to me that Michael [Grade] was the right guy to be director of programmes,' says Tesler. 'I always say I did it to get him out of light entertainment, because he was such an awful head of light entertainment. Michael seemed to be dedicated to making an international comedy star out of Arthur Mullard.'[26] Mullard was a flat-nosed cockney former boxer with a talent for mangling the English language. He had made a good career as a stooge to the likes of Tony Hancock, but was never leading-man material. In getting

Grade out of LE, Tesler had acted wisely, and the choice of producer David Bell to replace Grade in LE was another masterstroke. Bell promoted what John Kaye Cooper called a 'collegiate' atmosphere in the department, moving the offices from the tower to an adjoining half-timbered building, known among the producers as the Tudor Tea Rooms.

Although LWT made the lion's share of Saturday night programming for the ITV network, ATV still made some important contributions throughout the seventies. Chief among the company's LE hits was the Bob Monkhouse game show *Celebrity Squares*, while ATV also had major network success with its talent show, *New Faces*. Hosted by Derek Hobson, this was mainly memorable for the scathing verdicts handed down by one of the judges, composer and record producer Tony Hatch. Unlike the products of many modern talent shows, a considerable number of *New Faces* winners went on to enduring success in show business, among them the red-headed Sheffield-born comedienne Marti Caine and a young black comedian and impressionist from the Black Country, Lenny Henry. Caine was given her own ATV show almost immediately, while Henry worked his passage in the company's gloriously manic, slapstick-heavy, gunge-strewn Saturday morning children's show, *Tiswas*. Victoria Wood was another *New Faces* winner, but it took longer for her songs and observations to be fully appreciated.

★

In the days of the halls, entertainment had been the work of professionals, whose ranks the performers who took part in shows like *New Faces* and *Opportunity Knocks* were keen to join. With the arrival of television had come shows that allowed the British public to entertain each other, more or less. In time, these became known as people shows, arguably paving the way for so-called 'reality television' – although many involved in those early people shows will argue with equal passion that there is no relationship between the two.

The first 'people' show was *Ask Pickles*, produced by Brian Tesler at the BBC in the early fifties. '[Ronnie Waldman] introduced me to Wilfred and Mabel Pickles [stars of BBC Radio's *Have a Go*] and asked me to do a show with them,' Tesler recalls:

> [He said] 'Why don't you do a request show of some kind?' So I got a couple of researchers who had been researching panel shows – *Guess My Story* – for me, called Larry and Pauline Forrester. Larry Forrester was a tough little guy – he had been a fighter pilot in the war – and Pauline was an elegant woman. Larry went onto Hollywood, [where he] wrote stuff [and] also wrote a couple of rather exciting novels, one of which was filmed with Racquel Welch. The two of them were very good researchers – newshounds. Larry, Pauline and I would spend days going through the newspapers, looking for stories and making something out of them. People would request songs and performers, bits of old film, test match victories, heavyweight boxing. One viewer requested his brother's favourite tune before he went to Australia. He said 'I haven't seen him for twenty-five years, but we write to each other. He loved that song.' We thought 'Fine, we'll do that, but we'll also get the brother back and reintroduce them.' It was the first British show of that kind.[27]

Bruce Forsyth and the Generation Game was another true 'people' show, and its massive popularity aided the BBC in one of its most important matters of strategy. By the late sixties, Saturday nights had become the main battleground in the war of family entertainment, and the idea was that a balanced but enticing Saturday evening schedule should be constructed, so that as many viewers as humanly possible would be hooked from teatime until closedown. It helped that the BBC had, in that pre-satellite and subscription era, access to most of the major sporting events for *Grandstand*, ensuring a massive inheritance of viewers, chiefly the dads. ITV's sporting offerings were relatively meagre, as Brian Tesler was forced to acknowledge when ABC began producing *World of Sport* for the ITV network in 1965. From Len Marten reading the football results to *Parkinson*, via *The Gen Game* and *Doctor Who*, the BBC held all the cards on Saturday night.

The variety department was invariably responsible for BBC1 Saturday night comedy. Impressionist Mike Yarwood's series *Look – Mike Yarwood* and *Mike Yarwood in Persons* were important fixtures throughout the seventies, but the longest running and best remembered of all the Saturday night comedy shows was *The Two Ronnies*. The show's principals, the rotund, wordy Ronnie Barker and the small, but forceful Ronnie Corbett, had first been paired in *The Frost Report*, most famously with John Cleese in the 'I look up to him . . . I look down on him . . . I know my place' sketch on class, written by John Law and Marty Feldman. Prior to this, Corbett had been primarily a cabaret comedian and performer, working first at Winston's club in London's Clifford Street with female impersonator Danny La Rue and Barbara Windsor, then at La Rue's own club in Hanover Square. Meanwhile, Barker had been best known for a variety of roles on radio in *The Navy Lark* and his appearances in the Jimmy Edwards sitcom *Seven Faces of Jim*. Unsurprisingly, given the Frost connection, both Barker and Corbett had performed in their own shows for London Weekend. In 1969 and 1970, Barker had appeared as the lecherous peer Lord Rustless in two series of *Hark at Barker*, while Corbett had starred in *The Corbett Follies*, a series that showed off his cabaret pedigree.

Nonetheless, it was James Gilbert at the BBC who pulled off the coup of putting them together in their own show. Gilbert, who had been with the Corporation as a producer for a decade and was now climbing the executive ladder, did the commissioning and initial nurturing, but the production of the show was given to Terry Hughes. Hughes was one of the few BBC light entertainment producers to cross the variety and comedy divide. Although he cut his teeth on programmes like *The Val Doonican Show* and *Cilla*, working alongside John Ammonds and Michael Hurll, he brought Michael Palin and Terry Jones's *Ripping Yarns* to the screen in the late seventies. Consequently, he was the perfect producer for a show that combined comedy sketches that ranged from simple talking heads – such as Ronnie Corbett's chair monologues and Ronnie Barker's cod public information announcements – to lavish musical numbers, with a weekly filmed serial and special guests. 'Terry was very suave, laid-back, and very good with artists indeed,' says Marcus Plantin, who joined the show's production team in the mid-seventies. 'Some producers feel they have to impose themselves very heavily rather than delegate. He was a very good delegator. He knew how to get the right people. He certainly knew how to handle talent, very, very well.'[28] In later years, the guests were invariably female singers of the calibre of Barbara Dickson and Elaine Paige, but in the show's early years, there was also room for vocal groups and spesh acts, such as the novelty drummer Alfredo.

That was about the only change of format during the show's sixteen-year run. In the first edition, transmitted on 10 April 1971, the signature elements were all in place: the opening spoof news headlines, Ronnie Corbett's chair monologue, the filmed serial and the musical finale. In those early years, *The Two Ronnies* had a significant input from writers like Eric Idle, Michael Palin and Terry Jones, but the star of the writing team was indubitably Gerald Wiley – aka Ronnie Barker – who had used the pseudonym on the Frost shows at LWT to ensure that his scripts were selected on merit alone. In the production office, there was much fevered speculation as to the real identity of Wiley – his scripts were so good, he had to be a well-known name working under a pseudonym. Among those in the frame were the playwrights Peter Shaffer and Tom Stoppard. The truth was revealed when Wiley invited Frost and company to the Chinese restaurant opposite the LWT studios at Wembley. When Barker arose and announced that he was Wiley, one of the wags present declared that 'Nobody likes a smartarse.' The deception had been perfect. Barker the actor had been observed in rehearsals misinterpreting Wiley's lines and taking correction on the proper delivery.

Among Wiley's output for *The Two Ronnies* were the spoof public information broadcasts. These featured Barker, often as a pompous jargon-bound official spokesman explaining a ludicrous concept, or as someone making an appeal on behalf of a charitable cause, such as the Loyal Society for the Relief of Sufferers of Pismonunciation, 'people who cannot say their worms correctly, or who use the wrong worms entirely, so that other people cannot underhand a bird they are spraying'. As Wiley, Barker worked alone, and when the handwritten script for the famous 'Fork Handles/Four Candles' sketch – in which Corbett plays a hardware salesman tormented by Barker as an ambiguous customer – was auctioned in December 2007, it realized a price of £48,500. Complementing Barker's solo performances were Corbett's monologues, in which the diminutive Scottish comedian sat in a large leather armchair, and told a rambling, digressive story, written for many years by Spike Mullins, before David Renwick took over the job.

As the network's big hit Saturday night comedy show, *The Two Ronnies* could have what it wanted in terms of resources, Stanley Baxter's LWT spectaculars being perhaps the only shows that were more labour-intensive. 'One year, when I was the production manager, the filming was set in the south of France,' Plantin recalls. 'The script demanded it. Barker and Corbett were in their ascendancy and were very empowered with Bill [Cotton]. I don't mean that in the wrong way. They were bringing in the audience for the BBC and they could call the shots. It was a major piece of work. We were there probably a week and a half and we did the rest in the UK. We took down twenty people, we were shooting all over Marseilles, and it was very good fun. I can't deny it.'[29]

Nonetheless, Plantin maintains that it was money well spent, as these filmed elements were what made *The Two Ronnies* stand out from the other variety-led comedy shows of the time:

They were big budget shows, two days in the studio, at least. The element that became the differential, in my view, was the pre-filming, which was, I think, from the very early days, a month. A month's filming. This is an entertainment show. You had the running film story, 'Charley Farley', 'Piggy Malone' or whatever. They were big production numbers, like making a mini-film. I remember as a production manager once, driving to some location down in Dorset and thinking 'Fuck me' as I came over the hill and saw the crew and the gear. I thought 'It's like the circus has come to town.' It was big. There wasn't another show that was using proper lighting, proper costume design. This was very much driven by Barker and Corbett. A lot of people say that Barker was the only hammer there, but Corbett was [too], in a different way. He had very high standards. Everything would be rehearsed very, very thoroughly. He [Ronnie C.] was slick and thorough. At the end of the day, Terry Hughes, Barker and Corbett set the bar high. It paid off.[30]

Another important LE contribution to the BBC's Saturday night lockdown was *Jim'll Fix It*, a people show *par excellence*, which ran from 1975 to 1994. *Ask Pickles* had an element of wish fulfilment, whereas with *Jim'll Fix It*, that was the whole point. Reuniting brothers was just a matter of booking the right flights. In contrast, Jimmy Savile, indefatigable charity worker and marathon-running disc jockey, could make dreams come true. Already a major personality through his work on Radio Luxembourg, Radio 1 and *Top of the Pops*, *Jim'll Fix It* turned Savile into an icon – a surrogate mad uncle for at least two whole generations. Bedecked with jewellery and garish clothing in a manner that was a gift to lazy impressionists, those lucky enough to have their letter picked out and brought to life went home with a bit of Savile-style bling of their own, a gigantic, square silver medallion with the legend 'Jim Fixed It For Me' emblazoned on it.

Many were called, but few were chosen. To stand out from the thousands of letters that were destined for the pile of bin bags in producer Roger Ordish's office, a request had to be unusual, preferably with a strong visual aspect. The scouts who wanted to eat their lunch on a roller coaster were a perfect example of this. Some 'fixits' were unashamedly sentimental, for example the surprise that was arranged for a mad-keen Frankie Vaughan fan who played piano at an old people's home; courtesy of *Jim'll Fix It*, she got to meet her idol, the old folks got a cabaret performance from Vaughan and the home was given a new piano. Ordish also remembers with great fondness an opera-based fixit with Arthur Davis of the Welsh National Opera. 'There was a lovely little bit . . . when this beautiful little girl wanted to be Mimi [from *La Bohème*]. It was a clever choice, because Mimi doesn't actually sing during "Your Tiny Hand is Frozen". She just has to sit there and her hand is taken by him.'[31]

Ordish – or, as Savile always referred to him, 'Dr Magic' – was the producer for the show's entire nineteen-year run, and describes it as 'a wonderful thing to do'. He regards it as a perfect example of the pride that producers took in their work. 'It was very lowbrow, a very simple programme, but we always wanted it to be good. I really think that when I started there, most people thought "What I make is good, and I'm not going to make it if I don't think it's good."' Lowbrow it may have been, but Savile proved irresistible to some surprisingly elevated guests, including poet laureate Sir John Betjeman, who read a group of children the first poem he had ever written, at the age of six. 'That was terribly funny,' Ordish remembers. '"Ere John, I've got one for you," said Jim. "Roses are red, violets are grey, got the wrong colour, never mind, eh?" Betjers weeping with laughter: "Lovely, wonderful."'[32]

The producers behind most of these successful new shows were part of the generation that had joined the Corporation in the sixties, as Alan Boyd recalls. 'The seventh floor at Television Centre was where a lot of the younger entertainment producers were: the Alan Boyds, the Roger Ordishes, Vernon Lawrence, Brian Whitehouse, Jim Moir, Terry Hughes. The *Top of the Pops* floor, the *Jim'll Fix It* floor. The fourth floor were the senior ones – the John Ammonds and Michael Hurlls. The seventh floor was the noisy floor that was still going at eleven o'clock at night. We'd have a lot of funny lunches in those days. God knows how much we must have drunk at lunchtime, I hate to think.'[33]

Drinking was part of the working culture in those days. Leading by example, the head of light entertainment had his own private bar in the Television Theatre, known, from the days of Tom Sloan's leadership, as 'Uncle Tom's Cabin'. Back at the Centre, the Club bar was, in Jim Moir's description 'a marketplace. The back bar, until it was invaded by incomers from news, was very much the LE bar, and it was there that at lunchtime you would meet your colleagues. The bar was a social hub for the exchange of professional anecdotes, bonding, and which talent you should be allying yourself with. You would see artists in there before they went down to record shows. You'd hear what was going on. It was a rip and read newsroom for yourself for what was going on in light entertainment.'[34]

Some indulged more than others, among them Roger Ordish. 'I was a boozer, certainly, too much, excessive. It was a way of life. Everything you did concerned having a drink. Of course, you didn't have to drink. I think that if you think drunk and edit sober, you can get some good stuff, as with other mind-altering substances. But you must have the editing sober bit, that's very important. I was a bit of a barrack room lawyer as well. I wasn't a terrible troublemaker, but rather than say the right thing at a departmental meeting, I would say the wrong thing. I just had fun. I wanted to enjoy myself. I wasn't a layabout, because I worked very hard.'

Almost the only producer never to touch a drop was the suave, unflappable Terry Hughes. 'Terry Hughes never had a drink. He took a lot of stick for it, but good for him. Of course, I didn't think so at the time,' admits Roger Ordish.[35] Alan Boyd adds Jim Moir's affectionately mocking description of Hughes: 'He was the model in the shop window, he'd come out in the morning. He was always immaculate with the blazer and the freshly pressed jeans. He still is if you see him today. Terry was that then and had all the girls after him.'[36]

★

ITV's first serious attempt to dent the BBC's supremacy on Saturday nights came in 1978, when LWT director of programmes Michael Grade poached the *Generation Game* host Bruce Forsyth for £15,000 a programme, an unheard-of fee back then. Grade's big idea was to use Forsyth as the anchor for a complete evening of entertainment. Under the banner of *Bruce Forsyth's Big Night*, viewers could expect quiz games, celebrity guests and interviews, situation comedy and, Forsyth's forte, audience participation. The sitcom elements were to be shamelessly nostalgic, with revivals of 'The Glums' from *Take It From Here* – featuring Jimmy Edwards reprising his role as Pa Glum, aided by Ian Lavender and Patricia Brake – and Charlie Drake's sixties series *The Worker* alternating fortnightly. The main game show contribution was Steve Jones's *Pyramid Game*. Computer games like Space Invaders were all the rage at the time, and Brucie aimed to tap into the zeitgeist with 'Teletennis', in which members of the public attempted to control a bat and ball video game with their voice. Then there was the resident dance troupe, 32 Feet, under the direction of Brian Rogers. To get it all on screen needed three very experienced producers: David Bell – by now LWT's head of light entertainment – as executive producer with responsibility for the variety side, head of comedy Humphrey Barclay producing the sitcom segments and Richard Drewett in charge of the chat side of things. Then there were the writers, a stellar combination of established craftsmen like Barry Cryer and Garry Chambers with up-and-comers like Colin Bostock-Smith, Andrew Marshall and David Renwick. With a team like this, Forsyth a proven banker and something for everyone in the mix, the show couldn't possibly fail. Nonetheless, nothing was left to chance, and director Paul Smith remembers the preparations being long and arduous:

> The show started in September, and from April or May, I did nothing but sleep and do this show. I dedicated my entire life. It was David's concept, I think, and it was incredibly adventurous. I was the studio director [as well as doing] things like Rod Hull on location, and it was a massive undertaking. It was two and a half hours, absolutely enormous. It had to be a two-day recording. I had to post-produce it, rehearse the dancers and all that. I had no life at all. Great fun, but what hard work.[37]

Despite being one of LWT's junior LE staff, Smith's reputation was already very strong. He had worked with Birmingham-born comedian Jasper Carrott on a series and several successful specials, and he had persuaded director of programmes Michael Grade that there would be a large public audience for outtakes – previously a private pleasure for those working in television:

> It grew out of what we'll call the *Blue Peter* elephant [when a baby elephant disgraced herself all over the studio floor], which of course technically is not an outtake, because it appeared in the programme, but it wasn't intended. I saw it and it stuck in my mind. I used a short showreel made by a BBC VT engineer, even though I was selling it to ITV, because I didn't know how to go about collecting these clips. At least the BBC, because of the centralization, had collected them. They'd got about eight or ten clips. He edited them together for me, I took them to Michael and said that's what I want to do, and he got it immediately. He wanted Roy Castle to introduce it first of all, his first suggestion. In retrospect it wouldn't have been a good idea. It needed somebody who could cope with good narrative. I can't remember whether Roy Castle wasn't available, but Michael came back and said 'I've had a better idea – what about Denis Norden?' I was only a junior director/producer, so I said 'Sure Michael, whatever you want,' but he was the right choice, without a shadow of a doubt.
>
> At the same time, Michael said to me about Jasper Carrott. He'd seen him doing some after-dinner speaking, he asked me to go and see him, and see what I thought. I went to see him in Coventry and said sign him up. We did a transmittable pilot, which became one of a series of half hours called *An Audience with Jasper Carrott*. We did them back to back, one day Jasper Carrott, the next *It'll Be Alright on the Night*, in the same studio. Same set, just changed a couple of things. A very productive two days for London Weekend.[38]

Back at Television Centre, *Generation Game* producer Alan Boyd had to find a replacement for the departed Forsyth. To avoid invidious comparisons, he chose the antithesis of Brucie, the camp horse-toothed Midlands comedian Larry Grayson. 'It was counter scheduling against Bruce,' he explains. 'There was no point in doing a lookalike. You had to do it the opposite way.' The main difference between the two hosts lay in their respective grasp of the show's mechanics. Forsyth got it, Grayson didn't. 'Bruce was driving forward all the time. Larry we realized could half manage it if he was pointed. You literally had to manage him in his eyeline. If you see the tapes, you'll see him look off to camera right, you'll see him look – that's to the producer – "What do I do next?" or "Did I do right?"'[39] Marcus Plantin, who directed the Grayson *Gen Games* before becoming producer, reinforces Boyd's recollection: 'Bruce's ultimate skill is that, without savaging the public who take part, he can lift them, drive them and energize them. Bruce was producing it as he went along. It wasn't Larry's nature, he wasn't a driving force, he was reactive.'[40]

Bruce had also enjoyed the assistance of his wife, Anthea Redfern. Although Grayson was not the marrying kind, Boyd decided that a female foil was more necessary than ever. While he was trying to figure out who he could pair with Grayson, Boyd found himself having to pay a sudden visit to his ill father in Edinburgh:

He'd gone to bed, so I was watching television at eleven o'clock at night, and it was *The Birthday Show* or something, hosted by Isla St Clair. I thought 'Hmmm, that's interesting, wonder if she'd be right as the foil for Grayson?' So I got her down, interviewed her, liked her, saw that magic in her eye, thought 'Here's someone different, with a bit of bounce.' Had my father never had an attack of angina, it wouldn't have happened. I never knew of her until that day. She was the magic little girl next door. From Anthea, who was all dresses and twirls, here was the tomboy, who could do the games, where Larry couldn't. Isla was in control, not him. That was the clever part. Larry was just bumbling around having fun.[41]

Beginning his tenure as *Generation Game* host on 23 September 1978, Grayson had a couple of weeks' head start before the first *Bruce Forsyth's Big Night* on 7 October. Forsyth was his ebullient self from the off, opening with a check that all the regions were safely gathered in and 'Let's Get the Network Together', a jaunty song about the federal nature of ITV. Naturally, the viewing figures for Bruce's inaugural ITV show were high, but the following weeks saw vast numbers returning to the BBC. The show that couldn't fail had failed.

There were some good things in that first show, not least Forsyth's unorthodox interview with American singer/comedienne Bette Midler, in which both ended up crouching on the floor rather than using the plush chairs the props department had provided. The presence of Rod Hull and Emu brought a welcome element of danger, 'The Glums' proved as delightful as they had been thirty years earlier and *The Pyramid Game* showed the form that would eventually make it a hit show in its own right. Unfortunately, to get to these highlights, the viewer had to wade through large stretches of, at best, tedium and, at worst, some of the most cringingly embarrassing items ever mounted in the name of television entertainment. A segment at a bar where members of the public tried to impress Forsyth with their joke-telling fell into the tedium camp, while at the embarrassment end of the scale there was a fancy dress competition won by a woman dressed as the Post Office Tower. Somewhere in the middle, 'Teletennis' proved to be a very strange way of spending even part of a Saturday night, with the contestants whooping and yodelling to control their computerized paddles. Why they couldn't have just had joysticks like anybody else has never been adequately explained.

In retrospect, the show's biggest problem was that it attempted to be too many things at once. Not far behind that was the 'build it and they will come' mentality that seemed to pervade its genesis; keeping viewers' attention for two hours on a Saturday night took more than just the considerable force of Bruce Forsyth's personality, but for far too much of the programme, that was all they had. 'The show wasn't nailed down,' confesses director Paul Smith:

Here's how bad it was, honestly, and I kid you not. I would have Russ Abbot as a guest, say, and scripts would come over my left shoulder, as if I was directing the news. Myself and the vision mixer were reading them, ad-libbing [the shots]. Stuff was going on that no one had ever seen. I'm talking to the lighting director, everybody, because nobody knew what was going on. It was disorganized, because it was so ambitious. Bruce was being treated with huge kid gloves, and I think in the end there should have been more 'Listen, Bruce, you're a huge talent,' which he is, 'but come on, there needs to be a certain discipline here.'

Smith found the stress of fire-fighting far too much and soon decided to leave the show:

At the end of the second show, I thought 'I can't take this.' I'd given my life for it, I don't mind doing that, but I need to feel there's some kind of structure to what I'm doing. It was really getting to me. I went to see David after the second show had been taped, I went up to his office and said 'I'm terribly sorry, but I want to resign.' He said 'That's just as well, as I was going to fire you.' I said 'At least we agree on that one.' He took over, and then there was a huge furore in the press, about Bruce, about the ratings going down. It was nothing to do with me, but I learned for the first time what it's like to be the focus of press attention. Michael Grade said to me 'Why not go off to the States, just get away from it all?' So London Weekend paid for me to go off to the States. It was a sort of busman's holiday, as I ended up directing a series for cable television over there.[42]

★

The year that saw the *Big Night* take its bow also saw the final curtain for two warhorses of the light entertainment schedules, with the BBC broadcasting the last *Black and White Minstrel Show* on 21 July 1978 and Thames pensioning off the talent show *Opportunity Knocks* on 20 March 1978 after a seventeen-year run. Anachronistic even when it had started in 1958, by 1978, changing attitudes had rendered the *Black and White Minstrel Show* unacceptable and offensive. Many within BBC light entertainment had long felt uncomfortable with it. 'I remember saying that we shouldn't be doing the *Black and White Minstrel Show* on the grounds that it might be racially offensive, at a departmental meeting, which infuriated Bill Cotton,' recalls Roger Ordish, who was, at the time, seeing Gloria Stewart, a black actress, who had appeared in *Hair*. Stewart had hit the headlines in September 1969, when she auditioned for the show as a protest and was refused a part. The show was finally axed when James Gilbert – a producer with a distinguished record in comedy – became head of light entertainment in 1978, on Bill Cotton's elevation to BBC1 controller. 'I was embarrassed by the *Black and White Minstrel Show* and when I got into a strong enough position in the BBC, I had that show cancelled,' explained Gilbert in 2000.[43]

Many words have been written and spoken about the perceived evils of the programme, quite often by people who have never seen a complete edition, but if intent counts for anything, it was not a racist show. Its latter-day producer Ernest Maxin went on to produce *Kids International* with the express intention of promoting racial harmony, having seen the flipside himself, as a Jewish boy growing up in east London. The main problem seems to be that the show, having been created when blackface was still regarded as acceptable, then lived on into a time when this was no longer the case, with its continued success making BBC bosses reject reasoned and overdue requests for it to be taken off. Without the blackface make-up, the most offensive thing about the show would have been the corniness of the jokes told by toothy Birmingham comedian Don MacLean each week. Unfortunately, without the blackface, the show didn't work. A one-off had been made in 1968 under the title *Masquerade*, but it received a disappointing response and the idea was not pursued.

The evils of racism are self-evident, but by the end of his TV career, the toxicity of Hughie Green was proving almost as offensive to many who encountered him. The smarm, schmaltz and fake sincerity of his early years on television had given way to a far less palatable bitterness and a tendency to bring his right-wing political views into everything. The height of his hubris came in December 1976 when he closed one edition of *Opportunity Knocks* with a rendition of his patriotic anthem 'Stand Up and Be Counted', aided by the Wimbledon Operatic Society and a horde of sea and air cadets. Royston Mayoh, who had worked with Green since the ABC days, had tried to remind him gently that such antics had little to do with entertainment, but Green felt his massive ratings earned him the right to editorialize. He was allowed one outside broadcast per series, and Thames's former controller of programmes Jeremy Isaacs recalled in 2001 that 'he didn't suggest Battersea Park or Blackpool fairground or wherever. He would suggest a nuclear submarine base ... There was absolutely no way in which Hughie could be entitled to give vent to his political opinions in a show that was supposed to be about "was little Jeannie better than little Tommy at conjuring?".'[44]

It was Isaacs who finally wielded the axe. According to Thames producer Dennis Kirkland, a critical moment came when Green provoked Thames's head of light entertainment Philip Jones to a shuddering rage. Jones and Kirkland had been having a quiet drink in the bar at Teddington, while on the other side of the room sat a heavily inebriated Green. Green summoned Jones with a crooked finger, and Jones decided to ask Kirkland to accompany him for moral support. There was already bad blood between Green and Kirkland, stemming from a disagreement during Kirkland's brief association with *Opnox* (as the show was known within the industry), and as the pair approached the star, Green asked Jones 'Why have you brought that flat-footed cunt with you?' In an attempt to defuse the situation, Kirkland replied that he didn't have flat feet, but Jones told Green that he wouldn't hear anyone speaking of his producers in such a manner. Green had clearly thought he was unassailable. Never the pleasantest of men – the spectrum of show business loveliness running from Hattie Jacques at one end to Green at the other extreme – he had alienated and upset a great many people, to the point that when he pushed his luck once too often, there was no one willing to support him.

The final show went out on 20 March 1978, but he refused to go quietly. He masked his obvious upset by ramping up his trademark fake bonhomie and winking – which were by now so exaggerated that he was virtually a parody of himself. He also indulged in heavy self-justification, launching into speeches that reminded newspaper critics of the number of television stars and hit records that the show had produced. He told viewers that while the show was coming to an end he wasn't retiring, because 'I can't afford to'. In reality, the decision was made for him. Green had taken on the BBC and lost in 1949, when a radio version of *Opportunity Knocks* was dropped after just one series. During the court battle, head of variety Michael Standing went on record to describe Green as being 'vain as a peacock'. That time he had bounced back, but this time the phone never rang. His career was over. He was part of a consortium to oust both Thames and LWT in the 1980 franchise round, but the application was not taken seriously by the Independent Broadcasting Authority. Green's exit from the show was further marred by a drink-driving conviction and a legal action taken by a former contestant, who had been disqualified after alleged vote-rigging, concerning remarks made by Green to the studio audience off-air. His reputation was further harmed after his death, when it emerged that he had been violent and cruel to his family, while fathering a string of illegitimate offspring, including Paula Yates.

Thames' replacement for *Opnox* was a radical departure. In place of the winking, smirking, apparently wholesome Green came a cheeky, irreverent disc jockey with a penchant for 'naughty bits', fulfilled by the presence of a scantily clad multiracial dance troupe called Hot Gossip. *The Kenny Everett Video Show* was, in the eyes and ears of practically a whole generation, a vast improvement on the show that had preceded it. Green had oozed insincerity and made constant references to 'your show'. Everett eschewed a studio audience, and the only laughter to be heard came from the crew. That he could make jaded professionals continue to laugh on the second or third take is a testament to his own ability and that of his writers, Barry Cryer and Ray Cameron. Like Spike Milligan, Everett poked fun at his employers, making constant disparaging references to 'Lord Thames'. This not entirely accurate extract from his autobiography gives a flavour of the great man's attitude:

'My name is Philip Jones and I'd like you to do a TV show for Thames, starring you, with anything you'd like in it. We will, of course, pay you a vast amount of money for the privilege of using Your Extreme Wackiness on the tube.'

Me: 'Not today, thanks'.

Well, maybe it wasn't exactly like that, word for word, but you get the general gist. I really didn't want to do any television work . . . [but] he called again and offered even larger cheques . . . [and] I caved in under the weight of zeros.[43]

Everett, born Maurice Cole in Liverpool on Christmas Day 1944, had been an enfant terrible of broadcasting ever since he had been sacked from the pirate ship Radio London for sending up evangelist Garner Ted Armstrong, one of the station's regular advertisers. In 1970, he had been sacked by BBC Radio 1, ostensibly for making a remark about the Minister of Transport's wife passing her advanced driving test by bribery, but more likely because of his obvious distaste for the Musicians' Union and their rigid enforcement of 'needle time' restrictions on pop radio. Many looked for a motive behind his antics, and when he appeared at a Conservative Party event in 1983 advising the bombing of the Russians and kicking Michael Foot's walking stick away, it was thought that his true animus had been found. It seems likely, however, that Everett's only true motivation was mischief.

Even if Green had done himself out of a job, there was still a market for talent shows on television, as LWT showed when it launched *Search For A Star* just over a year after opportunity had knocked its last at Thames. The host was Steve Jones, fresh from *The Pyramid Game*, which had survived the collapse of *Bruce Forsyth's Big Night* to become a big hit in its own right. Television can be daunting for an inexperienced performer, so great pains were taken to ease participants in, as Steve Jones recalls:

Brian Rogers would choreograph [everyone], including the comics, showing them where to look and all that, for four or five days before we did the show. Then there would be a complete dress run the day before the show. They came on, we did the show, with mock juries – there was a real jury around the country on the night. We did the actual show, played it back the next day to the acts and said 'This is where you went wrong. This is why you shouldn't do that . . .' All of the advice from Brian Rogers, Alyn Ainsworth, and then the following night they'd record the show. You probably wouldn't get that now. They did the whole show twice, really.[46]

★

Back at the BBC in 1979, the victorious Alan Boyd had his plate full with the *Generation Game* and a new game show based on an American format called *The Match Game*, in which a contestant was given a sentence with a missing word, which they had to supply. They were faced with a panel of six celebrities, gaining points for each celebrity who supplied the same word. Boyd called in Terry Wogan from the Radio 2 breakfast show to host it, retitled it *Blankety Blank*, made a joke of the pitiful prizes the BBC was allowed to give out – worst of all being the *Blankety Blank* cheque book and pen consolation prize, a triumph of the nickel plater's art – and received flak from all angles. 'It was fun because the BBC weren't sure they wanted it,' he asserts. 'The board of governors were complaining, they didn't think it was really the BBC, and it was all silly. Bill Cotton got me in one day and said "Do we have to have this long thin microphone? Do we have to call it *Blankety Blank*?" We made it much funnier. The [American] producer came over and said "Ohh, you've destroyed my show."'[47]

Despite his reservations, Cotton was never one to turn up his nose at a palpable hit, so he entered into a small wager with Boyd, betting the producer a bottle of champagne if the ratings hit 10 million. 'One day, I was called into the office. It was Queenie [Lipyeat, PA to Tom Sloan then Bill Cotton]: "Bill Cotton wants to see you immediately." I thought "Oh shit, this is *Blankety Blank*. The board of governors have now decided it's gone too far." Bill just put two bottles of champagne on the table. I said "Well thank you, what's that?" He said "20 million. One for each 10." Nothing happened after that.'[48]

The original plan had been to nab Boyd for the *Big Night* at LWT, but he proved resistant to David Bell and Michael Grade's overtures. 'Michael Grade tried to get me in '78 [recalls Boyd]. They always said my name was in the telephone directory, because he was so sure I was coming.' By 1980, however, the lure of the South Bank proved too much. 'It was David [Bell] who persuaded me. One of the reasons they wanted me, Michael Grade said, and Brian Tesler eventually said, "You get Alan Boyd: A, you get the guy who's making the *Gen Game* and is killing us, and B, you hope to get another hit from him."'[49]

Plan B worked like a dream. Jeremy Fox, founder of the production company Action Time and son of former BBC1 controller Sir Paul Fox, brought Boyd a format called *The People Show*, based loosely on NBC's *Real People*, which introduced members of the public with unusual hobbies or interests to a US television audience. Boyd tinkered with the proposition, adding elements of the venerable American show *Truth or Consequences*, where contestants who answered questions wrongly had to perform a daft stunt as a forfeit, and the hidden camera aspect of *Candid Camera*. One of the elements that Boyd brought over from *Real People* was the idea of having four young, relatively unknown hosts. Selina Scott, then a newsreader at Grampian in Scotland, came down for two meetings, one with Boyd, one with David Nicholas at ITN, who offered her *News at Ten*. 'I thought "She's very posh, not going to get her hands dirty,"' admits Boyd, but fortunately, he had another candidate. 'I'd seen Sarah Kennedy on a telethon or something, and thought "She's mad, she'll roll her sleeves up." She came in and got interviewed in a funny big hat.' Next came bearded, gangling actor Matthew Kelly and Irish journalist Henry Kelly. The fourth position remained unfilled until one of the show's researchers, Jeremy Beadle, asked to be considered: 'He said can I be one of the hosts on the pilot? I can do all the games. He did the famous mouse in the box, and he did it so well, he looked at me and I said "Oh, all right then, Beadle, you can be the fourth host."'[50]

Before the programme made it to the airwaves, Boyd changed the title, albeit not quite in the way he intended originally. 'The night before we did the pilot, I couldn't sleep. Ray Moore, the sadly missed voice, who used to be one of my promotion voices when I was a trailer maker [was on the radio]. He suddenly said "Oh, you'll be good for a laugh." I thought "That's a good title," scribbled "Good for a laugh" and went to bed. I got in next morning, said to the graphics guys "I think I've got a title. Instead of *The People Show*, we'll call it this." I said "What is this? Good for a Laugh? Game for a Laugh? Game for a Laugh." I couldn't read my own handwriting. It changed entertainment for years afterwards.'[51]

Indeed it did, but some claimed it was not a change for the better. In the first show, transmitted on 26 September 1981, a crane smashed through a car roof in a hidden camera stunt, while presenter Sarah Kennedy judged a male beauty contest at a nudist colony. In show two, members of the audience were taken to sunbathe between the runways at Heathrow Airport. Meanwhile, in the studio on show seven of the run, members of the audience were asked to put their hands into boxes and feel the unknown objects, within one of which was the swimmer Duncan Goodhew's bald head. The show's detractors argued that these antics were cruel and exploitative. Meanwhile, the tabloid press latched onto the nudist colony item as an example of television at its most shocking, despite the fact that the item had been carefully filmed to show rather less than the same papers were used to displaying on their third page.[52] The viewing public en masse had no such qualms. *Game for a Laugh* finally wrested control of Saturday nights from the BBC after more than a decade. 'It destroyed my old show, the *Generation Game*, on the other side,' Boyd recalls with relish.[53]

CHAPTER NINE

Weekend world

By the time that ITV had taken ownership of Saturday nights, ATV – in name at least – was in its death throes, having been regulated out of existence by the Independent Broadcasting Authority in the 1980 franchise round. Representing the Midlands alone since 1968, the company still made most of its major productions outside the region at the Elstree studios, which had never gone down well with the regulator. The IBA decreed that ATV should close Elstree in favour of new studios in the east of its region at Nottingham,[1] that local investment should be sought and that a new name should be chosen. On 1 January 1982, ATV became Central.

There had been internal change before the franchise reshuffle. It was an IBA rule that no one over seventy was allowed to serve as a director of a programme contractor, so in 1977, Baron Grade of Elstree had resigned as chairman of ATV. Although he remained in charge of ATV's parent company, Associated Communications Corporation, he turned his attention increasingly towards film-making. Around the same time, Bill Ward, who had headed the production side of ATV since the start, also retired. Ward received a warm send-off in an Elstree studio where Jack Parnell and the massed ranks of producers sang 'Bill' from *Show Boat* to him, accompanied by the full ATV orchestra.

The new company inherited several hit shows from its predecessor, not least the Bob Monkhouse game show *Family Fortunes*, which had made its debut on Saturday nights in early 1980, before moving to Friday nights the following year. The idea was that two families competed against each other to guess the most likely responses to certain questions, as given by 100 people in a survey. The answers were displayed behind Monkhouse on a 'computer' display named Mr Babbage (actually just a graphical device driven by electrical relays, not unlike the pre-digital destination boards at major railway stations), and if an answer was given that had been mentioned by nobody in the survey, it was marked by a noise that can only be described as that made by a MiniMoog synthesiser on a baked bean binge.

The format had been originated in the States, under the title *Family Feud*. William G. Stewart had a strong track record in situation comedy and variety, but had never produced a game show until asked by ATV's director of production Francis Essex to visit America and see the show in action. At first he was baffled to be chosen, but the logic soon became clear. 'I asked "Why me? I don't do game shows." [Essex] said "Well the thing about these game shows, the big ones, is that the producer runs them from the floor." I'd run all my things from the floor and I was very good at warm-ups, having been a redcoat.' The prospect of an all-expenses paid trip to Los Angeles also appealed to Stewart as a fledgling independent producer with transatlantic contacts to maintain. 'I went, and I have to say I was so impressed with the slickness of how this thing was run. A man called Dickie Dawson was the presenter. I thought "Yeah, I could do this, and I'd enjoy it." I only went for the ticket, and when I came back, they told me it was Bob Monkhouse. Somebody at LWT wanted it for Bruce Forsyth. They tried to do a swap for *Play Your Cards Right*. Bob didn't want to do the swap. He also said "I don't like this title. What about *Family Fortunes* rather than *Feud*?" I liked Bob Monkhouse enormously, so I did it.'[2]

Stewart knew that between them, he and Monkhouse could make the show a big hit. As such, he felt entitled to be paid well, but even he was surprised with the outcome of the salary negotiations:

Billy Marsh, my agent, didn't know anything about negotiating for producers. Michael [Grade] had been my agent. Billy said 'What is the show?' I said 'It's a forty-five-minute game show, called *Family Fortunes*, it's going to be for twenty-five programmes or something like that.' He asked how much I was getting at the moment. I was getting about £1,200 a programme – this was a sitcom, you did one a week. Billy Marsh didn't know that. He said 'Will you be happy if I get you that?' I knew I was going to do twelve a week, but I didn't think he had in mind that I'd get that per programme. He turned round and said 'I've got it – £1,250 a programme.' I was doing twelve a week. No producer or director to this day gets paid per programme for game shows.

The thing about ATV was that there was an understanding, that if anybody's salary was above a certain amount, it had to go to the board for approval. My salary was going to come out at £30,000 for this series, and the maximum was £25,000. So, Jon Scoffield came to me and said 'How can we work it out?' I knew that I was going to get it off the ground, and when it's all up and running they'd get someone else in. I said 'How about this – if I agree to take the £25,000 instead of £30,000, I have first option on every other series?' Without a doubt, I was the highest paid producer in Britain by about eight miles because of what Billy had done.[3]

The anticipated success ensued, but Stewart's contract caused headaches when tensions grew between the producer and the host:

I really liked Bob, but I was very strict with him. I would not let him do his blue jokes on a family game show. One night, I was horrified. We had a celebrity edition and the two families were Lord Montagu and Lord Bath. It was for charity, but they wanted to do it because it was early in the spring and it was a plug for the houses for the summer. It was the old Lord Bath. The question was 'Can you name one of the films of Humphrey Bogart?' Someone said '*The African Queen*.' Bob looked up at the board and said 'Can we see Johnny Mathis up there?' I promise you. Everybody laughed. Of course they laughed. But in the break, I went up to him. I said to the floor manager 'I don't care, that's coming out, and Bob will do a retake saying "Can we see *The African Queen*?"' This happened on two or three occasions.[4]

At the end of the series, Jon Scoffield – by now head of light entertainment – called Stewart in and informed him that Monkhouse had asked for a new producer. Stewart replied that they had a deal. Faced with the choice between ditching a popular host from a big hit show and paying the producer a family fortune of his own not to produce the show, Scoffield took the latter option. Stewart returned as producer when Monkhouse moved to the BBC in 1983, and Max Bygraves took over as host. 'I said to Max "Don't take the job, because then I'll have to come back,"' Stewart jokes, adding that 'Max was not a success. Max will admit that it's not the kind of show he should do. With scripted material, Max would have the audience eating out of his hand.'[5]

The show was put on ice for a couple of years until it was revived in 1987 with Les Dennis as host, and still Stewart's original contract stood. 'Billy Marsh rang up and asked "Anything in this for Bill?" and another 35 grand came up. Billy said "Look, they're going to get fed up with this eventually. We're going to have to sort this out. I'll write a letter, and let's sell them this letter." Which we did for another £35,000. So I got paid for about five series I never did. It was great.'[6]

On balance, Stewart was a bargain for Central when he delivered another smash success US game show import for the Saturday night programme roster. *The Price is Right* had been a staple of the schedules for CBS in the US since 1972. The game itself, mostly based around the contestants trying to guess the value of the prizes, was almost irrelevant. What mattered was the show's wild atmosphere and raucous audience response. Each member of the audience was a potential contestant, and only knew they were taking part when the host Bob Barker called their name and invited them to 'Come on down!'

British executives had toyed with the idea of bringing the show over, but had dismissed the possibility, as Stewart relates:

The Price is Right had been hawked around in this country for quite a while, but nobody would touch it, [because] they didn't believe you could get British audiences to behave like that. I said 'You're mad. Firstly, I used to work at Butlins. Secondly, have you never seen "Last Night of the Proms"? There are middle-class kids standing there singing their heads off.' People will behave like that if you let them. But if you get 300 people in a TV studio, and the first thing you say to them is 'Before we start, in case of fire, the doors are over there and over there', immediately, you've got your work cut out. That's why you very rarely hear laughs in the first minute of a sitcom. Writers learn not to put them in. The audience is trying to get over a warm-up of dirty jokes and being reminded that there might be a fire in the place.[7]

By 1984, Britain was deemed ready for such a frenzy, but Stewart knew he needed a good host. His ideal candidate was Leslie Crowther, long-serving *Black and White Minstrel Show* comedian, sitcom actor and a seasoned ringmaster with several years' experience making children behave on *Crackerjack*. Unfortunately, Stewart's bosses dismissed Crowther as 'old hat'. Matthew Kelly was in the frame, but unavailable, while Russ Abbot was unwilling to make the three-year commitment that was being asked. Finally, Central suggested the affable rock and roller Joe Brown. Despite being, in Stewart's estimation, 'one of the nicest guys, and fun', the producer knew Brown would be wrong for the show. Eventually, Stewart suggested that two pilots should be made, one with Brown, the other with Crowther, and that Jon Scoffield should pick the best. In the interest of fair play, Stewart offered to let another producer make the Brown pilot, but Scoffield said he trusted Stewart to give both hosts 'a fair crack of the whip'. Scoffield had to admit that Stewart had been right about Crowther: 'Joe was smashing. He was fun and people liked him, but he wasn't in control, whereas Leslie [was] . . . When Leslie put his arm round an old lady and said "We want you to win that fridge," he meant it.'[8]

With Crowther in place as host, Stewart himself took charge of the warm-up. He spent some time thinking about how to get the audience ramped up to the required fever pitch, before inspiration struck:

> Leslie and I were out to dinner one night in Nottingham before the series started, just he and I, and there was a table with about twelve people on it. The bloke whose birthday it was looked to me like a military type. As the cake came out, all the people around the table suddenly started singing 'Land of Hope and Glory'. Not only did they do that, they were all standing up singing that. Suddenly, other people in the restaurant started joining in. I thought 'I've got it, that's what we'll do.' So the floor manager used to come out and, sweet phrase he used to use, 'Please be upstanding for our producer, William G. Stewart.' As they stood up, I played a recording from the Albert Hall of 'Land of Hope and Glory', so we had 8,000 people singing 'Land of Hope and Glory' and the people in the studio joined in. By the time Leslie came out, they were in a frenzy. I had also seen at Butlins that if people came to an event in groups, they were more likely to let their hair down. So three-quarters of that audience came in coach parties from all over. They were coming from Cornwall, Glasgow, Northern Ireland. It took them two days to get here for this bloody show. It was a phenomenon. It was huge fun.[9]

The patriotic choice of warm-up music might have surprised many at the IBA who regarded the programme as the brashest, most Americanized thing ever to appear on British television. The unease of the regulator was not matched by the viewing public. It alternated in the Saturday night schedules with Yorkshire Television's *3-2-1*, in which host Ted Rogers attempted to guide couples towards the star prize of a car or holiday and away from the booby prize of a dustbin, with the aid of guest stars who came on, did a turn, then read a hellishly cryptic riddle. The show had been going since 1978, and had continued to be very popular: during its 1983–1984 run it was almost always one of ITV's top ten programmes, usually occupying the number six spot with an audience of between 10 and 13.7 million. In its first week, *The Price is Right* matched *3-2-1*'s biggest audience. In week two, another 600,000 viewers had joined in. In week three, the unthinkable had happened, and *The Price is Right* had knocked *Coronation Street* sideways to clinch the top spot, with an audience of 16 million.

The show even went to Blackpool for a summer season, in 1985, but this venture proved to be a victim of its own success. It had been decided that the prizes had to be as good as those in the TV show, so Leslie Crowther's agent Jan Kennedy had arranged a deal with Great Universal Stores. Unfortunately, no one had reckoned with the Blackpool underworld, which produced crib sheets with the correct prices on, meaning that the prizes were always being won.

Eventually, the novelty wore off, but even at its lowest, *The Price is Right* was still good for an audience of 10 million. However, in 1988, Stewart was told by Central that they were going to try a season without *The Price is Right*. The first Crowther heard of it was when a journalist called at his house for a comment on Central's decision to drop the show.

The Price is Right was successful largely because it took to the air at the end of a massive recession and at the start of one of the most aggressively acquisitive times in our nation's history. The recession of the early eighties had affected ITV massively, with a downturn in advertising revenue. In 1982, Michael Grade left LWT to seek his fortune with the US production company Embassy, to be succeeded as director of programmes by former current affairs boss John Birt. Whereas Grade was an old-fashioned showman, Birt had become known for his relentless pursuit of logic. He was a man to whom hunches were anathema. Under Grade, the company might have pulled its horns in a little, and tried to trade through the slump, but Birt went for the scorched earth approach. As LWT's historian David Docherty put it, 'he believed that the only way to keep the company going was to assemble an emergency schedule of comparatively inexpensive, high-ratings programmes'.[10] Some already-recorded situation comedies and dramas were held over so that they would appear on the following year's balance sheet. The new economic climate meant that the massive variety spectaculars favoured by David Bell had fallen out of favour. In particular, the Birt purge marked the end of LWT's long, happy and fruitful association with Stanley Baxter.

In their place came game shows and people shows, very much the province of Alan Boyd, who was now head of light entertainment under controller of entertainment David Bell. Game shows, in particular, could be made on a production line basis, as William G. Stewart had found to his profit on *Family Fortunes*. Once the set, lighting, sound and equipment were primed for one show, several could be made in one session, with only minimal adjustments. Alan Boyd explains: 'Even when I was at the BBC, we would make four *Blankety Blanks* in a weekend: two on the Saturday, two on the Sunday. *Jeopardy* and some of these other shows, they were so designed by the American system to be manufactured at the rate of five or six a day.'[11] Bruce Forsyth made fun of the system in almost every edition of *Play Your Cards Right*, telling the audience that they were 'so much better than last week'. The punters roared with laughter and approval, secure in the knowledge that they *were* the previous week's audience and, depending on the workload in that particular session, probably the following week's too.

Cilla Black figured heavily in the eighties reinvention of LWT's light entertainment output. The Liverpool-born singer had moved from the BBC to ATV in the seventies, in an ill-advised shift away from variety into sitcom, with *Cilla's Comedy Six*. After that, her television work had been restricted to guest appearances, including one in the opening run of *Live from Her Majesty's*, LWT's successful eighties attempt to rekindle the spirit of *Sunday Night at the London Palladium*. Fortunately for her, she had a fan and ally at the top of LWT in the form of fellow Scouser John Birt, and it was a case of waiting for the right show to emerge. As Alan Boyd explains, that show turned out to be *Game for a Laugh*'s better-behaved sister:

The team, as they were developing *Game for a Laugh*, saw other ideas. We kept putting them aside, saying that's an idea for another show. It was originally called *The Good News Show*, and I didn't like the title. I said 'It's not about good news, it's about people who do wonderful things. They come and get a surprise, then they get a golden gong or something. We basically say "Surprise surprise, you've been good." There's a title in there.'[12]

Boyd arranged a meeting with Black and her husband/manager Bobby Willis. At first concerned about overexposure, Willis assented to a six-show run. Black's main concerns differed from those of her husband. 'She said "Can I sing?" I said "No,"' Boyd recalls. 'She said "Can I have a different costume every part?" I said "No, not on a show like this."' Boyd allowed her to sing the theme tune, a decision that became a gift to impressionists.

The first series, beginning on Sunday 6 May 1984, was to be transmitted live, and Boyd decided that Black needed a co-host, settling on rotund actor Christopher Biggins. 'I said "In live television you need a foil like the American talk shows. The Ed McMahon thing – when you're in trouble, you can use the foil to get yourself out of it." It was exactly as I had done with Larry and Isla, in reverse this time.' The end product had something for everyone. 'We had Cilla being put in the middle of a rock in the middle of the Channel somewhere, with helicopters saving her. We had Cabbage Patch kids, we had nuns,' Boyd relates.[13] The show was closer in spirit and intent to *Ask Pickles* than anything. It made a speciality of flying long-lost relatives from the other side of the world, in the interest of warming the hearts of the Sunday-night viewing millions. In so doing, it recast Cilla as the nation's nosey, but well-meaning auntie.

Unfortunately, while the show lasted for over fifteen years, the coupling of Black and Biggins was not destined to last more than two series. 'His agent wanted him to have equal billing, wanted it to be Cilla and Biggins' *Surprise Surprise*. I said no, Cilla's the star, Biggins, you're not. Biggins never knew this, to be fair. When eventually I said no, and the agent said "Well, we're not doing the deal," Biggins was very angry and sad that his agent had been demanding this. I think he left that agent shortly afterwards. Agents who push their luck with me get nowhere. I just say "Thank you, goodbye." They then try and rescind where we've got to and I say "You can't rescind. Bye."'[14]

With *Surprise Surprise* established and Cilla more bankable than she had been for years, the next step was *Blind Date*, synthesized from elements of an American show called *The Dating Game* and an Australian show called *Perfect Match*. In it, a contestant had to choose one of three potential suitors purely on the basis of their voice and the answers they gave to a series of loaded questions. Cilla was the natural choice, but Boyd decided to chance a pilot with somebody else. 'We hadn't gone for Cilla the first time for the simple reason that Bobby had said Cilla didn't want to do too many shows,' Boyd explains.[15]

The host for the pilot – which had been titled *It's a Hoot* – was comedian Duncan Norvelle, who had, in many ways, turned show business orthodoxy on its head. Over the years, there had been many privately gay performers who pretended to be heterosexual for fear that admitting otherwise would be career suicide. Danny La Rue's partner Jack Hanson was also his manager, but in press interviews La Rue stressed the professional nature of the relationship, and told journalists of his sadness at missing the boat when it came to marriage. In contrast, the heterosexual Norvelle camped it up something rotten in public, with his 'Chase me' catchphrase, and went to some pains to conceal the fact that he was happily married.

Norvelle's pilot was a disaster, Boyd recalls. 'He never understood the logistics. He'd look at the camera and say "Aren't I pretty?", he never understood the angles. It was hysterical. It took about six days to edit it. Gill Stribling-Wright [the show's producer] tried it and tore her hair out.' Even if Norvelle had handled the show with aplomb, there would have been other obstacles. John Birt let his inner Catholic prude get the better of him and had expressed grave reservations about the show. In turn, he had shown the tape to the Independent Broadcasting Authority's David Glencross, who echoed Birt's concerns about the tone

Above: Peter Cook and
Dudley Moore stage a
cricket match between good
and evil in *Not Only . . . But
Also . . .*, 1970

Right: Christmas sunshine
bringers Eric Morecambe
and Ernie Wise, as seen by
Barry Fantoni in 1978

The Comedians:
(from the top) Mike Reid,
Bryn Phillips, Jim Bowen,
Ken Goodwin, Colin Crompton,
George Roper, Bernard Manning,
Duggie Brown and producer
Johnnie Hamp

There is nothing like a dame:
Les Dawson in his dressing
room at the Richmond
Theatre, February 1982

Above: Lord Grade, Fozzie Bear and Muppeteer Frank Oz celebrate the success of *The Muppet Show*, February 1978

Right: Sir James Savile OBE KCSG and fixees outside the BBC Television Theatre, home of *Jim'll Fix It* and the base of BBC TV variety, 1953–1991

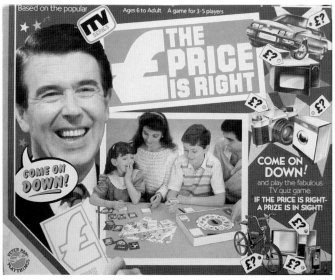

Come on down,
in the comfort of your
own home: variety
meets merchandising for
The Price is Right board
game, 1984

Mr Blobby and
friend invite you to
inspect Crinkley
Bottom, 1994

*Strictly Come
Dancing* champions
Darren Bennett and
Jill Halfpenny
tripping the light
entertainment
fandango, 2004

of the show, and the taste (or lack thereof) with which it was carried off. Boyd prepared himself for a hard sell to get his original choice as host, and was surprised by the receptive response:

> Bobby and Cilla came in, sat in my office at LWT and I said 'I've got a show for you.' Bobby said 'We've got a show we'd like to make.' I said 'Do you want to show me your show first, Bobby? Or shall I show you my show?' So, of course I put in the Australian show. It was called the *Perfect Match*. And he said 'But that's the show we want to make.' I said 'But I thought you didn't want to do more than twelve shows a year,' and he said 'Well, if we stop *Surprise Surprise* . . .' I said 'No, I don't want you to stop *Surprise Surprise*. Will you do this as well?' I told them the truth about Duncan Norvelle. I said 'We didn't come to you because we were led to believe that you wouldn't do more.' Bobby said 'Okay, we'll do twelve and we'll do sixteen *Blind Dates*.' We did it. We did two or three pilots, she got to learn the logic. No you can't sing, no you can't have different dresses.[16]

Boyd was certain that the presence of Gill Stribling-Wright, a Parkinson alumnus known affectionately to colleagues as 'Granny', as producer would reassure even the most vociferous doubters. Even so, and with his beloved Cilla at the helm, Birt remained unsure of the show. 'John Birt was very nervous: "They can't kiss, they must stay in separate hotels, are you sure we should be making this?"' says an amused Boyd. 'The great John Birt wasn't sure whether to commission it. I told a bit of a fib at this point, [that] I'd heard that Noel Edmonds was going to try a dating game on his show, so I said "If we don't air this, this autumn, the BBC will beat us with a very similar dating show." Which was rubbish. Later, John said "Was that true?" I said "No, but it got it shown." He would have stalled it. It was right in the middle of the mid-term review. It wasn't the done thing, he didn't want to be embarrassed by this tacky game show.' Even when the show opened to an audience just shy of 13 million viewers, Birt maintained the pressure on Boyd and his team. 'If I could only find some of my John

TURNED OUT NICE AGAIN

Birt little sticky notes that you used to get on a Monday morning – "A bit tacky, Alan." Cilla kept it clean. Any sign of any tackiness, Gill wouldn't have had it, we were in safe hands.'[17]

Bell's pet project as LWT's controller of entertainment in the dark days of retrenchment was the reintroduction of the big Sunday night variety show to the ITV schedules. Amazingly, with the savings being made in other areas, the funds were available to give the project a seven-week run at the start of 1983. Her Majesty's Theatre in London's West End was available, and so was Jimmy Tarbuck, one of the original hosts of *Sunday Night at the London Palladium*. The theatre had no other commitments, so Bill McPherson's glitzy sets could be left standing, and the show could benefit from three whole days of preparation, by then an unheard-of luxury back in the studios. On Friday, the technical set-up took place, with rehearsals following on Saturday and Sunday, before a live transmission on Sunday night. This level of preparation was crucial to Bell's stated desire to achieve a pre-recorded standard of slickness on a live production.

From the start, *Live from Her Majesty's* proved that there was still a massive audience for variety on television, pulling in between 12 and 13 million viewers week after week. The calibre of the guest artists helped, including transatlantic stars like soul group Gladys Knight and the Pips and crooner Jack Jones, as well as home-grown favourites like Des O'Connor, Max Bygraves, Cleo Laine and Dusty Springfield.

Sadly, the show is best remembered today for the tragic event that occurred on 15 April 1984. Tommy Cooper was in the middle of his act when he suffered a massive heart attack and slumped backwards into the curtains. Harold Fisher was the drummer in Alyn Ainsworth's band, with an uncomfortably close view of proceedings from the orchestra pit. 'I was just below him. The horrible thing was that the [sound] balancer who was outside in the scanner thought that it was part of the act. He sort of sank to his knees and what you were hearing was this death rattle, the poor sod. So, he turned it up. He did most of his act, as I remember and then he sank to his knees. They cued the

308

band and the adverts came on. It was unbelievable.'[18] Behind the scenes, Jimmy Tarbuck's manager Peter Prichard, a trained first-aider, did his best, but to no avail. The show had to continue in front of the curtain for some time after its resumption, because of the mayhem behind it.

Apart from supplying the music for *Live from Her Majesty's,* Alyn Ainsworth was producing music for most of LWT's big shows, having taken over as the company's main musical director from Harry Rabinowitz. The expansive, expensive Ainsworth sound was an integral part of LWT's light entertainment in the eighties, and the embodiment of the idea that while costs could be cut in other areas, some things required and justified a large, ongoing investment. Visiting American stars were all full of praise for his orchestra. Sometimes the big names would take issue with an aspect of the music, and it wasn't unknown for bandleaders to pass the blame very publicly and unfairly onto individual musicians. Ainsworth wasn't like that, as Harold Fisher – who, with bass player Paul Westwood and guitarists Paul Keogh and Chris Rae, formed Ainsworth's rhythm section for most of the time at LWT – remembers:

> He loved his band. He would never let somebody insult his band or try and take over. He would always take the can for the band and sort the problem, if there was one. With producers and artists, he was absolutely magnificent. He would never let you take shit. It was his band, he was so proud of it and he assumed responsibility. Quite often, you get bandleaders who pass the buck and let you roast. Throughout the eighties to 1990, we did so many TV shows – two or three a week. That band was a cracking band.[19]

★

Over at the BBC, magic was to become an important part of BBC1's counter-attack on ITV's new-found dominance of Saturday nights, but it had been a staple of television variety since the Alexandra Palace days. In particular, the close-up magic of card tricks and sleight of hand were suited to the intimacy of the medium. The Polish-born mental magician Chan Canasta had been a presence on BBC television since 1951, but television's first star magician was David Nixon. His initial small-screen success had nothing to do with his magic, coming as a result of being a panellist on *What's My Line*. Already well established as a conjuror on the variety circuit, his skills came before the television audience in the BBC series *It's Magic*. Later, he moved his shows over to Thames before the lung cancer that had dogged him for many years claimed him in December 1978. His demise coincided with the rise of his successor as the king of television magic, almost as though there was room for only one in the whole business.

Paul Daniels was, in some ways, Nixon's polar opposite. In the assessment of actor, comedian and variety historian Roy Hudd, 'David [Nixon] was not a great magician but his affability and warm personality made him an entertaining one.'[20] Daniels was and remains an excellent technician, but he lacks warmth. There is a touch of arrogance and aggression in his professional manner that means he is destined to be respected by audiences and colleagues, but never truly loved. To be fair, this may be a calamitous misjudgement of the man himself. A young magician, barely out of short trousers, met Daniels at a magic convention. He asked if he could show Daniels a trick. The professional watched patiently, then offered two pieces of advice. One was a technical tip on the trick itself. The other was never to work for free, at which Daniels handed the boy a pound.

The Middlesbrough-born son of a cinema projectionist, Daniels' interest in magic began as a schoolboy. After National Service, he turned professional, forming an act with his first wife. Following several years honing his act on the club circuit, his first television break came in 1970 with an appearance on *Opportunity Knocks*. This was followed by bookings on Granada's hit *Wheeltappers and Shunters Social Club*. It was the BBC, however, who gave Daniels his own series, beginning in 1979, under the auspices of producer John Fisher, himself a skilled magician.

Although Daniels was the headline act, *The Paul Daniels Magic Show* was also a showcase for the best magical talent from around the world.

One of the most memorable guests was San Francisco-based 'bubble magician' Tom Noddy, who appeared in October 1982, defying physics by blowing cube-shaped bubbles. 'It helped, I think, that I was a magician,' John Fisher explains. 'I had an editorial sense both of what Paul should be doing or could be doing, and of who was out there in the big, wide world, *vis-à-vis* magic guests and speciality acts. Sadly you can't earn a living in this country really as a spesh act, but if you go to Europe and America [you can]. The great thing was that we had a platform to give these acts time. "My god, did that guy really do that thing with those ten bubbles?" The following day, the whole country was talking about Tom Noddy, or Hans Moretti being pierced in a cardboard box with eighteen swords.'[21]

The show also contained a very strong historical element, with Daniels recreating great illusions from history, most famously the bullet-catching trick that had killed Chung Ling Soo at the Wood Green Empire in 1918. Daniels replicated it without incident in November 1982, aided by the late magician's original assistant, Jack Grossman. There was one occasion in 1987, however, when viewers were left with the unmistakable impression that something extremely unpleasant had happened to the star of the show, as John Fisher relates:

We were asked to do a live Halloween show. Paul and I said 'If we're going to do a Halloween show, we should attempt to send a shiver down the spine of the audience.' So we went to a National Trust property down at Godalming. We didn't have a proper audience. We had a group of twelve celebrities. John Humphrys was amongst them. We had an appropriate guest from America who specialized in macabre magic. We did a Houdini seance. All that sort of stuff was pretty standard, but we were going live, but the idea was to finish with Paul going into an iron maiden [with] inner spikes, and then the timer being set at the bottom of the screen. He had a minute, two minutes to get out, but we had no intention of bringing Paul out. The door slammed shut and nothing happened. Did we tell presentation? I don't think we did tell presentation. We might have given them a hint. We didn't play the sig. tune, I think we played some credits.

Suddenly the BBC switchboard went bananas. We'd obviously found a way to include an announcement later in the evening, but suddenly I was told I had to put Paul on camera fast and record him looking at the audience, so that could be played back in the next gap between programmes. I don't know how many complaints were registered, but I think it was some kind of record. Paul and I felt totally vindicated.[22]

The stunt and the reaction to it caused a predictable fuss. Fisher had the support of BBC1 controller Michael Grade, who had been warned about the plan by Fisher the night before, when he accompanied his uncle, Lew Grade, to an appearance on Terry Wogan's chat show, of which Fisher was executive producer. Nonetheless, Jim Moir called Fisher to express grave doubt that he would still be head of variety on Monday morning, and that, far worse, one of them would have to go on *Open Air*, a BBC1 daytime programme presented by Eamonn Holmes, which gave the green pen mob a chance to grill BBC executives on live television over perceived shortcomings in programming. On one edition, Bill Cotton had been pilloried over the *Black and White Minstrel Show*, even though the last series had been almost a decade earlier. Everyone dreaded the call to appear on it. Fisher calls it a 'stupid, misguided' programme, while Moir recalls the alternate title he gave it: 'I never called it *Open Air*. I called it *Open Wound*. [It] was a bit like [an] instantaneous magistrates court, or kangaroo court. It was a great thing apparently for governance and accountability, but it was occasionally hard enough to bear. It's bad enough to make errors, it's bad enough to have a professional catastrophe, without being paraded for a serious drubbing by Irate of Tunbridge Wells, with the gleeful co-operation of a production team [from] somewhere else [in the BBC]. There again, if you put yourself up there, you've got to take the flak.'[23]

Fisher remembers being in his office at 7am on the following Monday, determined to be in the building before Moir. From his office window, he could see Moir in his office, but had decided not to make the first move. 'He's going to have to call me. At quarter to eight, and normally I wouldn't be in the office until quarter to ten, the phone rings, and very nervously I pick up the phone. 'Can I speak to John Fisher? It's Lew Grade. I just want to thank you. You made me such a happy man on Friday night. To do the show was a wonderful experience. Anything I can do for you. I hope we meet again.' He didn't know I was in the office at that unearthly hour. It must have impressed him that at a time when no one else in the BBC was in their office, I was. Eventually, I don't know whether Jim Moir came up to see me or I wandered down to see him, but we both burst out laughing, because he had the *Radio Times* open in front of him.'[24] BBC1 was committed to a week of live outside broadcasts from the CBI Conference, and so *Open Air* was off-air. Moir and Fisher kept their jobs.

★

The Corporation's main response to ITV's sudden supremacy on Saturday nights had been to promote the man who had done so much to build up ratings on a Saturday morning with *Multi-Coloured Swap Shop* – Radio 1 disc jockey Noel Edmonds. Behind the move was Jim Moir, who had succeeded Robin Nash as head of variety[25] in November 1981, and Edmonds remembers 'the brief to me was to do the next generation Simon Dee show'. Like Dee, Edmonds was a major force on the wireless:

> All I ever wanted to do was be on the radio. I fell in love with the pirate ships, and the power of radio. There's a little bridge between *Swap Shop* and the *Late Late Breakfast Show*, where I was doing *Top Gear* and aviation programmes for the Beeb. Jim Moir sat me down and in that Jim Moir way, he said 'Look, do you want to be a television presenter or do you want to be a TV star?' I said 'I quite like doing my motoring programmes,' and he said 'Fine, I don't have a problem with that. You're an extremely good television presenter, but if you want to come into my department, you have to make the decision now.' He said 'I think you've reached that point in your career where you decide what you want to do, and I think I can make you highly successful in entertainment.' We had a running gag for twenty-odd years that we did quite well together.[26]

The job of producing this high-stakes show was given to tough old pro Michael Hurll, and the first *Late Late Breakfast Show* went out on Saturday 4 September 1982. Alongside the *Dee Time* aspects of celebrity guests, interviews and pop performances, were added hidden camera tricks played by Edmonds' 'Hit Squad' and breathtaking stunts performed by viewers in the 'Give It a Whirl' segment. Both features were a clear challenge to *Game for a Laugh*'s supremacy, and were popular from the start of the show's run. However, despite Hurll's experience and Edmonds' popularity, the first series failed to catch on in other ways. Edmonds had been given a girl Friday in the form of Scottish comedienne Leni Harper, but the chemistry was noticeably absent. 'I'm not quite sure what they were expecting of her,' muses Edmonds. 'Bless her, I don't think she had a specific role.' Perhaps most damning of all, she lacked glamour, Edmonds describing her as being 'quite like Olive Oyl'. Also involved was John Peel, a Radio 1 colleague but not a great show business mate of Edmonds', who took care of outside broadcasts, looking quite clearly as though he wished he were somewhere, anywhere else.

On its second run, beginning in the autumn of 1983, the show improved gradually. Peel was still on the OBs, still appearing to display a considerable distaste for what he was doing. Nonetheless, even that early on, many were wondering whether Hurll, the great risk-taker, wasn't pushing his luck with some of the stunts on the show. The matter came to a head in the edition of 10 September 1983. The previous week, the 'Whirly Wheel' had decided that a chosen punter would attempt to fly a one-man gyrocopter. While the wheel choosing the lucky viewer was legitimate, the wheel choosing the stunt was carefully rigged, so that the production team knew what they would be doing and where they would be next week. On this occasion, the wheel had malfunctioned – it had been intended to select a motoring stunt. The net result was that the gyrocopter stunt had to take place at Santa Pod racetrack, a venue of tangential relevance, where the following week's OB had already been arranged.

The chosen viewer's inability to get the gyrocopter more than a few feet in the air made it a weak sideshow compared to the real spectacle of experienced amateur racing drivers trying to leap over a line of cars. Numerous drivers attempted to break the record of 232 feet, including Richard Smith, whose only achievements turned out to be a fractured pelvis as well as head, neck and back injuries when he ploughed into the line of cars, rolled over and landed where spectators had been standing – until they saw his Jensen hurtling towards them. Peel was audibly shaken and heard to swear on the soundtrack, while Edmonds visibly changed from amused and amazed to horrified and stunned, as he tried to deal with the incident. The stunt resulted in serious questions being asked about the show internally and in the press. As is usually the way, this adverse coverage meant audience figures for the next show soared by over a million. By the time the show came off the air in 1986, a further 3 million had been added, taking the ratings over 13 million regularly, matching *Game for a Laugh* at its peak.

The growing popularity of the show saved it, and by the 1984 run, the show had found the formula that would last until its demise. Peel was replaced by fellow Radio 1 presenter Mike Smith – who was much more in tune with the host and tone of the show. Both were unashamed populists and both were nuts about helicopters. 'In the end, it worked brilliantly with Smitty and I, where he was on the OB.' Smith usually opened his contributions by complaining about being somewhere cold, wet and often dangerous, while Edmonds had a cushy number in the studio. Peel had done the same, but the difference was that he usually meant it. 'We had the slightly feisty thing with the big screen and it was decided that was how it would work, that apparently there was a bit of animosity there. There's nothing worse than working with people in a live context if you can't trust each other. Smitty and I did trust each other, and we didn't try and top each other.'[27]

Stunts and banter apart, the show's main selling point was the panoply of A-list guests it attracted, just as *Dee Time* had twenty years earlier. When Paul McCartney and Michael Jackson wanted to launch a new single in October 1983, McCartney put in a personal appearance with wife Linda on the *Late Late Breakfast Show*. The following week, Billy Joel was in town with product to shift, so he dropped in. With the stars of the day and physical stunts vying for airtime, this was a variety show in a sense that would have been recognizable to music hall audiences in the twenties.

The show would doubtless have continued if not for the tragic accident involving 'Whirly Wheeler' Michael Lush during rehearsals. On Thursday 13 November 1986, while preparing a trick in which he was to escape, Houdini-style, from a box suspended 120 feet above the ground, the 25-year-old Southampton builder fell to his death. The elasticated rope intended to break his fall had become detached, and a faulty clip was to blame. At first the BBC announced that the next edition of the show would be cancelled as an inquiry got underway, and that all future dangerous stunts would be dropped. On the Saturday, however, it was announced that the show would not return at all. The decision had been taken by Bill Cotton, by now managing director of BBC Television. Jim Moir, head of variety and just two months away from becoming BBC TV's last head of light entertainment group, remembers the meeting all too well:

> I can recall sitting with Bill Cotton, waiting for Noel to come in for the meeting, and Bill said 'The show will have to stop.' For ten seconds, I thought 'What?' and on the eleventh second, I realized he was absolutely right. You can't pick up a jolly entertainment – oops, sorry – as if nothing has happened. It has to be, when a human life is involved, complete and profound respect, so the show had to stop. It's as simple as that. It's irrelevant how well it was doing. It came to an end because it had to. There was no alternative. It was a very, very tragic thing to happen indeed. I can't look at anybody doing bungee jumping now. I can't do it. Whatever extenuating circumstances there may or may not have been, the fact [was] that a human being had perished, a family had lost a loved one. The rest is silence.[28]

Had Michael Hurll, the great risk-taker and showman, finally taken a risk too far? Lush had been thought ideal for a high-altitude stunt, because he had worked as a hod carrier on high-rise building sites. Nonetheless, there would be enough risks involved if a professional attempted the same stunt as Lush. Press reports hinted that corners had been cut, but the Health and Safety Executive official who investigated the accident, Maurice Pallister, said that, in designing the box, the BBC's visual effects designers 'had taken a high standard of safety and doubled that to ensure it was doubly safe'.[29] The weak link was the carabiner clip that had been meant to keep the elasticated rope attached, but which sprang loose. The HSE's senior scientific officer Graham Games had shown video evidence of twenty experiments involving a comparable clip and an elastic rope. The clip worked loose fourteen times out of twenty. A representative from the Dangerous Sports Club explained that they had eschewed clips in favour of shackles – always used in multiples for security – when attempting similar stunts. Other mistakes included the failure to check on the competence of the stunt arranger, who was an escapologist but not an acrobatics expert, and the failure to provide an airbag in case anything went wrong. The BBC was fined £2,000 for failing to take adequate safety provisions, and gave an *ex gratia* payment of £100,000 to Lush's family, but no one was judged to be responsible for the terrible outcome. More than twenty years on, Edmonds 'still find[s] it very difficult to talk about it':

I think that the way the media dealt with it was understandable, because actually no one was really found guilty. That was one of the extraordinary things. I was so stunned that somebody could lose their life in the name of light entertainment. Is television safer because of what happened? Procedures? Undoubtedly. It was a terrible, terrible accident, which shouldn't have happened, but it wasn't because there was a cavalier attitude to safety or that any of the experts involved were being reckless. I wasn't involved at all and I always said that, ignoring the obvious sensitivities, there's a big difference between something being someone's fault and their responsibility. If you've got your name up there on the show, I think it would have been totally inappropriate and monstrously callous for me to have almost shrugged my shoulders. I did, at the time, seriously think about stopping.[30]

The following winter, the BBC1 Saturday night schedules opened without a big variety-based show, but not without Edmonds, as his quiz *Telly Addicts* moved from a midweek slot. Russ Abbot, recently poached from LWT, took up the slack later in the evening with a sketch show similar to his LWT *Madhouse*. In 1988, however, Edmonds returned with a show that was recognizably related to the *Late Late Breakfast Show*, but different in several important details. Main among these was that *Noel Edmonds' Saturday Roadshow* was not live, but recorded. Michael Leggo remembers being informed that he was taking the project on – and being made responsible for defining the project:

> Jim Moir gave me a call, may even have sent me a memo saying 'You're producing and directing sixteen shows with Noel in the autumn, go away and think about something.' Shit. Noel and I sat down with literally a blank sheet of paper between us. One of the first things I wrote on the piece of paper was 'Live', and actually it ended up being one of the first things on the paper that I crossed off, because 'Why live?' unless you've got a reason to be live, if you can do it better, and give it better production values and choose the best bits if you record it.[31]

Leggo was nervous at the challenge, being still a fairly junior producer. 'You could count the number of things I'd produced on one hand,' he admits. However, he knew Edmonds from directing inserts for the *Late Late Breakfast Show* and a shared interest in fast cars. Their original plan was for a show in the mould of US chat king David Letterman's, but it mutated, and as it did, the outside broadcast element was sidelined, despite the show's title implying a certain amount of movement. Instead, a different, themed set based on a different location every week was built in the studio. For the first show, on 3 September 1988, the location was the Channel Tunnel, while later shows came from an ice station, a Bedouin tent and the Kremlin, without ever leaving Shepherd's Bush. Doing it this way was almost as expensive and arduous as decamping to the real locations, as Leggo explains, recalling the now almost-unthinkable cost. 'That was in the days when you could do that. We did have a modular set – the doors and the chat areas and the performing areas were common – but everything else around it changed.'[32]

The *Roadshow* was a respectable performer, ratings-wise, but it seems doomed to be forgotten, primarily because of what came immediately before and after it – overshadowed at the start by the Michael Lush tragedy and at the other end by the runaway success of Edmonds' Saturday night warhorse *Noel's House Party*. Nonetheless, elements of the *Roadshow* presaged the winning *House Party* formula. The idea of pretending the programme came from somewhere other than a television studio had been present in the earlier series. The 'Gotcha Oscars', in which hidden camera stunts were performed not on members of the public, but on celebrities, who were judged to be fair game, began as part of the *Roadshow*. *Noel's House Party* was to be set in a fictitious stately home in the hamlet of Crinkley Bottom, with the show's guests turning up at the door and being either invited in to do their turn or sent away by the host.

The main differences were that in *Noel's House Party*, the set did not change on a weekly basis, and that both producer and presenter had realized the value of doing the show live:

Mike Leggo and I reckoned we could add 2 million to Saturday evening and get back to those great big audience figures that the *Late Late Breakfast Show* had, if it was live. And so, together, we created *House Party*. It cost a fortune in bottles of Chardonnay, but we got there. We had it on a single sheet of A4, and we went to Jim Moir, who was then head of entertainment, and we said this is what we want to do, and it's live, and we guarantee that we'll put 2 million on what we were doing with *Roadshow*. Jim said 'What's it going to cost me?' For a non-transmission pilot, I think the figure was £350,000. He said 'Can it be a transmittable pilot?' We said 'No, because it's got to be live.' Jim said 'So, I'm going to give you £350,000 in order to make a pilot, and I'm never going to see that money again?' We said 'No, we'll get a hit show out of it.' And I remember it was like something out of one of those bad films where you know the person behind the desk is going to stop the person walking out of the door with one more line. And as we got to the door, he just said 'Guys.' We said 'Yes, Jim?' He said 'Don't fuck up.'[33]

Moir disputes the figure. 'It might have added up to that, but it wouldn't have been that in cash,' he observes. 'It makes for a good story, but it probably was far less than that in truth.' He also stresses that the whole process was far less cavalier than it sounds, being based on mutual trust and knowledge. 'You weren't investing in the unknown. Edmonds was extremely successful in those early evening slots. I had brought Edmonds into LE, it was me that promoted him. It wasn't some distant exec. saying "What are you chaps thinking of doing?" We were conspirators together and I wanted it to succeed. I would only have given it because I had it to give, and it would have been very carefully thought through and every penny accounted for by a chap called Tony James. He never gave anything away if we didn't have to.'[34]

The then BBC1 controller Jonathan Powell was from a drama background, and so he was largely happy to leave the LE experts to it, trusting them to deliver the hits, judging them only on results. Leggo recalls the lack of interference:

Almost as a courtesy, I said to Jonathan Powell 'Would you like to come and see what we're doing?' because we did a whole big non-transmission pilot with all the bells and whistles. Jonathan said 'Oh that would be very nice.' The afternoon of the recording he came down, I walked him round the set for about ten to fifteen minutes, he said 'Thanks very much,' went back to his office and the next thing we knew we did the series. It was all quite laid-back.[35]

Without a focus group or a demographic survey in sight, *Noel's House Party* took to the air on 23 November 1991. Edmonds and Leggo had been slightly out in their ratings estimates. Instead of the hoped-for 2 million 'we actually put 4 million on. It happened very quickly. I remember Mike coming down from the gallery after that first show, which for me was like a car crash, it was over so bloody fast, wow, what happened there? We're not really that tactile, but we both hugged each other, looked at each other and said "Whew, we got away with that, didn't we?" Within four weeks we had a hit. There are very, very few shows that are a hit out of the box and we were.'[36]

At its peak in 1993, *Noel's House Party* was regularly pulling in audiences of 15 million. When the National Lottery was launched the following year, the BBC won the contract to televise the Saturday night draws, and Edmonds was the natural choice for the gig, being Mr Saturday Night and highly adept at live television. The live element was a large part of *House Party*'s appeal, with the potential for things to go awry. Edmonds and Leggo weren't above rigging the odds on occasion:

> It was live and things went wrong. Occasionally they went wrong deliberately [admits Edmunds]. On one occasion, the front door fell off its hinges. Why would a front door fall off its hinges? I just said to one of the scene shifters in the afternoon, 'Do you fancy taking the top hinge off this door, so that the first time we open it, it'll fall off?' And it got such a bloody laugh. I can't remember who was at the door. I said 'Don't tell whoever's at the door.' I told Mike, obviously, so he could shoot it. The audience loved it, and we probably got a minute of complete mayhem while I and whoever it was at the door – I don't know why, but Russ Abbot comes to mind. I'd chosen the right person, I know that. It took us forever to put this bloody door back.
>
> The audience really felt they owned *House Party*. If the ding dong came in the wrong point, I got to the stage where I could look at the audience and say 'That's not meant to happen.' You'd get another laugh. Or they would miss the cue because I'd said something completely different, and I'd say 'The doorbell's going to ring in a minute.' It was pantomime.[37]

One of the elements that would not have been possible in a recorded show was NTV, where a secret camera was installed in a viewer's home, ready to display them, unwittingly, as they sat in front of the set. Technology had made the camera small enough to be hidden, but the concept was not a million miles from Cilla Black sending OB units to viewers' homes twenty-five years earlier. Unfortunately, not everyone realized the significance of NTV. 'One of my least favourite parts of the season was having to meet the press before we started,' Edmonds reveals. 'There were people like Charlie Catchpole, who were very nice to your face, but who absolutely hated the show. So, the moment the first show went out, they slashed it. There was a wonderful TV critic, Pat Codd, who used to work for the *Daily Star*, and Pat would always interview me and finish off by saying "Which night do you record it? I'd love to come along to a recording," and you go "Pat, it's live. It's been live for the last eighty performances. How do you think we do NTV?" "Oh yes." And you think, Oh God, your career's in the hands of people like that.'[38]

The Gotchas gave birth to the show's most infamous creation, a vile pink-and-yellow rubberized heap of boggle-eyed manic activity. Originally conceived as a throwaway device to allow Edmonds to be present at each Gotcha while remaining undetected until the very end when he removed the head of the costume, it soon became clear that Mr Blobby had legs, even if half the audience wanted them broken. Michael Leggo is perfectly willing to admit responsibility for being the terrible creature's father:

With the Gotchas the difficult bit always was getting Noel next to the subject rather than just at the end: 'Da da! Gotcha!' He's got a beard, it's blooming tricky. We once spent three hours in make-up with him, walked out and a friend of mine said 'Hello Mike, Hello Noel.' On the *Roadshow*, we'd done a Gotcha on Eamonn Holmes. It was supposed to be a training video for car salesmen and the customer was represented by this thing that looked a bit like the Sugar Puffs' Honey Monster. What Eamonn didn't know was that we were recording the rehearsals, where we had an actor, with just the furry brown trousers on. Then we went to the take, in which the actor puts on the top, and we substitute Noel. Now, the Honey Monster thing is being an arsehole, but it's Noel, and the audience know it is and it's a fantastic device. Dramatic irony, the audience is in on something that Eamonn isn't. It worked very well. Because the *House Party* was a very voracious machine, series two, I'm thinking what can I do that can get Noel into the Gotchas. So I started thinking about a character from a children's programme and I remembered this Eamonn Holmes thing. So, a lot of cheap alcohol and five minutes' doodling, and I came up with this thing in mauve felt-tip that was Mr Blobby. I was delighted at the time that I got eight Gotchas out of it, including Will Carling, Wayne Sleep, Val Singleton. Once they'd been transmitted, in terms of Gotchas, that's it, but it spawned a monster.[39]

A monster with numerous merchandizing opportunities, including a Christmas number one single, and theme parks at various sites around the UK, including one at Morecambe, which folded amid recriminations and legal action between Lancaster City Council and Edmonds' company Unique.

Noel's House Party is a good litmus test for the way the broadcasting environment changed during the nineties. At the time the show started in 1991, satellite television was in its infancy, with only 11.8 per cent of the UK's television-owning households having BSkyB or cable. By the time it finished in 1999, that figure was 25 per cent, and the average audience of *Noel's House Party* had dropped to 6.6 million, just over 8 million down on six years before. There had been a natural decline in the show's popularity, but the fragmentation of the audience caused by the take-up of multi-channel television must also bear partial responsibility. There was suddenly a lot more to compete with. Even though the dip had long been obvious to those most closely involved, the show had been too successful to kill off. Edmonds wishes it had gone out on a high:

In my ideal world, I wished it had ended after the fifth series in 1995/6. The components were still fresh. Certainly they'd matured, but they weren't getting stale. There was a ready supply of those running gags, the two guys from *The Bill* came to the door and all that sort of thing, and we were still able to get real stars to appear on the show. Now, when people say to me 'I'd love to have *House Party* on again', I want to say to them 'Ah, but who would you have coming to the door, that would make 350 people in the audience roar and make the viewer go "Who's that? Bloody hell, it's Dudley Moore." Who would you have now? Someone off *Big Brother* coming to the door? Or another tired soap performer?' I wouldn't want to be rude to any artists that appeared on it, but by the time that it finished in 1999, by then we were really scrabbling around to have people on the show that were a draw, and so I do remember that first five years with great affection and great gratitude. I got the opportunity to play around on the telly with some pretty impressive people. Working with Spike Milligan, Ken Dodd and people like this. Am I a grateful bunny? Yes.[40]

The show's demise was also marked by an acrimonious and very public dispute between Edmonds and BBC1 controller Peter Salmon, who had been, in Edmonds' view, less than robust with the press when they decided that the *House Party* fun had run its course:

It was inevitable that when I was billed as being the highest-paid entertainer on television, that the knives would come out. What was disappointing was that the BBC, going through this huge period of change, didn't have the confidence to get up and say 'This show is performing really well. Can't you see that we have changes in the broadcasting environment, and all channels are gradually clicking down?' And that's what was happening. When you look at the stats, we were no less successful, in terms of our decline, on a pro rata basis, than Cilla Black was. We had one really bad one, which I think was a 6.5 [million, but] ITV had a live blockbuster something, and the critics latched onto that. And because Peter Salmon was a coward, he didn't go public and say

'I'm very happy with *House Party*, it's still doing this, it's an important part of the schedule, this, that and the other' and I've always despised him for that. It wasn't just what happened to me, it was so demoralizing to the production team. We were made to feel as though we were a show in decline, when [it was] the whole genre.[41]

★

In the eighties and nineties, Cilla was not solely responsible for keeping ITV's end up on Saturday nights. LWT had also produced *You Bet*, first with Bruce Forsyth at the helm, then later with Matthew Kelly and Darren Day. The idea of the show was that members of the public bet a celebrity panel that they could undertake a strange, arcane, amusing or dangerous activity or challenge in a set amount of time. In one of the more sedate challenges, a contestant claimed to be able to distinguish different bass guitars by their sound alone, which he then attempted to do, aided by a blindfold and legendary session musician Herbie Flowers. Later, it added *Gladiators* – an endurance test in which Spandex-clad he-men and hardbody women attempted to knock each other out of contention with gigantic cotton buds – to its Saturday night roster, with massive success.

Meanwhile, in Manchester, Granada had latched onto a Dutch programme created by Joop van de Ende[42] called *The Soundmixshow*, in which contestants impersonated famous singers, aided by massive efforts of make-up and costume to make them look and sound like their heroes. Retitled *Stars In Their Eyes*, a pilot was made, but Granada's head of entertainment David Liddiment insisted on some changes before proceeding to a series:

[It] was a great idea, [and] it had worked in Holland. Having made the pilot, I believed I could see how we could make it better. We made a very conscious decision to invest very heavily in the show. It stood out on the screen in terms of production values – lighting, design, sound quality. It was an expensive show. In the original Dutch show, contestants had sung to pre-recorded backing tracks, effectively karaoke. We brought in

Ray Monk as musical director, absolutely recreated the sound of the original record. Everybody sung live, which we made a big deal of. I took a conscious decision to put that level of resources into it because we had, in my view, a long way to go to establish our credentials on the network as a major supplier of light entertainment. What was exciting was that the lighting design, the camerawork, everything on that show was done by Granada staff. We had a very highly skilled staff, because it was a fully staffed television station with four big studios and five crews. They were honed on drama because that was the company's specialism, but they loved doing music and entertainment more than anything else because it gave them more scope for creativity. We had a couple of lighting directors who loved to do light entertainment and worked very hard to get this glossy polished look.[43]

Liddiment also believes that the choice of presenter was crucial. Given that the show hinged on amateur performers giving a professional performance, Leslie Crowther stood out as the man most likely to set them at their ease, combining a wealth of show business experience – from *Crackerjack* to *The Price Is Right* – with an affable manner. Not that Crowther got the job without making some concessions. The terms were laid out at a highly memorable dinner at L'Escargot with Dianne Nelmes and Jane MacNaught from Granada, as his agent Jan Kennedy remembers: 'The West End was blanketed with snow, so bad I couldn't walk out in my stiletto heels, so I had two carrier bags on my feet, marching out like a washer woman with a scarf on. The reason we had that dinner was to tell Leslie he wasn't to dye his hair so much and he wasn't to wear glasses. Poor Leslie got hammered by us. It was hysterical.'[44]

Crowther kept dying his hair, but acquiesced on the glasses, and proved to be the perfect host for the show, which made its debut in July 1990. He would probably have continued to present it evermore, had he not been involved in a terrible car accident on the M5 in October 1992. Despite being an alcoholic – something he later conquered – on the day of the accident he had not touched a drop, and fatigue was identified as the cause. Russ Abbot came in as a temporary host of *Stars In Their Eyes*, but when it became clear that Crowther would not be able to return to the show, Matthew Kelly – who had made his name on *Game for a Laugh* – took over the job permanently. Despite being an actor by training rather than a comedian, Kelly shared Crowther's ability to set the contestants at ease, and hosted the show for eleven highly successful years before returning to the stage.

Throughout the eighties, the light entertainment establishment had been under assault from a new breed of performers and writers, who thought the old guard were, at best, outmoded and, at worst, offensive. The initial crucible of the revolution had been the Comedy Store, an unprepossessing room above a strip club in Soho. The infamously brutal master of ceremonies there was a Liverpudlian Communist called Alexei Sayle. Most prolific was Ben Elton, co-writer of *The Young Ones* and sole author of *Happy Families*. Almost all were university-educated, but not necessarily from an Oxbridge background. Almost all were very right-on and had a raft of jokes about the likes of Jimmy Tarbuck and Bruce Forsyth, their unashamed allegiance to the Conservative Party and their cosy, chummy world of golfing pals. One of the most barbed was this broadside from Alexei Sayle: 'Like all good comedians, I love a game of golf, and I often take part in the P.W. Botha Pro-Am Celebrity Golf Classic. You know the sort of thing. Strictly for charity, Water Rats versus Martin Bormann's Escaped Nazi War Criminal Showbiz Eleven.'[45]

The latex puppet-based satire series *Spitting Image* was no less brutal in its attitude to the elder statesmen of entertainment. In the mid-eighties, LWT had persuaded Jimmy Tarbuck to branch out into chat show territory with *Tarby and Friends*, which *Spitting Image* spoofed in April 1986 as *Tarby and Friend*, consisting of Tarbuck interviewing Michael Caine about the pay cheques he had received from his films, in front of a rank of audience seating that was empty apart from a puppet of Bruce Forsyth, clapping enthusiastically. In the same edition of *Spitting Image*, Tarby's fellow chat host Russell Harty was seen to be interviewing 'Page 3' model Samantha Fox's breasts, both of whom were considering solo careers. Another episode included a sketch about BBC LE music maestro Ronnie Hazlehurst's attempts to write a requiem mass.

It may come as a surprise, then, to learn that much of the ammunition aimed at the old-school variety dinosaurs was loaded by the same executives who employed them. At the BBC, each programme has a number. Shows made in London by the comedy department of the light entertainment group bore the prefix LLC. Variety shows were catalogued as LLV. Almost every ground-breaking comedy show made at the BBC in the eighties, and into the nineties, from *The Young Ones* to *A Bit of Fry and Laurie*, was a variety department production, classified LLV, and had been nurtured by head of variety Jim Moir. The motivation had been his desire to differentiate the BBC's two television channels. Through the seventies, and into the eighties, where BBC1 would have a full variety show, BBC2 tended towards intimate revue and singer-based programmes, but all were recognizably mainstream:

Controllers, from [Bryan] Cowgill onwards – certainly Paul Fox – realized that they needed to compete with ITV. They saw the worth of LE and placed it in their schedules to great effect. Particularly on BBC1 and also increasingly on BBC2. There was no real difference between entertainment on 1 and 2. It was the big stuff on 1, and the smaller stuff, the quirky stuff on 2. Not the big hitters. Stuff that would make you smile. I sat down and began to think that there was a need to differentiate entertainment on 2 from 1, and with Brian [Wenham – BBC2 controller from 1978 to 1982, then director of programmes, BBC TV, from 1982 to 1986]'s approval, I went out and got Rory Bremner, French and Saunders, Victoria Wood and Alexei Sayle. They began to transform BBC2 and it began to be a place that was identifiable for a particular form of comedy. It was clear to me that these people were definitely punching their weight, and I wanted them on my team. I had a meeting with French and Saunders, and it took me a year to bring that meeting to fruition. A year later they actually signed on the dotted line, and that's an association with the BBC that lasts today. Alexei Sayle was a difficult kettle of fish. I called him into my office. He sat there in front of me – he's a threatening looking chap, and I didn't know if he was going to become the mad axeman. I just said to him 'I really admire your talent, can we work together to make you a success on BBC2?' He said 'Thank you for that', went away and made *Alexei Sayle's Stuff* which was another piece of landmark BBC2 comedy. That's one of the joys of being a light entertainment impresario. Spotting the best talent and bringing it on from wherever it was.[46]

The first BBC TV light entertainment producer to spot the new wave of talent was Paul Jackson, the Bristol University-educated son of *What's My Line* and *This Is Your Life* producer T. Leslie Jackson and a successful producer of *The Two Ronnies* in his own right. Despite being steeped in traditional LE, Jackson lobbied hard to be allowed to bring new blood to the screen. His persistence resulted in two specials in 1980 and 1981 under the title *Boom Boom Out Go The Lights*, showcasing the likes of Alexei Sayle, Keith Allen and Tony Allen, not to mention Nigel Planer, Rik Mayall and Adrian Edmondson.

Planer, Mayall and Edmondson would, with Jackson as producer, take the alternative invasion of BBC television to the next level with *The Young Ones*, which made its BBC2 debut in 1982. A pilot had been made the previous year, but had not been given the green light to progress to a series until Channel 4 showed an interest in Edmondson, Mayall and Planer as part of the group that had broken away from the Comedy Store to found their own Comic Strip club. With a series of half-hour *Comic Strip* films in development for Channel 4 – the new network scheduled to bring minority interests, innovation and *Countdown* to television from November 1982 onwards – *The Young Ones* was rushed into production. Despite the panic, the series hit the screens in an assured, confident, noisy and, to many viewers, revolting manner. Set in a scrofulous student house, it concerned the petty squabbles of the four equally sociopathic but utterly different house-mates – pretentious poet Rick (played by Mayall), violent heavy metal fan Vyvyan (Edmondson), hippy Neil (Planer) and Mike 'the cool person' (played by Canadian actor Christopher Ryan) – and was a curiously effective hybrid of variety show and situation comedy. The central narrative of each episode was interrupted by musical interludes from bands of the day like Motorhead and Madness, and stand-up comedy from Alexei Sayle, nominally playing the housemates' sinister Polish landlord. Although the show came from within the heart of the BBC's variety department, the scripts by Mayall, his girlfriend Lise Mayer and their Manchester University contemporary Ben Elton, were full of digs at older LE stars. Rick's obsession with Cliff Richard was not meant to reflect well on the Christian singer. One episode turned into an homage to, then a demolition of, the cosy self-sufficiency sitcom *The Good Life*:

NEIL'S FATHER: Why can't you be in one of those decent situation comedies that your mother likes?

[*The Good Life* titles play, but Vyvyan emerges through them shouting]

VYVYAN: No, no, we are not watching the bloody *Good Life*. Bloody, bloody, bloody, bloody. It's so bloody nice. Felicity 'Treacle' Kendal and Richard 'Sugar-Flavoured Snob' Briers. What do they do now? Chocolate bloody Button ads, that's what. They're nothing but a couple of reactionary stereotypes confirming the myth that everyone in Britain is a lovable middle-class eccentric and I! HATE! THEM!

. . .

RICK: Well, you can just shut up, Vyvyan. You can just about blooming well shut up! Cause if you've got anything horrid to say about Felicity Kendal, you can just about bloomin' well say it to me first. All right?

VYVYAN: Rick, I just did.

RICK: Oh! Oh! You did, did you? Well, I've got a good mind to give you a ruddy good punch on the bottom for what you just said. You're talking about the woman I love.

NEIL: Yeah, and me. I love her too.

NEIL'S FATHER: Yes, well, I agree with the spotty twerps on that one. Felicity Kendall is sweetly pretty, and just what a real girlie should be. Why, speaking as a feminist myself, I can safely say this: that Felicity Kendal is a wonderful woman, and I want to protect her.

VYVYAN: Well, it's the first time I've ever heard it called *that*.[47]

Jackson also produced alternative comedy's debut on BBC1, collaborating with Geoff Posner, another open-minded young producer who had come up through the BBC LE ranks in the traditional manner. Having a decade of folk club and theatre experience under his belt, as well as a series and several successful specials for LWT, Jasper Carrott was far from a new face when he joined the BBC for *Carrott's Lib* in 1982. The crucial difference was that he was paired with younger performers like Nick Wilton and Rik Mayall, as well as new writers like Ian Hislop and Nick Newman, later to become founding writers for *Spitting Image* and the editorial backbone of *Private Eye*. 'The one person I went out and scalped, within eight weeks of being given the job of head of variety, was Jasper Carrott,' Moir recalls. 'I went up and met him in his agent's house near Birmingham. He didn't need the work. He was incredibly successful, he had an association with LWT. His concert tours were phenomenally successful. He didn't need the money or the exposure. I remember I cheekily said to him "Yes, but you do need to exercise your God-given talent before the biggest audience, so get off your rusty dusty and come and do some television for me."'[48]

The show was completely live on Saturday nights and unafraid of controversy, which was in plentiful supply in the immediate aftermath of the Falklands War. Listings writers are fond of referring to any comedy that isn't *Terry and June* as 'anarchic', but there was a genuine edge to *Carrott's Lib*. In many ways, it was the closest any broadcaster has ever come to channelling the original spirit of *TW3*. In Jim Moir's judgement, 'It was breathtakingly brilliant, because it was so funny, so contemporary. It hit all the nerve endings, it was sharp-edged. His show that went out just after the election – mind-bendingly good.'[49]

Between series of *The Young Ones*, Jackson left the BBC to set up his own company, Paul Jackson Productions, which developed a *Young Ones*-flavoured all-female sitcom called *Girls On Top* for Central Television – starring Tracey Ullman, Dawn French and Jennifer Saunders – and the Elton-penned family saga *Happy Families* for the BBC. However it was for LWT (who made it) and Channel 4 (which showed it) that Jackson produced the biggest alternative comedy showcase of all, *Saturday Live*. For this show, the cavernous studio 1 at LWT's complex on the South Bank of the Thames was filled with an audience, fairground rides and some of the most promising up and coming talent on the scene, both in the US and the UK. Over on BBC2, *Des O'Connor Tonight* and *The Bob Monkhouse Show* had been doing the same in their own relatively quiet way, giving comedians like Garry Shandling and Kelly Monteith their first UK television exposure, not to mention appearances from future US talk show demi-gods David Letterman and Jay Leno. However, while those programmes were chat shows, *Saturday Live* was a big, brash, noisy variety show. The pilot show was transmitted in January 1985: traditional in form, but amazingly revolutionary in content, the apex of everything that Jackson had been trying to bring to the small screen since *Boom Boom Out Go The Lights*.

Many performers came to prominence in *Saturday Live* and its successor *Friday Night Live*, not least Harry Enfield, in his regular spot as the Greek kebab shop owner-cum-philosopher Stavros. Stephen Fry and Hugh Laurie, who had first emerged in the Cambridge Footlights class of '81 – appearing in *The Cellar Tapes* at the Edinburgh Festival along with Penny Dwyer,[50] Paul Shearer, Tony Slattery and Emma Thompson – had also consolidated their television experience with regular appearances on *Saturday Live*. By 1987, their literate, absurdist humour was thought ripe for its own showcase, and a pilot show was commissioned. The choice of Roger Ordish, best known for his work on chat shows and *Jim'll Fix It*, as producer may have come as a surprise to some observers, but in many ways he was perfect for the job. He had been schooled in university revue at Trinity College, Dublin, in the early sixties, before performing in a mid-sixties ATV stab at satire called *Broad and Narrow*. Ordish recalls how it came about: 'Jim Moir was trying to find the right person to do them, and he was talking to John Lloyd. He said "You ought to try Roger Ordish. He's their kind of person." Jim was a bit surprised. I said "I'd love to," and he said "Well, let's see if it works." I suppose I was identified with another kind of thing, whereas I felt that this was my sort of thing and the others weren't.'[51] The pilot went out on BBC1 on Boxing Day 1987 in a late-night slot. It went well enough to lead to a BBC2 series just over a year later in the prime 9pm comedy slot.

In its own way, *A Bit of Fry and Laurie* was as subversive a show as any of the more obviously abrasive offerings. Under the veneer of well-spoken wordplay and absurdity was a pure and rather beautiful rage against the machine of late eighties/early nineties Britain. Under the Thatcher government, the market was God and businessmen the new religious leaders. As a counterbalance, Fry and Laurie depicted businessmen as clueless idiots who swaggered around the boardroom swigging Scotch like it was going out of fashion, and saying 'Damn' rather a lot. As the Thatcher government was privatizing everything it thought it owned and making much of the word 'choice', BBC2 viewers were treated to sketches in which government ministers, dining in posh restaurants, had their cutlery taken away and replaced with hundreds of plastic coffee-stirrers. All were completely useless for the job in hand, but the diner had so much more choice than before.

Less subtle but equally funny was a Fry monologue about his vision of Britain, closing one of the second series shows. 'I see many towns and many villages, and I see family heritage amusement theme fun parks, which will smell of urine and vomit.... As yet, it is only a vision, a vision of family heritage urine and fun amenity vomit. But soon, soon, with luck, sincerity and steadfast voting, it may become a reality.'[52]

The stars and writers of the show felt very comfortable with Ordish as director, but wondered if they had his full attention, given the year-round slog of fielding the *Jim'll Fix It* postbag. 'It was such an institution that it never stopped. The mailbags never stopped coming in, it was always ticking over. It certainly got up Hugh Laurie's nose that I was always also doing something to do with *Jim'll Fix It* while I was doing their shows. Which was a shame, because I loved doing that stuff. We did a Christmas show and then I did two series, so it wasn't as though there was a terrible rift.'[53] For the second series, Ordish co-produced with Fry and Laurie's Cambridge contemporary Nick Symons, while continuing to direct the show. A third and fourth series were made, both wonderful, but not quite as wonderful as their predecessors.

If, however, a single series had to be chosen to represent the demise of the old school of light entertainment and the rise of the new order, it was *Filthy Rich and Catflap*, a situation comedy written by Ben Elton, aired on BBC2 in early 1987 and never repeated. It was sold as the sequel to *The Young Ones*, and, while it contained three of that series' principals, and placed that show's disdain for mainstream entertainment at the centre of the stage, it stands alone, requiring no prior knowledge. The Rich of the title was Richie Rich, a vain, pompous, talentless, hammy has-been/never-was former continuity announcer, unafraid to use illegal tactics to get his pasty, pig-nosed face on television. Played by Rik Mayall with manic glee, he was accompanied by his unsanitary, resentful minder and flatmate Eddie Catflap, played by Adrian Edmondson, and a show business agent, the alcoholic roué and pornographer, Ralph Filfthy, who made Max Bialystock look like Mother Theresa ('Look, daughter, I'm a dying man. I may not live through this fag.') and was portrayed beautifully by Nigel Planer.

During the course of the six episodes, Rich was: blackmailed by the Nolan Sisters after being found in their dressing room; booked very reluctantly as the replacement for Bernie Winters on *Ooer Sounds a Bit Rude* – a game show bearing more than a passing resemblance to *Blankety Blank*; and moved to throw a dinner party for Tarby and Brucie to celebrate his decade in show business. ('The years and the tears. Come and celebrate Richie Rich's ten fabulous years of success, from third dummy in the window in *Are You Being Served* to his very own carpet ad.') He was also: inclined to kill his own father for financial gain; booked to appear as a stand-up comic in a Soho peep show ('A peep show, Filthy. What if Tarby finds out? I shall be thrown out of the Royal Order of the Charitable Self-Publicizing Showbiz Bog Otters.'); and finally rewarded with his own show, after he becomes a tabloid journalist and forces every other entertainer into hiding by writing lies about their private lives.

The targets were obvious, but the whole matter was set out explicitly by Catflap in episode three, in response to Rich's proclamation of platonic love for Jimmy Tarbuck, 'the cheeky chap from the' Pool, everybody's pal, the jolly, gap-toothed Scouser with a twinkle in his eye and a smile for every honest Englishman'. The minder declares:

> Look, if there's one thing I hate in British entertainment more than you, it's that vast army of ex-stand-up comics who did one half-funny gag on *Sunday Night at the London Palladium* in the middle sixties, and have made a fortune doing game shows ever since. 'Oh, good evening, your name is Cynthia, and you'd like me to patronize and humiliate you on the off-chance of winning a Teasmade.' Cheeky chappies? More like complete and utter bastards, if you ask me.[54]

Although Ralph Filthy, Richie Rich and Eddie Catflap were fictional characters, played by comic actors, and much of what they said was motivated by the simple desire to get laughs, there can be little doubt that there was a kernel of very genuine anger at both the comic and political establishment. And yet, the show was a BBC variety department production, nurtured by Jim Moir and produced by Paul Jackson, who had demonstrated his continuing commitment to mainstream comedy by producing Cannon and Ball at LWT. Moir's faith was repaid by the presence in episode four of Jumbo Whiffy, the BBC's bluff, matey, portly, bum-slapping, drink-sodden 'head of nice entertainment', to whom Rich attempts to sell his quiz show format, *All-Star Golfing Secrets*. 'It's meant to be me,' admits Moir, still clearly amused by the whole matter. 'It was Ben Elton pulling my leg. I know Ben Elton very well and like him very much. I was honoured it was played by Mel Smith. It's up to us to say if it's a caricature or if it bears any resemblance to the real person. But Jumbo Whiffy was a head of light entertainment somewhere in the BBC who may or may not have talked like this. The real Jumbo Whiffy commissioned *Filthy Rich and Catflap*, and read all the scripts beforehand, so was well aware.'[55]

As television edged into the nineties, its entertainment side had remained largely true to the pattern set by Ronnie Waldman in the fifties. The executives who gave the dangerous new talents of the alternative comedy scene their breaks were, at most, one degree of separation away from Waldman himself, having been appointed by his appointees. Variety was a broad church, and it had proved able to withstand almost every pressure exerted on it, internal or external, by adapting seamlessly to every new development in entertainment. It seemed to be an impregnable fortress, but soon the whole broadcasting establishment was under siege, from both without and within.

CHAPTER TEN

Goodbye to all that

For much of the eighties and early nineties, the whole broadcasting establishment was under political siege. The Conservative government was quick to regard every critical comment made in a programme as evidence of an insidious left-wing bias. Moreover, having taken on the miners and the newspaper print workers, by 1987, Mrs Thatcher was gunning for the broadcasting unions, referring at one Downing Street meeting to the television industry as 'the last bastion of restrictive practices'. As with Fleet Street, these unions wielded a lot of power and sought to keep salaries artificially high. One industry joke stated that the difference between an LWT videotape editor and an Arab oil sheikh was that the sheikh didn't get London Weighting. An end to the unions' stranglehold on the industry would be welcome news to senior television executives. Indeed, when members of the ACTT (the Association of Cinematograph Television and Allied Technicians) walked out at TV-am – the ITV breakfast contractor – in 1987, chief executive Bruce Gyngell kept the station on the air with management and administrative staff taking over technical duties, and sacked all of the strikers. Gyngell's actions were a bloody nose for the strikers who felt sure that the management would return to the table, desperate to minimize losses. However, the TV-am strike-breaking avoided a catastrophic loss of advertising revenue and proved that a service could be maintained with minimal skilled staff. The development was an important fillip to the reforming Thatcher administration, but few in television were prepared for the root and branch reforms that transpired.

Ever since the Pilkington Report, commercial television had been tightly regulated and expected to make its fair share of unprofitable programmes, under the banner of public service television. Mrs Thatcher saw no reason why the television industry should not be completely market driven. The Broadcasting Act of 1990, steered through by home secretary David Waddington, was the means by which her end was achieved. It abolished the Independent Broadcasting Authority, replacing it with the Independent Television Commission and the Radio Authority, which were to be far less interventionist bodies. Most crucially, whereas franchises had previously been awarded on the basis of programming proposals and boardroom clout, the Act ruled that they were to go to the highest bidder in each case, as long as a vague, nebulous quality threshold was passed. The main concerns for quality were whether what the ITC judged to be a tolerable service could be sustained. This ruled out several of the highest bidders, whose financial commitments to the Treasury would, in the ITC's view, be too onerous to allow a proper level of programme investment. After extensive lobbying from the Campaign for Quality Television, a pressure group that included several television executives and the comedians Rowan Atkinson and Terry Jones, Home Office junior minister David Mellor managed to include an 'exceptional circumstances' clause which allowed the ITC a degree of discretion in awarding the franchises.

Unfortunately for them, two of the Act's strongest supporters within the television industry ended up being its victims, when the results of the franchise applications were announced in October 1991. TV-am lost its breakfast television franchise, its £14.13 million bid having been bested by the consortium that was to become GMTV, with a £34.61 million bid. Thatcher famously wrote Bruce Gyngell a letter apologizing for the unintended consequences of the legislation with regard to his company, which came as cold comfort indeed. Television South (TVS), which had taken over the south of England from Southern in 1982, lost its franchise in 1991, despite its chief executive James Gatward being partially responsible for the legislation in the first place.

Gatward had long thought that his company should be admitted to the top table of the ITV network, with Thames, LWT, Granada, Central and Yorkshire. TVS, by virtue of the affluence of its audience, was one of the network's biggest generators of advertising revenue. Brian Tesler, deputy chairman of LWT at the time of the franchise battle, takes up the story:

It was Jimmy Gatward's fault. TVS was the second highest earner of net revenue on the network, and he had no guarantee of any shows, because the big five were guaranteed. He was furious. We needed him at the weekend because the other guys, the seven-day contractors, were making all their money during the week. The weekend didn't matter to them, and we couldn't make everything. We couldn't guarantee that everything we made was going to be a smash, so I needed help from the regions – TVS, Scottish, Anglia. We encouraged them to make things: *Sale of the Century*, *Tales of the Unexpected*. The others were happy to sell their shows in. James wanted a guarantee. He called the managing directors of the majors in for dinner: 'Before we sit down to eat, I'd like to make a little presentation to you.' Now he's got Bryan Cowgill – Thames; Paul Fox – Yorkshire; David Plowright – Granada; Bob Phillis – Central; and me. He does a presentation with slides, to people like Cowgill and Fox, showing how well TVS is doing. Its share of this, its share of that, therefore it should be the sixth major. Unbelievable, and of course [it] totally put the backs up of Fox, Plowright and Cowgill. Didn't put my back up because I wanted his shows, but I'd said to him 'They won't buy this, James. Do a deal with me, which guarantees that you have part of my output for the network. You'll never be a sixth major. They won't buy it, but we can arrange it so that you get your shows on. I need your shows, for Heaven's sake, so you'll be all right.' But he was 'No'. He had every right to be. Second wealthiest company in the whole system. At the dinner afterwards there was a bit of a frost.

Three days afterwards, he says 'I'm having lunch with [home secretary]

Douglas Hurd and I'm going to put my ideas to him. Would you like to come along?' I said 'Oh, why, do you know Douglas?' He said 'No, I've never met him before in my life. I phoned him and I said I have some ideas.' The chutzpah of this guy. And he put his case to Douglas, and Douglas Hurd said 'What do you think?' I said 'Well it is true that he makes more money than anybody else except Thames, and he has a case, but a) the other guys won't agree and b) I don't think it's necessary to go that far. There are other ways of doing it. Working in liaison with another major, ideally us, because we're the smallest.' Douglas went away and that started the hare running.[1]

Gatward's downfall had been his expansion into America, buying Mary Tyler Moore's MTM production company at the height of the market for $320 million, far more than it turned out to be worth. Despite topping all other bids for the franchise at £59.76 million, TVS did not pass the quality threshold, as it was felt that it would be paying out too much to maintain programme quality. LWT itself survived with a bid of £7.58 million, its only rival London Independent Broadcasting having bid £35.41 million, but failed to pass the quality threshold. LWT had undergone extensive reorganization, dividing into three separate businesses – an ITV franchisee, a production arm and a studio facilities company – as well as arranging a 'golden handcuffs' deal of share options for its senior executives.

Previously an unthinkable outcome, Thames – the warhorse of the network – failed to retain the London weekday franchise, being outbid by Carlton, which had begun as a technical facilities provider and studio owner. It differed in one important aspect from its predecessor. Thames had been a fully staffed and equipped television company, whereas Carlton was to be a publisher-broadcaster, buying in all of its programming from independent producers, just as Channel 4 had since 1982. This was despite having as experienced a producer/director as Paul Jackson in the job of programme director. Central looked to be sitting pretty, having correctly gauged that it would be unopposed and bid a mere £2,000, but when ownership rules were relaxed in 1993, allowing companies to own more than one franchise, Central became vulnerable to a takeover, Carlton being the victor in 1994. At the same time, London Weekend succumbed to a hostile takeover bid from Granada, always its biggest rival in the ITV network, which also took over Yorkshire and Tyne Tees.

These takeovers, and the handover of commissioning and scheduling to the new ITV Network Centre, caused a massive shift in the light entertainment power base of the ITV network. Central – as might be expected from ATV's successor – and LWT had been the two main providers of LE, but now they were owned and controlled by companies whose strengths were in other areas. Granada was noted for its drama and documentaries, while Carlton had not distinguished itself particularly in anything, and was proving to be a sitting duck for critics. The traditional LWT corporate attitude had been to spend whatever it took to get a show right. The Granada culture had been, even in the days when ITV had been that infamous licence to print money, more parsimonious. Marcus Plantin, who worked for LWT as a head of LE, then Granada as a head of production, observes that 'the fiscal control at Granada is quite something'.[2]

Prior to the Granada takeover, John Kaye Cooper, as LWT's controller of entertainment, had presided over a stable of hit shows. *You Bet* was still running, and it had been joined by *The Brian Conley Show*, a Saturday night variety show with music and sketches, featuring Conley as various characters like stuntman Dangerous Brian and puppet-beating children's TV presenter Nick Frisbee. However, LWT's biggest hitters at this time were the impressionist and comedian Michael Barrymore and the sporting endurance contest *Gladiators*.

Kaye Cooper had been one of Barrymore's great sponsors, first using him in *Russ Abbot's Madhouse* at the end of the seventies. Through the eighties, Barrymore made guest appearances on other people's shows and was the host of the Thames game show *Strike It Lucky*, so he was a well enough known name to fill theatres nationwide. It wasn't until the early nineties, however, that his manic intensity was harnessed successfully for TV. The winning formula had been to pair him with members of the public, firstly in *Barrymore*, then *My Kind of People* and *My Kind of Music*. He shared with Bruce Forsyth the ability to set non-performers at ease, while sending them up gently with asides and looks, but he also had a vulnerability that the ultra-professional Forsyth has never displayed. Forsyth always remained a star, an untouchable, but, for many punters, Barrymore was 'one of us'.

Even when Barrymore came out as homosexual, a situation that many closeted performers avoided, fearing that it would end their careers, the reserves of affection held by a vast majority of the viewing public did not run dry. Stewart Morris was directing Barrymore's first day of location filming after the news had broken, and thought there was potential for a frosty response:

> When the gay bit first hit the press, I was filming him the next day in the Whitgift Centre in Croydon, for *My Kind of Music*. I thought 'What is going to happen?' There must have been 300 press. I've never seen so many cameras and film cameras. I thought 'They're going to crucify him.' And the Whitgift Centre was crowded to capacity. The room used as a dressing room was right at the top and as he started coming down the staircase, the applause went on for several minutes. They loved him and it never stopped. No matter what he did, they still loved him.[3]

*

The early nineties changes in the ITV network's working practices were mirrored by similar upheavals at the BBC. In 1987, LWT's director of programmes John Birt had joined the Corporation as deputy director general, tasked with getting the news and current affairs output – thought by many on the Conservative side to be a hotbed of left-wing bias – under control. In 1993, he succeeded Michael Checkland as DG and turned his attention to all aspects of programming. In Birt's view, the Corporation was a mass of inefficiency. Internal markets – under the heading of 'Producer Choice' – were the answer. Many of those who preceded him cavil at the suggestion that the BBC was a wasteful organization. 'We were a tight ship,' says Jim Moir:

We fought for those budgets in the commissioning process, and then used bottom line accounting to balance the books. Nevertheless, if you have won a pot of gold in the commissioning process and came out evens it begs the question did you win too big a pot of gold at the commissioning process? And by taking that pot of gold, were you denying some of the bars to other departments? There was a concern and there always will be a tension in organizations, that LE have upped the ante: 'No wonder they can bring it in, because they're too well-funded.' That I think is what controllers are there for, to make sure that their bottom line accounting is correct between light entertainment, drama, news, etc. We lobbied hard as well, in order to give the very best of shows. Once we had our budgets agreed, we policed them very vigorously indeed.[4]

Doubtless there were efficiencies that could have been made, but there was a perception that Birt was putting in place a bureaucracy to police the new order, funded by money that would have been better spent on programming. One who perceived this from the sharp end was Roger Ordish:

The rot started with Birt, there's absolutely no question about it. The whole thing was wrecked by one man. It was incredible. It was ludicrous. The things that I know are facts, are so incredible that people wouldn't believe them. In our department, the only bit I can vouch for, there was a head of variety, a head of comedy and a head of the group. Birt arrived, everybody had to be swept away, even Jim Moir. David Liddiment arrived, with the encouragement of Birt. We had nine people called head of something, of whom Michael Leggo was one. You can't be head of something unless you have an office with an outer office and a secretary who says 'He's in a meeting.'

Then, useful places were removed. We had a room and it had in it all the media you could want, so if you had a tape from Japan or Madagascar you could look at it, you could convert it to something else. Gone. To make way for the head of thinking about what I do or whatever it is. Unbelievable. We had a man called Tony James who was brilliant at sorting out your budget on the back of a cigarette packet. He'd say 'We can do it, you can do each show for £8,000, provided you don't try and spend up to the £8,000, give me back what you can because we can use that on something else.' It worked. He was replaced with fourteen people. All of whom had to have offices and computers and so on. How can Birt say 'We are now spending more money on programmes than we used to'? That's the biggest lie. 'I have increased the number of heads in light entertainment from three to nine, and that's cutting down on bureaucracy.' Is it?[5]

In 1993, Jim Moir was ousted as head of light entertainment, having held the post for six years and been head of variety for five years before that. It was the end of an era. From Pat Hillyard onwards, all BBC Television heads of light entertainment had been internal appointments, steeped in the lore of the Corporation, men who knew the system and how to work it to the advantage of their staff. 'There was an ethos, an atmosphere, a collegiality, a feeling of the regiment within light entertainment group,' Moir observes. 'I wasn't there under Ronnie Waldman, but I was a successor in the group that he ran, I worked with people he'd worked with, so I felt the spirit had been handed on. We all thought of ourselves as being part of the family firm.'[6]

Moir's replacement, David Liddiment, had spent his entire career at Granada, taking over as head of entertainment in 1987 when Johnnie Hamp retired (Birt himself had been a Granada trainee, having been passed over for a BBC traineeship). Liddiment had a good record for commissioning hit shows and nurturing talent. He did a lot to bring future influential performers like Steve Coogan, Caroline Aherne and John Thomson to television, originally in north-west-only regional shows. With his credentials not being at issue, his appointment went down badly mainly thanks to the universal esteem in which his predecessor was held by his colleagues. Liddiment also suffered because he was perceived to represent the ill wind of needless change.

He maintains that the change was necessary. 'I joined the

entertainment department, which was in decline,' he says. He also notes that there were massive financial differences between his two employers. 'People were paid more money. Certainly stars were paid more money. Not being a commercial environment, the money consciousness that was part of the Granada culture – Granada was quite a mean company, it always looked after costs very tightly – wasn't there at the BBC. We still had a deal with Jimmy Savile for *Jim'll Fix It*, which was past its sell-by date. We still had *The Paul Daniels Magic Show*, which was past its sell-by date.'[7]

One of his first moves was to rename the light entertainment group. 'He arrived, and he sent out a memo to the staff where he said "The light has to go," and my feeling is that he spoke truer than he knew,' quips Jim Moir, who had moved to become deputy director of corporate affairs.[8] Liddiment stayed just two years at the BBC, returning to Granada as director of programmes at the newly acquired LWT. 'I found the BBC a very political place, a lot of people spent a lot of time plotting their next move, their next foot on the career ladder. I wouldn't have missed it for the world, but there was an opportunity to go back to Granada, and as somebody who had worked a lot in entertainment, London Weekend was an exciting place to go to and I was working with a group of people I'd worked with for many years. I wouldn't have left if I'd been happy. I went to the BBC probably expecting to be there for the rest of my life. Anybody of my generation who grew up in television, the BBC was the pinnacle.'[9]

Just as Liddiment was abandoning the BBC, Jim Moir staged a remarkable resurgence, becoming controller of BBC Radio 2 and giving it a profile it hadn't possessed since the days of the Light Programme. Moir was both clever and lucky to survive. In light entertainment, Birt's reforms had come just as some of the most experienced producers were retiring. Stewart Morris had retired in 1991, bowing out with a Bruce Forsyth special before heading into an Indian summer of freelancing for LWT, and Yvonne Littlewood produced her last show in 1990 – a gala for the Queen Mother's ninetieth birthday. Others, who could normally have expected to spend another decade or more at the

Corporation, took early retirement when it was offered, among them Roger Ordish, who left the Corporation in 1996, after producing *Paul Daniels' Secrets*, the magician's BBC swansong. In the Liddiment reforms, the old head of variety job had been renamed head of light entertainment and been given to Michael Leggo. Leggo had worked under Ordish at the start of his career, and this led to friction when the roles were reversed, as Ordish recalls:

> It was Leggo. They say 'Sorry. We have no shows to give you,' and you say 'Yes, but that's only because you won't give them to me. You've got shows to give to other people. What you're saying is "I don't want you here."' That's always the problem. You get a new boss and they want their producers to be people whom they appointed, who are grateful to them, to put it mildly. [People who] will look to their leader rather than saying 'I taught you everything you know.' There's that terrible hurt of not being wanted, but really of course it's a much better thing to do.[10]

★

Panel games continued to thrive throughout the 1990s, particularly those made by Hat Trick, the company founded by former BBC radio LE trainee Jimmy Mulville and his then wife, Denise O'Donoghue. For Channel 4, they made *Whose Line Is It Anyway?*, an improvisation show hosted by former barrister Clive Anderson. It made the reputation of south London-born comedian Paul Merton, who consolidated his fame as a panellist on the topical quiz *Have I Got News For You*.

A Hat Trick production, it began on BBC2 on 28 September 1990, with Angus Deayton – from Radio 4's *Radio Active* – as host, and *Private Eye* editor Ian Hislop as Merton's rival team captain. There was very little particularly original about the format: Radio 4's *The News Quiz* had been running since 1977. Meanwhile, at BBC Bristol in 1981 and 1982, Colin Godman had produced two series of a topical BBC2 quiz called *Scoop*, with contributions from film critic Barry Norman, musical comedian Richard Stilgoe, humorist Miles Kington and Hislop's *Private Eye* elders Willie Rushton and Barry Fantoni. *Have I Got News For You* simply had the advantage to emerge at a time when regulation in broadcasting was being loosened, making it possible for satirists to get away with more than had previously been possible. The second series of *Scoop* had coincided with the Falklands War, and some of the most important stories of the week had been declared off-limits, much to Godman's frustration.

Have I Got News For You made full use of its freedom, and proved popular enough to make the move to BBC1 in 2000. Along the way, it had substituted a tub of lard for an absent Roy Hattersley, had former spy David Shayler contribute to the show by satellite as he was not permitted to enter the UK, and brought the word 'allegedly' into national usage as a disclaimer for any dubious proclamations. The show survived Deayton's sacking in 2002, following a sex and drugs scandal, and continues with guest hosts, contracted until the end of 2009. Deayton's firm grip on the proceedings is, however, often missed, and the quality of the guest-hosted editions is wildly variable.

As the nature of mainstream television entertainment changed during the nineties, elements of old-school variety re-emerged in Channel 4's comedy output, previously the heartland of 'alternative' humour. The most literal manifestation was a 1991 series, *Packet of Three*, and its sequel *Packing Them In*, starring Frank Skinner, Jenny Eclair, Henry Normal and, later, Kevin Eldon. Part-sitcom set in a down-at-heel provincial variety theatre, part stand-up comedy-led variety show, it ran for two series but was overshadowed by another Channel 4 series of the era.

On 25 May 1990, *Vic Reeves Big Night Out* sprang onto British screens for the first time, its star already billed as 'Britain's top light entertainer and singer'. At first, the epithet appeared ironic, but as the series unfolded, it became apparent that a very deep and real love of traditional variety underpinned the surreal flights of Reeves' creator Jim Moir (no relation), and his comedy partner, former solicitor Bob Mortimer. In its gorgeously warped way, each half hour was pure LE: Reeves' entrance each week, singing an unlikely song – such as The Smiths' 'Sheila Take a Bow' or 'We Plough the Fields and Scatter' – in

347

cabaret style, was a tip of the hat to every male singer who ever had his own show from Andy Williams to Val Doonican. In best chat show tradition, there was a house band, albeit dressed as jockeys for no apparent reason, and a gigantic host's desk, clad with horse brasses. The mock-talent show 'Novelty Island' was *Opportunity Knocks'* deranged cousin, the brown raincoat-wearing voyeur and pervert Graham Lister trying week after week to score a victory. There was also Judge Nutmeg's 'Wheel of Justice', with overtones of Noel Edmonds' 'Whirly Wheel'; not to mention the ill-concealed plugs for dubious meat products and dangerous gewgaws made by Reeves and Mortimer's own company, an echo of every star who ever took a freebie. The high-pitched, mithering Stott brothers, Donald and Davey, returned regularly in a variety of LE-related guises: as inept magicians, chat show hosts and as the presenters of *This Is Your Life*. Then there were the random 'acts' or 'turns' who cropped up, all played by Reeves and Mortimer. Among them were Talc and Turnips, the Aromatherapists, and a performance art duo called Action Image Exchange, whose long, pretentious introductions were followed by meaningless dances while wearing home-made Sean Connery masks.

Perhaps the clearest indication of Reeves and Mortimer's sense of comic heritage came at the end of the second show of series one. Bob, claiming to be eighties pop star Rick Astley, was all set to close proceedings with a rendition of 'She Wants to Dance With Me'. Midway through the song, Reeves emerged from the background, dressed in flat cap, horn-rimmed glasses and brown raincoat, holding a carrier bag, just as Eric Morecambe had in the later Thames shows. Shouting 'Wahey' and slapping Mortimer's face, Reeves brought the show to a grinding halt.

Although Moir's Vic Reeves act had been honed and developed in South London pubs, such as the Goldsmith's Tavern in New Cross, his and Mortimer's comic outlook was recognizably north-eastern, from the Teesside hinterland between Tyneside and North Yorkshire. Jimmy James had occupied similar absurd ground fifty years earlier. The club influence is obvious: the line about Asbley being a treat for pensioners is straight from the vocabulary of a working men's club entertainments secretary. Reeves and Mortimer, aided by Harry Enfield's scriptwriters Paul Whitehouse and Charlie Higson, as well as Fred Aylward as the lab-coated mute savant Les, celebrated that whole earthy world of entertainment, but with a post-modern spin.

By 1993, Reeves and Mortimer had taken their world of surreal LE to BBC for *The Smell of Reeves and Mortimer*, the spoof panel game *Shooting Stars*, and 1999's underrated *Bang Bang It's Reeves and Mortimer*, where clubland surfaced again in a spoof documentary set in a Hull nightspot. Various attempts to entertain the punters fail miserably. One of these is an 'erotic' night with 'rude food', including a vodka-based cocktail called 'Simply the Breast', garnished with an umbrella and an uncooked chicken breast. Later, the club's resident compère 'Kinky' John Fowler, played by Reeves, runs a disastrous talent night and forms a boy band called Mandate, before running amok in the club with a gun.

A decade after Reeves and Mortimer made their Channel 4 debut, another young comedian, Peter Kay, was on the channel displaying his allegiance to clubland, north-western style, in the situation comedy *Phoenix Nights*. Kay himself played the petty, mean, pompous, wheelchair-bound club owner Brian Potter, but the contribution of his co-writer Dave Spikey, playing the compère Jerry Dignan – known professionally as Jerry 'the Saint' St Clair – must not be overlooked. Potter has almost no scruples, Jerry is a hypochondriac, a worrier and a man of conscience. In many ways, *Phoenix Nights*, in its affectionate presentation of the club scene, is a direct descendant of the *Wheeltappers and Shunters Social Club*.

The main difference is that the comic artifice of the *Wheeltappers* was a frame within which genuine acts performed, while *Phoenix Nights* was completely fictional, and the acts were creations of Kay, Spikey and their collaborator Neil Fitzmaurice. Among them was the stunningly tactless psychic (spelled on a hand-painted banner as 'pyskick') Clinton Baptiste, played by Alex Lowe.

After offending everyone he picks on, with the disclaimer 'I'm only telling you what the spirits are telling me', Baptiste gets his come-uppance by choosing a burly audience member and declaring that he was 'getting the word . . . nonce'.

★

While younger comedians were happy to take their cues from traditional LE through the nineties, mainstream TV entertainment producers tried to distance themselves from the big shows that had gone before. By 1999, even *Noel's House Party*, once the iron horse of the BBC1 Saturday night schedules, was declared past its sell-by date. The manner in which the decision was reached and handled continues to rankle with Noel Edmonds:

> The last two years were hell, because the Birt thing had really kicked in, we didn't have enough money to do what we wanted to do, the viewer doesn't go 'Oh that's quite a nice Gotcha bearing in mind that Noel's had 15 per cent year-on-year cuts in the budget. They're all doing very well.' They just look at it and think 'It's not as good as it used to be'. It [the BBC] was a rudderless ship, and all of the key people eventually went. There was just a lack of confidence within the BBC, and I'm not the only person – a lot of people in current affairs, sports department – listen to Des Lynam about it, that's why he was off. It was an unhappy end.[11]

However, the clearest indication for Edmonds that BBC LE wasn't the big happy family it had once been came from some way below senior executive level:

> They outsourced all of the security and reception at Television Centre. One Saturday, I turned up and the girl behind the desk asked me who I was and which production. I thought 'Hmm, I've done 150 of these shows.' It still was the premier entertainment show, and just behind her on the wall was a picture of me.

As *Noel's House Party* was waning, a major hit was waxing at ITV, in the form of the quiz show *Who Wants to Be a Millionaire?*. In 1997, David Liddiment had replaced Marcus Plantin as director of programmes at the ITV Network Centre, and it was to him that the independent producer Celador took a quiz format called *Cash Mountain*, developed by David Briggs, Steve Knight and Mike Whitehill, who had been creating competitions for Chris Tarrant's breakfast show on London's Capital FM. The quiz itself wasn't the innovation – it bore a striking resemblance to *Double Your Money*; it was the size of the prize. Also new was the presence of three lifelines: 'Phone a Friend', '50/50' and 'Ask the Audience'. Throughout the history of British television, prize levels had lagged behind those offered in the US. For many years, the Independent Broadcasting Authority had set the value of a small British family car as the upper limit. The BBC could not justify using licence money to buy big prizes, and could not accept obvious freebies under product placement rules, and so was forced to be even less generous than ITV. Some hosts, such as Terry Wogan and Les Dawson on *Blankety Blank*, made a running joke out of the poor quality of the prizes. In 1993, the Independent Television Commission removed the upper limit. It was theoretically possible for a show to offer a top prize as large as £1 million, but nobody was in a position to do so. Celador finally hit on the idea of recruiting contestants via premium rate telephone lines.

At first, Liddiment was unconvinced, despite the enthusiastic backing of ITV's head of entertainment Claudia Rosencrantz, but when Celador's founder, ex-LWT producer Paul Smith, invited him to play the game with £250 of his own money, against a potential top prize of £2,000, Liddiment grasped the idea. Unsure of which answer to pick, he phoned a friend, then went 50/50 before deciding that an Aborigine was most likely to live in a wurley, rather than eat it, hunt with it or play it. He was right, and he doubled his money. A pilot programme misfired due to inappropriate incidental music and over-bright lighting, but once these had been fixed, Liddiment was ready to commission the show to run five nights a week, hosted by Chris Tarrant:

Who Wants to Be a Millionaire? was probably the most exciting new innovation in light entertainment [Liddiment recalls]. You can see where its roots are, but as a format it's near perfect and as a scheduling idea it was revolutionary. It's a brilliant quiz show, but the money's important; it's about creating in close-up real-life drama, and the money, the jeopardy, is what creates the drama. When you're faced with 'Get this wrong and I might lose £100,000 but if I get it right I'll make £250,000', those are big moments and it's very exciting television.[12]

The success of *Millionaire* was followed by the revival of the talent show, in the form of *Popstars*, which emanated from the Spice Girls' creator Simon Fuller's pop management company. As well as creating the groups Hear'Say, Liberty X and Girls Aloud, the show made a star of Nigel Lythgoe, the show's executive producer, whose critical comments earned him the press nickname of 'Nasty Nigel'. Lythgoe had begun his career as a dancer with the Young Generation troupe, before moving into choreography. He had then worked his way through the ranks at ATV, Central and TVS, eventually becoming a producer, before joining LWT. In the mid-nineties, he had been the prime mover behind *Gladiators*, and when John Kaye Cooper left as controller of entertainment, Lythgoe had been appointed as his successor.

Since then, ITV and Fuller, in combination with record company executive Simon Cowell and Alan Boyd at the production company Fremantle Media, have filled Saturday nights with more variations on the talent show theme: *Pop Idol*, *The X Factor* and *Britain's Got Talent*. These shows, along with *Millionaire* and the BBC's *Weakest Link*, have changed the dynamic of format sales in television worldwide. Traditionally, all formats came from the US, and Britain was a net importer of formats for many years. Now, many of the most successful and lucrative shows are British in origin, and even Goodson-Todman Productions – the home of *What's My Line, The Price Is Right* and other major shows – is now under European ownership, as part of Fremantle Media.

Meanwhile, the BBC has not been without success in the new wave of entertainment programmes. Stewart Morris remembers one particular conversation between several veterans: 'Bill Cotton was here for dinner, and I think Terry Wogan was here too. We were all discussing the non-appearance of variety. Bill said "The day somebody comes up with a good idea, the audience will be enormous." Shortly after that, *Strictly Come Dancing* began, and it wiped ITV off the screen.'[13] Not only was the combination of celebrities and ballroom dancing a domestic hit, but it also allowed the BBC to move into US TV production, with an American version of the show, titled *Dancing With The Stars*. Other newer BBC1 Saturday night shows such as *How Do You Solve A Problem Like Maria?* have taken the talent initiative, finding new stars for West End musicals.

However, the biggest current stars of Saturday night television are on ITV, even though their career progression mirrors that of a former BBC golden boy almost exactly. Noel Edmonds made his TV reputation hosting a Saturday morning children's show, BBC1's *Multi-Coloured Swap Shop*, while Ant McPartlin and Declan Donnelly established themselves as presenters on a similar vehicle, *SMTV*, which ran on ITV from 1998 to 2003. There are other parallels, as Edmonds notes approvingly:

> I like what Ant and Dec do. The only time that I'm just incredulous watching television is when people in light entertainment make basic errors. Insult the audience, nick ideas and don't do them very well. I've had the tabloid press trying to wind me up about Ant and Dec, but I won't, because I think they do it very well. Yes, they've taken a number of things from *House Party*. They admit it, they've sat down and watched all the tapes. If people do it well, full marks. Have I ever done that? Too bloody right I have. It's when people do it badly [that] it's really irritating.[14]

★

Successes like *Ant and Dec's Saturday Night Takeaway*, which launched in 2002, must not distract from the fact that smaller audiences mean smaller revenues. A few flagship programmes still get big budgets, but at the expense of other shows, which now have to be made as cheaply as possible. There is no longer the same breadth of entertainment, but while television variety may now be a shadow of what it was twenty years ago, the genre is far from dead. Under the layers of ironic detachment and supposed 'ediness' that festoon much modern television are concepts and methods that date back to Alexandra Palace or even earlier. However, those early pioneers and their successors thrived on adrenalin and danger. The world of modern business is risk-averse, and television is no exception. Many of the greatest performers and producers in the history of light entertainment would argue that nothing worthwhile can be achieved without taking a few risks and enjoying your work. Perhaps the last word should go to Sir Bill Cotton:

> I'm very careful about talking to people, because what I say can be construed as a bloke who thinks that he's absolutely marvellous, and nobody knows how to do it now, and all that. You just get yourself kicked to death. 'Oh, that old fart walking around saying all these things.' The fact is, not only in television, but in so many things in modern life, things are too serious, or are made out to be too serious. Where there was fun to be had in work, there's not the same type of fun now.[15]

Notes

INTRODUCTION

1 Denis Norden, Sybil Harper and Norma Gilbert (eds.), *Coming to You Live!* (Methuen, London, 1985), p. 7.

CHAPTER ONE

1 *Illustrated London News*, December 1856, quoted in Raymond Mander and Joe Mitchenson, *British Music Hall* (rev. edn, Gentry Books, London, 1974), p. 23.
2 Raymond Mander and Joe Mitchenson, *British Music Hall* (rev. edn, Gentry Books, London, 1974), p. 23.
3 Classified advertisement, *The Times*, 24 August 1835, p. 1.
4 Douglas Jerrold, *Mrs Caudle's Curtain Lectures* (Prion Books, London, 2000), pp. 13–17.
5 Gavin Weightman, *Bright Lights, Big City: London Entertained 1830–1950* (Collins & Brown, London, 1992), p. 20.
6 *The Times*, 26 November 1912, p. 15.
7 *The Times*, 10 January 1942, p. 6.
8 Author's interview with Peter Prichard, 18 November 2004.
9 In 1970, *Dad's Army* co-creator Jimmy Perry collaborated with BBC Head of Comedy Michael Mills to stage an authentic nineteenth century music hall night for BBC2. Transmitted on 26 December, *Wilton's – The Handsomest Hall in Town* featured Spike Milligan as Mackney and Peter Sellers as Ross. Happily, this tribute by now-dead legends to artists who died long before they were

born still exists, and while Milligan acquits himself well enough in bringing the Robinson's marmalade jar golliwog to life, Sellers' performance of 'Sam Hall' is mesmerizing, sinister and superb.

10 Known on their bill matter, respectively, as 'the Dandy Coloured Coon', 'the White-Eyed Kaffir' and 'the Chocolate Coloured Coon'.

11 'The Beefeater' by Dan Leno, recorded *circa* November 1901, as reissued on the LP *Music Hall: Top of the Bill* (World Records SHB22).

12 One of the brothers, George Ganjou, became an agent when he retired from performing, and represented the young Cliff Richard.

13 I am indebted to Roy Holliday, Burnand's great-nephew, who dropped this information casually into conversation one day. Roy's father also worked the halls as a comedian under the name Charlie Kenny, with his bill matter – 'Fit for your front room' – indicating that his act contained no dubious material.

14 Author's interview with Jack Parnell, 24 January 2004.

15 Quoted in Mander and Mitchenson, *British Music Hall* (1974), p. 107.

16 Quoted in Midge Gillies, *Marie Lloyd: The One and Only* (Victor Gollancz, London, 1999), p. 119.

17 *The Times*, 1 November 1904, p. 6.

18 Quoted in Peter Honri, *Music Hall Warriors* (Greenwich Exchange, London, 1997), p. 7.

19 Ibid., p. 49.

20 Cited in Weightman, *Bright Lights, Big City* (1992), p. 81.

21 Mrs Laura Ormiston Chant's testimony to the LCC licensing committee, 10 October 1894, reported in *The Times*, 11 October 1894, p. 7.

22 *The Times*, 22 October 1894, p. 7.

23 Author's interview with Peter Prichard, 18 November 2004.

24 According to listings in *The Times*, Naughton and Gold were doubling up at the Holborn Empire that week too.

25 Roy Hudd, with Philip Hindin, *Roy Hudd's Cavalcade of Variety Acts* (Robson Books, London, 1997), p. 133.

26 From *Naughton and Gold in Search of the Loch Ness Monster* (Decca F3843) [78 rpm disc].

27 Naughton was born in 1887, Gold in 1886. Nervo was born in 1897, Knox in 1896.

28 Maureen Owen, *The Crazy Gang: A Personal Reminiscence* (Weidenfeld & Nicolson, London, 1986), p. 63.

29 Ibid., p. 64.

30 Sid Colin, *And the Bands Played On* (Elm Tree Books, London, 1977), p. 102.

31 The London and Manchester stations opened on 14 November 1922.
32 Eric Maschwitz, *No Chip On My Shoulder* (Herbert Jenkins, London, 1957), p. 49.
33 The Footlights influence on show business didn't begin with Peter Cook and Jonathan Miller. Maschwitz was one of the writers of the 1922 revue, while brothers Jack and Claude Hulbert dominated the society just before and after the First World War, respectively. Davy Burnaby of the Co-Optimists was another Footlighter, performing in the 1901 show *The Oriental Trip*.
34 Maschwitz, *No Chip On My Shoulder* (1957), p. 54.
35 Ibid., p. 69.
36 Ibid., pp. 70, 69, 71.
37 It was possible to record the 30-line image on a gramophone record, and, amazingly, a fragment of this show survives in this form. Donald McLean deserves a great deal of respect for retrieving images from these surviving discs: the results can be viewed at his website, http://www.tvdawn.com.
38 *Picture Page* resumed in 1946, continued until 1952, and a handful of recordings from the tail-end of the run survive.
39 *Radio Times Television Supplement*, 19 February 1937, p. 4.
40 Fred Barnes was a very interesting performer, as openly gay as it was possible to be in that pre-Wolfenden age. He is commemorated in Paul Bailey, *Three Queer Lives* (Hamish Hamilton, London, 2001).
41 'Television News by "The Scanner"', *Radio Times*, 1 September 1939, p. 15.
42 The closedown did not occur, as is popularly believed, in the middle of the Mickey Mouse cartoon.
43 John Watt, *Radio Variety* (J.M. Dent & Sons, London, 1939), p. ix.
44 From *Bandwaggon*, broadcast on the BBC Home Service, 30 September 1939.
45 Author's interview with John Ammonds, 14 April 2005.
46 Ibid.

CHAPTER TWO

1 From the script of *V-ITMA* (BBC Home Service, tx: 10 May 1945); published in Ted Kavanagh, *The ITMA Years* (Woburn Press, London, 1974), p. 92.
2 Author's interview with Sir Bill Cotton, 29 September 2004.
3 In return for their investment, Sid and Phil Hyams received a 50 per cent stake in the new agency. Their cinemas included the Gaumont State, Kilburn.
4 Author's interview with Peter Prichard, 18 November 2004.
5 Author's interview with Sir Bill Cotton, 29 September 2004.

6 Author's interview with John Fisher, 11 May 2006.

7 *Take It From Here* (BBC Light Programme, tx: 18 April 1958).

8 He can be seen doing this on a grainy excerpt from an unidentified late-sixties ATV variety show, much to the delight of the musicians on the rostrum behind him. The ATV identification is possible because the conductor is obviously Jack Parnell.

9 After retiring from show business, Brough returned to run his family's textile firm, while Horne was a senior executive with the safety glass manufacturer Triplex.

10 *Variety Bandbox* (BBC Light Programme, tx: 22 January 1950).

11 Ibid.

12 Author's interview with John Ammonds, 14 April 2005.

13 D.G. Bridson, *Prospero and Ariel: The Rise and Fall of Radio – A Personal Recollection* (Gollancz, London, 1971), pp. 178–9.

14 Quoted in Barry Took, *Laughter in the Air* (Robson Books, London, 1976), p. 87.

15 Ibid., p. 86.

16 Roger Wilmut, *The Goon Show Companion* (Robson Books, London, 1976), p. 34.

17 Author's interview with Roger Ordish, 22 October 2004.

18 Bob Monkhouse, *Crying with Laughter* (Arrow, London, 1994), p. 68.

19 David Bradbury and Joe McGrath, *Now That's Funny: Writers on Writing Comedy* (Methuen, London, 1998), p. 31.

20 Eric Sykes, *If I Don't Write It, Nobody Else Will* (Fourth Estate, London, 2005), pp. 218–9.

21 Author's interview with Yvonne Littlewood, 24 February 2005.

22 Ibid.

23 Ibid.

24 'Infamy, infamy, they've all got it in for me!' as delivered by Kenneth Williams in *Carry On Cleo* is remembered as one of the most famous lines that Rothwell ever wrote, so it may be a surprise to learn that it was in fact given to him by his friends Frank Muir and Denis Norden, who had used it in *Take It From Here* a decade earlier.

25 Author's interview with Richard Greenough, 8 April 2006.

26 Ibid.

27 Michael Mills, quoted in Denis Norden, Sybil Harper and Norma Gilbert (eds.), *Coming To You Live!* (Methuen, London, 1985), p. 219.

28 Quoted in ibid., p. 10.

29 Author's interview with Yvonne Littlewood, 24 February 2005.

30 Ibid.

31 Author's interview with Brian Tesler, 23 February 2005.

32 Ibid.

33 Ibid.

34 Author's interview with Ernest Maxin, 9 November 2005.

35 Ibid.

36 Ibid.

37 Ibid.

38 Attenborough needs no introduction, Peacock will pop up later as the controller of BBC1, BBC2 and managing director of London Weekend.

39 Author's interview with Brian Tesler, 24 February 2005.

40 Ibid.

41 Author's interview with Ernest Maxin, 9 November 2005.

42 Author's interview with Brian Tester, 24 February 2005.

43 *The Times*, 6 January 1948, p. 6.

44 *The Times*, 4 February 1948, p. 2.

45 Ibid.

46 Roy Castle, *Now and Then* (Pan, London, 1995), pp. 73–74.

47 Many famous variety routines have disappeared forever. Fortunately, a version of this one survives in the recording of *The Big Show*, Tyne Tees Television's opening attraction in 1959, and it is from this that I quote.

48 Vivian Van Damm, *Tonight and Every Night* (Stanley Paul & Co., London, 1952), p. 86.

CHAPTER THREE

1 Report of Harold Macmillan's Bedford speech, 20 July 1957, *The Times*, 22 July 1957, p. 4.

2 Always referred to as Ian, he was known in the Commons at this time as Charles Ian Orr-Ewing, to avoid confusion with his relative Sir Ian Orr-Ewing, MP for Weston-super-Mare. After the elder man's death in 1958, he reverted to using his middle name.

3 Quoted in H.H. Wilson, *Pressure Group: The Campaign for Commercial Television* (Secker & Warburg, London, 1961), p. 100.

4 *The Times*, 25 August 1954, p. 1.

5 Born Gomer Berry in Swansea, much of Lord Kemsley's success had derived from being the younger brother of William Berry, later Lord Camrose, owner of the *Daily Telegraph* since 1928.

6   *The Times*, 27 October 1954, p. 6.

7   Quoted in Bernard Sendall, *Independent Television in Britain: Volume 1 – Origin and Foundation, 1946–1962* (Macmillan Press, London, 1982), p. 83.

8   *The Times*, 6 July 1954, p. 15.

9   Tony Ryan (ed.), *Fleet Street Remembered* (Heinemann, London, 1990), p. 298.

10 Author's interview with Richard Greenough, 8 April 2006.

11 Sadly this show seems not to have survived, unlike Hill's speech.

12 'Opinion', *Daily Express*, 22 September 1955.

13 'Comment', *Daily Mirror*, 22 September 1955, p. 4.

14 *Daily Mirror*, 23 September 1955, p. 1.

15 David Croft, *You Have Been Watching . . .* (BBC Books, London, 2004), p. 135.

16 All quoted in Pamela W. Logan, *Jack Hylton Presents* (British Film Institute, London, 1995), pp. 21, 52, ibid., ibid.

17 *Daily Mirror*, 30 September 1955, quoted in Logan, *Jack Hylton Presents* (1995), p. 5.

18 Quoted in Logan, *Jack Hylton Presents* (1995), pp. 32–3.

19 Eric Sykes, *If I Don't Write It, Nobody Else Will* (Fourth Estate, London, 2005), p. 315.

20 Ibid., p. 316.

21 Denis Forman, *Persona Granada* (Andre Deutsch, London, 1997), p. 91.

22 Ibid., p. 92.

23 Ibid., pp. 97–8.

24 Author's interview with Stanley Baxter, 31 May 2006.

25 Also reported as 'Fuck!' and 'Oh ma goad'.

26 The characters had been originated by Stanley Baxter and Rikki Fulton, but it was the Milroy and Fulton partnership that is best remembered.

27 Author's interview with Stanley Baxter, 31 May 2006.

28 Ibid.

29 Author's interview with Brian Tesler, 23 February 2005.

30 Author's interview with Ernest Maxin, 9 November 2005.

31 Ibid.

32 Ibid.

33 Ibid.

34 Author's interview with Brian Tesler, 23 February 2005.

35 The television *Billy Cotton Band Show* is very badly served by the BBC archives with a mere five shows remaining from twelve years. The first show was recorded for posterity, but has since disappeared without trace. However, the last survivor, from 10 May 1964, is a corker. Cotton opens the show by

announcing that he's going to Italy on his holidays, a cue for a big production number based around 'Papa Piccolino'. Grisha Farfel and drummer Kenny Clare rip into 'Swing Low, Sweet Chariot', complete with added Beatle quotes, and are followed by Spike Milligan in rare stand-up comedian mode. Russ Conway, Kathie Kay, Ted Rogers and Frankie Vaughan also feature. Rogers overstays his welcome, but it's all still terrific fun.

36 Jack Good, speaking in *A Good Man Is Hard To Find* (BBC2, tx: 16 January 2005).

37 'Disgusted of Tunbridge Wells' was another Muir and Norden creation, by the way. The English language owes them both a great debt.

38 This was the first of two trial shows, before the series proper began on Saturday 13 September. The show later moved to the Hackney Empire, ABC borrowing ATV's facilities because it did not yet have a London base of its own.

39 'Oh Boy! – It's A Musical Powerhouse ... With The Accent On Vitality', *TV Times*, 13 June 1958, pp. 8–9.

40 Author's interview with Brian Tesler, 23 February 2005.

41 Ibid.

42 Ibid.

43 An unsubstantiated story runs that Trinder made some ill-advised anti-Semitic remarks.

44 Author's interview with Brian Tesler, 23 February 2005.

45 Ibid.

46 Author's interview with Yvonne Littlewood, 24 February 2005.

47 Author's interview with Sir Bill Cotton, 29 September 2004.

48 Author's interview with Yvonne Littlewood, 24 February 2005.

49 Author's interview with Sir Bill Cotton, 29 September 2004.

50 Ibid.

51 The Jack Benny shows were an even harder editing job, being sponsored by Lucky Strike cigarettes, which were mentioned in links and sketches.

52 Author's interview with Yvonne Littlewood, 24 February 2005.

53 Ibid.

54 Author's interview with William G. Stewart, 23 March 2006.

55 Author's interview with Stewart Morris, 1 April 2005.

56 Ibid.

57 Author's interview with Yvonne Littlewood, 24 February 2005.

58 Author's interview with Sir Bill Cotton, 29 September 2004.

59 Ibid.

60 *Hancock's Forty-Three Minutes* (BBC TV, tx: 23 December 1957). Available now on DVD after nearly fifty years of sitting on a shelf in the BBC archives.

61 Ibid.
62 *The Times*, 19 May 1967, p. 3.
63 Author's interview with Rosalyn Wilder, 21 January 2005.
64 Ibid.
65 Ibid.

CHAPTER FOUR

1 Neither Took nor Feldman were gay themselves. Polari was also adopted by theatricals and market traders.
2 Author's interview with Roger Ordish, 22 October 2004.
3 Ibid.
4 'BBC Networks by Numbers', *The Times*, 28 July 1967, p. 3.
5 Frank Muir, *A Kentish Lad* (Bantam Press, London, 1997), p. 227.
6 Ibid., p. 228.
7 Author's interview with Sir Bill Cotton, 29 September 2004.
8 Author's interview with William G. Stewart, 22 March 2006.
9 Author's interview with Richard Greenough, 2 April 2006.
10 Two of the best trumpeters Britain ever produced.
11 Author's interview with Jack Parnell, 22 January 2004.
12 From a tribute to Roger Moffat, compiled by Keith Skues and broadcast on Radio Hallam in Sheffield on 9 August 1987.
13 *Make Way for Music* (BBC TV, tx: 9 August 1960).
14 Author's interview with John Ammonds 14 April 2005.
15 *The Times*, 17 May 1960, p. 16.
16 Rather cheekily, the bass drum has the legend 'Hot Pyes' daubed on it, a reference not to fast food, but to Donegan's ATV-controlled record label.
17 *The Times*, 17 May 1960, p. 16.
18 Howard Thomas, *With an Independent Air* (Weidenfeld & Nicolson, London, 1977), p. 176.
19 Author's interview with Brian Tesler, 24 February 2005.
20 Ibid.
21 The Pigalle was in the building now occupied by BAFTA.
22 Author's interview with Brian Tesler, 24 February 2005.
23 Ibid.
24 Ibid.
25 Ibid.
26 Thomas, *With an Independent Air* (1977), p. 163.

27 Ibid., p. 165.

28 Mike and Bernie Winters, *Shake a Pagoda Tree: Mike and Bernie's Autobiography* (W.H. Allen, London, 1976), pp. 44–5.

29 Despite the long-standing rivalry between Lancashire and Yorkshire, Morecambe was for many years the holiday destination of choice for the vast majority of Leeds families, thanks to railway links.

30 Author's interview with John Ammonds, 14 April 2005.

31 *People,* 25 April 1954, p. 8, quoted in Graham McCann, *Morecambe and Wise* (Fourth Estate, London, 1998), p. 109.

32 Bob Monkhouse, *Crying with Laughter* (Arrow, London, 1994), p. 117.

33 Bruce Forsyth, *Bruce: The Autobiography* (Sidgwick & Jackson, London, 2001), p. 195.

34 Author's interview with Jan Kennedy, 20 April 2005.

35 *The Morecambe and Wise Show* (ATV, tx: 26 February 1966).

36 On the recording, he fluffs the line, and it comes out as 'If you don't want the show to close . . . finish early, yes.'

37 Ibid.

38 *The Morecambe and Wise Show* (ATV, tx: 18 April 1964).

39 Ibid.

40 Author's interview with Eric Geen, 10 March 2006.

41 The BBC had begun test transmissions from Alexandra Palace, using the American NTSC system, in October 1955.

42 Author's interview with Richard Greenough, 8 April 2006.

43 Thomas, *With an Independent Air* (1977), p. 195.

44 Quoted in Forsyth, *Bruce: the Autobiography* (2001), p. 129.

45 There were only five studios open at the Centre in 1963. The gigantic TC1 had yet to be equipped. That evening's other big live production, *That Was The Week That Was*, came from TC2.

46 Author's interview with Yvonne Littlewood, 24 February 2005.

47 Author's interview with Roger Ordish, 22 October 2004.

48 Author's interview with Terry Henebery, 6 November 2004.

49 Author's interview with Roger Ordish, 22 October 2004.

50 Author's interview with Terry Henebery, 6 November 2004.

51 Author's interview with Roger Ordish, 22 October 2004.

52 Author's interview with Marcus Plantin, 4 March 2005.

53 Quoted in Harry Thompson, *Peter Cook: A Biography* (Hodder & Stoughton, London, 1997), p. 114.

54 The prime example is the Defence of the Realm Act 1914, passed to ensure munitions workers' attendance at work, by limiting pub opening hours. DORA

affected the licensing of alcohol sales for a further ninety years.

55 Author's interview with Elkan Allan, 25 October 2005.

56 'Notes On Broadcasting: Satire In The Age Of Television', *The Times*, 15 December 1962.

57 Author's interview with Elkan Allan, 25 October 2005.

58 Although, in his autobiography, he claims that he did. Presumably, he was unaware of the machinations required to secure his position.

59 Author's interview with Elkan Allan, 25 October 2005.

60 Ibid.

61 Quoted in David Frost, *David Frost: An Autobiography – Part One: from Congregations to Audiences* (HarperCollins, London, 1993), p. 46.

62 Frost and Birdsall were both Cambridge graduates, Levin went to the London School of Economics.

63 Interview with Jack Duncan, 4 November 2004.

64 Quoted in Frost, *An Autobiography – Part One* (1993), p. 54.

65 If anyone wants further proof of their non-racist intent, the singers also once accompanied blues singer Josh White on a Light Programme broadcast.

66 Author's interview with Jack Duncan, 4 November 2004.

67 'I got a lot of mates – Johnny Speight, Galton and Simpson, Frank Muir and Denis Norden, Barry Took and Marty Feldman – to give me bits and pieces which I worked up into an act': Frankie Howerd, *The Times*, 6 August 1977, p. 6. Galton, Simpson, Took and Feldman are absent from the show's credits.

68 Quoted in Roger Wilmut, *From Fringe to Flying Circus* (Methuen, London, 1980), p. 61.

69 Quoted in Frost, *An Autobiography: Part One* (1993), p. 61.

CHAPTER FIVE

1 Author's interview with Elkan Allan, 25 October 2005.

2 Ibid.

3 Ibid.

4 Ibid. A nice easy job for reporters at ITN, which shared the building with Rediffusion.

5 Author's interview with Sir Bill Cotton, 29 September 2004.

6 Author's interview with Elkan Allan, 25 October 2005.

7 Ibid.

8 'Ginger Judas', *Private Eye*, issue 103, 26 November 1965, p. 5. A former Rediffusion cameraman has suggested to me that in the original version of

the joke, Allan was advised to go to the party not as an armpit, but as 'a fox's arse'.

9   Author's interview with Elkan Allan, 25 October 2005.

10 Author's interview with Terry Henebery, 6 November 2004.

11 Ibid.

12 Author's interview with Sir Bill Cotton, 29 September 2004.

13 Committee members included Joyce Grenfell and Peter Hall, then the director of the Shakespeare Memorial Theatre.

14 BBC1 and ITV remained exclusively on 405-line VHF until 15 November 1969, when their colour services launched. The 405-line transmitter network was finally closed in January 1985.

15 Author's interview with Terry Henebery, 6 November 2004.

16 Author's interview with John Ammonds, 14 April 2005.

17 Author's interview with Terry Henebery, 6 November 2004.

18 Ibid.

19 A surprising and gratifying amount of *Jazz 625* survives, simply because videotape machines were at a premium, resulting in many editions of the show being 'telerecorded' on film for transmission. For many years the film recording systems available had not been regarded as of sufficient quality for transmission, but by the mid-sixties, the new fast pull-down system was capable of very high-quality pictures indeed. In general, the editions made on VT were wiped subsequently, tape being regarded as a reusable medium, while the films were kept.

20 Author's interview with Terry Henebery, 6 November 2004. This edition was long thought lost until a copy with Spanish subtitles turned up.

21 Ibid.

22 *Not Only ... But Also ...* (BBC2, tx: 9 January 1965).

23 Excerpt from the London Television Consortium's application to the ITA, quoted in David Docherty, *Running the Show* (Boxtree, London, 1990), p. 20.

24 Although the company was called London Weekend Television, its on-air identity was simply London Weekend for the first decade of its life. The station identification was initially plain white text on a black background, but in 1969, a more ornate logo came into use, with the station name inside a graphic device resembling a TV screen. It wasn't until 1970 that the long-serving and famous 'River' ident came into service.

25 Quoted in Docherty, *Running the Show* (1990), p. 23.

26 Author's interview with William G. Stewart, 23 March 2006.

27 Ibid.

28 'Television's New Look', *The Times*, 20 July 1968, p. 17.

29 An ABC-branded clock was exhumed for time checks, the ABC triangle only partially obscured by masking tape.

30 'The New Television Programme Companies After A Year In Business', *The Times*, 6 August 1969, p. 8.

31 Barry Took, *A Point of View* (Duckworth, London, 1990), p. 142.

32 Ibid.

33 Author's interview with Terry Henebery, 6 November 2004.

34 Ibid.

35 Author's interview with Paul Smith, 20 May 2005.

36 'The Man Who Has Kept Britain Laughing For Half A Century', *The Independent*, 8 January 2007, p. 10.

37 Author's interview with Sir Bill Cotton, 29 September 2004.

38 Author's interview with Jim Moir, 19 July 2006.

39 Ibid.

40 Author's interview with Stewart Morris, 1 April 2005.

41 Ibid.

42 Ibid.

CHAPTER SIX

1 Author's interview with Brian Tesler, 23 February 2005.

2 *The Eamonn Andrews Show* (ABC, tx: 1 May 1966).

3 Bill Cotton, *Double Bill* (Fourth Estate, London, 2000), p. 126.

4 Author's interview with Terry Henebery, 6 November 2004.

5 Ibid.

6 Author's interview with Roger Ordish, 22 October 2004.

7 Author's interview with Jim Moir, 19 July 2006.

8 Author's interview with Terry Henebery, 6 November 2004.

9 Ibid.

10 Ibid. The much-missed Ray Moore had been the show's announcer in Manchester.

11 Henebery was lucky to survive: three other motorists died in the accident.

12 Author's interview with Roger Ordish, 22 October 2004.

13 Ibid.

14 Ibid.

15 *Dee Time*, 21 September 1968. The bass player in question is likely to have been Joe Mudele.

16 Author's interview with Roger Ordish, 22 October 2004. The full performance was finally transmitted in a compilation of highlights from the show.

17 Author's interview with Sir Bill Cotton, 29 September 2004.

18 Ibid.

19 Author's interview with Roger Ordish, 22 October 2004.

20 *The Times*, 20 February 1971, p. 17.

21 Author's interview with Sir Bill Cotton, 29 September 2004.

22 Ibid.

23 Ibid.

24 Easy enough now, but in the pre-Sunday trading and cashpoints world of 1973, it was a considerable achievement.

25 Author's interview with John Fisher, 11 May 2006.

26 Ibid.

27 Ibid.

28 *Parkinson* (BBC1, tx: 6 March 1982).

29 Author's interview with John Fisher, 11 May 2006.

30 Alan Bennett, *Writing Home* (Faber & Faber, London, 1997), p. 63.

31 Author's interview with Marcus Plantin, 4 March 2005.

32 Bob Monkhouse, *Crying with Laughter* (Arrow, London, 1994), p. 263.

33 Author's interview with Sir Bill Cotton, 29 September 2004.

34 Author's interview with Jim Moir, 19 July 2006.

35 Author's interview with Roger Ordish, 22 October 2004.

CHAPTER SEVEN

1 Author's interview with John Ammonds, 14 April 2005.

2 Author's interview with Sir Bill Cotton, 29 September 2004.

3 Author's interview with John Ammonds, 14 April 2005.

4 Author's interview with Sir Bill Cotton, 29 September 2004.

5 Author's interview with John Ammonds, 14 April 2005.

6 It also cropped up on the 1964 HMV LP *Mr Morecambe Meets Mr Wise*. Their last Christmas special, made in 1983 for Thames, is in places a shot-for-shot remake of their 1976 BBC Christmas show, with different guest stars, such as Peter Skellern standing in for Elton John. Now, I love Peter Skellern, but I can't help but think that even he'd admit that he's a bit of a comedown.

7 Author's interview with John Ammonds, 14 April 2005.

8 Ibid.

9   Ibid.
10 Author's interview with Ernest Maxin, 9 November 2005.
11 Ibid.
12 Author's interview with John Ammonds, 14 April 2005.
13 'Christmas Specials', *Televisual*, December 1985, p. 20.
14 Author's interview with Bernie Clifton, 12 August 2005.
15 Author's interview with Johnnie Hamp, 4 July 2007.
16 Ibid.
17 Ibid.
18 Ibid.
19 Ibid.
20 *Wheeltappers and Shunters Social Club*, series 1, show 3 (Granada, tx: 27 April 1974).
21 *Wheeltappers and Shunters Social Club*, series 1, show 2 (Granada, tx: 20 April 1974).
22 Author's interview with Johnnie Hamp, 4 July 2007.
23 Author's interview with David Liddiment, 3 March 2005.
24 'Great Service, Great Sets, That's Granada' to the tune of the thirties song 'Granada' being their advertising slogan.
25 Author's interview with Jan Kennedy, 20 April 2005.
26 Ibid.
27 Author's interview with Stewart Morris, 1 April 2005.
28 Ibid.
29 Ibid.
30 Author's interview with Jack Parnell, 22 January 2004.
31 Lew Grade, *Still Dancing: My Story* (Collins, London, 1987), p. 233.
32 David Nobbs, *I Didn't Get Where I Am Today* (Arrow, London, 2004), p. 245.
33 Les Dawson, *A Clown Too Many* (Elm Tree Books, London, 1985), p. 111.
34 Author's interview with Jack Duncan, 4 November 2004.
35 Dawson, *A Clown Too Many* (1985), p. 127.
36 Nobbs, *I Didn't Get Where I Am Today* (2004), p. 259.
37 Author's interview with Ernest Maxin, 9 November 2005.
38 Author's interview with Stewart Morris, 1 April 2005.
39 Ibid.
40 Author's interview with John Fisher, 11 May 2006.
41 'No Rationing for Mr Dodd', *The Times*, 21 April 1965, p. 13.

CHAPTER EIGHT

1   David Docherty, *Running the Show* (Boxtree, London, 1990), p. 74.
2   Author's interview with John Kaye Cooper, 2 March 2006.
3   Ibid.
4   Author's interview with Stanley Baxter, 31 May 2006.
5   Author's interview with John Kaye Cooper, 2 March 2006.
6   Ibid.
7   Author's interview with Stanley Baxter, 31 May 2006.
8   Author's interview with Alan Boyd, 8 June 2005.
9   Author's interview with Stanley Baxter, 31 May 2006.
10 Ibid.
11 *Stanley Baxter's Christmas Box* (LWT, tx: 26 December 1976).
12 *Stanley Baxter on Television* (LWT, tx: 1 April 1979).
13 Author's interview with John Kaye Cooper, 2 March 2006.
14 Author's interview with Marcus Plantin, 4 March 2005.
15 Author's interview with Stanley Baxter, 31 May 2006.
16 Author's interview with Brian Tesler, 24 February 2005.
17 Ibid.
18 Some weeks, this would be followed by a mass chorus of 'Never heard of him/her' – usually when it was a war hero's turn – and an immediate switch-over to another channel, the wireless or various other nourishing pursuits.
19 Archive interview with T. Leslie Jackson, excerpted in *Archive Hour: This Is Your Life at 50* (BBC Radio 4, tx: 28 September 2002).
20 *The Times* of 7 February 1961 reports that the replacement was 'a programme which told the story of Dr Robert Fawcus, of Chard, Somerset'. It is unclear whether this was an edition of *This Is Your Life* or not.
21 Denis Norden, Sybil Harper and Norma Gilbert (eds.), *Coming To You Live!* (Methuen, London, 1985), pp. 206–7.
22 Ibid.
23 Author's interview with Brian Tesler, 23 February 2005.
24 Ibid.
25 Ibid.
26 Ibid.
27 Ibid.
28 Author's interview with Marcus Plantin, 4 March 2005.
29 Ibid.
30 Ibid.
31 Author's interview with Roger Ordish, 22 October 2004.

32 Ibid.

33 Author's interview with Alan Boyd, 8 June 2005.

34 Author's interview with Jim Moir, 19 July 2006.

35 Author's interview with Roger Ordish, 22 October 2004.

36 Author's interview with Alan Boyd, 8 June 2005.

37 Author's interview with Paul Smith, 20 May 2005.

38 Author's interview with Paul Smith, 9 June 2005.

39 Author's interview with Alan Boyd, 8 June 2005.

40 Author's interview with Marcus Plantin, 4 March 2005.

41 Author's interview with Alan Boyd, 8 June 2005.

42 Author's interview with Paul Smith, 20 May 2005.

43 Paul Hamilton, Peter Gordon and Dan Kieran (eds.), *How Very Interesting: Peter Cook's Universe and All That Surrounds It* (Snowbooks, London, 2006), pp. 127–8.

44 Jeremy Isaacs, speaking on *The Real Hughie Green* (Channel 4, tx: 7 August 2001).

45 Kenny Everett, with Simon Booker, *The Custard Stops at Hatfield* (Collins Willow, London, 1982), p. 110.

46 Author's interview with Steve Jones, 10 November 2005.

47 Author's interview with Alan Boyd, 8 June 2005.

48 Ibid.

49 Ibid.

50 Ibid.

51 Ibid.

52 In any case, it was twenty-five years too late to be outraged, as Dan Farson had reported from a nudist colony in his 1950s Associated-Rediffusion show *Out of Step*.

53 Author's interview with Alan Boyd, 8 June 2005.

CHAPTER NINE

1 The special cyclorama lighting trough was replicated at the new premises.

2 Author's interview with William G. Stewart, 22 March 2006.

3 Ibid.

4 Ibid.

5 Ibid.

6 Ibid.

7 Ibid.

8 Ibid.

9 Ibid.

10 Docherty, *Running the Show* (1990), p. 160.

11 Author's interview with Alan Boyd, 8 June 2005.

12 Ibid.

13 Ibid.

14 Ibid.

15 Ibid.

16 Ibid.

17 Ibid.

18 Author's interview with Harold Fisher, 17 November 2004.

19 Ibid.

20 Roy Hudd, with Philip Hindin, *Roy Hudd's Cavalcade of Variety Acts* (Robson Books, London, 1997), p. 138.

21 Author's interview with John Fisher, 11 May 2006.

22 Ibid.

23 Author's interview with Jim Moir, 19 July 2006.

24 Author's interview with John Fisher, 11 May 2006.

25 Nash remains the only man to have been both head of comedy and head of variety at the BBC.

26 Author's interview with Noel Edmonds, 29 September 2004.

27 Ibid.

28 Author's interview with Jim Moir, 19 July 2006.

29 'Maximum Fine For The BBC Over TV Death Plunge Stunt', *The Times*, 17 April 1987.

30 Author's interview with Noel Edmonds, 29 September 2004.

31 Author's interview with Michael Leggo, 20 October 2004.

32 Ibid.

33 Author's interview with Noel Edmonds, 29 September 2004.

34 Author's interview with Jim Moir, 19 July 2006.

35 Author's interview with Michael Leggo, 20 October 2004.

36 Author's interview with Noel Edmonds 29 September 2004.

37 Ibid.

38 Ibid.

39 Author's interview with Michael Leggo, 20 October 2004.

40 Author's interview with Noel Edmonds, 29 September 2004.

41 Ibid.

42 Later to become one half of the partnership behind Endemol.

43 Author's interview with David Liddiment, 3 March 2005.

44 Author's interview with Jan Kennedy, 20 April 2005.
45 *Alexei Sayle's Stuff*, series 3, Show 1 (BBC, tx: 3 October 1991).
46 Author's interview with Jim Moir, 19 July 2006.
47 *The Young Ones*, 'Sick' (BBC2, tx: 12 June 1984).
48 Author's interview with Jim Moir, 19 July 2006.
49 Ibid.
50 Penny Dwyer went on to become an eminent metallurgist before dying in 2003, far too young.
51 Author's interview with Roger Ordish, 22 October 2004.
52 *A Bit of Fry and Laurie* series 2, show 6 (BBC2, tx: 13 April 1990)
53 Author's interview with Roger Ordish, 22 October 2004.
54 *Filthy Rich and Catflap*, (BBC2, tx: 21 January 1987).
55 Author's interview with Jim Moir, 19 July 2006.

CHAPTER TEN

1 Author's interview with Brian Tesler, 23 February 2005.
2 Author's interview with Marcus Plantin, 4 March 2005.
3 Author's interview with Stewart Morris, 1 April 2005.
4 Author's interview with Jim Moir, 19 July 2006.
5 Author's interview with Roger Ordish, 22 October 2004.
6 Author's interview with Jim Moir, 19 July 2006.
7 Author's interview with David Liddiment, 3 March 2005.
8 Author's interview with Jim Moir, 19 July 2006.
9 Author's interview with David Liddiment, 3 March 2005.
10 Author's interview with Roger Ordish, 22 October 2004.
11 Author's interview with Noel Edmonds, 29 September 2004.
12 Author's interview with David Liddiment, 3 March 2005.
13 Author's interview with Stewart Morris, 1 April 2005.
14 Author's interview with Noel Edmonds, 29 September 2004.
15 Author's interview with Sir Bill Cotton, 29 September 2004.

Bibliography

While I have aimed to be comprehensive in this book, space constraints mean that it is not exhaustive. Fortunately, many aspects of light entertainment history have been covered in loving detail by other books, many of which I have consulted. Anyone wanting to know more about specific acts is advised to track down copies of Mander and Mitchenson's *British Music Hall*, Roy Hudd's *Cavalcade of Variety Acts* and Roger Wilmut's typically thorough and engrossing *Kindly Leave the Stage*, all of which are heavily illustrated. Apart from the books listed below, I drew extensively on listings magazines, particularly the *Radio Times* and *TV Times*, and industry journals like *Broadcast*, *The Stage* and *Televisual*. I have also watched and listened to many hours of archive material. Some of this is commercially available and I'll be keeping track of relevant archive DVD releases, online clips and other developments at my website http://www.louisbarfe.com.

Anderson, Jean (ed.), *Late Joys at the Players' Theatre* (T.V. Boardman, London, 1943)

Bailey, Paul, *Three Queer Lives* (Hamish Hamilton, London, 2001)

Barker, Felix, *The House That Stoll Built* (Frederick Muller, London, 1957)

Bennett, Alan, *Writing Home* (Faber & Faber, London, 1997)

Bradbury, David, and Joe McGrath, *Now That's Funny: Writers on Writing Comedy* (Methuen, London, 1998)

Bridson, D.G., *Prospero and Ariel: The Rise and Fall of Radio – A Personal Recollection* (Gollancz, London, 1971)

Briggs, Asa, *History of Broadcasting in the United Kingdom*, 5 vols (Oxford University Press, Oxford 1961–79)

Campey, George, *The BBC Book of That Was the Week That Was* (BBC, London, 1963)

Carpenter, Humphrey, *That Was Satire That Was: The Satire Boom of the 1960s* (Victor Gollancz, London, 2000)

Cherry, Simon, *ITV: The People's Channel* (Reynolds & Hearn, London, 2005)

Colin, Sid, *And the Bands Played On* (Elm Tree Books, London 1977)

Cotton, Bill, *Double Bill* (Fourth Estate, London, 2000)

Croft, David, *You Have Been Watching . . .* (BBC Books, London, 2004)

Crompton, Colin, and John Hamp, *The Wheeltappers and Shunters Social Club Members' Handbook* (Pentagon Books, Pinner, 1976)

Cryer, Barry, *You Won't Believe This, But . . .: An Autobiography of Sorts* (Virgin, London, 1998)

Currie, Tony, *The Radio Times Story* (Kelly Publications, Tiverton, 2001)

Davidson, Andrew, *Under the Hammer* (William Heinemann, London, 1992)

Davies, Russell (ed.), *The Kenneth Williams Diaries* (HarperCollins, London, 1994)

Dawson, Les, *A Clown Too Many* (Elm Tree Books, London, 1985)

Dawson, Les, *No Tears for the Clown* (Robson Books, London, 1992)

Docherty, David, *Running the Show* (Boxtree, London, 1990)

Donaldson, Marie (ed.), *Both Sides of the Camera: A Souvenir Book of Television Programmes and the People Who Make Them* (Weidenfeld & Nicolson, London, 1960)

Donovan, Paul, *The Radio Companion* (HarperCollins, London, 1991)

Earl, John, and Michael Sell (eds.), *The Theatres Trust Guide to British Theatres 1750–1950* (A&C Black, London, 2000)

Everett, Kenny, with Simon Booker, *The Custard Stops at Hatfield* (Collins Willow, London, 1982)

Eyles, Allen, *Gaumont British Cinemas* (Cinema Theatre Association, Burgess Hill, 1996)

Fisher, John, *Tommy Cooper: Always Leave Them Laughing* (HarperCollins Entertainment, London, 2006)

Forman, Denis, *Persona Granada* (Andre Deutsch, London, 1997)

Forsyth, Bruce, *Bruce – the Autobiography* (Sidgwick & Jackson, London, 2001)

Foster, Andy, and Steve Furst, *Radio Comedy 1938–1968* (Virgin, London, 1996)

Frost, David, *David Frost: An Autobiography – Part One: From Congregations to Audiences* (HarperCollins, London, 1993)

Gillies, Midge, *Marie Lloyd: The One and Only* (Victor Gollancz, London, 1999)

Grade, Lew, *Still Dancing: My Story* (Collins, London, 1987)

Hamilton, Paul, Peter Gordon and Dan Kieran (eds.), *How Very Interesting: Peter Cook's Universe and All That Surrounds It* (Snowbooks, London, 2006)

Hewison, Robert, *Footlights: A Hundred Years of Cambridge Comedy* (Methuen, London, 1983)

Honri, Peter, *Music Hall Warriors: A History of the Variety Artists' Federation 1906–1967* (Greenwich Exchange, London, 1997)

Howard, Diana, *London Theatres and Music Halls 1850–1950* (Library Association, London, 1970)

Hudd, Roy, with Philip Hindin, *Roy Hudd's Cavalcade of Variety Acts* (Robson Books, London, 1997

Jerrold, Douglas, *Mrs Caudle's Curtain Lectures* (Prion Books, London, 2000)

Kavanagh, Ted, *The ITMA Years* (Woburn Press, London, 1974)

La Rue, Danny, *From Drags to Riches* (Viking, London, 1987)

Levin, Richard, *Television by Design* (The Bodley Head, London, 1961)

Lewisohn, Mark, *The Radio Times Guide to TV Comedy* (BBC, London, 1998)

Lister, David, *In the Best Possible Taste: the Crazy Life of Kenny Everett* (Bloomsbury, London, 1996)

Logan, Pamela W., *Jack Hylton Presents* (British Film Institute, London, 1995)

McCann, Graham, *Morecambe and Wise* (Fourth Estate, London, 1999)

McCann, Graham, *Frankie Howerd: Stand-Up Comic* (Fourth Estate, London, 2004)

Mander, Raymond, and Joe Mitchenson, *British Music Hall* (rev. edn, Gentry Books, London, 1974)

Maschwitz, Eric, *No Chip On My Shoulder* (Herbert Jenkins, London, 1957)

Maxwell, John, *The Greatest Billy Cotton Band Show* (Jupiter Books, London, 1976)

Monkhouse, Bob, *Crying With Laughter* (Arrow, London, 1994)

Muir, Frank, *A Kentish Lad* (Bantam Press, London, 1997)

Mullins, Spike, *Me, To Name But A Few* (M&J Hobbs/Michael Joseph, London, 1979)

Murray, George T., *The United Kingdom: An Economic and Marketing Study Prepared for the Research Section of Rediffusion Television Ltd* (Marketing Economics, London, 1964)

Nobbs, David, *I Didn't Get Where I Am Today* (Arrow, London, 2004)

Norden, Denis, Sybil Harper and Norma Gilbert (eds.), *Coming to You Live!* (Methuen, London, 1985)

Owen, Maureen, *The Crazy Gang: A Personal Reminiscence* (Weidenfeld & Nicolson, London, 1986)

Palin, Michael, *Diaries 1969–1979* (Weidenfeld & Nicolson, London, 2006)

Peter, Bruce, *Scotland's Splendid Theatres* (Polygon, Edinburgh, 1999)

Ryan, Tony (ed.), *Fleet Street Remembered* (Heinemann, London, 1990)

Sendall, Bernard, *Independent Television in Britain: Volume 1 – Origin and Foundation, 1946–1962* (Macmillan Press, London, 1982)

Skues, Keith, *Pop Went the Pirates* (Lamb's Meadow, Sheffield, 1994).

Skues, Keith, *That's Entertainment: the Chelsea Lodge Story* (Lamb's Meadow, Horning, 2004).

Sloan, Tom, *BBC Lunch-time Lectures Eighth Series – 2: Television Light Entertainment* (BBC, London, 1970)

Sykes, Eric, *If I Don't Write It, Nobody Else Will* (Fourth Estate, London, 2005)

Thomas, Howard, *With an Independent Air* (Weidenfeld & Nicolson, London, 1977)

Thompson, Harry, *Peter Cook: A Biography* (Hodder & Stoughton, London, 1997)

Took, Barry, *Laughter in the Air* (Robson, London, 1976)

Took, Barry, *A Point of View* (Duckworth, London, 1990)

Van Damm, Vivian, *Tonight and Every Night* (Stanley Paul & Co., London, 1952)

Watt, John, *Radio Variety* (J.M. Dent & Sons, London, 1939)

Weightman, Gavin, *Bright Lights, Big City: London Entertained 1830–1950* (Collins & Brown, London, 1992)

Wilmut, Roger, *The Goon Show Companion* (Robson, London, 1976)

Wilmut, Roger, *Tony Hancock – Artiste* (Methuen, London, 1978)

Wilmut, Roger, *From Fringe to Flying Circus* (Methuen, London, 1980)

Wilmut, Roger, *Kindly Leave the Stage: The Story of Variety 1919–1960* (Methuen, London, 1985)

Wilson, H.H., *Pressure Group: The Campaign for Commercial Television* (Secker & Warburg, London, 1961)

Winters, Mike, and Bernie Winters, *Shake a Pagoda Tree: Mike and Bernie's Autobiography* (W.H. Allen, London, 1976)

Index